Anniversary Party Pâté, Pork Fajita Pitas, Sausage Bread, Apple-Cheddar Turnovers, Crabmeat-Stuffed Flounder, Scallop and Bacon Sauté, Chocolate-Peanut Butter Cups, Sweet Potato Chips, Fruit-Walnut Stuffing, Herbed Cheese Dip, Hot Buttered Rum, Cran-Raisin Muffins

You'll find easy-to-follow recipes for these
and many other delectable, nutritious dishes in
WEIGHT WATCHERS QUICK AND EASY MENU COOKBOOK.
Now there's no more deprivation! And no more holiday
dieting blues—ever! You'll feast all year long on the
freshest, most nutritious foods of the season
while shedding those extra pounds safely
and painlessly!

WEIGHT WATCHERS

QUICK AND EASY
MENU COOKBOOK

WEIGHT WATCHERS®

QUICK AND EASY
MENU COOKBOOK

Over 250 Seasonal Recipes and Menus
Based on The Quick Success® Program

Photography by Steven Mark Needham

A PLUME BOOK

Published simultaneously in Canada by Penguin Books Canada Ltd.

Designed by Julian Hamer

Food stylist: Nina Procaccini

Prop stylist: Nancy Mernit

Illustrations by Dolores R. Santoliquido

Nutrition analysis by Hill Nutrition Associates, Inc.

For kindly lending us serving pieces and other props for photography we thank:
Bennington Potters, Vermont; Christofle; Country Floors, New York, N.Y.;
Hutschenreuther; Georg Jensen Silversmiths, New York, N.Y.; Mood Indigo,
New York, N.Y.; Oneida; Pan American Phoenix, New York, N.Y.;
Thaxton & Co., New York, N.Y.

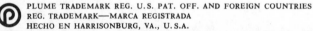

PLUME TRADEMARK REG. U.S. PAT. OFF. AND FOREIGN COUNTRIES
REG. TRADEMARK—MARCA REGISTRADA
HECHO EN HARRISONBURG, VA., U.S.A.
SIGNET, SIGNET CLASSIC, MENTOR, ONYX, PLUME, MERIDIAN and NAL BOOKS
are published *in the United States* by New American Library, a division of
Penguin Books USA Inc., 1633 Broadway, New York, New York 10019, and *in Canada*
by Penguin Books Canada Limited, 2801 John Street, Markham, Ontario L3R 1B4

Library of Congress Cataloging-in-Publication Data

Weight Watchers quick and easy menu cookbook.

    Includes Index.
      1. Low-calorie diet — Recipes.   2. Menus.
3. Weight Watchers International.   I. Needham,
Steven Mark.   II. Weight Watchers International
III. Title: Quick and easy menu cookbook.
RM222.2.W324   1988   641.5′635   87-20426
ISBN 0-453-01015-6
ISBN 0-452-26248-8 (pbk.)

First Printing, January, 1988

6 7 8 9 10 11 12

PRINTED IN THE UNITED STATES OF AMERICA

ACKNOWLEDGMENTS

Putting a cookbook together requires patience, dedication, cooperation, insight, stamina, and an occasional bout of insomnia. Just ask the hard-working staff of professionals here at Weight Watchers. Their individual and collective talents have made the Quick and Easy Menu Cookbook the special volume that it is, and we'd like to thank them all for a job well done.

First, we'd like to extend our gratitude to Eileen Pregosin under whose direction the staff of the Publication Services Department has produced a cookbook we can all be proud of.

To Nina Procaccini, Christy Foley McHale, and Judi Rettmer, our sincere appreciation for their countless hours of recipe development, testing, and revision. They were also responsible, along with Susan Haines, for the food styling for all of the photography in this book.

Our thanks to Patricia Barnett, Anne Neiwirth, Harriet Pollock, Elizabeth Resnick-Healy, and April Rozea, who handled the huge task of researching, writing, editing, and proofreading the manuscript, as well as seeing it through various stages of production. A great big thank-you also goes to AnnMarie Clarke, Isabel Fleisher, and Jodi Ann Lisa. Whether it was word processing, photocopying, or proofreading, our secretaries were always there when we needed them.

And so, in this 25th anniversary year, we thank our dedicated staff for their inspiration and support. Here's to many more cookbooks!

WEIGHT WATCHERS INTERNATIONAL

Contents

APRIL 89

MAY 113

JUNE 137

NOVEMBER   251

DECEMBER   275

A Letter from Jean Nidetch

Dear Friends,

"I'm too busy to fuss. . . ." Isn't that the password these days? Especially for the multitude of people juggling job/home/family. So ease and speed have to be prime ingredients in menu planning, since <u>that's</u> a juggling act, too! That's why Weight Watchers — which has always been attuned to your life-style needs — has come up with this Silver Jubilee cookbook to help celebrate our 25th anniversary. It contains over 250 recipes that can each be prepared in <u>an hour or less</u>! And they're all based on our exciting new 1988 Quick Success® Food Plan, which makes losing weight not only faster but more appetizing than ever.

Our recipes include quick breakfast items for those who "don't have time to eat" (but should!), totable lunches, convenient dinners, plus an array of handy snacks. To enhance your weekend and holiday dining, there is a variety of slightly more elaborate menus, including delectable brunches and <u>non</u>-portable lunches to be enjoyed at home.

We've done your planning for you, too! Every recipe is "partnered" with a complete full-day menu. You'll also find six 7-day menus that show you how flexibly you can dine on a weekly basis. All the recipes indicate Food Plan Exchanges, as well as the first week on the Food Plan that the dish can be eaten.

To keep pace with your busy calendar, the book is organized by months, and includes hints for special days; for instance, we highlight a December meal that would make a delightful Christmas brunch, and a spring menu appropriate for Passover. We've included ways to effortlessly whip together leftovers, too (how about Turkey Cutlets with Orange-Cranberry Sauce to lighten your post-Thanksgiving schedule?). Sprinkled throughout are special Silver Jubilee treats, especially in May, to help you celebrate our 25th anniversary with us on May 15th!

You'll find savvy suggestions for expediting your efforts, including a wealth of do-ahead tips. For example, you can breakfast on an Orange-Pecan Waffle that was prepared and frozen ahead of time, so all you have to do is let it warm in your toaster- or microwave oven. (Isn't that a scrumptious way to greet the day?)

But with all our time-savers, we haven't cut any corners on nutrition! Our menus take advantage of in-season fruits and vegetables, along with monthly lists of the best buys in seasonally available produce. You'll also find nutrition data as well as recommendations for the most nutritious methods of preparing foods.

We're supplying you with guidelines to kitchen shortcuts, too, plus the best ways to use such aids as food processors, blenders, pressure cookers, and microwave ovens. And we give carry-along lunch tips, information about food storage and shopping, and a host of other suggestions for streamlining your schedule.

It all adds up to making your weight-loss life-style more rewarding and easier than ever — but that's been the story behind the Weight Watchers organization since we began. So how fitting that this book is appearing as Weight Watchers celebrates its silver anniversary. In these 25 exciting years, we've grown from a handful of people meeting in my living room to over <u>27 million</u> enrollments — including men and women from their teens to their nineties. Today, more than three-quarters of a million members gather in weekly meetings that span 22 countries. Of course, Weight Watchers is more than the meetings; we have other products and services designed to add convenience to your weight-loss efforts. We offer a popular line of convenience foods, best-selling cookbooks, resorts and spas, children's camps, magazines, a national health and fitness newsletter, video cassettes (hosted by Lynn Redgrave) — with others on the horizon for our <u>next</u> quarter of a century!

What our members are discovering — and what you'll find as you sample these pages — is that weight-control meals can be tasty, nutritious, and interesting. Our new Food Plan, while offering faster weight loss, is also in step with the latest nutritional findings, and is supervised by our medical advisor and staff of nutritionists. Working in tandem with them, our expert chefs, home economists, writers, and editors have lent their skills to creating this book. Every recipe in it was developed and prepared in the test kitchen of Weight Watchers International.

The result is a culinary guide that blends ease, simplicity, and variety into your life-style. The only thing missing is hassle!

Isn't that a delicious way to celebrate a four-star event?

Love,

Jean Nidetch

Introduction

THE ORGANIZED COOK: MENU PLANNING FOR THE '80s AND BEYOND

Dieting demands organization. "Too difficult," you say. "I'm just not an organized person."

Being an organized cook doesn't have to be difficult, as you'll see when you read this section. On the next few pages you'll find a host of hints on how to follow the menus in this book, as well as how to use the items we've included on the menus.

You'll discover the best methods of cooking vegetables, how to use seasonal produce, and how much a bagel should weigh. You'll learn how to pack a portable lunch and how to use diet foods.

Read this section carefully before you begin following the menus. You'll pick up dozens of valuable tips and soon you'll be on your way to becoming a more organized cook.

Fruits and Vegetables

When we developed our menus, we kept in mind the seasonal availability of certain fresh fruits and vegetables. When fresh produce is not available, feel free to substitute frozen or canned; just be sure these products have no sugar added.

Tips for Using Fruits

- When the menu calls for half a banana, you may wonder what to do with the other half. Sprinkle the cut side with lemon juice, wrap the banana in plastic wrap, and save for another day.
- If grapefruit with sugar appears on a breakfast menu, section it the night before, sprinkle with sugar, wrap in plastic wrap, and refrigerate. The sugar will become syrupy and sweeten the grapefruit.

1

Steaming Vegetables

The preferred method for cooking vegetables is steaming, which preserves more of the valuable nutrients than other cooking methods. Steaming requires a covered pan with a steamer basket or insert so that the cooking water does not touch the vegetables. This method takes a bit longer than boiling but is well worth it in terms of taste, color, texture, and nutrient value. You can shorten the steaming time by cutting the vegetables into smaller, thinner pieces.

The following vegetables are well suited to steaming: artichokes, asparagus, broccoli, brussels sprouts, cabbage, carrots, cauliflower, green beans, onions, peas, potatoes, summer squash, and turnips.

HOW TO STEAM VEGETABLES

1. Fill a saucepan or the bottom of a steamer pot with one to two inches of water.

2. Place the vegetables in a steamer basket (or in the insert of a steamer pot) and set over the water in the pan (or pot). The water should not touch the bottom of the steamer basket or insert.

3. Cover the saucepan (or pot), bring the water to a boil over medium heat, and steam the vegetables until they are tender-crisp (this means they can be pierced with a fork but are still slightly firm).

Vegetables and the Microwave Oven

We've included a variety of cooked vegetables, and if you own a microwave oven, you may want to use it for cooking them. Because the cooking time is brief and very little water is needed, vegetables come to the table bright in color and crisp in texture, as well as retaining valuable nutrients.

For best results, consider the following when microwaving vegetables:

■ Cut vegetables into uniform size and thickness for even microwaving.

■ Asparagus tips and broccoli florets are tenderer than the stalks and require less energy to cook. Arrange them in the center of the dish.

■ Arrange whole or halved vegetables in a circle on a dish, leaving space between each. They will cook more evenly.

■ Skins on whole vegetables (such as potatoes and winter squash) should be pierced with a fork before microwaving to permit steam to escape and to prevent the vegetable from exploding.

HOW TO MICROWAVE VEGETABLES

1. Arrange vegetables in a microwave-safe container, add a few tablespoons of water, and cover with a lid or plastic wrap. The water will provide steam, resulting in quick and even cooking.

2. Microwave on High for the amount of time the manufacturer or the recipe directs.

3. Halfway through cooking, stir, rearrange, or turn vegetables over.

4. Most instructions specify standing time, since the vegetables will continue cooking after microwaving is completed. This important step helps to avoid overcooking and permits vegetables to become tender without losing their texture.

Boiling Vegetables

Any vegetable that can be steamed may be boiled instead. For best results, use as little water as possible — just enough to cover the vegetables — and cook in a pan with a tight-fitting lid to prevent steam from escaping. Drain as soon as cooking is completed, since any vegetable kept in hot water continues to cook. Don't discard the cooking liquid, though — it's a flavorful and nutrient-rich base for soups. Freeze the liquid in ice cube trays to make portioning easy.

Baking Vegetables

This method is more time-consuming than others, but if you bake several things at the same time, you'll save energy in the process. You can also prepare other parts of the meal while your dishes are in the oven. Baking is an excellent method for cooking eggplant, potatoes, winter squash, and tomatoes.

Braising Vegetables

Braising is a slow cooking method in which the vegetable is cooked in a covered saucepan with a minimal amount of water. Leeks, mushrooms, potatoes, and summer squash are all delicious cooked this way.

Another way to braise a vegetable is to parboil it, then finish cooking it in a small amount of liquid over low heat. The vegetable will soak up the liquid as it finishes cooking. Try this using brussels sprouts, cabbage, celery, leeks, onions, or potatoes.

Meat, Poultry, and Fish

The weights we've listed on the menus for meat, poultry, and fish are skinned, boned, and cooked weights, unless we've indicated otherwise. Before eating poultry, be sure to remove and discard the skin.

When we developed the menus, we kept in mind the seasonal availability of fresh saltwater fish. However, if fresh fish is not available in your area, you may substitute canned or frozen fish.

When tuna, salmon, or sardine salads or sandwiches appear on a lunch menu, we are referring to the canned product. Canned fish should be well drained before weighing.

Snacks

Foods listed on the menus as snacks may be eaten with any of the day's meals instead of being taken as snacks.

Low-Calorie and Reduced-Calorie Products and Sugar Substitutes

Diet foods (low- and reduced-calorie) have been included in some of the menus to add variety and interest to your meals. We have included the calories for these items in the Total Optional Calories that appear on each menu. In calculating these figures, we used the following calories for each item:

- Reduced-calorie spread
  16 calories per 2 teaspoons
- Low-calorie gelatin
  8 calories per ½-cup serving
- Diet soda
  0 calories
- Reduced-calorie salad dressings

Blue cheese	40 calories per tablespoon
Buttermilk	30 calories per tablespoon
Creamy bacon	30 calories per tablespoon
Creamy cucumber	30 calories per tablespoon
Creamy Italian	30 calories per tablespoon
French	30 calories per tablespoon
Italian	6 calories per tablespoon
Russian	25 calories per tablespoon
Thousand Island	30 calories per tablespoon

If the products you use have a different caloric content, adjust the number of Total Optional Calories as necessary.

- Reduced-calorie margarine comes in sticks or tubs. Our menus call for the kind that comes in a plastic tub.
- The use of sugar substitutes and low-calorie sweeteners on the Weight Watchers food plan is entirely optional. Natural sweetness is available in the form of fruits and honey as well as white and brown sugar, fructose, molasses, syrup, jams, jellies, and preserves. The decision about using sugar substitutes and low-calorie sweeteners should be made by you and your physician.

Other Foods

- Eggs should be prepared without fat unless the menu indicates a specific amount. Use a nonstick skillet or nonstick cooking spray.
- Bagels, English muffins, and hamburger and frankfurter rolls should weigh 2 ounces each; a half of each should weigh one ounce.
- Cocktail breads should weigh ¾ ounce for 2 slices.
- The buttermilk flaky biscuits called for on menus are the refrigerated, ready-to-bake biscuits found in the dairy case of the supermarket.
- Graham crackers should each be 2½ inches square.
- Dietary frozen dessert should contain 100 calories per 3-ounce serving.
- Wherever ½ cup of skim milk has been included on the menu, it may be combined in the blender with 1 cup of cold diet soda to make a creamy, frothy beverage. Raspberry, chocolate, coffee, black cherry, orange, or cherry-cola diet sodas are all delicious when combined with milk.
- Prepare popcorn following package directions, or use a hot-air popper or microwave popcorn. For added flavor sprinkle on one of these seasonings: chili powder, curry powder, garlic powder, grated Parmesan cheese, cinnamon-sugar mixture, or ginger-garlic powder mixture.
- Vary the type of mustard you use to add interest to the menu. Dijon-style, coarse grain, deli mustard, and spicy brown mustard are all good choices.

Portable Lunches

Most of the lunches on our menus are designed to be packed and carried to work or school. Our more elaborate brunch/lunch menus were meant to be enjoyed on weekends, when most people can relax and enjoy a leisurely meal.

Here are some hints to help make preparation and packing of portable lunches easy and convenient.

- Prepare a week's worth of vegetable accompaniments on Sunday evening. Chop celery, cut carrot sticks, slice cucumber, etc., and store in the crisper. For super-simple salads and vegetable accompaniments, you can purchase ready-prepared ingredients from your supermarket's salad bar.
- Sandwiches made the night before should be kept in the refrigerator until you're ready to take them with you in the morning.
- Wrap sandwiches and vegetable accompaniments in aluminum foil or plastic wrap.
- Pack salads (minus dressing) in resealable plastic containers. Bring your own dressing in a small, empty spice jar or similar small container for easy toting.

■ Carry lunches in insulated bags to prevent spoilage of perishable items.

■ If your lunchroom has a microwave or toaster-oven, try some of our sandwich suggestions heated. Cheese is especially delicious when it's hot and bubbly.

■ Pack lettuce and tomato separately; add them to your sandwich at lunchtime. (This helps prevent soggy sandwiches.)

■ If hot water is available at your place of business, add it to one packet of reduced-calorie hot cocoa mix. Count it as 1 Milk Exchange (adjust your daily menu accordingly). Or take one packet of instant broth and seasoning mix, add hot water, and enjoy a cup of hot soup (count as 10 Optional Calories).

■ Low-calorie fruit-flavored gelatin is available in 1-cup foil-sealed servings that need no refrigeration. Pack one with your lunch for a change-of-pace dessert (count toward Optional Calories).

■ Skim milk is available in 8-ounce paper cartons that are processed under ultra-high temperatures (UHT) and need no refrigeration. If you wish, pack one along with your lunch — it's easier than carrying an insulated vacuum container (count as 1 Milk Exchange, and adjust daily menu accordingly).

THE EDUCATED COOK: USING THE RECIPES AND INGREDIENTS

When you look through the recipes in this book, you'll find that they are well organized and easy to follow. But if you're like many people, you want to know more about ingredients, cooking methods, nutrition — in short, you want to become an educated cook. The information in this section will help you do just that. You'll learn how to get the most from this cookbook, which, in turn, will help you in your weight-loss efforts.

The Recipes

■ You'll notice that each recipe is designated with a week number, indicating the first week that the recipe may be used on the Weight Watchers food plan. The menu for the day is based on that same week. Be sure to keep this in mind when you choose recipes. If you are on a more advanced week than the recipe indicates, you may choose to alter the recipe or menu to include food that you are permitted to have.

■ Nonstick cookware means you can cook without fat. If you don't own cookware with a nonstick surface, spray an ordinary pan with nonstick cooking spray.

■ The nutrition information for recipes containing cooked rice or pasta has been calculated on the assumption that no extra salt or fat has been added during cooking.

Some Basic Ingredients

■ The weights of fruits and vegetables in the recipes are the weights as you would buy the items; that is, they are the weights before peeling, cutting, or any other procedure has been done. For example, if a recipe calls for 1 pound of apples, cored, pared, and sliced, you should purchase 1 pound of apples, then proceed according to directions.

■ Canned fruit and juice should have no sugar added. Canned fruit may be packed in its own juice or another fruit juice, in a juice blend, in water, and with artificial sweetener. Apple cider should be unfermented.

■ We've used fresh vegetables in our recipes unless otherwise indicated. If you substitute frozen or canned vegetables, you will have to adjust the cooking times.

■ Hot chili peppers are not only hot to the taste buds; their volatile oils can make your skin and eyes burn, too. Wear rubber gloves and be careful not to touch your face or eyes while working with these peppers. Before continuing with the recipe, wash your hands, knife, and cutting board thoroughly to remove all traces of the pepper.

■ Some of our recipes call for shredded cheese. Many cheeses are sold in shredded form, but at an extra cost to the consumer. To save time and money, shred your own cheese at the beginning of the week and refrigerate it in a resealable plastic bag or container.

■ You've probably noticed that there are many types of vegetable oils on the market today. Some have certain characteristics that make them appropriate for specific needs, but very often one can easily be substituted for another. If no particular type is specified, you can use safflower, sunflower, soybean, corn, cottonseed, or any of these combined. Since olive oil, Chinese sesame oil, walnut oil, and peanut oil have distinctive flavors, they have been specifically indicated. There are two types of sesame oil: light and dark. The light oil is relatively flavorless and may be used as a substitute for any other vegetable oil. When sesame oil is specified, use the dark variety. This product, made from toasted sesame seed, has a rich amber color and a characteristic sesame flavor.

■ If you store nut and seed oils (such as walnut, hazelnut, peanut, almond, and sesame) in the refrigerator after opening, they won't become rancid or develop odors. These items are generally more expensive, too, so buy them in small quantities and store them appropriately.

Herbs and Spices

Herbs and spices can add zest and flavor to many kinds of foods. These guidelines will help you use them to best advantage.

■ Our recipes call for dried herbs, unless otherwise indicated. If you are substituting fresh herbs, use approximately four times the dried amount (for example, 1 teaspoon of chopped fresh basil instead of 1/4 teaspoon of dried basil leaves). If you are substituting ground (powdered) herbs for dried leaves, use approximately half the dried amount (for example, 1/4 teaspoon of ground thyme instead of 1/2 teaspoon of dried thyme leaves).

■ If you are substituting fresh spices for ground, use approximately eight times the ground amount (for example, 1 teaspoon of minced fresh ginger root instead of 1/8 teaspoon of ground ginger).

■ Dried herbs and spices usually lose their potency after about a year. A good way to check on this is to date the container when you buy it. Open it now and then to see if the herb or spice is aromatic. If so, it is still potent; if the aroma has diminished, the recipe may require a larger amount of the seasoning.

Shelling and Deveining Shrimp

When a recipe calls for shelled and deveined shrimp, you can save time and hassle by buying already shelled and deveined shrimp, although it does cost a bit more. If you'd like to do it yourself, here's how:

1. Hold tail end of shrimp in one hand. Slip thumb of other hand under the shell, between the feelers, and lift off shell segments. Then, firmly hold tail in one hand and gently pull shrimp free of remaining shell, making sure to keep tail meat intact.

2. To devein a shelled cooked shrimp, pull a narrow strip off back (outside curve) of shrimp, peeling strip down to tail. Using a small, pointed knife, remove and discard the vein.

3. To devein a shelled raw shrimp, using small, pointed knife, cut lengthwise along back (outside curve), just deep enough to expose vein but not all the way through, about 1/8 inch deep; remove and discard vein.

Boneless Chicken Breasts and Cutlets

Some of our recipes call for chicken cutlets, which tend to be costly when purchased at the supermarket or butcher shop. To save money, you can buy cutlets in quantity when they are on sale and freeze them.

Boneless chicken breasts are a less expensive alternative to cutlets, but they can sometimes be too thick for stuffing and rolling. To turn them into cutlets, place the package of chicken breasts in the freezer for about 30 minutes. They'll chill just enough to make slicing with a sharp knife easier. Cut them in half lengthwise; then, unless you plan to use them immediately, wrap in moisture- and vapor-resistant paper and freeze.

When stuffing chicken cutlets, to make rolling easier, flatten cutlets to about 1/4-inch thickness by pounding with a wet meat mallet. Wetting the mallet helps to prevent particles of meat from sticking to it. (This procedure may also be used with veal.)

HOW TO BONE CHICKEN BREASTS

Boning chicken breasts yourself will save you some money, so it may be well worth the extra time it takes. And it isn't hard to do. There's also the bonus of saving the bones to use for making stock. Just place them in a resealable plastic bag and store in the freezer; soon you'll have enough for a potful of stock.

Follow these step-by-step instructions for boning chicken breasts:

1. Place chicken breast on cutting board, skin-side down. With tip of a sharp knife, cut through gristle at neck end. (A boning knife makes the job easier.) Bend chicken breast backward until keel bone (dark bone in center) "pops" up. Loosen bone with index fingers and pull out.

2. Work on each side of breast separately. Insert tip of knife under long rib bone. Work knife beneath bone, separating it from meat. Lift bone and cut meat from rib cage. Remove bones. Repeat on the other side of breast.

3. Scrape meat away from ends of wishbone. Cut out bone. Slip knife beneath tendons (long white fibers) on both sides of breast. Loosen and pull out tendons. Remove skin.

The Exchange and Nutrition Information

Each recipe in this book is followed by an Exchange Information statement. This statement tells you how one serving prepared from that recipe fits into the Weight Watchers food plan. You will find this information useful whether you follow our menus or develop your own. If you make any changes in the recipes, be sure to adjust the Exchange Information accordingly.

Since many people are also concerned about nutrition, we have included per-serving nutrition analyses for calories, protein, fat, carbohydrate, calcium, sodium, and cholesterol. These figures were calculated using the most up-to-date data available; they will change if the recipe is altered, even if the alteration does not affect the Exchange Information.

Nutrition Notes

The foods we eat provide the nutrients we need to stay healthy — about 40 in all, including proteins, fats, carbohydrates, vitamins, minerals, and water. Our bodies use these nutrients for energy, growth, repair of body tissue, and regulation and control of body processes. It is the amount of proteins, fats, and carbohydrates in foods that determine their caloric content.

■ Proteins are necessary for building and maintaining body tissue. The best sources of protein are poultry, meat, fish, eggs, milk, and cheese.

■ Fats and carbohydrates provide energy and assist other body functions. Fruits, vegetables, cereals, and grains are excellent sources of carbohydrates. Margarine, vegetable oils, poultry, meat, and fish supply fats.

■ Sodium is a significant factor in weight control since it affects the body's water balance. Sodium occurs naturally in some foods, and additional amounts are often added in processing prepared foods.

■ Calcium builds and maintains strong bones and teeth, and is essential throughout your life to prevent osteoporosis in later years. The best sources of calcium are, of course, milk and other dairy products. But calcium is also found in sardines and salmon (canned with bones); tofu and cooked soybeans; and in certain fruits, such as oranges, and vegetables, such as cooked collard, turnip and mustard greens, broccoli, and spinach.

■ Cholesterol is an essential part of all body tissue and is found in foods of animal origin. However, high blood cholesterol has been associated with an increased risk of heart disease. To lower your cholesterol intake, choose low-fat dairy products; trim all visible fat from meats; cook meats on a rack (bake, roast, or broil); and select poultry or fish in place of meats.

The objective of daily menu planning is to provide yourself with basic nutrients while staying within your caloric limit. Remember that no single food supplies all the essential nutrients in the amounts needed, and that variety is the key to success. The greater the variety of food, the less likely you are to develop a deficiency or an excess of any nutrient, and the more interesting and attractive your diet will be.

Recipe Symbols

We have included symbols throughout the book to indicate recipes that can be prepared extra-fast or that are budget stretchers.

This symbol indicates that the recipe can be prepared in 30 minutes or less.

This symbol indicates a budget recipe.

THE QUICK COOK: FAST-FIX HINTS FOR TODAY'S BUSY LIFE-STYLES

Convenience is today's watchword. And it's sure to be tomorrow's, too, as women and men everywhere juggle jobs, families, and other commitments. Their busy life-styles leave precious little spare time, so when it comes to meals, they want to get in and out of the kitchen fast. Yet these quick cooks also want wholesome, nutritious foods the whole family will enjoy.

Enter Weight Watchers. In addition to the scores of easy-to-prepare recipes in this cookbook, you'll find dozens of quick-fix convenience tips in this section. If you own or are considering the purchase of a microwave oven, then this section is a must-read. It's packed with ideas on how to get the most mileage from your microwave oven.

You'll also find hints on using your blender, pressure cooker, slow cooker, or food processor to streamline meal preparation. Plus, we'll let you in on some kitchen shortcuts our chefs swear by. And we'll show you how your freezer can become a storehouse of home-cooked foods for meals at virtually a moment's notice. Now that's convenience!

Convenience Equipment

Food Processor

The versatile and hard-working food processor can blend, chop, grate, shred, mix, slice, knead, and make crumbs quickly and efficiently. Once considered chefs' specialty equipment, food processors are now widely available and enormously popular. They are available in large-capacity models as well as in new compact ones that take up very little counter space and are perfect for small amounts of an ingredient.

These tips will help you make the most of your food processor:

■ Slice or chop salad vegetables in quantity using the processor; store prepared vegetables in covered containers or plastic bags in the refrigerator.

■ Chop large quantities of onion, celery, and green pepper; freeze in premeasured amounts for use in cooking.

■ Process dry foods before moist ones, even if the dry ones are needed last. You won't have to wash the work bowl as often.

■ Rinse blades and bowl immediately after use for easier cleanup.

■ If you accidentally overprocess a food, don't throw it out — find another use for it. Fruits can be used as sauces; vegetables can be seasoned and served as a side dish.

Blender

Before the food processor there was the basic blender. If your blender is stashed away in a cabinet, get it out, put it on the counter, and rediscover what it can do for you.

■ Whip up shakes and mixed drinks
■ Prepare salad dressings and mayonnaise
■ Make tomato sauce
■ Puree fruits and vegetables

When processing liquids, never fill your blender to the top, and always start on low speed, gradually increasing to the desired speed.

Slow Cooker

The slow cooker helps eliminate mealtime hassles by cooking your dinner all day long while you're busy or away. Some recipes call for as much as 10 hours of cooking time, which you can do without any bother at all. When using your slow cooker, keep these tips in mind:

■ If you own a large cooker, you can double or triple your recipe and freeze the extras.

■ Plug the cooker into an automatic timer and set it to go on while you're away. Do remember, though, that most uncooked foods should not stand in the cooker for more than two hours before the cooker goes on.

■ To avoid having to scrub off hardened food residue, add warm water to the cooker immediately after removing the food. Don't wait for the cooker to cool. Some cookers have a removable liner that can be immersed in the sink for washing.

Pressure Cooker

Pressure cookers have been around for many decades — your mother probably had one and used it often. It's still a time and energy saver since foods cook in about one-third of their regular cooking times. That's because the pressure of built-up steam inside the cooker produces higher temperatures than would be produced under regular cooking conditions.

Pressure cookers also preserve valuable nutrients, since foods cook for a short time in a small amount of liquid. Excellent for vegetables, the pressure cooker will also tenderize less tender cuts of meat.

Microwave Oven

The microwave oven is swiftly becoming the most popular appliance on the market today, and with good reason. It's quick, cool, and clean. A microwave oven does the job of a conventional oven in about one-fourth the time, using much less energy. It doesn't heat up your kitchen — a definite "plus" in warm weather. And it's easy to clean with a sponge and warm, soapy water. In fact, cleanup is a breeze if you cook on disposable paper or plastic instead of the traditional utensils.

Micro-convection ovens do the quick-cooking job of a microwave oven but, because they use circulating hot air, will also brown the food the way a convection oven does.

CONVENIENCE TIPS FOR THE MICROWAVE
- Always be sure to follow the manufacturer's directions regarding use and care of your microwave oven.
- Before buying special microwave-safe cookware, test the cookware you already own to determine if it is safe for the microwave oven (metal and metal-trimmed cookware should never be used in the microwave oven). Suppose you want to test one of your ceramic casseroles. Place it in the oven along with a glass 1-cup liquid measure filled with water. Microwave on High for 1 minute. If the water is warm and the casserole is cool, the casserole is safe for use in the oven. If the casserole is warm or hot, it is absorbing microwaves and should not be used in the oven, as it may break. Microwave absorption by cookware also means less efficient cooking of foods.
- Make after-dinner cleanup easier by micro-cooking and serving in the same dish. Try reheating individual portions right on the dinner plate.
- Many foods cooked in the microwave oven continue to cook after being removed from the oven. For this reason, remove them while they are still slightly undercooked, and allow for "standing time" to complete the cooking process. Use the standing time to finish preparing the rest of the meal or to microwave another food.

HOW THE MICROWAVE OVEN CAN MAKE LIFE EASIER

▪ The microwave oven speeds meal preparation. Did you forget to take out that piece of meat or poultry from the freezer in time for it to thaw? Don't worry — the microwave thaws it in minutes. And cooked dishes can be reheated in the time it takes to set the table.

▪ Use the microwave oven to increase the amount of juice that can be squeezed from oranges, lemons, limes, and grapefruits. Before cutting and squeezing, microwave on High until the fruit is slightly warm to the touch, 20 to 25 seconds.

▪ When making flavored vinegars, speed the release of flavors with the microwave oven. Combine the vinegar and herb in a well-washed ketchup or other condiment bottle and microwave until slightly warm (<u>not hot</u>).

▪ To soften and warm tortillas, place 4 tortillas between damp paper towels and microwave on High until warm to the touch, 20 to 40 seconds.

▪ Use your microwave oven to melt chocolate, butter, or margarine. Because the microwave energy penetrates from all sides rather than just the base, as in range-top cooking, the food will melt faster than it would in a double boiler. You don't even have to wait until the food is completely melted — just stir the last small pieces into the already-melted part until it is completely smooth.

▪ Use the microwave to toast coconut. Spread a tablespoon of coconut evenly on a glass plate and microwave on High for 40 to 50 seconds, checking and stirring every 20 seconds.

▪ Plump raisins and other dried fruit in water just to cover in a microwave-safe bowl.

▪ Start cooking chicken or potatoes in the microwave; finish them in a conventional or convection oven, or even on the barbeque, for browning and crispness.

▪ Breads and rolls can be defrosted and warmed in seconds in the microwave oven. Wrap bread in paper towels and microwave <u>just until warm</u> (Overheating will toughen the bread.) Serve immediately, while still warm.

▪ Remember that anything sugary, such as dried fruit, becomes hot very quickly, so time these items carefully to avoid overcooking. Wrap in paper towels to absorb moisture before placing in the microwave oven.

▪ For people on the move, "no time for breakfast" is no longer an acceptable excuse when a microwave oven is available. Hot cereals are seconds away, as are eggs — yes, eggs. Of course, you may not be able to prepare a skillet-type sunny-side-up egg in the microwave oven, but if you want an egg breakfast in a flash, it's a small sacrifice to make.

▪ For a delicious scrambled egg, break the egg into a small, microwave-safe bowl, add 2 tablespoons of skim, low-fat, or whole milk or water, ½ teaspoon of margarine or butter, and a dash of seasoning. Stir as you would for scrambled eggs. Microwave, partially covered, for 1 minute on Medium-High, stir, and continue to microwave on Medium-High, partially covered, until almost set, $\frac{1}{2}$ to 1 minute longer. Let stand $\frac{1}{2}$ to 1 minute before serving. Serve with a slice of toast spread with margarine, butter, or reduced-calorie fruit-flavored spread, and a piece of fruit or a glass of fruit juice. Add a beverage and you have a delicious full meal to start the day, with no skillet to clean.

■ <u>Never</u> microwave eggs in the shell and <u>never</u> microwave a whole egg without pricking the yolk with a toothpick to break the outer membrane. If you forget to do this the egg may explode, making a real mess. (This also applies to foods such as potatoes, eggplant, and winter squash.)

■ Microwave ovens without browning units will not give foods the characteristic, appetizing color we have come to expect from conventional ovens. To add some color, try sprinkling food with seasonings or herbs before microwaving.

■ Top-of-the-range isn't the only way to sauté. When a recipe calls for sautéing, combine the food with the margarine, butter, or oil in a microwave-safe bowl or casserole. Microwave, stirring occasionally, until cooked as desired. Then add other ingredients directly to bowl or casserole and continue cooking. (You can even serve in the same bowl or casserole.) No messy skillet to clean.

The microwave oven does more than cook. It speeds up some tasks which take more time using conventional appliances. The following chart is a guide to some of its many uses.

Reheating or Warming	Melting	Softening	Defrosting
Cup of tea or coffee	Butter/ margarine	Dietary frozen dessert, ice milk, or ice cream	Meats
Liqueurs for flaming	Cheeses	Hardened brown sugar	Poultry
Sauces for pancakes or desserts	Chocolate	Frozen whipped topping	Frozen vegetables
Individual servings of food right on serving plate or in bowl (slice of pie; cup of soup)		Cream cheese (remove foil wrap first)	Frozen baked goods
Warming egg whites — if whites need to be at room temperature for beating		Refrigerated peanut butter (for ease in spreading)	

Freezer Facts

Your freezer is an appliance you probably take for granted, but living without one would certainly be quite inconvenient. Just think back to the days of the "icebox," when people had to buy ice regularly and shop for fresh foods nearly every day. Long-term freezing was virtually unheard of.

Today there are literally thousands of frozen convenience foods in the frozen foods section of large supermarkets. And, for many people, convenience also means preparing home-cooked meals in advance and freezing them.

When wrapping foods (such as meats) for the freezer, be sure to use moisture- and vapor-resistant wrap that molds easily to the shape of the food. Let hot items cool before freezing so you get the most efficient performance from your freezer. Fill freezer containers as close to the top as possible to keep air out. (If filling with liquid, be sure to leave room for expansion that occurs during the freezing process.) A layer of plastic wrap placed directly on the food surface will help prevent ice crystals from forming.

Here are some more tips for turning your freezer into an even greater timesaver.

- Prepare breakfast foods such as pancakes and muffins in advance and freeze. Then just pop them into the microwave oven or toaster-oven to reheat in a flash.

- Casseroles and stews of poultry, fish, or meat with vegetables or pasta freeze well because they are usually coated with sauce. (Cooked potatoes, however, tend to lose their shape and texture when frozen, so avoid freezing dishes containing potatoes.) And, remember, serving-size portions thaw faster.

- Pasta side dishes like lasagna or baked ziti are perfect to prepare ahead and freeze. Don't try freezing a pasta salad, though. The vegetables and dressing will not be appetizing when you serve it.

- Soups and sauces freeze well. For faster thawing, freeze in individual portions (especially welcome on cold days). Don't freeze creamed soups or sauces — you can always add the milk later.

- Desserts such as cakes, cookies, fruit pies, and cobblers not only freeze well but also enable you to prepare in advance so desserts are available when guests drop by.

- Pastry and cookie dough can be prepared whenever you have the time, then frozen, which makes homemade baking a snap!

- Coffee (beans, ground, instant, or freeze-dried) stays fresh for months in the freezer. You can buy it on sale — no more running to the store when you're down to your last potful.

- Flour also can be kept in the freezer for months.

- Don't throw away meat scraps, bones, and pieces of raw vegetables — freeze them for use in making stock.

■ With the aid of your freezer you're no longer limited to enjoying fresh herbs when you have a garden full. Harvest your herbs when they are plentiful or buy them from the local supermarket or greengrocer, snip off the leaves, and seal them in plastic freezer bags. Freeze them and you'll have them on hand whenever a recipe calls for fresh herbs (don't plan to use them for garnish since the freezing process will leave them wilted-looking and, therefore, not as attractive).

The Busy Person's Guide to Kitchen Shortcuts

Following the Weight Watchers food plan means shopping for, preparing, and serving nutritious meals for yourself and your family, as well as for company. But does it have to mean spending endless hours in the supermarket or kitchen? Of course not! Just follow these helpful hints and you'll be able to whiz through your mealtime chores lickety-split.

Shopping

■ Shopping's a breeze when you organize your list so that it corresponds to the aisles in the supermarket. No more doubling back for forgotten items.

■ Take advantage of your supermarket salad bar, where you can find fresh, cut-up vegetables and fruits for salads, soups, stews, stir-fries, and more.

■ Purchase hard-to-find ingredients in quantity; you'll save time by having them on hand when you need them.

■ Planning a special holiday dinner? Do your grocery shopping well in advance to avoid pre-holiday crowds and long lines at the checkout counter.

■ Before you leave on a trip, stock up on staples such as coffee, dry cereal, instant nonfat dry milk powder or UHT skim milk, canned goods, and frozen vegetables. That way, you won't have to run out to the market as soon as you return.

Preparation

■ Assemble all recipe ingredients and do all required preparation (chopping, slicing, etc.) in advance. When you're ready to begin cooking or baking, you'll have everything you need right at your fingertips.

■ It's easier and faster to chop with a sharp knife than a dull one, so why not invest in some of the new knives that never need sharpening.

■ Collecting and measuring out all the ingredients is often the most time-consuming part of preparing a recipe. But you can save time if you measure out another set of dry ingredients, label them, and store them for future use. It makes for speedier preparation the next time around.

- Coordinate the timing of your entire menu so that all dishes are ready at the same time.
- Double or triple salad dressing ingredients and use your blender to combine them. Refrigerate extra dressing in a tightly covered jar.
- Need room-temperature eggs fast? Put them in a bowl of warm (not hot) water.
- When preparing chicken stock, leave the skin on the onions, then strain to remove. They add a golden color to the stock.
- When preparing biscuits, make square ones rather than round so you won't have any dough scraps to re-roll.

Serving

- No time to prepare fancy food for company? Use garnishes to add an elegant touch to simple dishes and platters. Try radish roses, carrot curls, parsley sprigs, or lemon slices dipped in paprika on one half, parsley on the other. Artistic and easy!
- Keep your camera handy to shoot pictures of an attractive table setting or a special dish you've prepared. Date the photos and file them for future reference.

Cleanup

- If you use a charcoal grill, line it with foil before adding charcoal. When you're through cooking and the coals and ashes have cooled, just lift out the foil and throw it away. Your grill will be cleaner and ready to cook your next meal.

Ready to Begin

As you turn the pages of this cookbook, you're bound to find recipe after recipe that you and your family will enjoy. And the menus are sure to make your meals more interesting, and preparation quick and easy. Use this book often and you'll definitely be a mealtime whiz!

January

Lentils, Rice, and Vegetables

JANUARY'S BEST BUYS FOR FRUITS AND VEGETABLES

alfalfa sprouts	cauliflower	leeks	pineapples
avocados	celery	lettuce	potatoes
bananas	Chinese pea pods	mandarin oranges	radishes
bean sprouts	eggplants	mushrooms	scallions (green onions)
Belgian endives	escarole	mustard greens	spinach
bell peppers	grapefruit	onions	sweet potatoes
broccoli	kale	oranges	Swiss chard
brussels sprouts	kiwi fruit	parsnips	tangerines
cabbage	kohlrabi	pears	yams
carrots	kumquats		

BREAKFAST

½ medium Banana, sliced
½ cup Cooked Cereal
½ cup Skim Milk
Coffee or Tea

LUNCH

Roast Beef Sandwich (2 ounces roast
  beef with 2 *each* tomato slices and
  lettuce leaves and 1 teaspoon
  reduced-calorie mayonnaise on
  2 slices reduced-calorie wheat
  bread)
6 *each* Carrot and Zucchini Sticks
1 small Orange
Coffee, Tea, or Mineral Water

DINNER

1 serving **Cauliflower au Gratin Soup**
3 ounces Broiled Chicken Breast
½ cup Cooked Chopped Spinach
1½ cups Mixed Green Salad with
  1 tablespoon Creamy Italian
  Dressing and 1 teaspoon *each*
  Imitation Bacon Bits and Grated
  Parmesan Cheese
12 large Grapes
½ cup Skim Milk
Coffee or Tea

SNACKS

½ cup Low-Calorie Lemon-Flavored
  Gelatin; ½ cup Skim Milk

Total Optional Calories: 85

Cauliflower au Gratin Soup Ⓒ

2 teaspoons reduced-calorie margarine (tub)
½ cup diced onion
2 cups cauliflower florets
¾ cup water
1 packet instant chicken broth and seasoning mix
⅛ teaspoon ground nutmeg
1 cup skim milk
¼ cup half-and-half (blend of milk and cream)
2 ounces Swiss cheese, shredded
3 tablespoons plain dried bread crumbs
Garnish: chopped fresh parsley

In 2-quart saucepan heat margarine until bubbly and hot; add onion and sauté until golden. Add cauliflower, water, broth mix, and nutmeg and bring to a boil. Reduce heat and let simmer until cauliflower is tender, about 15 minutes. Remove from heat and let cool slightly.

Pour half of cauliflower mixture into blender container and, using an on-off motion, process at low speed until cauliflower is finely chopped (<u>do not puree</u>). Transfer mixture to medium bowl and repeat procedure with remaining cauliflower mixture; return chopped cauliflower mixture to saucepan. Add milk and half-and-half and heat (<u>do not boil</u>).

In small bowl combine cheese and bread crumbs. Ladle soup into 2 flameproof soup bowls and sprinkle each with half of the cheese mixture. Arrange bowls on baking sheet and broil until cheese is melted and golden brown. Serve garnished with chopped parsley.

MAKES 2 SERVINGS, ABOUT 1¼ CUPS EACH

Each serving provides: 1 Protein Exchange; ½ Bread Exchange;
  2½ Vegetable Exchanges; ½ Fat Exchange; ½ Milk Exchange;
  55 Optional Calories
Per serving: 284 calories; 17 g protein; 14 g fat; 23 g carbohydrate;
  505 mg calcium; 770 mg sodium; 40 mg cholesterol

TIP: Transform this soup into a real budget-stretcher by substituting vegetables you have on hand for the cauliflower. Try sliced carrots, mushrooms, onions, or chopped spinach or broccoli.

BREAKFAST

½ cup Orange Sections
⅓ cup Cottage Cheese
½ small Bagel, toasted, with
  2 teaspoons Reduced-Calorie
  Orange Marmalade
1 cup Skim Milk

LUNCH

Tuna in a Pita (2 ounces tuna with
  1 tablespoon diced celery, ¼ cup
  alfalfa sprouts, 2 tomato slices,
  ¼ cup shredded lettuce, and
  1 teaspoon reduced-calorie
  mayonnaise in 1-ounce pita bread)
6 *each* Cucumber Spears and Green
  Bell Pepper Strips
1 small Apple
Coffee, Tea, or Mineral Water

DINNER

1 serving **Roasted Vegetable Bisque**
3 ounces Roast Veal
3 ounces Baked Potato topped with
  ¼ cup Plain Low-Fat Yogurt and
  Chopped Chives
½ cup Cooked Sliced Carrot
1½ cups Tossed Salad with
  1 tablespoon Russian Dressing
Cinnamon-Spiced Tea

SNACKS

½ cup Canned Pineapple Chunks

Total Optional Calories: 30

Roasted Vegetable Bisque

A hearty creamed soup that's sure to warm up a cold winter day.

2 medium thoroughly washed leeks (white portion only)
1 <u>each</u> medium eggplant (1 to 1¼ pounds), medium zucchini, and medium red bell pepper
2 teaspoons margarine
½ cup finely chopped celery
1 tablespoon chopped shallots
2 garlic cloves, minced
2 cups <u>each</u> low-fat milk (1% milk fat) and water
2 packets instant chicken broth and seasoning mix
1 medium tomato, blanched, peeled, seeded, and finely chopped
1 tablespoon <u>each</u> minced fresh basil and fresh parsley
¼ teaspoon salt
Dash pepper

Preheat broiler. On baking sheet lined with heavy-duty foil broil leeks, eggplant, zucchini, and bell pepper, turning frequently, until vegetables are charred on all sides; let stand until cool enough to handle, 15 to 20 minutes.

In 3- or 4-quart saucepan heat margarine over medium-high heat until bubbly and hot; add celery, shallots, and garlic and sauté, stirring occasionally, until vegetables are softened, 1 to 2 minutes. Stir in milk, water, and broth mix, stirring to dissolve broth mix; remove from heat and set aside.

Peel roasted vegetables and remove and discard stem ends. Cut eggplant and bell pepper into halves and remove and discard seeds. Coarsely chop 1 eggplant half and the zucchini; transfer to blender container or work bowl of food processor, add 1 cup milk mixture, and process until smooth. Return pureed mixture to saucepan with remaining milk mixture. Finely chop remaining roasted vegetables and add to saucepan along with tomato and seasonings; cook over medium heat until flavors blend and mixture is thoroughly heated, 10 to 15 minutes (<u>do not boil</u>).

MAKES 4 SERVINGS, ABOUT 1½ CUPS EACH

Each serving provides: 3½ Vegetable Exchanges; ½ Fat Exchange; ½ Milk Exchange; 15 Optional Calories
Per serving: 136 calories; 7 g protein; 4 g fat; 21 g carbohydrate; 230 mg calcium; 739 mg sodium; 5 mg cholesterol

1 medium Kiwi Fruit, sliced
Mushroom Omelet (1 egg and ¼ cup
   cooked sliced mushrooms,
   prepared with 1 teaspoon
   reduced-calorie margarine)
½ English Muffin, toasted
½ cup Skim Milk
Coffee or Tea

LUNCH

Peanut Butter and Jelly Sandwich
   (2 tablespoons peanut butter with
   2 teaspoons reduced-calorie grape
   spread on 2 slices reduced-calorie
   white bread)
1 large Tangerine
Coffee, Tea, or Mineral Water

DINNER

3 ounces Roast Chicken
½ cup Cooked Rice sprinkled with
   Chopped Parsley
½ cup Cooked Kale with Lemon Juice
2 cups Tossed Salad with
   1 tablespoon French Dressing
½ cup Skim Milk
Coffee or Tea

SNACKS

Horseradish Dip (½ cup plain low-fat
   yogurt mixed with 1 teaspoon
   horseradish) with 6 Green Bell
   Pepper Strips, 8 Cucumber Slices,
   and ½ cup Cauliflower Florets;
   1 serving **Party Bologna Stacks**

Total Optional Calories: 110

Party Bologna Stacks ◐◑

Beautiful, colorful, and delicious. Makes a great
hors d'oeuvre or snack!

3 tablespoons whipped cream cheese
1 tablespoon plus 1 teaspoon mayonnaise
1 tablespoon chopped chives
½ teaspoon prepared mustard
1 to 2 drops hot sauce
8-ounce package sliced bologna (1-ounce slices)
½ medium cucumber, cut into 8 thin slices
⅓ cup drained canned pimientos, cut into 16 small pieces

In small mixing bowl combine first 5 ingredients, mixing to
form a smooth paste. Spread 1 bologna slice with ⅙ of
cream cheese mixture (about 2 teaspoons); top with
another bologna slice. Continue spreading and stacking 2
more times, ending with the fourth bologna slice. Using
remaining bologna and cream cheese mixture, repeat
procedure. Arrange stacks on freezer-safe plate; cover with
plastic freezer wrap and freeze for 10 minutes.

   Set chilled bologna stacks on cutting board and, using a
sharp knife, carefully cut each stack into 8 wedges. Cut each
cucumber slice in half and arrange 1 slice on each wedge;
top each with a piece of pimiento. Using a decorative
toothpick, secure cucumber and pimiento to each wedge;
arrange wedges on serving platter. Serve immediately or
cover and refrigerate until ready to serve.

MAKES 8 SERVINGS, 2 WEDGES EACH

Each serving provides: 1 Protein Exchange; ¼ Vegetable Exchange;
   ½ Fat Exchange; 15 Optional Calories
Per serving: 122 calories; 4 g protein; 11 g fat; 2 g carbohydrate;
   9 mg calcium; 322 mg sodium; 21 mg cholesterol

Italian Potato Casserole ⓒ

1 ⅓ cups potato flakes (instant mashed potatoes)
**1 tablespoon plus 1 teaspoon reduced-calorie
    margarine (tub)**
¼ cup finely chopped onion
1 garlic clove, minced
½ cup part-skim ricotta cheese
1 egg, lightly beaten
½ ounce grated Parmesan cheese
2 tablespoons chopped fresh parsley
½ teaspoon salt
⅛ teaspoon pepper
2 ½ ounces mozzarella cheese, shredded

In 1-quart saucepan bring 1¾ cups water to a boil; remove from heat, add potato flakes, and stir until mixture is smooth and no lumps remain.

Preheat oven to 350°F. In 8-inch skillet heat margarine over medium-high heat until bubbly and hot; add onion and garlic and sauté until softened, 1 to 2 minutes. Transfer to medium mixing bowl; add potatoes and remaining ingredients except mozzarella cheese, mixing well.

Spray 1-quart casserole with nonstick cooking spray; spread half of the potato mixture in bottom of casserole. Sprinkle half of the mozzarella cheese over potato mixture in casserole; top with remaining potato mixture, then sprinkle with remaining cheese. Bake until top is lightly browned, 25 to 30 minutes.

MAKES 4 SERVINGS

Each serving provides: 1½ Protein Exchanges; 1 Bread Exchange;
    ⅛ Vegetable Exchange; ½ Fat Exchange
Per serving: 390 calories; 15 g protein; 11 g fat; 58 g carbohydrate;
    263 mg calcium; 593 mg sodium; 95 mg cholesterol

BREAKFAST

½ cup Orange Juice
Lox 'n' Bagel (½ small bagel topped with 2 tablespoons whipped cream cheese and 1 ounce smoked salmon)
1 cup Skim Milk

LUNCH

Egg Salad Sandwich (2 hard-cooked eggs, chopped, with 1 tablespoon *each* chopped pickle, onion, and celery, 2 lettuce leaves, and 2 teaspoons reduced-calorie mayonnaise on 2 slices reduced-calorie wheat bread)
½ cup Broccoli Florets and 6 Cherry Tomatoes
1 large Tangerine
Coffee, Tea, or Mineral Water

DINNER

1 serving **Lentils, Rice, and Vegetables**
1 cup Cooked Chopped Spinach
1½ cups Mixed Green Salad with 1 teaspoon Grated Parmesan Cheese and 1½ teaspoons Italian Dressing mixed with 2 teaspoons Red Wine Vinegar
½ cup Low-Calorie Lemon-Flavored Gelatin topped with 1 tablespoon Whipped Topping
Coffee or Tea

SNACKS

½ cup Fruit Salad; 1 serving Reduced-Calorie Chocolate Dairy Drink

Total Optional Calories: 135

Lentils, Rice, and Vegetables ⊄

A wonderful prepare-ahead meal because it is even better a day or two after it's prepared. Just reheat and serve.

2 teaspoons olive <u>or</u> vegetable oil
2 cups thinly sliced onions
½ cup <u>each</u> thinly sliced red and yellow bell peppers (thin strips)
1 small garlic clove, minced
2 cups water
3 ounces sorted uncooked lentils, rinsed
2 ounces uncooked brown rice
1 packet instant chicken broth and seasoning mix
2 tablespoons sour cream
2 teaspoons chopped fresh Italian (flat-leaf) parsley

In 2-quart saucepan heat oil over high heat; add onions, peppers, and garlic and cook, stirring frequently, until tender, 8 to 10 minutes. Remove 1 cup of vegetable mixture to small bowl; set aside and keep warm.

Add water, lentils, rice, and broth mix to vegetable mixture remaining in saucepan and cook, stirring occasionally, until mixture comes to a boil. Reduce heat to low, cover, and let simmer until lentils and rice are tender, about 40 minutes. Transfer to serving platter and top with reserved vegetable mixture; spoon sour cream onto vegetable mixture and serve sprinkled with parsley.

MAKES 2 SERVINGS, ABOUT 1½ CUPS EACH

Each serving provides: 2 Protein Exchanges; 1 Bread Exchange; 3 Vegetable Exchanges; 1 Fat Exchange; 40 Optional Calories
Per serving: 390 calories; 16 g protein; 9 g fat; 63 g carbohydrate; 106 mg calcium; 523 mg sodium; 6 mg cholesterol

BREAKFAST

½ medium Banana, sliced
¾ ounce Cold Cereal
½ cup Skim Milk
Coffee or Tea

LUNCH

Ham Sandwich (2 ounces baked ham
    with 3 tomato slices and 1 tea-
    spoon mayonnaise on 2 slices
    reduced-calorie rye bread)
½ cup Cauliflower Florets and
    6 Radishes
1 small Apple
Coffee, Tea, or Mineral Water

DINNER

1 serving **Seafood Stew**
1 cup Cooked Cut Green Beans with
    1 teaspoon Margarine
1½ cups Tossed Salad with
    1 tablespoon Reduced-Calorie
    Blue Cheese Dressing
Gelatin 'n' Yogurt (½ cup low-calorie
    cherry-flavored gelatin topped
    with ¼ cup plain low-fat yogurt)
Cinnamon-Apple Tea

SNACKS

½ cup Reduced-Calorie Butterscotch
    Pudding; 1 small Orange

Total Optional Calories: 50

Seafood Stew

Cod, scrod, or red snapper fillets are all excellent choices in this hearty and satisfying stew. To prepare in quantity to freeze, or to serve a larger group, just double the recipe.

1 tablespoon plus 1 teaspoon olive _or_ vegetable oil
½ cup _each_ diced onion, celery, carrot,
    and green bell pepper
1 garlic clove, minced
2 cups canned Italian tomatoes (with liquid); drain and
    chop tomatoes, reserving liquid
1½ cups water
6 ounces pared potato, cut into cubes
1 tablespoon chopped fresh Italian (flat-leaf) parsley
1 packet instant chicken broth and seasoning mix
1 bay leaf
¼ teaspoon thyme leaves
⅛ teaspoon pepper
10 ounces firm white fish fillets, cut into chunks
5 ounces shelled and deveined medium shrimp

In 2-quart saucepan heat oil; add onion, celery, carrot, bell pepper, and garlic and sauté until tender-crisp, about 5 minutes. Add remaining ingredients except fish and shrimp and bring to a boil. Reduce heat, cover, and let simmer until potatoes are tender, 20 to 25 minutes. Add fish and shrimp and stir to combine; cook until fish flakes easily when tested with a fork and shrimp just turn pink, about 5 minutes. Remove and discard bay leaf before serving.

MAKES 4 SERVINGS, ABOUT 1½ CUPS EACH

Each serving provides: 3 Protein Exchanges; ½ Bread Exchange;
    2 Vegetable Exchanges; 1 Fat Exchange; 3 Optional Calories
Per serving with cod or scrod: 217 calories; 23 g protein; 6 g fat;
    18 g carbohydrate; 88 mg calcium; 579 mg sodium; 81 mg cholesterol
With red snapper: 224 calories; 24 g protein; 6 g fat; 18 g carbohydrate;
    88 mg calcium; 588 mg sodium; 89 mg cholesterol

BREAKFAST

Oatmeal 'n' Raisins (½ cup cooked
oatmeal with 2 tablespoons raisins,
1 teaspoon reduced-calorie
margarine, and ½ teaspoon honey)
1 serving Reduced-Calorie
Hot Cocoa

LUNCH

Chicken Salad (2 ounces diced
chicken with ½ cup *each* bean
sprouts and broccoli florets, ¼ cup
alfalfa sprouts, 2 lettuce leaves,
and 1½ teaspoons Italian dressing
mixed with 2 teaspoons red wine
vinegar)
¾ ounce Flatbread
½ medium Banana
Coffee, Tea, or Mineral Water

DINNER

1 serving **Shrimp and Vegetable Sauté**
½ cup Cooked Leeks with Chopped
Parsley
Bibb Salad (1½ cups torn Bibb lettuce
with ¼ cup shredded carrot plus
red wine vinegar and herbs)
Kiwi 'n' Sherbet (½ cup lemon sherbet
topped with 1 medium kiwi fruit,
sliced)
½ cup Skim Milk
Coffee or Tea

SNACKS

1 cup Strawberries; ½ cup Skim Milk

Total Optional Calories: 270

Shrimp and Vegetable Sauté

1 tablespoon margarine
1 cup quartered mushrooms
½ cup diced shallots or onion
2 tablespoons drained capers, rinsed
½ pound shelled and deveined large shrimp (tail feathers left on)
1 cup each thawed frozen artichoke hearts, cut into quarters, and canned Italian tomatoes (with liquid); drain and chop tomatoes, reserving liquid
4 slices crisp bacon, crumbled
2 tablespoons dry white table wine
2 large pitted black olives, cut into quarters
Dash each salt, pepper, and lemon juice
1 cup cooked long-grain rice (hot)
Garnish: 1 each lemon twist and Italian (flat-leaf) parsley sprig

In 10-inch nonstick skillet heat margarine until bubbly and hot; add mushrooms, shallots (or onion), and capers and cook until shallots (or onion) are translucent, 1 to 2 minutes. Add shrimp and cook, stirring frequently, just until shrimp turn pink, 1 to 2 minutes. Add remaining ingredients except rice and garnish and stir to combine; continue cooking until mixture is heated through, about 5 minutes. Transfer shrimp mixture to serving platter. Arrange rice in a circle around shrimp mixture; garnish with lemon twist and parsley sprig.

MAKES 2 SERVINGS

Each serving provides: 3 Protein Exchanges; 1 Bread Exchange;
    3½ Vegetable Exchanges; 1½ Fat Exchanges; 110 Optional Calories
Per serving: 467 calories; 35 g protein; 15 g fat; 46 g carbohydrate;
    149 mg calcium; 1,065 mg sodium; 172 mg cholesterol

BREAKFAST

⅓ cup Pineapple Juice
Swiss and "Bacon" Melt (½ English
    muffin, toasted, topped with
    1 ounce Swiss cheese and
    1 teaspoon imitation bacon bits
    and broiled)
½ cup Skim Milk
Coffee or Tea

LUNCH

Chick-Pea and Green Bean Toss
    (2 ounces canned chick-peas with
    1 cup chilled cooked cut green
    beans and 1 teaspoon vegetable
    oil mixed with 2 teaspoons red
    wine vinegar plus seasonings)
1 large Tangerine
Coffee, Tea, or Mineral Water

DINNER

1 serving **Anniversary Party Pâté**
    with 6 Saltines
3 ounces Roast Veal
½ cup Cooked Noodles sprinkled
    with 1 teaspoon Poppy Seed
½ cup Cooked Sliced Carrot
1½ cups Mixed Green Salad with
    1 tablespoon Russian Dressing
½ cup Reduced-Calorie Chocolate
    Pudding topped with 1 tablespoon
    Aerosol Instant Whipped Cream
Coffee or Tea

SNACKS

Orange 'n' Yogurt (½ cup orange
    sections topped with ¼ cup plain
    low-fat yogurt and sprinkled with
    1 teaspoon shredded coconut)

Total Optional Calories: 120

Anniversary Party Pâté ◑

Delicious as a spread on melba rounds or saltines or serve on a bed of lettuce with chopped hard-cooked egg and red onion.

1 tablespoon plus 1 teaspoon lightly salted butter, divided
10 ounces chicken cutlets, cut into 2-inch cubes
¼ cup chopped shallots
2 tablespoons cognac <u>or</u> brandy
1 tablespoon whipping cream
Dash <u>each</u> salt, pepper, and thyme leaves

In small nonstick skillet heat 2 teaspoons butter until bubbly and hot; add chicken and shallots and sauté, stirring occasionally, until chicken is browned, 10 to 15 minutes. Transfer mixture to work bowl of food processor; set aside.

To same skillet add cognac (or brandy) and cook over medium-high heat, using a wooden spoon to scrape particles from sides and bottom of pan, until mixture is slightly reduced, 1 to 2 minutes. Add to mixture in food processor and let cool slightly. Using an on-off motion, process mixture until well blended (<u>do not puree</u>); add remaining 2 teaspoons butter along with the cream and seasonings and process just until thoroughly combined, about 1 second. Using a rubber scraper, transfer mixture to serving bowl; serve immediately or cover and refrigerate until chilled.

MAKES 4 SERVINGS, ABOUT ¼ CUP EACH

Each serving provides: 2 Protein Exchanges; ⅛ Vegetable Exchange;
    65 Optional Calories
Per serving: 150 calories; 17 g protein; 6 g fat; 2 g carbohydrate;
    16 mg calcium; 121 mg sodium; 57 mg cholesterol

TIP: Leftover pâté may be stored in the refrigerator, in a covered container, for up to 1 week. Let stand at room temperature for 10 minutes before serving.

Capered Turkey Amandine ◖

**¼ cup canned ready-to-serve chicken broth
2 tablespoons dry white table wine
1½ teaspoons lemon juice
¼ teaspoon Dijon-style mustard
1 teaspoon <u>each</u> vegetable oil and margarine
½ pound turkey cutlets, cut into ¼-inch-thick slices
½ ounce sliced almonds
1 teaspoon all-purpose flour
1 tablespoon drained capers
½ teaspoon minced fresh parsley**

In 1-cup liquid measure combine broth, wine, lemon juice, and mustard; set aside.

In 9- or 10-inch nonstick skillet heat oil and margarine together over medium-high heat until margarine is bubbly and mixture is hot; add turkey and sauté, turning once, until lightly browned and cooked through, 2 to 3 minutes on each side. Transfer turkey to serving platter; set aside and keep warm.

In same skillet sauté almonds over medium-high heat, stirring frequently, until lightly browned, 1 to 2 minutes; sprinkle with flour and stir quickly to combine. Gradually stir in broth mixture. Reduce heat to medium; add capers and parsley and cook, stirring frequently, until mixture thickens, 3 to 5 minutes. Pour almond mixture over turkey and serve immediately.

MAKES 2 SERVINGS

Each serving provides: 3 Protein Exchanges; 1 Fat Exchange; 70 Optional
    Calories
Per serving: 230 calories; 28 g protein; 10 g fat; 3 g carbohydrate;
    37 mg calcium; 354 mg sodium; 70 mg cholesterol

BREAKFAST

½ medium Banana, sliced
½ cup Cooked Cereal
1 cup Skim Milk
Coffee or Tea

LUNCH

Tuna Salad (2 ounces tuna with
2 tablespoons *each* chopped onion
and celery and 1 tablespoon
reduced-calorie mayonnaise
on 4 lettuce leaves)
6 *each* Radishes and Cucumber
Spears
1 small Orange
Coffee, Tea, or Mineral Water

DINNER

¾ cup Chicken Bouillon
1 serving **Chili Cups**
1 cup Cooked Broccoli Florets
1½ cups Mixed Green Salad with
1½ teaspoons Italian Dressing
mixed with 2 teaspoons Red Wine
Vinegar
½ cup Low-Calorie Lime-Flavored
Gelatin
Cinnamon-Spiced Tea

SNACKS

½ cup Reduced-Calorie Vanilla
Pudding; ½ cup Canned Fruit
Cocktail

Total Optional Calories: 20

Chili Cups

1 teaspoon olive <u>or</u> vegetable oil
7 ounces ground veal
¼ cup <u>each</u> diced onion and green bell pepper
½ small jalapeño pepper, seeded and minced
1 small garlic clove, minced
1½ teaspoons chopped fresh cilantro (Chinese parsley)
½ cup canned Italian tomatoes (with liquid); drain and chop tomatoes, reserving liquid
¼ teaspoon <u>each</u> salt and chili powder
Dash pepper
2 ready-to-bake refrigerated buttermilk flaky biscuits (1 ounce each)
1 ounce Monterey Jack cheese, shredded

In small nonstick skillet heat oil; add veal, onion, bell pepper, jalapeño pepper, garlic, and cilantro and cook, breaking up large pieces of veal with a wooden spoon, until veal is crumbly and lightly browned and vegetables are soft, about 5 minutes. Stir in tomatoes, reserved liquid, and seasonings and bring to a boil. Reduce heat and let simmer, stirring occasionally, until liquid has evaporated, 3 to 5 minutes. Remove from heat and set aside.

Preheat oven to 400°F. Into each of two 10-ounce flameproof custard cups place 1 biscuit; press biscuit into bottom and up sides of cup to form a crust. Spoon half of veal mixture into each cup; top each portion with ½ ounce cheese. Place cups on baking sheet and bake until crust is browned, 10 to 12 minutes. Turn oven control to broil and broil until cheese begins to brown, about 1 minute.

MAKES 2 SERVINGS, 1 CUP EACH

Each serving provides: 3 Protein Exchanges; 1 Bread Exchange;
1⅛ Vegetable Exchanges; ½ Fat Exchange
Per serving: 354 calories; 25 g protein; 20 g fat; 18 g carbohydrate;
144 mg calcium; 840 mg sodium; 83 mg cholesterol

TIP: The flavor of chili improves when prepared in advance, so take advantage of this time-saving tip — prepare veal mixture a day or two before serving. Then just shape the cups, fill, and bake.

BREAKFAST

Pineapple Cheese (⅓ cup cottage
  cheese mixed with ½ cup canned
  crushed pineapple and ½ teaspoon
  honey)
¼ cup Skim Milk
Coffee or Tea

LUNCH

Turkey Sandwich (2 ounces sliced
  turkey with ¼ cup grated carrot,
  2 lettuce leaves, and 2 teaspoons
  mayonnaise on 2 slices reduced-
  calorie multi-grain bread)
6 *each* Red Bell Pepper Strips and
  Celery Sticks
Coffee, Tea, or Mineral Water

DINNER

1 serving **Pork Fajita Pitas**
1 cup Cooked Cut Green Beans
1½ cups Mixed Green Salad with
  1½ teaspoons French Dressing
  mixed with 2 teaspoons Red Wine
  Vinegar and ¼ teaspoon Mustard
2-inch wedge Honeydew Melon
½ cup Skim Milk
Coffee or Tea

SNACKS

1 serving Reduced-Calorie Chocolate
  Dairy Drink; 1 small Orange

Total Optional Calories: 15

Pork Fajita Pitas

**2 tablespoons <u>each</u> red wine vinegar, Worcestershire
  sauce, and water**
Salt and pepper
4 small garlic cloves
15 ounces pork cutlets
**4 small plum tomatoes, blanched, peeled, seeded, and
  chopped**
¼ cup <u>each</u> minced onion and green bell pepper
1 small jalapeño pepper, seeded and minced
**1 tablespoon <u>each</u> chopped fresh cilantro (Chinese
  parsley) and ketchup**
4 pita breads (1 ounce each), heated
½ cup plain low-fat yogurt
Garnish: cilantro sprig (Chinese parsley)

In small saucepan combine vinegar, Worcestershire sauce,
water, and ¼ teaspoon <u>each</u> salt and pepper. Mash 2 garlic
cloves; add to saucepan and cook, stirring occasionally, until
mixture is heated through, about 2 minutes. Pour into heat-
resistant bowl (not aluminum*); add pork, turn to coat with
marinade, and let stand at room temperature for 5 minutes.

In medium bowl combine tomatoes, onion, bell pepper,
jalapeño pepper, cilantro, ketchup, and dash <u>each</u> salt and
pepper. Mince remaining garlic cloves; add to vegetable
mixture and stir to combine. Cover bowl with plastic wrap
and refrigerate until ready to serve.

Remove pork from marinade, reserving marinade. Set
pork on rack in broiling pan and broil, turning several times
and basting with reserved marinade, until pork is browned
and thoroughly cooked, 8 to 10 minutes.

To serve, transfer pork to work surface and thinly slice. Cut
each pita in half crosswise, making 8 halves; open each half
to form a pocket. Fill each half with ⅛ of the pork slices and
⅛ of the tomato mixture. Arrange on serving platter and
serve with yogurt. Garnish with cilantro.

MAKES 4 SERVINGS

Each serving provides: 3 Protein Exchanges; 1 Bread Exchange;
  ¾ Vegetable Exchange; ¼ Milk Exchange; 5 Optional Calories
Per serving: 329 calories; 32 g protein; 10 g fat; 26 g carbohydrate;
  73 mg calcium; 597 mg sodium; 85 mg cholesterol

*It's best to marinate in glass or stainless-steel containers; acidic ingredients
  such as vinegar may react with aluminum, causing color and flavor changes
  in foods.

Sausage, Apple, and Cheddar Bake

A lovely winter weekend lunch.

1½ pounds Granny Smith apples, cored, pared, and cut
  into ¼-inch-thick slices
1 tablespoon lemon juice
2 ounces cooked veal sausage, cut into ½-inch-thick
  slices
¼ cup chopped scallions (green onions)
2 slices white bread, made into fine crumbs or ⅓ cup
  plus 2 teaspoons plain dried bread crumbs
2 ounces Cheddar cheese, shredded
2 tablespoons firmly packed dark brown sugar
¼ teaspoon ground cinnamon
2 tablespoons plus 2 teaspoons reduced-calorie
  margarine (tub), melted

Preheat oven to 350°F. In medium mixing bowl combine
apples and lemon juice, tossing to combine; add sausage
and scallions and mix well. Spray 8 x 8 x 2-inch baking
pan with nonstick cooking spray and spread apple
mixture evenly in bottom of pan; set aside.

In small mixing bowl combine bread crumbs, cheese,
sugar, and cinnamon, mixing well until thoroughly
combined; add margarine and stir until moistened.
Sprinkle crumb mixture evenly over apple mixture and
bake until apples are tender and topping is lightly
browned, 20 to 30 minutes.

MAKES 4 SERVINGS

Each serving provides: 1 Protein Exchange; ½ Bread Exchange;
  ⅛ Vegetable Exchange; 1 Fat Exchange; 1½ Fruit Exchanges;
  30 Optional Calories
Per serving with bread: 267 calories; 9 g protein; 11 g fat; 35 g
  carbohydrate; 131 mg calcium; 422 mg sodium; 30 mg cholesterol
With dried bread crumbs: 271 calories; 9 g protein; 11 g fat; 36 g
  carbohydrate; 132 mg calcium; 430 mg sodium; 30 mg cholesterol

Variation: Bacon, Apple, and Cheddar Bake (Week 5) —
substitute 2 ounces diced Canadian-style bacon for the
veal sausage.

Per serving with bread: 256 calories; 8 g protein; 11 g fat; 35 g
  carbohydrate; 131 mg calcium; 432 mg sodium; 22 mg cholesterol
With dried bread crumbs: 265 calories; 8 g protein; 11 g fat; 36 g
  carbohydrate; 133 mg calcium; 459 mg sodium; 24 mg cholesterol

Kasha Stuffing

An excellent side dish with roast chicken or
Cornish hen.

**4 ounces uncooked coarse-grain buckwheat groats
   (kasha)**
1 egg, lightly beaten
1 teaspoon salt
½ teaspoon pepper
1 tablespoon vegetable oil
1 teaspoon margarine
½ pound Granny Smith apples, cored, pared, and diced
½ cup <u>each</u> diced onion and green bell pepper
2 cups water
2 packets instant chicken broth and seasoning mix
¼ cup dark raisins
⅛ teaspoon <u>each</u> thyme leaves and ground sage

In 4-quart saucepan combine kasha, egg, salt, and pepper
and cook over medium heat, stirring constantly, until grains
of kasha are dry and separated and egg is set; remove from
heat and set aside.

   In 10-inch skillet heat oil and margarine together until
margarine is bubbly and mixture is hot; add apples, onion,
and bell pepper and cook, stirring occasionally, until onion is
translucent and apples are softened, 3 to 4 minutes. Add
apple mixture, water, broth mix, raisins, thyme, and sage to
kasha mixture and stir to combine; bring to a boil. Reduce
heat to low, cover, and let simmer until liquid is absorbed
and kasha is soft.

MAKES 4 SERVINGS, ABOUT ¾ CUP EACH

Each serving provides: 1 Bread Exchange; ½ Vegetable Exchange; 1 Fat
   Exchange; 1 Fruit Exchange; 25 Optional Calories
Per serving: 223 calories; 6 g protein; 7 g fat; 38 g carbohydrate; 58 mg
   calcium; 1,076 mg sodium; 69 mg cholesterol

BREAKFAST

⅓ cup Apple Juice
Lox 'n' Bagel (½ small bagel topped with 2 tablespoons whipped cream cheese and 1 ounce smoked salmon)
1 cup Skim Milk

LUNCH

Chick-Pea 'n' Egg Combo (2 ounces canned chick-peas with 1 hard-cooked egg, sliced, 1 cup torn spinach, 6 tomato wedges, 1 teaspoon imitation bacon bits, and 1½ teaspoons French dressing mixed with 2 teaspoons lemon juice and ¼ teaspoon mustard)
¾ ounce Crispbread
1 small Orange
Coffee, Tea, or Mineral Water

DINNER

4 ounces Broiled Swordfish with Lemon Wedge
1 serving **Pasta with Roasted Pepper Sauce**
½ cup *each* Cooked Chinese Pea Pods and Sliced Bamboo Shoots
1½ cups Mixed Green Salad with 1½ teaspoons Olive Oil mixed with 2 teaspoons Tarragon Vinegar plus Seasonings
½ cup Low-Calorie Lemon-Flavored Gelatin topped with 1 tablespoon Whipping Cream
Coffee or Tea

SNACKS

Prune Yogurt (½ cup plain low-fat yogurt mixed with 3 medium prunes, chopped, sprinkled with cinnamon)

Total Optional Calories: 140

Pasta with Roasted Pepper Sauce

Roasting helps develop the rich flavor of peppers. You'll love what it does to this sauce.

1 medium red bell pepper
2 teaspoons olive or vegetable oil
1 garlic clove, sliced
½ cup canned Italian tomatoes (with liquid); drain and chop tomatoes, reserving liquid
1 tablespoon drained capers
2 drained canned anchovy fillets, diced
2 pitted black olives, chopped
¼ teaspoon each salt and oregano leaves
Dash pepper
2 cups cooked fettuccine or spaghetti (hot)
1½ teaspoons chopped fresh Italian (flat-leaf) parsley

Preheat broiler. On baking sheet lined with heavy-duty foil broil pepper 3 inches from heat source, turning frequently, until charred on all sides; let stand until cool enough to handle, 15 to 20 minutes.

Peel pepper; remove and discard stem ends and seeds. Chop pepper and set aside.

In 9- or 10-inch nonstick skillet heat oil over medium heat; add garlic and sauté, stirring frequently, until browned (be careful not to burn). Add tomatoes and reserved liquid and cook, continuing to stir frequently, until mixture is heated through, 5 to 7 minutes; add roasted pepper, capers, anchovies, olives, and seasonings and let simmer until thoroughly heated, 3 to 5 minutes. Serve sauce over pasta and sprinkle with parsley.

MAKES 4 SERVINGS

Each serving provides: 1 Bread Exchange; ¾ Vegetable Exchange; ½ Fat Exchange; 5 Optional Calories
Per serving: 117 calories; 3 g protein; 3 g fat; 19 g carbohydrate; 24 mg calcium; 272 mg sodium; 1 mg cholesterol

Variation: Pasta with Pignolia Pepper Sauce (Week 8) — Sauté ½ ounce pignolias (pine nuts) along with the garlic; proceed as directed. Increase Optional Calories to 25.

Per serving: 135 calories; 4 g protein; 5 g fat; 19 g carbohydrate; 25 mg calcium; 272 mg sodium; 1 mg cholesterol

BREAKFAST

BREAKFAST

½ cup Orange Sections
Cheese and "Bacon" Melt (½ English
  muffin, toasted, topped with
  1 ounce American cheese and
  1 teaspoon imitation bacon bits
  and broiled)
½ cup Skim Milk
Coffee or Tea

LUNCH

Turkey "Reuben" (2 ounces sliced
  turkey with ¼ cup sauerkraut and
  1½ teaspoons Russian dressing on
  2 slices reduced-calorie rye bread)
6 *each* Carrot and Green Bell Pepper
  Sticks
1 small Apple
Coffee, Tea, or Mineral Water

DINNER

3 ounces Broiled Veal Chop
1 serving **Spaghetti with Garlic-
  Hazelnut Sauce**
1 cup Cooked Chopped Spinach
  with 1 teaspoon Reduced-Calorie
  Margarine
1½ cups Shredded Romaine Lettuce
  with 2 Pitted Black Olives, sliced,
  and 1 tablespoon Reduced-Calorie
  Italian Dressing
Apricot Yogurt (½ cup plain low-fat
  yogurt mixed with 4 dried apricot
  halves, diced, and 1 teaspoon
  reduced-calorie apricot spread)
4 fluid ounces Dry White Wine
Coffee or Tea

SNACKS

1 medium Kiwi Fruit; ½ cup
  Skim Milk

Total Optional Calories: 180

Spaghetti with Garlic-Hazelnut Sauce

This delicately flavored side dish is a delicious addition to an Italian meal.

2 to 3 unpeeled garlic cloves
¾ ounce shelled hazelnuts
2 tablespoons olive oil
¼ teaspoon salt
Dash pepper
2 cups cooked thin spaghetti (hot)
1 tablespoon plus 1 teaspoon grated Parmesan cheese
2 teaspoons chopped fresh Italian (flat-leaf) parsley

Preheat broiler. On baking sheet lined with heavy-duty foil broil garlic cloves 4 to 5 inches from heat source, turning frequently, until charred on all sides; let stand until cool enough to handle, at least 10 minutes.

Turn oven control to 300°F. Arrange hazelnuts on separate baking sheet and roast, shaking pan frequently, until browned on all sides, about 10 minutes. Transfer nuts to center of clean kitchen towel; rub with ends of towel to remove skins. Finely chop nuts and set aside.

Remove and discard skins from garlic cloves (garlic will have a pastelike consistency) and transfer to small bowl; add oil and, using a fork, mash until combined. Heat 8-inch nonstick skillet; add garlic mixture and cook over medium heat for 1 minute, stirring constantly. Add salt and pepper and stir to combine; remove from heat.

To serve, in medium bowl top spaghetti with hazelnuts, garlic mixture, and Parmesan cheese; using 2 forks, toss well until spaghetti is thoroughly coated. Serve sprinkled with parsley.

MAKES 4 SERVINGS

Each serving provides: 1 Bread Exchange; 1½ Fat Exchanges; 45 Optional
  Calories
Per serving: 182 calories; 4 g protein; 11 g fat; 18 g carbohydrate; 44 mg
  calcium; 168 mg sodium; 1 mg cholesterol

BREAKFAST

¾ ounce Cold Cereal
½ cup Skim Milk
1 serving **Easy Pineapple "Danish"**
Coffee or Tea

LUNCH

Chicken-Vegetable Platter (2 ounces
   sliced chicken with 8 tomato
   wedges, 6 cucumber slices,
   3 sliced radishes, and 1 tablespoon
   reduced-calorie mayonnaise on
   1½ cups torn lettuce)
2 Melba Slices
1 small Orange
Coffee or Tea

DINNER

4 ounces Broiled Bluefish Fillets
1 cup Cooked Cauliflower Florets
   with ¼ cup Chopped Pimientos
½ cup Cooked French-Style Green
   Beans
1½ cups Tossed Salad with
   1½ teaspoons Italian Dressing
   mixed with 2 teaspoons Red Wine
   Vinegar
½ cup Low-Calorie Strawberry-
   Flavored Gelatin
Coffee or Tea

SNACKS

Banana 'n' Yogurt (½ medium banana,
   sliced, topped with ¼ cup plain
   low-fat yogurt); ¾ cup Skim Milk

Total Optional Calories: 30

Easy Pineapple "Danish" ⓒ ◑

Treat yourself to a leisurely weekend breakfast
featuring this tasty "Danish."

¼ cup plain low-fat yogurt
2 teaspoons granulated sugar
¼ teaspoon vanilla extract
**2 slices reduced-calorie white bread (40 calories
   per slice)**
1 teaspoon margarine, melted
**1 cup drained canned crushed pineapple
   (no sugar added)**

In small bowl combine yogurt, sugar, and vanilla; set aside.
   Brush 1 side of each slice of bread with half of the
margarine; place bread margarine-side up on baking sheet.
Broil until bread is lightly browned, 1 to 2 minutes. Spread
each bread slice with ½ cup pineapple and continue broiling
until pineapple is heated through, 2 to 3 minutes. Top each
"Danish" with half of the yogurt mixture; serve immediately.

MAKES 2 SERVINGS, 1 "DANISH" EACH

Each serving provides: ½ Bread Exchange; ½ Fat Exchange; 1 Fruit
   Exchange; ¼ Milk Exchange; 20 Optional Calories
Per serving: 168 calories; 4 g protein; 2 g fat; 35 g carbohydrate;
   90 mg calcium; 138 mg sodium; 2 mg cholesterol

BREAKFAST

½ medium Grapefruit
¾ ounce Cold Cereal
1 cup Skim Milk
Coffee or Tea

LUNCH

Salmon Sandwich (2 ounces salmon
    with 1 tablespoon chopped celery,
    2 lettuce leaves, and 1 teaspoon
    reduced-calorie mayonnaise on
    2 slices reduced-calorie white
    bread)
6 *each* Red and Green Bell Pepper
    Strips
Coffee, Tea, or Mineral Water

DINNER

4 ounces Broiled Steak
½ cup *each* Stewed Tomatoes,
    Cooked Mushroom Caps, and
    Sliced Onion
Cucumber-Radish Salad
    (6 cucumber slices with 6 sliced
    radishes and 1 tablespoon
    creamy Italian dressing on 1 cup
    shredded lettuce)
1 serving **Bananas with Maple-Yogurt
    Sauce**
Coffee or Tea

SNACKS

¾ cup Skim Milk; ½ cup Low-Calorie
    Cherry-Flavored Gelatin

Total Optional Calories: 50

Bananas with Maple-Yogurt Sauce ⊙◑

A wonderful combination of warm bananas and cool sauce.

2 medium bananas (about 6 ounces each)
1 teaspoon <u>each</u> margarine, melted, and lemon juice
¼ cup plain low-fat yogurt
1 tablespoon plus 1 teaspoon maple syrup
Dash ground cinnamon

Peel bananas and cut into halves lengthwise, then cut each half in half crosswise; arrange banana pieces in 1½-quart flameproof casserole. In cup or small bowl combine margarine and lemon juice and, using a pastry brush, brush mixture evenly over bananas. Broil 5 to 6 inches from heat source until bananas are lightly browned and heated through, 3 to 4 minutes.

While bananas are broiling, in small bowl combine yogurt and maple syrup, stirring well until thoroughly blended; set aside. Transfer bananas and any liquid remaining in pan to 2 dessert dishes. Top each portion with half of the yogurt mixture and sprinkle with cinnamon; serve while bananas are warm.

MAKES 2 SERVINGS

Each serving provides: ½ Fat Exchange; 2 Fruit Exchanges;
    ¼ Milk Exchange; 40 Optional Calories
Per serving: 173 calories; 3 g protein; 3 g fat; 37 g carbohydrate;
    74 mg calcium; 45 mg sodium; 2 mg cholesterol

BREAKFAST

½ cup Orange Sections
¼ cup Part-Skim Ricotta Cheese
   topped with 2 teaspoons Reduced-
   Calorie Strawberry Spread
1-ounce Pita Bread
½ cup Skim Milk
Coffee or Tea

LUNCH

Open-Face Sardine Sandwich
   (2 ounces sardines with 4 tomato
   slices, 2 onion slices, 2 lettuce
   leaves, and 1 teaspoon mayonnaise
   on 1 slice pumpernickel bread)
6 *each* Carrot and Zucchini Sticks
1 small Apple
Coffee, Tea, or Mineral Water

DINNER

¾ cup Chicken Bouillon
3 ounces Baked Chicken Breast
½ cup *each* Cooked Wax Beans and
   Sliced Beets
Iceberg-Sprout Salad (iceberg lettuce
   wedge with ¼ cup alfalfa sprouts
   and 1 tablespoon Russian dressing)
Jasmine Tea

SNACKS

1 serving **Maple-Banana Parfaits**;
   ½ cup Skim Milk

Total Optional Calories: 65

Maple-Banana Parfaits ⊂◑

Makes a fast and elegant dessert or snack.

1 cup plain low-fat yogurt
2 tablespoons plus 2 teaspoons reduced-calorie
   pancake syrup (60 calories per fluid ounce)
1 medium banana (about 6 ounces), peeled and sliced
2 graham crackers (2½-inch squares), made into crumbs

Into each of 2 parfait glasses spoon ¼ cup yogurt, 1
tablespoon syrup, and ¼ of the banana slices. Top each
portion with ¼ cup yogurt, then half of the remaining
banana slices. Sprinkle each portion with half of the graham
cracker crumbs and drizzle each with 1 teaspoon syrup.
Cover with plastic wrap and refrigerate for 1 hour.

MAKES 2 SERVINGS, 1 PARFAIT EACH

Each serving provides: ½ Bread Exchange; 1 Fruit Exchange;
   1 Milk Exchange; 40 Optional Calories
Per serving: 191 calories; 7 g protein; 3 g fat; 36 g carbohydrate;
   214 mg calcium; 128 mg sodium; 7 mg cholesterol

BREAKFAST

½ cup Canned Peach Slices
½ cup Cooked Cereal
1 cup Skim Milk
Coffee or Tea

LUNCH

Turkey Sandwich (2 ounces sliced
    turkey with 4 tomato slices, ¼ cup
    shredded lettuce, and 1 teaspoon
    mayonnaise on 2 slices reduced-
    calorie wheat bread)
3 Pickle Spears and 6 Celery Sticks
Coffee, Tea, or Mineral Water

DINNER

1 cup Chilled Tomato Juice with
    Celery Stick
4 ounces Broiled Flounder Fillet
    with Lemon Wedge
½ cup *each* Cooked Broccoli and
    Cauliflower Florets
Mushroom-Watercress Salad (½ cup
    watercress with ¼ cup sliced
    mushrooms and 1 tablespoon blue
    cheese dressing)
1-ounce Roll
Cinnamon-Apple Tea

SNACKS

1 serving **Party Popcorn Snack;**
    1 serving Reduced-Calorie
    Chocolate Dairy Drink

Total Optional Calories: 120

Party Popcorn Snack ◑

4 cups plain prepared popcorn
8 dried apricot halves, diced
2 tablespoons <u>each</u> dark and golden raisins
1 tablespoon sunflower seed
¼ cup light corn syrup
3 tablespoons firmly packed light brown sugar
1 teaspoon vanilla extract

In large mixing bowl combine popcorn, apricots, raisins, and sunflower seed; set aside.

In small saucepan combine remaining ingredients; set candy thermometer in pan and cook over medium-high heat until thermometer reaches 230°F.* Pour sugar mixture over popcorn mixture and toss quickly to thoroughly coat.

Spray 8 x 8 x 2-inch baking pan with nonstick cooking spray; turn popcorn mixture into pan and, using back of spoon, press mixture into pan. Let stand until mixture cools, 5 to 10 minutes. Invert onto serving dish and cut into four equal portions.

MAKES 4 SERVINGS

Each serving provides: ½ Bread Exchange; 1 Fruit Exchange; 120 Optional
    Calories
Per serving: 182 calories; 2 g protein; 1 g fat; 42 g carbohydrate;
    29 mg calcium; 19 mg sodium; 0 mg cholesterol

*If candy thermometer is not available, cook until a drop of hot mixture
    spins a 2-inch thread when dropped into cold water (thread stage).

BREAKFAST

½ cup Grapefruit Sections
Mushroom Omelet (1 egg with ¼ cup chopped mushrooms)
1 slice Whole Wheat Bread, toasted, with 1 teaspoon Margarine
½ cup Skim Milk
Coffee or Tea

LUNCH

Chicken in a Pocket (2 ounces sliced chicken with 2 *each* lettuce leaves and tomato slices and 1 teaspoon mustard in 1-ounce whole wheat pita bread)
6 *each* Zucchini Sticks and Red Bell Pepper Strips
1 small Apple
Coffee, Tea, or Mineral Water

DINNER

3 ounces Broiled Veal Patty
½ cup *each* Cooked Diced Carrot and Chopped Spinach
Lettuce and Tomato Salad (1½ cups torn Boston lettuce with 3 tomato slices and 1 tablespoon buttermilk dressing)
Peach Yogurt (½ cup plain low-fat yogurt mixed with ½ cup canned peach slices and 1 teaspoon honey)
Peppermint Tea

SNACKS

1 serving **Brazilian Cocoa 'n' Crème**

Total Optional Calories: 120

Brazilian Cocoa 'n' Crème ⊙◐

¼ cup __each__ granulated sugar and unsweetened cocoa
1⅛ teaspoons ground cinnamon, divided
⅛ teaspoon ground nutmeg
2 cups skim milk
1 cup strong coffee
½ cup thawed frozen dairy whipped topping

In 1½-quart saucepan combine sugar, cocoa, 1 teaspoon cinnamon, and the nutmeg; add milk and coffee and cook over medium heat, stirring frequently, until cocoa and sugar are dissolved and mixture is heated through, 4 to 5 minutes (__do not boil__). Divide into 4 mugs. Spoon ¼ of the whipped topping onto each serving of cocoa or fit a pastry bag with a star tip, fill bag with topping, and pipe topping onto cocoa. Sprinkle each serving with ¼ of the remaining cinnamon and serve immediately.

MAKES 4 SERVINGS

Each serving provides: ½ Milk Exchange; 100 Optional Calories
Per serving: 132 calories; 5 g protein; 3 g fat; 24 g carbohydrate; 166 mg calcium; 75 mg sodium; 2 mg cholesterol

Variation: Brazilian Cocoa (Week 1) — Omit whipped topping. Decrease Optional Calories to 75.

Per serving: 108 calories; 5 g protein; 1 g fat; 22 g carbohydrate; 166 mg calcium; 65 mg sodium; 2 mg cholesterol

February

**Chicken and Vegetables
in Lemon-Mustard Sauce**

FEBRUARY'S BEST BUYS FOR FRUITS AND VEGETABLES

alfalfa sprouts	carrots	kohlrabi	parsnips
avocados	cauliflower	kumquats	pineapples
bananas	celery	leeks	potatoes
bean sprouts	Chinese pea pods	lemons	radishes
Belgian endives	eggplants	mandarin oranges	scallions (green onions)
bell peppers	escarole	mushrooms	spinach
broccoli	grapefruit	mustard greens	sweet potatoes
brussels sprouts	kale	onions	Swiss chard
cabbage	kiwi fruit	oranges	yams

½ cup Orange Juice
⅓ cup Cottage Cheese
1 slice Raisin Bread, toasted
¾ cup Skim Milk

LUNCH

Tuna in a Pita (2 ounces tuna with
    1 teaspoon reduced-calorie
    mayonnaise, 3 tomato slices, and
    ¼ cup *each* alfalfa sprouts and
    shredded lettuce in 1-ounce pita
    bread)
½ cup Broccoli Florets and 6 Red
    Bell Pepper Strips
Coffee, Tea, or Mineral Water

DINNER

1 serving **Creamed Onion Soup**
3 ounces Roast Pork
½ cup Cooked Brown Rice with
    ¼ cup Cooked Sliced Mushrooms
½ cup Cooked Chopped Spinach
1½ cups Tossed Salad with
    1 tablespoon Russian Dressing
½ cup Applesauce
Coffee or Tea

SNACKS

Pear-Yogurt Delight (2 canned pear
    halves topped with ½ cup plain
    low-fat yogurt and 1 teaspoon
    each sunflower seed and toasted
    shredded coconut)

Total Optional Calories: 120

Creamed Onion Soup

1 teaspoon margarine
1 cup halved and thinly sliced onions
½ garlic clove, minced
1 tablespoon all-purpose flour
1½ cups water
1 tablespoon plus 1½ teaspoons dry sherry
**1½ packets (about 1½ teaspoons) instant beef broth and
    seasoning mix**
½ cup low-fat milk (1% milk fat)
3 tablespoons sour cream
Dash white pepper

In 1½- or 2-quart saucepan heat margarine over medium-high heat until bubbly and hot; add onions and garlic and sauté, stirring occasionally, until onions are softened, 2 to 3 minutes. Sprinkle with flour and stir quickly to combine; cook, stirring constantly, for 1 minute. Continuing to stir, gradually add water; add sherry and broth mix, stirring to dissolve broth mix. Bring to a boil. Reduce heat to low, stir in milk, and cook, stirring occasionally, until slightly thickened, about 20 minutes.

Remove 1 cup soup from pan and, in small bowl, combine with sour cream, mixing well; add mixture to soup along with pepper and continue cooking, stirring frequently, until thoroughly heated, 2 to 3 minutes.

MAKES 2 SERVINGS, ABOUT 1 CUP EACH

Each serving provides: 1 Vegetable Exchange; ½ Fat Exchange; ¼ Milk
    Exchange; 90 Optional Calories
Per serving: 153 calories; 5 g protein; 7 g fat; 15 g carbohydrate;
    124 mg calcium; 764 mg sodium; 12 mg cholesterol

BREAKFAST

½ cup Orange Sections
½ cup Cooked Cereal
¼ cup Skim Milk
Coffee or Tea

LUNCH

Peanut Butter and Jelly Sandwich
    (2 tablespoons peanut butter with
    2 teaspoons reduced-calorie
    raspberry spread on 2 slices
    reduced-calorie white bread)
½ medium Banana
Coffee, Tea, or Mineral Water

DINNER

1 serving **Creamy Cauliflower Soup**
4 ounces sliced Roast Beef
3 ounces Mashed Potato with
    1 teaspoon Margarine
1 cup Cooked Chinese Pea Pods
Escarole-Onion Salad (1½ cups torn
    escarole with ¼ cup sliced red
    onion and 1½ teaspoons blue
    cheese dressing mixed with
    2 tablespoons plain low-fat yogurt
    plus garlic powder)
½ medium Grapefruit
Coffee or Tea

SNACKS

1 serving Reduced-Calorie Vanilla
    Dairy Drink

Total Optional Calories: 160

Creamy Cauliflower Soup

Other vegetables can be substituted for the cauliflower. Try broccoli, asparagus, or any other favorite.

2 teaspoons margarine
2 tablespoons <u>each</u> finely chopped leek, carrot, and celery
2 garlic cloves, minced
1 tablespoon all-purpose flour
1½ cups water
1 cup low-fat milk (1% milk fat)
1½ packets (about 1½ teaspoons) instant chicken broth and seasoning mix
1¼ cups small cauliflower florets
2 tablespoons whipped cream cheese
2 teaspoons chopped fresh parsley
Dash <u>each</u> ground nutmeg and ground red pepper

In 1½-quart saucepan heat margarine over medium-high heat until bubbly and hot; add leek, carrot, celery, and garlic and sauté until vegetables are softened, 2 to 3 minutes. Sprinkle vegetables with flour and stir quickly to combine; continuing to stir, gradually add water. Add milk and broth mix, stirring to dissolve broth mix; add cauliflower. Reduce heat to low and cook until cauliflower is tender and mixture thickens slightly, 15 to 20 minutes.

Transfer half of soup to work bowl of food processor; add cream cheese and process until pureed. Return to saucepan; add parsley, nutmeg, and pepper and cook, stirring frequently, until heated through, 3 to 4 minutes (<u>do not boil</u>).

MAKES 2 SERVINGS, ABOUT 1½ CUPS EACH

Each serving provides: 1½ Vegetable Exchanges; 1 Fat Exchange; ½ Milk Exchange; 65 Optional Calories
Per serving: 167 calories; 8 g protein; 8 g fat; 16 g carbohydrate; 193 mg calcium; 905 mg sodium; 14 mg cholesterol

BREAKFAST

½ cup Grapefruit Juice
1 Soft-Cooked Egg
1 slice Whole Wheat Bread, toasted, with 1 teaspoon Reduced-Calorie Margarine
1 cup Skim Milk

LUNCH

Tuna-Vegetable Salad (2 ounces tuna with ½ cup torn lettuce, ¼ cup *each* diced tomato and green bell pepper, and 1½ teaspoons Russian dressing mixed with 2 tablespoons plain low-fat yogurt and ¼ teaspoon mustard)
3 Sesame Melba Rounds
1 small Apple
Coffee, Tea, or Mineral Water

DINNER

¾ cup Onion Bouillon with 1 serving **Garlic Toast**
3 ounces Baked Chicken
½ cup Cooked Sliced Carrot drizzled with ½ teaspoon Honey
½ cup Cooked Cauliflower Florets
Boston-Zucchini Salad (1½ cups torn Boston lettuce with ½ cup sliced zucchini, ¼ cup diced red bell pepper, and 1 teaspoon olive oil mixed with 2 teaspoons red wine vinegar plus seasonings)
Herb Tea

SNACKS

Peach "Melba" (2 canned peach halves topped with 2 teaspoons reduced-calorie raspberry spread); ¾ cup Skim Milk

Total Optional Calories: 40

Garlic Toast ◐ ◑

Add this delicious toast to your favorite soup or salad. It can be prepared 1 or 2 days in advance and stored in a resealable plastic bag.

8 slices Italian bread (½ ounce each)
1 tablespoon plus 1 teaspoon margarine
1 garlic clove, minced
2 teaspoons grated Parmesan cheese
1 teaspoon chopped fresh Italian (flat-leaf) parsley

Preheat oven to 350°F. On baking sheet bake bread until crisp and lightly browned, 8 to 10 minutes.

In small saucepan heat margarine until bubbly and hot; add garlic and sauté for 1 minute. Using a pastry brush, brush ⅛ of the garlic mixture onto each slice of bread; sprinkle each with ¼ teaspoon cheese and ⅛ teaspoon parsley. Bake until cheese is lightly browned, 2 to 3 minutes.

MAKES 8 SERVINGS, 1 SLICE EACH

Each serving provides: ½ Bread Exchange; ½ Fat Exchange; 3 Optional Calories
Per serving: 59 calories; 1 g protein; 2 g fat; 8 g carbohydrate; 10 mg calcium; 113 mg sodium; 0.5 mg cholesterol

BREAKFAST

½ cup Orange Juice
1 serving **Lox, Dill, and Onion Spread**
   on ½ small Bagel
1 cup Skim Milk

LUNCH

Turkey 'n' Swiss Sandwich (2 ounces
   sliced turkey with ½ ounce
   julienne-cut Swiss cheese and
   1 teaspoon *each* mustard and
   reduced-calorie mayonnaise on
   2 slices reduced-calorie
   pumpernickel bread)
6 *each* Zucchini Sticks and Green
   Bell Pepper Strips
1 large Mandarin Orange
Coffee, Tea, or Mineral Water

DINNER

3 ounces Smoked Beef Sausage
3 ounces Cooked Potato with
   1 teaspoon Reduced-Calorie
   Margarine and Chopped Parsley
½ cup Sauerkraut sprinkled with
   ½ teaspoon Caraway Seed
½ cup *each* Cooked Chopped
   Spinach and Sliced Mushrooms
1 cup Mixed Green Salad with
   1 tablespoon Caesar Dressing
½ cup Low-Calorie Strawberry-
   Flavored Gelatin
Coffee or Tea

SNACKS

1 small Apple, baked; ½ cup
   Reduced-Calorie Chocolate
   Pudding

Total Optional Calories: 120

Lox, Dill, and Onion Spread ◑

This spread is delicious with bagels and equally as good with melba rounds or as a stuffing for celery or cherry tomatoes; it can be stored in the refrigerator for up to 1 week.

½ cup cream cheese, softened
2 ounces smoked salmon (lox)
2 tablespoons finely chopped red onion
1 tablespoon chopped fresh dill

In work bowl of food processor* combine cream cheese and lox, processing until light and fluffy; stir in onion and dill. Transfer to small bowl; cover with plastic wrap and refrigerate until chilled, about 30 minutes.

MAKES 4 SERVINGS, ABOUT 2 TABLESPOONS EACH

Each serving provides: ½ Protein Exchange; 100 Optional Calories
Per serving: 126 calories; 5 g protein; 11 g fat; 1 g carbohydrate;
   29 mg calcium; 968 mg sodium; 37 mg cholesterol

*If food processor is not available, use electric mixer at low speed and beat cheese mixture until light and fluffy; proceed as directed.

BREAKFAST

1 medium Kiwi Fruit, sliced
1 serving **Country Cookin' Omelet**
½ English Muffin, toasted, with
  1 teaspoon Reduced-Calorie
  Margarine
¼ cup Skim Milk
Coffee or Tea

LUNCH

Tuna in a Pita (2 ounces tuna with
  ¼ cup *each* chopped celery and
  shredded lettuce and 1 teaspoon
  mayonnaise in 1-ounce whole
  wheat pita bread)
3 Pickle Spears and 6 Red Bell
  Pepper Strips
Coffee, Tea, or Mineral Water

DINNER

3 ounces Baked Veal Chop
1 cup Cooked Fettuccine with ¼ cup
  Tomato Sauce
3 Cooked Broccoli Spears
1½ cups Tossed Salad with
  1½ teaspoons Buttermilk Dressing
  mixed with 2 tablespoons Plain
  Low-Fat Yogurt and ¼ teaspoon
  Mustard
½ cup Fruit Salad
Coffee or Tea

SNACKS

Banana Yogurt (¼ cup plain low-fat
  yogurt mixed with ½ medium
  banana, sliced); 1 serving Reduced-
  Calorie Vanilla Dairy Drink

Total Optional Calories: 65

Country Cookin' Omelet

When preparing this delicious weekend breakfast, to help make separating the eggs easier, use cold eggs.

4 eggs, separated (at room temperature)
2 tablespoons maple syrup, divided
1 teaspoon vanilla extract
Dash salt
1 tablespoon plus 1 teaspoon reduced-calorie
  margarine (tub)
¼ ounce sliced almonds
2 slices crisp bacon, crumbled

In small bowl beat together egg yolks, 2 teaspoons maple syrup, and the vanilla until blended; set aside.

Preheat oven to 350°F. In medium mixing bowl combine egg whites and salt and, using electric mixer at high speed, beat until whites are stiff but not dry. Fold a few spoonfuls of yolk mixture into beaten whites, then fold remaining yolk mixture into whites; set aside.

In 9-inch nonstick skillet that has an oven-safe or removable handle heat margarine over medium-low heat until bubbly and hot; add almonds and spread in a single layer over bottom of pan. Spread egg mixture over almonds and cook until bottom is lightly browned, 1 to 2 minutes. Transfer skillet to oven and bake until omelet is puffed and golden brown, 8 to 10 minutes. Remove skillet from oven and sprinkle omelet with crumbled bacon. Using a spatula, loosen omelet around edges; then, using a pancake turner, fold omelet in half and slide onto warmed plate. Cut into 4 equal wedges and serve each with 1 teaspoon of the remaining syrup.

MAKES 4 SERVINGS

Each serving provides: 1 Protein Exchange; ½ Fat Exchange; 65 Optional
  Calories
Per serving: 153 calories; 7 g protein; 10 g fat; 8 g carbohydrate;
  44 mg calcium; 194 mg sodium; 277 mg cholesterol

BREAKFAST

½ medium Grapefruit
1 serving **Apple-Cheddar Turnovers**
¼ cup Skim Milk
Coffee or Tea

LUNCH

Chef's Salad (1 ounce julienne-cut
   turkey with ½ ounce *each* julienne-
   cut Swiss cheese and roast beef,
   6 *each* tomato wedges, cucumber
   slices, red onion slices, and celery
   sticks, and 2 tablespoons reduced-
   calorie Italian dressing on 1½ cups
   shredded lettuce)
Coffee, Tea, or Mineral Water

DINNER

¾ cup Chicken Bouillon
3 ounces Roast Veal
½ cup Cooked Sliced Carrot
½ cup Cooked Diced Red and Green
   Bell Pepper
1½ cups Torn Escarole with
   1 tablespoon French Dressing
1-ounce Roll with 1 teaspoon
   Reduced-Calorie Margarine
½ cup Reduced-Calorie Butterscotch
   Pudding
Coffee or Tea

SNACKS

½ medium Banana; ¾ cup Skim Milk

Total Optional Calories: 20

Apple-Cheddar Turnovers ◖◑

Spark up a chilly, drab weekend by serving these delicious turnovers for breakfast. In less than 30 minutes you can sit down to a real treat.

1 teaspoon margarine
1 small apple (about ¼ pound), cored, pared, and diced
1 tablespoon diced onion
Dash ground cinnamon
2 ready-to-bake refrigerated buttermilk flaky biscuits (1 ounce each)
2 ounces Cheddar cheese, shredded

In small skillet heat margarine until bubbly and hot; add apple and onion and sauté until soft, about 3 minutes. Sprinkle with cinnamon and stir to combine; set aside.

Preheat oven to 400°F. Roll each biscuit between 2 sheets of wax paper, forming two 5-inch circles. Spread half of each circle with half of the apple mixture; top each with 1 ounce cheese. Fold each circle in half, enclosing filling and, using the tines of a fork, press edges to seal; transfer turnovers to sheet of foil or nonstick baking sheet and bake in middle of center oven rack until golden brown, about 10 minutes.

MAKES 2 SERVINGS, 1 TURNOVER EACH

Each serving provides: 1 Protein Exchange; 1 Bread Exchange;
   ½ Fat Exchange; ½ Fruit Exchange
Per serving: 246 calories; 9 g protein; 15 g fat; 20 g carbohydrate;
   209 mg calcium; 492 mg sodium; 30 mg cholesterol

BREAKFAST

½ cup Orange Sections
¾ ounce Cold Cereal
½ cup Skim Milk
Coffee or Tea

LUNCH

¾ cup Chicken Bouillon
1 serving **Cheese Wedges**
Cabbage and Carrot Slaw (½ cup
    each shredded green cabbage and
    carrot with 1 tablespoon reduced-
    calorie mayonnaise on 2 lettuce
    leaves)
½ cup Reduced-Calorie Vanilla
    Pudding
Coffee, Tea, or Mineral Water

DINNER

Broiled Dijon Shrimp (5 ounces raw
    shelled and deveined shrimp,
    broiled and basted with mixture
    of 1 teaspoon *each* lemon juice,
    Dijon-style mustard, and reduced-
    sodium soy sauce)
1 cup Cooked Broccoli Florets
½ cup Cooked Sliced Mushrooms
1 medium Tomato, cut into wedges,
    topped with 2 teaspoons Reduced-
    Calorie Mayonnaise and 1 tea-
    spoon grated Parmesan Cheese
2 Melba Slices
Pineapple 'n' Yogurt (½ cup canned
    crushed pineapple topped with
    ¼ cup plain low-fat yogurt)
Coffee or Tea

SNACKS

½ cup Canned Peach Slices; ½ cup
    Low-Calorie Lemon-Flavored
    Gelatin

Total Optional Calories: 30

Cheese Wedges ⓒ ◑

Makes a wonderful weekend winter lunch.

2 ounces extra-sharp Cheddar cheese, shredded
1 teaspoon margarine, softened
1 to 2 drops hot sauce (optional)
1 pita bread (1 ounce), cut in half horizontally and
    toasted

In small bowl thoroughly combine cheese, margarine, and if
desired, hot sauce; spread each pita half with half of cheese
mixture, covering entire surface of pita. Set pita halves on
baking sheet and broil until cheese is melted and lightly
browned, 2 to 3 minutes. Cut each half into 4 equal wedges
and serve hot.

MAKES 2 SERVINGS, 4 WEDGES EACH

Each serving provides: 1 Protein Exchange; ½ Bread Exchange;
    ½ Fat Exchange
Per serving: 175 calories; 8 g protein; 11 g fat; 10 g carbohydrate;
    208 mg calcium; 289 mg sodium; 30 mg cholesterol

Variation: Nutty Cheese Wedges (Week 8) — Add ½ ounce
ground walnuts and 1 teaspoon sweet sherry or Madeira to
cheese mixture; proceed as directed. Add 50 Optional
Calories to Exchange Information.

Per serving: 224 calories; 9 g protein; 16 g fat; 11 g carbohydrate;
    214 mg calcium; 290 mg sodium; 30 mg cholesterol

Bourbon Chicken

1 tablespoon <u>each</u> olive <u>or</u> vegetable oil and margarine
2¼ pounds chicken parts, skinned
1 teaspoon salt
½ teaspoon pepper
½ cup bourbon, divided
¼ cup chopped shallots
2 to 3 tablespoons chopped fresh parsley
1 teaspoon thyme leaves
½ cup half-and-half (blend of milk and cream)

In 12-inch nonstick skillet heat together oil and margarine until margarine is bubbly and mixture is hot; add chicken pieces, sprinkle with salt and pepper, and brown well on all sides. Add ¼ cup bourbon; using a long match, ignite mixture. When flame goes out, add remaining ¼ cup bourbon along with the shallots, parsley, and thyme. Reduce heat to low, cover, and let simmer until chicken is tender and, when pierced with a fork, juices run clear, 20 to 25 minutes. Using slotted spoon, remove chicken to serving platter; keep warm.

Add half-and-half to pan juices in skillet and let simmer, stirring frequently, until mixture thickens slightly; pour over chicken and serve immediately.

MAKES 4 SERVINGS

Each serving provides: 3 Protein Exchanges; ⅛ Vegetable Exchange;
    1½ Fat Exchanges; 125 Optional Calories
Per serving: 331 calories; 26 g protein; 16 g fat; 4 g carbohydrate;
    64 mg calcium; 672 mg sodium; 87 mg cholesterol

BREAKFAST

½ cup Canned Peach Slices
⅓ cup Cottage Cheese
½ English Muffin, toasted
½ cup Skim Milk
Coffee or Tea

LUNCH

Egg Sandwich (1 hard-cooked egg, sliced with 2 *each* tomato slices and lettuce leaves on 2 slices reduced-calorie rye bread)
6 *each* Zucchini and Yellow Squash Slices
1 small Orange
Coffee, Tea, or Mineral Water

DINNER

¾ cup Onion Bouillon
1 serving **Chicken and Vegetables in Lemon-Mustard Sauce**
¾ cup Cooked Broccoli Florets
Spinach-Radish Salad (1½ cups torn spinach with ¼ cup sliced radishes, 2 red onion slices, and 1½ teaspoons olive oil mixed with 2 teaspoons white wine vinegar plus seasonings)
½ cup Skim Milk
Coffee or Tea

SNACKS

½ cup Reduced-Calorie Vanilla Pudding topped with 1 tablespoon Whipped Topping; 1 small Apple, baked

Total Optional Calories: 45

Chicken and Vegetables in Lemon-Mustard Sauce

1½ teaspoons olive <u>or</u> vegetable oil
2 chicken cutlets (¼ pound each)
1½ teaspoons margarine
½ cup <u>each</u> sliced onion, carrot, celery, and red <u>or</u> green bell pepper
1 small garlic clove, sliced
2 tablespoons dry sherry
½ cup water
2 teaspoons spicy brown mustard
1 tablespoon lemon juice
1 packet instant chicken broth and seasoning mix
6 ounces pared potato, cut into cubes

In 9-inch skillet heat oil; add chicken and cook, turning once, until browned, 2 to 3 minutes on each side. Transfer chicken to plate and set aside.

In same skillet heat margarine until bubbly and hot; add vegetables and garlic and sauté, stirring frequently, until onions are translucent, 4 to 5 minutes. Add sherry and bring to a boil; stir in water, mustard, lemon juice, and broth mix. Add potatoes and chicken to skillet and return mixture to a boil. Reduce heat, cover, and let simmer until chicken is tender and, when pierced with a fork, juices run clear, 15 to 20 minutes.

MAKES 2 SERVINGS

Each serving provides: 3 Protein Exchanges; 1 Bread Exchange; 2 Vegetable Exchanges; 1½ Fat Exchanges; 20 Optional Calories
Per serving: 320 calories; 30 g protein; 8 g fat; 27 g carbohydrate; 55 mg calcium; 700 mg sodium; 66 mg cholesterol

BREAKFAST

½ medium Banana, sliced
¼ cup Part-Skim Ricotta Cheese
1 slice Reduced-Calorie Wheat
   Bread, toasted
Coffee or Tea

LUNCH

Salmon in a Pita (2 ounces salmon
   with 2 tablespoons *each* chopped
   onion and green bell pepper and
   2 teaspoons reduced-calorie
   mayonnaise in 1-ounce pita bread)
¾ cup Cauliflower Florets and 6 Red
   Bell Pepper Strips
1 medium Kiwi Fruit, sliced
Coffee, Tea, or Mineral Water

DINNER

1 serving **Madeira Chicken with
Shiitakes**
½ cup Cooked Rice
¾ cup Cooked Julienne-Cut Yellow
   Squash
Mandarin Salad (1 cup torn Boston
   lettuce with ½ cup *each* mandarin
   orange sections and alfalfa sprouts
   and 1½ teaspoons Italian dressing
   mixed with 2 teaspoons red wine
   vinegar)
½ cup Reduced-Calorie Butterscotch
   Pudding
Coffee or Tea

SNACKS

½ cup Applesauce; 1 cup Skim Milk

Total Optional Calories: 100

Madeira Chicken with Shiitakes

Shiitake mushrooms are Oriental mushrooms with wide brown caps. They have a distinctive beefy flavor and are a unique addition to this elegant dish.

2 chicken cutlets (¼ pound each), pounded to ½-inch thickness
2 tablespoons all-purpose flour
2 teaspoons reduced-calorie margarine (tub)
1 teaspoon olive oil
1 cup shiitake mushrooms, sliced
6 small chestnuts, roasted, shelled, and cut into halves
1 tablespoon minced shallots
1 garlic clove, minced
¼ cup dry Madeira wine
¾ cup canned ready-to-serve chicken broth
1 tablespoon whipping cream

On sheet of wax paper or a paper plate dredge cutlets in flour, lightly coating both sides and reserving remaining flour.

In 12-inch nonstick skillet heat margarine and oil together over medium heat until margarine is bubbly and mixture is hot; add cutlets and sauté, turning once, until lightly browned, 2 to 3 minutes on each side. Transfer chicken to plate; set aside.

In same skillet combine mushrooms, chestnuts, shallots, and garlic and sauté until shallots are softened, about 1 minute. Sprinkle with reserved flour and stir quickly to combine; continuing to stir, gradually add wine. Stir in broth and cook, stirring occasionally, until sauce has thickened, 3 to 4 minutes. Return chicken to skillet and continue cooking until chicken is cooked through, 2 to 3 minutes longer. Transfer chicken to serving platter and keep warm. Add cream to skillet and stir to combine; cook, stirring frequently, until heated through (<u>do not boil</u>). Pour sauce over chicken and serve immediately.

MAKES 2 SERVINGS

Each serving provides: 3 Protein Exchanges; ½ Bread Exchange;
   1 Vegetable Exchange; 1 Fat Exchange; 100 Optional Calories
Per serving: 321 calories; 30 g protein; 9 g fat; 20 g carbohydrate;
   38 mg calcium; 501 mg sodium; 76 mg cholesterol

Chili Dogs ©◑

An excellent way to use up leftover ground beef.

1 teaspoon margarine, divided
1 tablespoon <u>each</u> chopped onion and green bell
    pepper
1 cup canned Italian tomatoes (with liquid), pureed
    and strained (discard seeds)
2 ounces drained canned red kidney beans
1 ounce cooked ground beef, crumbled
1 tablespoon ketchup
1½ teaspoons Worcestershire sauce
½ teaspoon chili powder
⅛ teaspoon powdered mustard
2 beef frankfurters (2 ounces each)
2 frankfurter rolls (2 ounces each)
1 ounce Cheddar cheese, shredded

In 8-inch nonstick skillet heat ½ teaspoon margarine over
medium-high heat until bubbly and hot; add onion and bell
pepper and sauté, stirring frequently, until vegetables are
tender, 1 to 2 minutes. Add tomatoes, beans, beef, ketchup,
Worcestershire sauce, chili powder, and mustard, mixing
well. Reduce heat to low and let simmer, stirring frequently,
until flavors are blended, 5 to 7 minutes. Set aside and keep
warm.

In separate 8-inch skillet heat remaining ½ teaspoon
margarine over medium heat until bubbly and hot; add
frankfurters and cook, turning frequently, until lightly
browned and heated through, 5 to 6 minutes.

To serve, set 1 frankfurter into each roll, then top each with
½ of the bean mixture (about ⅓ cup) and sprinkle with ½
ounce cheese.

MAKES 2 SERVINGS, 1 CHILI DOG EACH

Each serving provides: 3½ Protein Exchanges; 2 Bread Exchanges;
    1⅛ Vegetable Exchanges; ½ Fat Exchange; 10 Optional Calories
Per serving: 538 calories; 22 g protein; 29 g fat; 47 g carbohydrate;
    206 mg calcium; 1,415 mg sodium; 64 mg cholesterol

BREAKFAST

Cottage-Raisin Toast (⅓ cup cottage cheese mixed with 2 tablespoons raisins, chopped, and cinnamon on 1 slice toasted pumpernickel bread)
1 cup Skim Milk

LUNCH

Chick-Pea Salad (2 ounces canned chick-peas with 1 ounce shredded Fontina cheese, ¼ cup *each* sliced mushrooms and diced red bell pepper, 1 teaspoon grated Parmesan cheese, and 1½ teaspoons Italian dressing on 3 romaine lettuce leaves)
1 medium Kiwi Fruit
Coffee, Tea, or Mineral Water

DINNER

1 serving **Mexican Joes**
½ cup Coleslaw
1½ cups Mixed Green Salad with 1 teaspoon Olive Oil mixed with 2 teaspoons Red Wine Vinegar plus Seasonings
½ cup Grapefruit Sections
Diet Soda

SNACKS

½ cup Reduced-Calorie Vanilla Pudding; 2 Honey Graham Crackers

Total Optional Calories: 135

Mexican Joes ◑

2 teaspoons olive or vegetable oil
½ cup diced onion
1 small mild or hot green chili pepper, seeded and minced
1 small garlic clove, minced
5 ounces cooked ground beef, crumbled
½ cup tomato sauce
1 tablespoon taco seasoning mix
2 hamburger rolls (2 ounces each), split and toasted
1 ounce Monterey Jack cheese, shredded
½ cup shredded lettuce
½ medium tomato, diced
1 tablespoon plus 1 teaspoon sour cream
2 large pitted black olives, sliced

In small nonstick skillet heat oil; add onion, pepper, and garlic and sauté until softened. Stir in ground beef, tomato sauce, and seasoning mix and cook over low heat until heated through, about 5 minutes.

To serve, on each of 2 individual serving plates place bottom half of each roll; top each with half of the meat mixture. Sprinkle each portion with ½ ounce cheese, then top with ¼ cup lettuce, half of the tomato, 2 teaspoons sour cream, half of the olive slices, and top half of roll.

MAKES 2 SERVINGS, 1 MEXICAN JOE EACH

Each serving provides: 3 Protein Exchanges; 2 Bread Exchanges; 2¾ Vegetable Exchanges; 1 Fat Exchange; 25 Optional Calories
Per serving: 574 calories; 30 g protein; 28 g fat; 50 g carbohydrate; 204 mg calcium; 1,701 mg sodium; 82 mg cholesterol

Variation: Tacos (Week 5) — Omit hamburger rolls. For each serving fill 2 heated taco shells with ¼ of the meat mixture each. Top each filled taco shell with ¼ ounce cheese, 2 tablespoons lettuce, ¼ of the tomato, 1 teaspoon sour cream, and ¼ of the olives.

Per serving: 505 calories; 26 g protein; 29 g fat; 32 g carbohydrate; 162 mg calcium; 1,414 mg sodium; 78 mg cholesterol

BREAKFAST

½ medium Grapefruit
½ cup Cooked Cereal with
 1 tablespoon Whipping Cream
1 serving Reduced-Calorie
 Hot Cocoa

LUNCH

Chicken in a Pita (2 ounces sliced
 chicken with 3 tomato slices,
 ½ cup shredded lettuce, ¼ cup
 alfalfa sprouts, and 1 teaspoon
 each mayonnaise and mustard
 in 1-ounce pita bread)
6 *each* Carrot and Celery Sticks
1 small Apple
Coffee, Tea, or Mineral Water

DINNER

1 serving **Anniversary Steaks Flambé**
½ cup Cooked Noodles with
 1 teaspoon Margarine and
 Chopped Parsley
¾ cup Cooked Broccoli
Romaine and Pepper Salad (2 cups
 torn romaine lettuce with 4 red bell
 pepper rings, 1 teaspoon imitation
 bacon bits, and 1½ teaspoons
 Italian dressing mixed with
 2 teaspoons red wine vinegar)
½ cup Fruit Salad
2 Amaretti Cookies (¼ ounce each)
Coffee or Tea

SNACKS

1 medium Kiwi Fruit; 1 cup Skim
 Milk

Total Optional Calories: 195

Anniversary Steaks Flambé ◑

**2 beef tenderloin steaks _or_ boneless rib steaks
 (¼ pound each)
1 teaspoon salt (optional)
2 tablespoons dry sherry
1 tablespoon _each_ chopped chives and steak sauce
2 tablespoons brandy**

If desired, sprinkle steaks evenly with salt. On rack in broiling
pan broil steaks, turning once, until done to taste. Transfer to
serving platter; set aside and keep warm.

 In small saucepan combine sherry, chives, and steak sauce
and cook until hot, 1 to 2 minutes; pour evenly over steaks.

 In separate small saucepan heat brandy over low heat
until warm and vapors rise (<u>do not boil</u>). Using long match,
ignite brandy and, wearing oven mitt, pour flaming mixture
over steaks. Serve immediately after flame goes out.

MAKES 2 SERVINGS

Each serving provides: 3 Protein Exchanges; 60 Optional Calories
Per serving without salt: 334 calories; 21 g protein; 20 g fat;
 3 g carbohydrate; 9 mg calcium; 188 mg sodium; 0.7 mg cholesterol
With salt: 334 calories; 21 g protein; 20 g fat; 3 g carbohydrate;
 16 mg calcium; 1,289 mg sodium; 0.7 mg cholesterol

BREAKFAST

½ cup Orange Sections
⅓ cup Cottage Cheese
2 slices Reduced-Calorie Wheat
    Bread, toasted
Coffee or Tea

LUNCH

Cheese Sandwich (2 ounces sharp
    Cheddar cheese with 3 tomato
    slices and 1 teaspoon *each*
    reduced-calorie mayonnaise and
    mustard on 2 slices reduced-calorie
    multi-grain bread)
¾ cup Cauliflower Florets and
    6 Cucumber Spears
½ medium Banana
Coffee, Tea, or Mineral Water

DINNER

1 serving **Veal with Creamy Mustard
    Sauce**
3 ounces Baked Potato topped with
    2 tablespoons Plain Low-Fat
    Yogurt
1 cup Cooked Brussels Sprouts
1½ cups Mixed Green Salad with
    1½ teaspoons Thousand Island
    Dressing mixed with 2 tablespoons
    Plain Low-Fat Yogurt and
    ¼ teaspoon Mustard
½ cup Reduced-Calorie Vanilla
    Pudding
Coffee or Tea

SNACKS

1 cup Melon Balls; ½ cup Skim Milk

Total Optional Calories: 65

Veal with Creamy Mustard Sauce ◖

1 tablespoon all-purpose flour
¼ teaspoon salt
Dash pepper
2 veal cutlets (¼ pound each)
1½ teaspoons _each_ vegetable oil and margarine
½ cup _each_ sliced onion and quartered mushrooms
¼ cup half-and-half (blend of milk and cream)
1 tablespoon _each_ chopped fresh parsley and Dijon-style mustard
1½ teaspoons lemon juice

Preheat oven to 200°F. On sheet of wax paper or a paper plate combine flour, salt, and pepper; dredge veal in flour mixture, coating both sides.

In 9-inch nonstick skillet heat oil over medium heat; add veal and cook, turning once, until browned on both sides and cooked throughout, 1 to 2 minutes on each side. Transfer veal to oven-safe serving platter; set in oven and keep warm.

In same skillet heat margarine over high heat until bubbly and hot; add onion and mushrooms and sauté until lightly browned. Reduce heat to low; add half-and-half, parsley, mustard, and lemon juice and cook, stirring constantly, until mixture comes to a boil and is slightly thickened. Remove veal from oven, top with sauce, and serve immediately.

MAKES 2 SERVINGS

Each serving provides: 3 Protein Exchanges; 1 Vegetable Exchange;
    1½ Fat Exchanges; 65 Optional Calories
Per serving: 314 calories; 25 g protein; 19 g fat; 10 g carbohydrate;
    61 mg calcium; 620 mg sodium; 92 mg cholesterol

Variation: Chicken with Creamy Mustard Sauce (Week 3) — Substitute chicken cutlets for the veal cutlets.

Per serving: 263 calories; 28 g protein; 12 g fat; 10 g carbohydrate;
    61 mg calcium; 615 mg sodium; 77 mg cholesterol

BRUNCH

Orange Juice Spritzer (½ cup *each*
  orange juice and club soda)
Scrambled Egg (1 egg scrambled
  in 1 teaspoon reduced-calorie
  margarine)
1 serving **Sausage Bread**
1½ cups Mixed Green Salad with
  1½ teaspoons Buttermilk Dressing
  mixed with 2 tablespoons Plain
  Low-Fat Yogurt and ¼ teaspoon
  Mustard
Café au Lait (½ cup *each* hot coffee
  and skim milk with cinnamon stick)

DINNER

3 ounces Roast Chicken
½ cup *each* Cooked Sliced
  Mushrooms and Onion
Vegetable Medley (¾ cup *each*
  cooked broccoli florets, red bell
  pepper strips, and sliced carrots)
½ cup Sliced Cucumber with
  1½ teaspoons Blue Cheese
  Dressing
½ cup Canned Pineapple Chunks
  topped with 1 teaspoon *each*
  Wheat Germ, toasted, and Honey
Coffee or Tea

SNACKS

1 small Apple, diced, topped with
  2 tablespoons Plain Low-Fat
  Yogurt; 1 serving Reduced-Calorie
  Vanilla Dairy Drink

Total Optional Calories: 30

Sausage Bread

This bread may be frozen; to serve, thaw at room temperature, then heat. Perk up a gray Sunday by getting the gang together and serving this for brunch.

2 teaspoons <u>each</u> margarine and olive oil
1 small garlic clove, minced
1 loaf frozen bread dough (1 pound), thawed
3 ounces thinly sliced provolone cheese
10 ounces cooked veal sausage, finely chopped
3 ounces mozzarella cheese, shredded

In small saucepan heat margarine and oil together over medium heat until margarine is bubbly and mixture is hot; add garlic and sauté until golden, about 1 minute.

Preheat oven to 350°F. On work surface, press bread dough into a 17 x 10-inch rectangle; using pastry brush, brush dough with half of the garlic mixture. Arrange provolone cheese over dough; top with sausage, then sprinkle with mozzarella cheese. Firmly press cheeses and sausage into dough. Starting from wide end, roll dough jelly-roll fashion to enclose filling; pinch each narrow end to seal and tuck ends underneath loaf.

Transfer loaf, seam-side down, to nonstick baking sheet. Using pastry brush, brush remaining garlic mixture over bread; bake 30 to 35 minutes (until golden brown). If bread is browning too quickly, cover with foil. Transfer bread to wire rack and let cool 15 minutes before serving. To serve, cut into 16 equal slices.

MAKES 8 SERVINGS, 2 SLICES EACH

Each serving provides: 2 Protein Exchanges; 2 Bread Exchanges;
    ½ Fat Exchange
Per serving: 321 calories; 19 g protein; 15 g fat; 27 g carbohydrate;
    159 mg calcium; 893 mg sodium; 54 mg cholesterol

Variation: Prosciutto Loaf (Week 2) — Reduce sausage to ½ pound and add 2 ounces thinly sliced prosciutto (Italian-style ham) to recipe. Proceed as directed, topping sausage layer with prosciutto slices.

Per serving: 315 calories; 18 g protein; 14 g fat; 28 g carbohydrate;
    159 mg calcium; 553 mg sodium; 51 mg cholesterol

BREAKFAST

½ cup Canned Peach Slices
½ cup Cooked Cereal
½ cup Skim Milk
Coffee or Tea

LUNCH

Greek Salad (2 ounces crumbled feta
    cheese with 1 cup torn spinach,
    ¼ cup *each* sliced celery and
    radishes, and 1 teaspoon olive oil
    mixed with 2 teaspoons red wine
    vinegar plus seasonings)
1-ounce Whole Wheat Pita Bread
Coffee, Tea, or Mineral Water

DINNER

1 serving **Pork Chops in Tomato Sauce**
1 cup Cooked Sliced Zucchini with
    1½ teaspoons Margarine
2 cups Mixed Green Salad with
    1 tablespoon Reduced-Calorie
    Italian Dressing
½ medium Grapefruit sprinkled with
    ½ teaspoon Brown Sugar
Sparkling Mineral Water

SNACKS

Fruited Yogurt (¾ cup plain low-fat
    yogurt mixed with ½ cup canned
    fruit cocktail)

Total Optional Calories: 15

Pork Chops in Tomato Sauce ©

Makes a colorful meal when served with a green salad.

2 teaspoons reduced-calorie margarine (tub)
½ cup onion wedges
½ to 1 small garlic clove, minced
½ cup canned Italian tomatoes (with liquid), pureed
1½ teaspoons chopped fresh Italian (flat-leaf) parsley
½ teaspoon Italian seasoning
¼ teaspoon grated lemon peel
Dash <u>each</u> salt and pepper
2 pork chops (5 ounces each), broiled until rare

In 8-inch nonstick skillet heat margarine until bubbly and hot; add onion and garlic and sauté until lightly browned, about 2 minutes. Add remaining ingredients except pork chops and stir to combine; bring mixture just to a boil. Reduce heat to low; add pork chops to skillet, spooning sauce over chops. Cover and let simmer, stirring occasionally, until pork is tender, 35 to 40 minutes. Arrange pork chops on serving platter and top with sauce.

MAKES 2 SERVINGS

Each serving provides: 3 Protein Exchanges; 1 Vegetable Exchange;
    ½ Fat Exchange
Per serving: 242 calories; 28 g protein; 11 g fat; 6 g carbohydrate;
    33 mg calcium; 276 mg sodium; 83 mg cholesterol

Variation: Pork Chops 'n' Pasta (Week 2) — Arrange 1 cup hot cooked spaghetti on serving platter. Arrange pork chops on spaghetti and top with sauce. Add 1 Bread Exchange to Exchange Information.

Per serving: 397 calories; 33 g protein; 12 g fat; 38 g carbohydrate;
    45 mg calcium; 277 mg sodium; 83 mg cholesterol

BREAKFAST

½ medium Banana, sliced
¾ ounce Cold Cereal
½ cup Skim Milk
Coffee or Tea

LUNCH

Tuna Sandwich (2 ounces tuna with
    3 tomato slices, ¼ cup shredded
    lettuce, and 2 teaspoons reduced-
    calorie mayonnaise on 2 slices
    reduced-calorie multi-grain bread)
6 *each* Celery and Zucchini Sticks
1 small Orange
Coffee, Tea, or Mineral Water

DINNER

4 ounces Roast Cornish Hen
1 serving **Green Rice**
¾ cup *each* Cooked Sliced Carrots
    and Cut Green Beans
1½ cups Tossed Salad with
    1½ teaspoons Italian Dressing
    mixed with 2 teaspoons Red Wine
    Vinegar
1 cup Strawberries
½ cup Skim Milk
Coffee or Tea

SNACKS

1 cup Skim Milk; ½ cup Low-Calorie
    Cherry-Flavored Gelatin

Total Optional Calories: 20

Green Rice ©

A Mexican specialty.

1 medium green bell pepper
½ cup canned ready-to-serve chicken broth
¼ cup chopped fresh parsley
2 tablespoons chopped onion
½ medium canned jalapeño pepper, seeded and
    chopped
½ garlic clove, chopped
¼ teaspoon salt
Dash freshly ground pepper
2 teaspoons olive oil
2 ounces uncooked regular long-grain rice

Preheat broiler. On baking sheet lined with heavy-duty
foil broil bell pepper 3 inches from heat source, turning
frequently, until charred on all sides; let stand until cool
enough to handle, 15 to 20 minutes. Peel pepper; remove
and discard stem ends and seeds. Transfer pepper to
blender container; add broth, parsley, onion, jalapeño
pepper, and seasonings and process at high speed until
pureed.

In small saucepan heat oil over medium-high heat; add
rice and cook, stirring constantly, until rice is coated with
oil, about 2 minutes (do not brown). Add pureed pepper
mixture and stir to combine. Reduce heat to lowest possible
setting, cover pan, and cook until liquid is absorbed and rice
is tender, about 15 minutes.

MAKES 2 SERVINGS

Each serving provides: 1 Bread Exchange; 1½ Vegetable Exchanges;
    1 Fat Exchange; 10 Optional Calories
Per serving: 168 calories; 3 g protein; 5 g fat; 27 g carbohydrate;
    29 mg calcium; 656 mg sodium; 0 mg cholesterol

BREAKFAST

½ medium Grapefruit
Cinnamon-Yogurt Cereal
  (½ cup cooked cereal topped with
  2 tablespoons plain low-fat yogurt
  and cinnamon)
½ cup Skim Milk
Coffee or Tea

LUNCH

Turkey in a Pita (2 ounces sliced
  turkey with 2 tomato slices, ¼ cup
  alfalfa sprouts, and 1 teaspoon
  mayonnaise in 1-ounce whole
  wheat pita bread)
6 Carrot Sticks and 3 Pickle Spears
1 large Mandarin Orange
Coffee, Tea, or Mineral Water

DINNER

3 ounces Sliced Steak
1 serving **Spinach Gratinée**
1 cup Cooked Cauliflower Florets
1½ cups Mixed Green Salad with
  1½ teaspoons Thousand Island
  Dressing mixed with 2 tablespoons
  Plain Low-Fat Yogurt and
  ¼ teaspoon Mustard
1 small Apple
Coffee or Tea

SNACKS

1 serving Reduced-Calorie Vanilla
  Dairy Drink; ¾ ounce Breadsticks

Total Optional Calories: 55

Spinach Gratinée ©

1 tablespoon plus 1 teaspoon margarine, divided
½ cup finely chopped onion
1 small garlic clove, minced
¾ cup part-skim ricotta cheese
¼ cup grated Parmesan cheese
1 egg, beaten
⅛ teaspoon pepper
4 cups cooked fresh spinach,* well drained and chopped
3 tablespoons plain dried bread crumbs

Preheat oven to 375°F. In 8-inch nonstick skillet heat 1 teaspoon margarine over medium-high heat until bubbly and hot; add onion and garlic and sauté until softened, 1 to 2 minutes. Transfer to medium mixing bowl; add cheeses, egg, and pepper and mix well. Add spinach and mix until thoroughly combined. Spray 1-quart casserole with nonstick cooking spray; add spinach mixture and spread evenly. Set aside.

In small saucepan melt remaining tablespoon margarine. Remove pan from heat; add bread crumbs and stir to combine. Sprinkle crumb mixture over spinach mixture and bake until topping is lightly browned and spinach mixture is thoroughly heated, 35 to 40 minutes.

MAKES 4 SERVINGS

Each serving provides: 1 Protein Exchange; 2¼ Vegetable Exchanges;
  1 Fat Exchange; 55 Optional Calories
Per serving: 208 calories; 15 g protein; 11 g fat; 15 g carbohydrate;
  459 mg calcium; 373 mg sodium; 87 mg cholesterol

*Thawed and well-drained frozen chopped spinach may be substituted for
  the cooked fresh.

Per serving: 219 calories; 16 g protein; 11 g fat; 18 g carbohydrate;
  492 mg calcium; 411 mg sodium; 87 mg cholesterol

BREAKFAST

1 small Orange
¾ ounce Cold Cereal
¾ cup Skim Milk
Coffee or Tea

LUNCH

Chicken-Vegetable Combo
(2 ounces julienne-cut chicken
with 1 cup torn lettuce, ¼ cup
each sliced scallion and
cucumber, 6 tomato slices, and
1½ teaspoons blue cheese
dressing mixed with 2 tablespoons plain low-fat yogurt plus
garlic powder)
½ medium Banana
Coffee, Tea, or Mineral Water

DINNER

Tofu and Vegetable Stir-Fry
(9 ounces diced tofu with ½ cup
each broccoli florets, red bell
pepper strips, sliced onion, and
sliced bamboo shoots stir-fried in
1 teaspoon vegetable oil and
1 tablespoon reduced-sodium soy
sauce)
1 cup Cooked Short-Grain Rice
1 serving **Sprout Slaw with Ginger
Dressing**
Tea

SNACKS

1 small Apple; ½ cup Reduced-
Calorie Chocolate Pudding

Total Optional Calories: 5

Sprout Slaw with Ginger Dressing ◐

1 cup _each_ bean sprouts and alfalfa sprouts
½ cup shredded carrot
**¼ cup _each_ diagonally sliced scallions (green onions)
and diced red _or_ green bell pepper**
1½ teaspoons _each_ rice vinegar, water, and vegetable oil
**½ teaspoon _each_ Chinese sesame oil, salt, and firmly
packed brown sugar**
½-inch piece pared ginger root, chopped
½ small garlic clove
Dash pepper

In medium bowl combine sprouts, carrot, scallions, and bell
pepper; set aside.

In blender container combine remaining ingredients and
process until combined, scraping down sides of container as
necessary; pour over sprout mixture and toss to coat. Cover
bowl with plastic wrap and refrigerate until mixture is chilled;
toss again before serving.

MAKES 2 SERVINGS, ABOUT 1 CUP EACH

Each serving provides: 3 Vegetable Exchanges; 1 Fat Exchange;
5 Optional Calories
Per serving: 85 calories; 3 g protein; 5 g fat; 9 g carbohydrate;
34 mg calcium; 563 mg sodium; 0 mg cholesterol

Gala Chocolate Nut-Crust Custard

May be served warm or chilled.

4 eggs
1 cup skim milk
½ cup evaporated skimmed milk
2 tablespoons <u>each</u> granulated sugar and almond <u>or</u> chocolate liqueur
1 ounce sliced almonds
½ ounce semisweet chocolate, shaved or grated

Preheat oven to 350°F. In medium bowl combine all ingredients except almonds and chocolate and, using a fork or wire whisk, beat until well blended. Into each of four 6-ounce custard cups pour ¼ of mixture; sprinkle each portion with ¼ of the almonds and ¼ of the chocolate. Set cups in 8 x 8 x 2-inch baking pan and pour hot water into pan to a depth of about 1 inch; bake in middle of center oven rack for 30 to 35 minutes (until a knife, inserted in center of custard, comes out clean). Remove baking pan from oven and cups from water bath; set cups on wire rack and let cool.

MAKES 4 SERVINGS, 1 CUSTARD EACH

Each serving provides: 1 Protein Exchange; ½ Milk Exchange; 115 Optional Calories
Per serving with almond liqueur: 232 calories; 12 g protein; 11 g fat; 26 g carbohydrate; 216 mg calcium; 138 mg sodium; 276 mg cholesterol
With chocolate liqueur: 236 calories; 12 g protein; 11 g fat; 27 g carbohydrate; 216 mg calcium; 138 mg sodium; 276 mg cholesterol

Variation: Cream-Topped Chocolate Custard (Week 8) — Top each custard with 1 tablespoon thawed frozen dairy whipped topping. Increase Optional Calories to 130.

Per serving with almond liqueur: 244 calories; 12 g protein; 12 g fat; 27 g carbohydrate; 216 mg calcium; 143 mg sodium; 276 mg cholesterol
With chocolate liqueur: 248 calories; 12 g protein; 12 g fat; 29 g carbohydrate; 216 mg calcium; 143 mg sodium; 276 mg cholesterol

BREAKFAST

Banana Yogurt (¼ cup plain low-fat
   yogurt mixed with ½ medium
   banana, sliced)
1 slice Raisin Bread, toasted
Coffee or Tea

LUNCH

Salmon in a Pita (2 ounces salmon
   with 2 tablespoons chopped onion,
   ½ cup alfalfa sprouts, and
   2 teaspoons reduced-calorie
   mayonnaise in 1-ounce pita bread)
3 Pickle Spears and 6 Celery Sticks
1 small Orange
Coffee, Tea, or Mineral Water

DINNER

3 ounces Broiled Lamb Chop
¾ cup Cooked Sliced Fennel
½ cup Stewed Tomatoes
Spinach-Radish Salad (1½ cups torn
   spinach with ¼ cup sliced radishes
   and 1 tablespoon Thousand Island
   dressing)
1 serving **Ricotta-Peach Pie**
½ cup Skim Milk
Coffee or Tea

SNACKS

½ cup Canned Crushed Pineapple;
   ¾ cup Buttermilk

Total Optional Calories: 50

Ricotta-Peach Pie ☉

**4 ready-to-bake refrigerated buttermilk flaky biscuits
   (1 ounce each)**
**2 cups drained canned peach halves (no sugar added),
   thinly sliced**
2 eggs
½ cup part-skim ricotta cheese
¼ cup skim milk
**1 tablespoon _each_ firmly packed light brown sugar and
   granulated sugar**
1 teaspoon vanilla extract
¼ teaspoon grated lemon peel
**⅛ teaspoon _each_ ground cinnamon, ground nutmeg,
   and ground ginger**

Preheat oven to 375°F. Carefully separate each biscuit into
4 thin layers of dough.* In 8-inch pie plate arrange biscuits,
with edges overlapping slightly, over bottom and up sides
of plate; using fingers, spread to form crust, pressing edges
of biscuits together to seal. Place sheet of foil onto pie shell
and fill with uncooked dry beans; bake for 5 minutes.
Remove beans and foil. Arrange peach slices in pie crust; set
aside.

   In blender container combine remaining ingredients and
process until thoroughly combined, scraping down sides of
container as necessary. Pour over peaches; set pie plate on
baking sheet and bake at 375°F. in middle of center oven
rack for 45 minutes (until lightly browned and a knife,
inserted in center, comes out clean). Transfer to wire rack
and let cool slightly before serving.

MAKES 8 SERVINGS

Each serving provides: ½ Protein Exchange; ½ Bread Exchange;
   ½ Fruit Exchange; 20 Optional Calories
Per serving: 115 calories; 5 g protein; 4 g fat; 15 g carbohydrate;
   62 mg calcium; 190 mg sodium; 73 mg cholesterol

*Separate dough into layers as soon as it is removed from refrigerator; it
   will be difficult to work with if allowed to come to room temperature.

TIP: Filling the unbaked pie shell with dry beans will prevent bubbling
during baking; save the beans since they can be used repeatedly for this
purpose. This pie is delicious served warm or chilled.

March

Orange-Pecan Waffles

MARCH'S BEST BUYS FOR FRUITS AND VEGETABLES

alfalfa sprouts	brussels sprouts	kiwi fruit	oranges
artichokes	cabbage	kohlrabi	parsnips
asparagus	carrots	kumquats	peas
avocados	cauliflower	leeks	pineapples
bananas	celery	lettuce	potatoes
bean sprouts	Chinese pea pods	mushrooms	radishes
beets	eggplants	mustard greens	rhubarb
Belgian endives	escarole	new potatoes	scallions (green onions)
bell peppers	grapefruit	okra	spinach
broccoli	kale	onions	Swiss chard

Fruit 'n' Cheese Breakfast (2 canned
    peach halves topped with ⅓ cup
    cottage cheese and 2 teaspoons
    reduced-calorie raspberry spread)
4 Melba Slices
½ cup Skim Milk
Coffee or Tea

LUNCH

Roast Beef on Rye (1 ounce sliced
    roast beef with 2 tomato slices,
    2 lettuce leaves, and 2 teaspoons
    reduced-calorie mayonnaise on
    2 slices reduced-calorie rye bread)
6 *each* Carrot and Celery Sticks
Coffee, Tea, or Mineral Water

DINNER

1 serving **Vegetable-Cheddar Soup**
3 ounces Broiled Flounder Fillet
½ cup Cooked Broccoli Florets with
    1 teaspoon Margarine
Red Bell Pepper Salad (1½ cups
    shredded lettuce with ½ cup red
    bell pepper rings and 1 tablespoon
    reduced-calorie Thousand Island
    dressing)
½ medium Grapefruit sprinkled with
    ½ teaspoon Confectioners' Sugar
Coffee or Tea

SNACKS

½ cup Canned Fruit Cocktail;
    1 serving Reduced-Calorie Vanilla
    Dairy Drink

Total Optional Calories: 80

Vegetable-Cheddar Soup ⓒ ◑

Warm up with this creamy and colorful soup.
The recipe can easily be doubled so you can keep extra
portions on hand. Just reheat over low heat.

2 teaspoons margarine
½ cup diced carrot
¼ cup <u>each</u> diced green bell pepper, celery, and onion
1½ teaspoons all-purpose flour
⅛ teaspoon powdered mustard
Dash ground red pepper
1 cup low-fat milk (1% milk fat)
½ cup water
1 packet instant chicken broth and seasoning mix
2 ounces sharp Cheddar cheese, shredded
Garnish: chopped fresh parsley

In 1-quart saucepan heat margarine over medium-high heat
until bubbly and hot; add vegetables and sauté, stirring
occasionally, until tender-crisp, 3 to 5 minutes. Reduce heat
to medium; cover and let cook until vegetables are soft,
about 5 minutes longer. Sprinkle flour, mustard, and pepper
over vegetables and stir quickly to combine; cook,
uncovered, stirring constantly, for 1 minute. Continuing to
stir, gradually add milk; add water and broth mix and, stirring
constantly, bring just to a boil. Reduce heat to low; stir in
cheese and cook, continuing to stir, until cheese is melted
and soup is thickened. Serve sprinkled with parsley.

MAKES 2 SERVINGS

Each serving provides: 1 Protein Exchange; 1¼ Vegetable Exchanges;
    1 Fat Exchange; ½ Milk Exchange; 25 Optional Calories
Per serving: 239 calories; 13 g protein; 15 g fat; 14 g carbohydrate;
    377 mg calcium; 803 mg sodium; 35 mg cholesterol

Sausage, Chicken, and Rice Soup ⊙

A great way to use up leftovers.

6 ounces cooked smoked beef sausage
1 tablespoon plus 1 teaspoon olive <u>or</u> vegetable oil
½ cup <u>each</u> diced onion and red <u>or</u> green bell pepper
2 to 3 garlic cloves, minced
4 ounces uncooked regular long-grain rice
2 tablespoons chopped fresh Italian (flat-leaf) parsley
1 tablespoon chopped fresh basil
2 packets instant chicken broth and seasoning mix
1 quart water
6 ounces skinned and boned cooked chicken,
   cut into strips
Dash pepper

In 1-quart saucepan combine sausage and enough water to cover and bring to a boil; cook for 10 minutes. Drain and slice sausage; set aside.

In 4-quart saucepan heat oil over high heat; add onion, bell pepper, and garlic and sauté until onion is lightly browned. Stir in rice, parsley, basil, and broth mix and cook, stirring constantly, for 1 minute; add water and bring to a boil. Reduce heat to low; cover and let simmer until rice is tender, about 20 minutes. Stir in sausage, chicken, and pepper and let simmer until meats are heated through, about 5 minutes.

MAKES 4 SERVINGS

Each serving provides: 3 Protein Exchanges; 1 Bread Exchange;
   ½ Vegetable Exchange; 1 Fat Exchange; 5 Optional Calories
Per serving: 382 calories; 21 g protein; 20 g fat; 28 g carbohydrate;
   31 mg calcium; 953 mg sodium; 50 mg cholesterol

Ham 'n' Cheese Muffins ©

A real crowd pleaser. Prepare these savory muffins in advance, then, just before serving, reheat in conventional or microwave oven. Freeze leftovers in resealable plastic freezer bags.

1½ cups all-purpose flour
3 tablespoons granulated sugar
2 teaspoons powdered mustard
1½ teaspoons double-acting baking powder
1¼ teaspoons baking soda
⅛ teaspoon pepper
5 ounces finely diced cooked smoked ham or Canadian-style bacon
3 ounces Cheddar cheese, shredded
1½ ounces (¼ cup) uncooked yellow cornmeal
1 cup buttermilk
2 eggs
3 tablespoons plus 1 teaspoon vegetable oil

Preheat oven to 400°F. In medium mixing bowl sift together flour, sugar, mustard, baking powder, baking soda, and pepper; add ham (or bacon), cheese, and cornmeal, mixing well.

In separate medium mixing bowl, using a wire whisk, beat together buttermilk, eggs, and oil; add to ham mixture and stir just until thoroughly combined (do not overmix). Spray ten 2½-inch-diameter muffin pan cups with nonstick cooking spray; spoon ¹/₁₀ of batter into each sprayed cup (each will be about ¾ full) and partially fill remaining cups with water (this will prevent pan from burning and/or warping). Bake in middle of center oven rack for 20 to 25 minutes (until muffins are lightly browned and a toothpick, inserted in center, comes out dry). Remove pan from oven and carefully drain off water (remember, it will be boiling hot). Remove muffins from pan and set on wire rack to cool slightly; serve warm.

MAKES 10 SERVINGS, 1 MUFFIN EACH

Each serving provides: 1 Protein Exchange; 1 Bread Exchange;
    1 Fat Exchange; 30 Optional Calories
Per serving with smoked ham: 219 calories; 9 g protein; 10 g fat;
    23 g carbohydrate; 132 mg calcium; 462 mg sodium; 71 mg cholesterol
With Canadian-style bacon: 223 calories; 9 g protein; 10 g fat;
    23 g carbohydrate; 133 mg calcium; 459 mg sodium; 72 mg cholesterol

BREAKFAST

BREAKFAST

1 cup Low-Calorie Cranberry Juice
½ small Bagel, toasted, with
   1 tablespoon Cream Cheese
½ cup Skim Milk
Coffee or Tea

LUNCH

Liverwurst Sandwich (1 ounce sliced
   liverwurst with 3 tomato slices,
   2 lettuce leaves, and 2 teaspoons
   mustard on 2 slices reduced-calorie
   rye bread)
6 *each* Carrot and Celery Sticks
Coffee, Tea, or Mineral Water

DINNER

3 ounces Broiled Veal Chop
1 serving **Swiss Chard Gnocchi in Tomato-Cream Sauce**
1 cup Cooked Cubed Eggplant
Bibb Salad (1 cup torn Bibb lettuce
   with ¼ cup *each* sliced mushrooms
   and shredded carrot, 2 teaspoons
   imitation bacon bits, and
   1 tablespoon Italian dressing)
½ medium Grapefruit drizzled with
   ½ teaspoon Honey
Coffee or Tea

SNACKS

Pudding 'n' Banana (½ cup reduced-
   calorie vanilla pudding mixed with
   ½ medium banana, sliced); ½ cup
   Skim Milk

Total Optional Calories: 160

Swiss Chard Gnocchi in Tomato-Cream Sauce

2 teaspoons margarine
2 tablespoons minced shallots
¾ cup each all-purpose flour and part-skim ricotta cheese
2 ounces plus 2 teaspoons grated Parmesan cheese, divided
1 egg, lightly beaten
¼ cup well-drained cooked chopped Swiss chard
⅛ teaspoon ground nutmeg
Dash white pepper
2 to 3 quarts water
Tomato-Cream Sauce (see page 83)
Garnish: basil leaves

In 8-inch skillet heat margarine over medium-high heat until bubbly and hot; add shallots and sauté until softened, 1 to 2 minutes. Transfer shallots to medium mixing bowl; add flour, ricotta cheese, 2 ounces Parmesan cheese, the egg, Swiss chard, nutmeg, and pepper and mix well to form dough.

Divide dough into 4 equal portions and roll each into a rope about ¾ inch in diameter; cut each rope into ½-inch lengths and, using your thumb and forefinger, press the middle of each piece together to form an indent.

In 3- or 4-quart saucepan bring water to a boil; drop in gnocchi, a few at a time (water should continue to boil as gnocchi are added); when gnocchi rise to the surface, cook until al dente, 5 to 7 minutes. Using slotted spoon, remove gnocchi from water and arrange on serving platter. Top with Tomato-Cream Sauce and, using 2 spoons, toss to combine; sprinkle with remaining 2 teaspoons Parmesan cheese and garnish with basil leaves.

MAKES 4 SERVINGS

Each serving (including Tomato-Cream Sauce) provides: 1½ Protein
   Exchanges; 1 Bread Exchange; 2 Vegetable Exchanges; 1 Fat Exchange;
   80 Optional Calories
Per serving: 330 calories; 14 g protein; 16 g fat; 33 g carbohydrate;
   297 mg calcium; 628 mg sodium; 102 mg cholesterol

Variation: Spinach Gnocchi (Week 3) — Substitute
well-drained cooked chopped spinach for the Swiss chard.

Per serving: 331 calories; 14 g protein; 16 g fat; 33 g carbohydrate;
   306 mg calcium; 616 mg sodium; 102 mg cholesterol

BREAKFAST

½ medium Grapefruit
Peanut Butter Grahams (1 tablespoon
    peanut butter on 2 graham
    crackers)
1 serving Reduced-Calorie Hot
    Cocoa

LUNCH

Shrimp Salad (2 ounces tiny shrimp
    with 2 tablespoons chopped
    celery, ¼ cup alfalfa sprouts,
    and 2½ teaspoons mayonnaise
    on 2 lettuce leaves)
6 Zucchini Sticks and ½ cup Cauliflower
    Florets
¾ ounce Breadsticks
20 small Grapes
Coffee, Tea, or Mineral Water

DINNER

Bouillon Surprise (¾ cup chicken
    bouillon with 1½ ounces diced tofu
    and ¼ cup chopped spinach)
1 serving **Greek Vegetarian Pitas**
½ cup Cooked Sliced Beets
1½ cups Mixed Green Salad with
    1 tablespoon Reduced-Calorie
    Buttermilk Dressing
Peach 'n' Yogurt (2 canned peach
    halves topped with ¼ cup plain
    low-fat yogurt and 1 teaspoon
    wheat germ)
Herb Tea

SNACKS

½ cup Low-Calorie Strawberry-
    Flavored Gelatin; ½ cup Skim Milk

Total Optional Calories: 125

Greek Vegetarian Pitas ◑

Tahini is a paste made from sesame seeds. Once
opened, it should be kept refrigerated in a covered
container. Stir before using.

½ cup shredded lettuce
2 tablespoons thinly sliced seeded cucumber
1 tablespoon <u>each</u> chopped green bell pepper and red
    onion
2 teaspoons lemon juice, divided
1 teaspoon <u>each</u> olive oil and red wine vinegar
½ teaspoon water
¼ teaspoon <u>each</u> oregano leaves and chopped fresh
    parsley
Dash pepper
2 ounces drained canned chick-peas (garbanzo beans)
1 tablespoon <u>each</u> tahini and plain low-fat yogurt
½ teaspoon chopped fresh mint
½ small garlic clove, chopped
2 pita breads (1 ounce each), lightly toasted
1 ounce feta cheese, crumbled

In small mixing bowl combine lettuce, cucumber, bell
pepper, and onion. In separate small bowl combine ½
teaspoon lemon juice with the oil, vinegar, water, oregano,
parsley, and pepper; pour over vegetables and toss to coat.
Set aside.

  In blender container combine chick-peas, tahini, yogurt,
mint, garlic, and remaining 1½ teaspoons lemon juice and
process until smooth, scraping down sides of container as
necessary.

  Cut each pita bread in half crosswise and gently open
each half to form a pocket. Spread ¼ of chick-pea mixture
(about 1 tablespoon) inside each pita half; fill each half with
¼ of the vegetable mixture (about 2 tablespoons) and ¼ of
the feta cheese.

MAKES 2 SERVINGS, 2 FILLED PITA HALVES EACH

Each serving provides: 1½ Protein Exchanges; 1 Bread Exchange;
    ¾ Vegetable Exchange; ½ Fat Exchange; 25 Optional Calories
Per serving: 241 calories; 9 g protein; 10 g fat; 30 g carbohydrate;
    154 mg calcium; 452 mg sodium; 13 mg cholesterol

BREAKFAST

1 medium Kiwi Fruit, sliced
1 Poached Egg
½ English Muffin, toasted
1 cup Skim Milk

LUNCH

Turkey "Reuben" Sandwich (2 ounces
  sliced turkey with ¼ cup sauerkraut
  and 1½ teaspoons Russian dressing
  on 2 slices reduced-calorie rye
  bread)
6 *each* Red and Green Bell Pepper
  Strips
¾ ounce Mixed Dried Fruit
Coffee, Tea, or Mineral Water

DINNER

1 serving **Salmon with Creamy Lime
  Sauce**
½ cup Cooked Fettuccine sprinkled
  with 1 teaspoon Grated Parmesan
  Cheese
1 cup Cooked Julienne-Cut Carrots
1½ cups Mixed Green Salad with
  1 tablespoon French Dressing
4 fluid ounces Dry White Wine
Coffee or Tea

SNACKS

½ cup Applesauce; 1 cup Skim Milk

Total Optional Calories: 210

Salmon with Creamy Lime Sauce

4 salmon fillets (5 ounces each)
1 tablespoon <u>each</u> tequila and lime juice (no sugar added)
½ cup sour cream
2 tablespoons chopped fresh parsley
1 tablespoon chopped chives
½ teaspoon grated lime peel
Dash <u>each</u> salt and white pepper
2 tablespoons whipped butter, melted
**Garnish: lemon and lime slices and Italian (flat-leaf)
  parsley sprigs**

In glass or stainless-steel container (not aluminum) that
is large enough to hold salmon in a single layer arrange
salmon. In cup or small bowl combine tequila and lime juice;
pour over fillets and turn to coat. Cover with plastic wrap
and refrigerate for 30 minutes.

In blender container combine sour cream, parsley, chives,
lime peel, salt, and pepper and process until smooth; set
aside.

Preheat broiler. Transfer salmon to broiling pan, reserving
marinade. Pour marinade into bowl; add butter and stir to
combine. Broil salmon, basting with marinade mixture, until
fish flakes easily when tested with a fork, 3 to 4 minutes
(depending on thickness of fillet).

Transfer salmon to serving platter; top with any juices from
bottom of broiling pan and any remaining marinade mixture.
Spoon sour cream mixture over fillets and garnish with lemon
and lime slices and parsley sprigs.

MAKES 4 SERVINGS

Each serving provides: 4 Protein Exchanges; 100 Optional Calories
Per serving: 404 calories; 33 g protein; 28 g fat; 2 g carbohydrate;
  150 mg calcium; 184 mg sodium; 76 mg cholesterol

*It's best to marinate in glass or stainless-steel containers; acidic ingredients
  such as lime juice may react with aluminum, causing color and flavor
  changes in foods.

½ cup Canned Peach Slices
½ cup Cooked Cereal
½ cup Skim Milk
Coffee or Tea

LUNCH

Chicken Salad (2 ounces diced
   chicken with ¼ cup *each* broccoli
   and cauliflower florets, 6 tomato
   wedges, and 1 tablespoon buttermilk dressing)
1-ounce slice French Bread
1 small Orange
Coffee, Tea, or Mineral Water

DINNER

1 serving **Prosciutto-Wrapped Shrimp**
½ cup Cooked Rice
½ cup *each* Cooked Mushroom Caps
   and Sliced Zucchini with
   1 teaspoon Reduced-Calorie
   Margarine
Romaine and Cucumber Salad
   (1½ cups shredded romaine lettuce
   with ½ cup sliced cucumber and
   1 tablespoon reduced-calorie
   Italian dressing)
Cappuccino (½ cup *each* hot espresso
   and hot skim milk with cinnamon
   stick)

SNACKS

½ medium Banana; ½ cup Reduced-
   Calorie Vanilla Pudding

Total Optional Calories: 15

Prosciutto-Wrapped Shrimp

12 large (26–30s*) shrimp (about 7 ounces)
2 ounces mozzarella cheese, cut into 12 cubes
2 ounces prosciutto (Italian-style ham), cut into twelve
   3 x ¾-inch strips
1 teaspoon olive <u>or</u> vegetable oil
1 tablespoon plus 1 teaspoon dry white table wine
2 teaspoons <u>each</u> lemon juice and water
1 teaspoon Dijon-style mustard
½ teaspoon <u>each</u> chopped fresh basil and parsley
½ garlic clove, minced
Dash pepper

Preheat oven to 450°F. Shell and devein shrimp, leaving last segment and tail in place. Using a sharp knife, butterfly shrimp by splitting each along back, down to tail, cutting as deep as possible without going through to the other side; spread shrimp open so they lie flat. Onto center of each shrimp place 1 cheese cube; roll 1 strip of prosciutto around each shrimp, enclosing cheese and tucking ends of prosciutto under shrimp.

   Grease 2 individual 1¾-cup casseroles with ½ teaspoon oil each; set 6 shrimp, prosciutto-ends down, in each casserole. Fold tail over prosciutto strip and press down to hold in place. In small bowl combine remaining ingredients; pour half of mixture over each portion of shrimp and bake until shrimp turn pink and cheese is melted, 8 to 10 minutes.

MAKES 2 SERVINGS

Each serving provides: 4 Protein Exchanges; ½ Fat Exchange; 10 Optional
   Calories
Per serving: 220 calories; 25 g protein; 11 g fat; 3 g carbohydrate;
   219 mg calcium; 602 mg sodium; 122 mg cholesterol

*This indicates the approximate number of shrimp per pound before
   cooking, shelling, and deveining; 1 dozen shrimp will yield about ¼ pound
   cooked seafood.

TIP: To save time, shell and devein shrimp, then arrange 6 in each greased
casserole. Shred cheese and sprinkle over shrimp, then top with prosciutto.
Combine remaining ingredients and proceed as directed.

BREAKFAST

½ cup Applesauce
Lox 'n' Bagel (½ small bagel topped
  with 1 tablespoon cream cheese
  and 1 ounce smoked salmon)
1 cup Skim Milk

LUNCH

Vegetable-Egg Salad (1 hard-cooked
  egg, cut into wedges, with 1 cup
  torn lettuce, ½ cup *each* alfalfa
  sprouts and sliced zucchini, and
  1 tablespoon Italian dressing)
6 *each* Carrot and Celery Sticks
1-ounce Roll
Coffee, Tea, or Mineral Water

DINNER

Orange Spritzer (½ cup *each* orange
  juice and club soda)
1 serving **Herb Cheese-Stuffed Chicken**
6 Cooked Asparagus Spears
Boston Lettuce Salad (1 cup torn
  Boston lettuce with 6 cherry
  tomatoes plus lemon juice and
  herbs)
Coffee or Tea

SNACKS

Prune Yogurt (½ cup plain low-fat
  yogurt mixed with 3 medium
  prunes, pitted and chopped);
  ½ cup Low-Calorie Lemon-
  Flavored Gelatin

Total Optional Calories: 120

Herb Cheese-Stuffed Chicken

¼ cup cream cheese
1 teaspoon water
1 tablespoon <u>each</u> chopped scallion (green onion),
  chopped fresh dill, and chopped fresh parsley
⅛ teaspoon <u>each</u> minced fresh garlic, salt, and white
  pepper
Dash hot sauce
4 chicken cutlets (5 ounces each)
⅓ cup plus 2 teaspoons buttermilk
3 ounces (1¼ cups) cornflake crumbs
1 tablespoon plus 1 teaspoon vegetable oil, divided

Preheat oven to 450°F. In small mixing bowl combine cream
cheese and water and, using electric mixer at medium
speed, beat until light and fluffy; stir in scallion, seasonings,
and hot sauce and set aside.

Using a sharp knife, cut a 2 x 2-inch pocket into thickest
portion of each cutlet; spoon ¼ of cheese mixture (about 1
tablespoon) into each and gently press edges of each
pocket to enclose filling. Dip each cutlet into buttermilk,
then into cornflake crumbs, coating thoroughly and pressing
any remaining crumbs firmly into chicken to adhere and seal
stuffed pockets. Set coated cutlets on nonstick baking sheet
and drizzle each with ½ teaspoon oil. Bake until lightly
browned, 8 to 10 minutes; turn chicken over, drizzle each
with ½ teaspoon oil, and bake until chicken is tender and
coating is crisp, about 10 minutes longer.

MAKES 4 SERVINGS

Each serving provides: 4 Protein Exchanges; 1 Bread Exchange;
  1 Fat Exchange; 60 Optional Calories
Per serving: 339 calories; 36 g protein; 11 g fat; 20 g carbohydrate;
  61 mg calcium; 493 mg sodium; 99 mg cholesterol

TIP: No need to buy cornflake crumbs if you have cornflakes in the house.
Just process them in blender or food processor until finely crumbled.

BREAKFAST

2 tablespoons Raisins
¾ ounce Cold Cereal
½ cup Skim Milk
Coffee or Tea

LUNCH

Ham and Cheese Sandwich (1 ounce
    each sliced ham and Cheddar
    cheese with ¼ cup shredded lettuce
    and 2 teaspoons mustard on
    2 slices reduced-calorie rye bread)
6 *each* Red and Green Bell Pepper
    Strips
Coffee, Tea, or Mineral Water

DINNER

1 serving **Festive Honey-Pecan Chicken**
¾ cup Cooked Noodles with
    1½ teaspoons Margarine
½ cup Cooked Artichoke Hearts with
    ¼ cup Chopped Pimientos
2 Cooked Asparagus Spears
1½ cups Tossed Salad with
    1 tablespoon Reduced-Calorie
    Russian Dressing
½ cup Orange Sections
½ cup Skim Milk
Coffee or Tea

SNACKS

1 piece Angel Food Cake (¹⁄₁₂ of
    9-inch cake); ½ cup Raspberries;
    1 cup Skim Milk

Total Optional Calories: 290

Festive Honey-Pecan Chicken

¾ cup plain dried bread crumbs
8 thinly sliced chicken cutlets (¼ pound each)
¼ cup all-purpose flour
2 eggs, lightly beaten
¼ cup vegetable oil, divided
1½ ounces pecan halves
1 cup canned ready-to-serve chicken broth
¼ cup honey
2 tablespoons lemon juice
2 teaspoons minced fresh parsley
1 teaspoon cornstarch
¼ teaspoon <u>each</u> grated orange peel and salt
⅛ teaspoon pepper
1 small orange (about 6 ounces), cut crosswise into
    8 thin slices

On sheet of wax paper or a paper plate spread bread crumbs. Sprinkle cutlets evenly with flour, coating both sides; dip each cutlet into beaten egg, then into crumbs, coating both sides and pressing crumbs to adhere.

In 12-inch nonstick skillet heat 2 tablespoons oil over medium-high heat; add half of the chicken and cook, turning once, until lightly browned, 3 to 4 minutes on each side. Remove chicken to serving platter and keep warm. Repeat procedure using remaining oil and chicken cutlets.

In same skillet sauté pecans until lightly toasted, 1 to 2 minutes. In small bowl combine remaining ingredients, except orange slices, stirring to dissolve cornstarch; add to pecans in skillet and, stirring constantly, bring to a boil. Reduce heat and let simmer until mixture thickens, 4 to 5 minutes.

To serve, arrange orange slices on platter with chicken and top with pecan mixture.

MAKES 8 SERVINGS

Each serving provides: 3 Protein Exchanges; ½ Bread Exchange;
    1½ Fat Exchanges; 110 Optional Calories
Per serving: 337 calories; 30 g protein; 14 g fat; 22 g carbohydrate;
    42 mg calcium; 355 mg sodium; 135 mg cholesterol

TIP: Orange peel adds a fresh citrus flavor to this dish. The next time you eat an orange, first grate the peel. Wrap in plastic freezer wrap and freeze. Then you'll have it on hand when you're ready to prepare this extra-special dinner.

BREAKFAST

½ cup Grapefruit Sections
⅓ cup Cottage Cheese
1 slice Raisin Bread, toasted
½ cup Skim Milk
Herb Tea

LUNCH

Tuna Sandwich (2 ounces tuna with
    3 tomato slices, 2 lettuce leaves,
    and 1 teaspoon mayonnaise on
    2 slices reduced-calorie wheat
    bread)
6 Cucumber Spears and ½ cup
    Cauliflower Florets
Coffee, Tea, or Mineral Water

DINNER

1 serving **Sweet 'n' Sour Chicken**
Stir-Fried Broccoli (½ cup *each*
    broccoli florets and bamboo shoots
    stir-fried in 1 teaspoon vegetable
    oil)
1½ cups Mixed Green Salad with
    Lemon Juice and Herbs
½ cup Skim Milk
Tea

SNACKS

1 small Apple, cut into wedges,
    sprinkled with Nutmeg; 1 serving
    Reduced-Calorie Chocolate Dairy
    Drink

Total Optional Calories: 15

Sweet 'n' Sour Chicken ◑

1 teaspoon <u>each</u> margarine and vegetable oil
½ pound chicken cutlets, cut into cubes
½ cup <u>each</u> sliced green <u>or</u> red bell peppers, sliced
    onion, and quartered mushrooms
1 small garlic clove, sliced
½ cup drained canned crushed pineapple
    (no sugar added)
1½ teaspoons ketchup
1 teaspoon <u>each</u> firmly packed light <u>or</u> dark brown
    sugar and cider vinegar
½ packet (about ½ teaspoon) instant chicken broth
    and seasoning mix
1 large plum tomato, blanched, peeled, seeded,
    and sliced
¼ cup diagonally sliced scallions (green onions)

In 9- or 10-inch skillet heat margarine and oil together
until margarine is bubbly and mixture is hot; add chicken
and sauté, stirring frequently, until lightly browned, about
5 minutes. Add peppers, onion, mushrooms, and garlic
and cook, stirring occasionally, until vegetables are
tender-crisp, about 5 minutes.

In blender container combine pineapple, ketchup,
sugar, vinegar, and broth mix and process until pureed,
scraping down sides of container as necessary. Pour
pureed mixture over chicken and vegetables in skillet and
stir to combine; bring to a boil. Reduce heat to low; add
tomato and scallions, stir to combine, and cook until
flavors blend, about 5 minutes.

MAKES 2 SERVINGS

Each serving provides: 3 Protein Exchanges; 2¼ Vegetable
    Exchanges; 1 Fat Exchange; ½ Fruit Exchange; 15 Optional Calories
Per serving: 249 calories; 28 g protein; 6 g fat; 21 g carbohydrate;
    49 mg calcium; 394 mg sodium; 66 mg cholesterol

TIP: Plan ahead and prepare this the day before you're going to serve it.
This will give the flavors a chance to blend, so the dish will taste even
better. Just reheat and serve.

BREAKFAST

½ cup Canned Pineapple Chunks
⅓ cup Cottage Cheese
½ cup Skim Milk
Coffee or Tea

LUNCH

Dijon-Turkey Salad (2 ounces diced
turkey with ¼ cup sliced celery
and 2 teaspoons *each* Dijon-style
mustard and reduced-calorie
mayonnaise)
6 *each* Cherry Tomatoes and
Cucumber Spears
1 small Apple
Coffee, Tea, or Mineral Water

DINNER

1 serving **Blue Cheese-Stuffed Burgers**
1 cup Cooked Cauliflower
Tossed Salad with 1 tablespoon
Russian Dressing
1 small Orange, sliced, sprinkled
with Cinnamon
Coffee or Tea

SNACKS

½ cup Reduced-Calorie Chocolate
Pudding; ½ cup Skim Milk

Total Optional Calories: 0

Blue Cheese-Stuffed Burgers ◖

For an extra-special burger, try this recipe using Gorgonzola cheese.

7 ounces ground beef sirloin
2 tablespoons finely chopped scallion (green onion)
1 tablespoon Worcestershire sauce
½ teaspoon chili powder
⅛ teaspoon pepper
1 ounce blue cheese, crumbled
2 hamburger rolls (2 ounces each), split

In small mixing bowl combine beef, scallion, Worcestershire sauce, chili powder, and pepper, mixing well. Divide mixture into 4 equal portions and shape each into a patty about ¼ inch thick. Onto center of each of 2 patties arrange ½ ounce cheese, then top each with a remaining patty, firmly pressing edges of patties together to seal. Transfer patties to rack in broiling pan; broil 4 to 6 inches from heat source, turning once, for 3 to 4 minutes on each side or until done to taste. Serve each stuffed burger on a hamburger roll.

MAKES 2 SERVINGS, 1 BURGER EACH

Each serving provides: 3 Protein Exchanges; 2 Bread Exchanges;
⅛ Vegetable Exchange
Per serving: 410 calories; 34 g protein; 15 g fat; 33 g carbohydrate;
132 mg calcium; 630 mg sodium; 90 mg cholesterol

BREAKFAST

Peach 'n' Yogurt (½ cup canned peach
  slices topped with ¼ cup plain
  low-fat yogurt)
1 slice Whole Wheat Bread, toasted
Coffee or Tea

LUNCH

Open-Face Tuna Sandwich (2 ounces
  tuna with ¼ cup *each* chopped
  onion and celery, 2 lettuce leaves,
  and 1 teaspoon mayonnaise on
  1 slice reduced-calorie multi-grain
  bread)
6 *each* Red and Green Bell Pepper
  Strips
1 small Orange
Coffee, Tea, or Mineral Water

DINNER

1 serving **Steak au Gratin**
1 cup Cooked Chopped Spinach
  with ½ teaspoon Olive Oil plus
  Minced Garlic
1 cup Cooked Cauliflower
1½ cups Tossed Salad with
  1½ teaspoons Buttermilk Dressing
  mixed with 2 tablespoons Plain
  Low-Fat Yogurt and ¼ teaspoon
  Mustard
½ cup Reduced-Calorie Butterscotch
  Pudding
Coffee or Tea

SNACKS

Gelatin 'n' Fruit (½ cup low-calorie
  strawberry-flavored gelatin and
  ½ medium banana, sliced, topped
  with 2 tablespoons plain low-fat
  yogurt)

Total Optional Calories: 35

Steak au Gratin ◑

½ **pound boneless sirloin steak**
2 **teaspoons reduced-calorie margarine (tub)**
1 **cup sliced onions**
1 **garlic clove, minced**
½ **cup canned ready-to-serve beef broth**
1 **tablespoon red wine vinegar**
2 **teaspoons Dijon-style mustard**
3 **tablespoons plain dried bread crumbs**
1 **tablespoon <u>each</u> chopped fresh parsley and grated
  Parmesan cheese**

On rack in broiling pan broil steak until rare, 3 to 4 minutes
on each side.

While steak is cooking, in 10-inch nonstick skillet heat
margarine over high heat until bubbly and hot; add onions
and garlic and sauté, stirring occasionally, until onions are
tender-crisp, 2 to 3 minutes. Stir in broth, vinegar, and
mustard and continue cooking until liquid is reduced by
half, 3 to 4 minutes longer.

Transfer steak to 9 x 9 x 2-inch flameproof baking dish
and top with onion mixture. In small bowl combine bread
crumbs, parsley, and cheese, mixing well; sprinkle over
onion mixture and broil until topping is lightly browned,
1 to 2 minutes.

MAKES 2 SERVINGS

Each serving provides: 3 Protein Exchanges; ½ Bread Exchange;
  1 Vegetable Exchange; ½ Fat Exchange; 25 Optional Calories
Per serving: 287 calories; 30 g protein; 12 g fat; 15 g carbohydrate;
  80 mg calcium; 596 mg sodium; 78 mg cholesterol

Variation: Steak in Onion-Wine Sauce (Week 2) — Add
¼ cup dry red wine along with the beef broth to skillet;
proceed as directed. Increase Optional Calories to 55.

Per serving: 312 calories; 30 g protein; 12 g fat; 16 g carbohydrate;
  83 mg calcium; 598 mg sodium; 78 mg cholesterol

BRUNCH

1 medium Kiwi Fruit, sliced
Cheese and Mushroom Omelet
 (2 eggs with ¼ cup sliced
 mushrooms and 1 ounce shredded
 Cheddar cheese, prepared in
 1 teaspoon margarine)
1 serving **Leeks with Hot Bacon
 Vinaigrette**
½ small Bagel, toasted, with
 2 teaspoons Reduced-Calorie
 Raspberry Spread
1 cup Skim Milk

DINNER

4 ounces Sliced Roast Turkey Breast
3 ounces Baked Potato with
 1 teaspoon Margarine
½ cup Cooked Baby Carrots
6 Cooked Asparagus Spears
1½ cups Mixed Green Salad with
 1 tablespoon Reduced-Calorie
 Buttermilk Dressing
Apple-Raisin Yogurt (½ cup plain
 low-fat yogurt mixed with ¼ cup
 applesauce and 1 tablespoon
 raisins)
Coffee or Tea

SNACKS

2 cups Plain Popcorn; 2 Dates

Total Optional Calories: 95

Leeks with Hot Bacon Vinaigrette ◖

Serve this elegant side dish at your next Sunday brunch.
Chill leftovers and serve cold later in the week.

8 medium leeks
¾ cup water
¼ cup dry white table wine
1 small garlic clove
2 to 3 peppercorns
3 slices crisp bacon, crumbled
2 tablespoons red wine vinegar
1 tablespoon plus 1 teaspoon olive oil
**1 tablespoon <u>each</u> lemon juice and chopped fresh
 parsley**
1 teaspoon Dijon-style mustard
½ garlic clove, minced
¼ teaspoon <u>each</u> granulated sugar and salt
Dash pepper

Using sharp knife, cut off and discard stem and tough green
leaves from each leek. Slice each leek in half lengthwise;
wash thoroughly to remove sand. Drain leeks and set aside.
 In 10-inch skillet combine water, wine, the whole garlic
clove, and the peppercorns and cook over high heat until
mixture comes to a boil; add leeks, cover skillet, and cook
until tender-crisp, 2 to 3 minutes. Using slotted spoon,
transfer leeks to serving platter; keep warm. Continue
cooking mixture in skillet, uncovered, until liquid is reduced
to about ¼ cup; remove and discard peppercorns and
garlic. Reduce heat to low; add remaining ingredients and
cook, stirring occasionally, until heated through, 3 to 5
minutes. Top leeks with bacon mixture.

MAKES 4 SERVINGS

Each serving provides: 2 Vegetable Exchanges; 1 Fat Exchange;
 50 Optional Calories
Per serving: 149 calories; 3 g protein; 7 g fat; 17 g carbohydrate;
 68 mg calcium; 272 mg sodium; 4 mg cholesterol

BREAKFAST

BREAKFAST

Tropical Breakfast Crunch (½ cup plain low-fat yogurt mixed with ¾ ounce cold cereal and ½ cup canned crushed pineapple)
Coffee or Tea

LUNCH

Salmon Salad (2 ounces salmon with 1 cup torn lettuce, 2 red onion slices, and 2½ teaspoons mayonnaise)
½ cup Cauliflower Florets and 6 Whole Radishes
1 slice Pumpernickel Bread
1 small Apple
Coffee, Tea, or Mineral Water

DINNER

3 ounces Broiled Steak
1 serving **Nacho Potato Wedges**
1 cup Cooked Cut Green Beans
2 cups Tossed Salad with 1 tablespoon Reduced-Calorie Blue Cheese Dressing
8 fluid ounces Beer

SNACKS

1 small Orange, cut into wedges; ½ cup Reduced-Calorie Butterscotch Pudding

Total Optional Calories: 140

Nacho Potato Wedges ⊙ ◐

They'll say "olé" when you turn leftover baked potato into this spicy appetizer or side dish.

6 ounces baked potato (with skin), cut lengthwise into wedges
1 teaspoon margarine, melted
Dash pepper
1 ounce Monterey Jack <u>or</u> sharp Cheddar cheese, shredded
1 tablespoon thinly sliced scallion (green onion)
¼ to ½ teaspoon seeded and minced hot <u>or</u> mild green chili pepper

On baking sheet arrange potato wedges in a single layer, skin-side down. Using pastry brush, brush wedges with margarine, then sprinkle with pepper; broil until browned, about 10 minutes.

In small bowl combine cheese, scallion, and chili pepper; sprinkle evenly over potato wedges and broil until cheese is melted, 1 to 2 minutes.

MAKES 2 SERVINGS

Each serving provides: ½ Protein Exchange; 1 Bread Exchange; ½ Fat Exchange
Per serving with Monterey Jack cheese: 164 calories; 6 g protein; 6 g fat; 22 g carbohydrate; 117 mg calcium; 105 mg sodium; 12 mg cholesterol
With Cheddar cheese: 168 calories; 6 g protein; 7 g fat; 22 g carbohydrate; 114 mg calcium; 117 mg sodium; 15 mg cholesterol

½ medium Grapefruit
½ cup Cooked Cereal
1 cup Skim Milk
Coffee or Tea

LUNCH

Sardines in a Pita (2 ounces sardines
    with 3 tomato slices, 2 red onion
    rings, 2 lettuce leaves, and
    1 teaspoon mayonnaise in 1-ounce
    pita bread)
½ cup Broccoli Florets and 6 Celery
    Sticks
1 small Apple
Coffee, Tea, or Mineral Water

DINNER

3½ ounces Roast Cornish Hen
6 Cooked Asparagus Spears with
    1 teaspoon Margarine
1 cup Cooked Sliced Carrots
1 serving **Endive, Pepper, and Blue
    Cheese Salad**
½ cup Low-Calorie Strawberry-
    Flavored Gelatin
Coffee or Tea

SNACKS

½ cup Reduced-Calorie Vanilla
    Pudding drizzled with 1 teaspoon
    Strawberry Syrup; ⅛ medium
    Pineapple

Total Optional Calories: 30

Endive, Pepper, and Blue Cheese Salad ◑

3 medium Belgian endives (about 3 ounces each)
1 cup julienne-cut red bell pepper (thin strips)
2 ounces blue cheese, crumbled
2 tablespoons Italian dressing

Separate each endive into individual leaves. On large
serving platter decoratively arrange leaves, curved-side up;
place an equal amount of pepper strips in each leaf, then
sprinkle evenly with blue cheese. Drizzle dressing evenly
over salad and serve immediately.

MAKES 4 SERVINGS

Each serving provides: ½ Protein Exchange; 1¼ Vegetable Exchanges;
    1 Fat Exchange
Per serving: 100 calories; 4 g protein; 8 g fat; 4 g carbohydrate;
    89 mg calcium; 261 mg sodium; 11 mg cholesterol

BREAKFAST

½ cup Orange Sections
¾ ounce Cold Cereal
1 cup Skim Milk

LUNCH

Fish Salad (2 ounces fish with
   2 tablespoons chopped celery and
   1½ teaspoons creamy Italian
   dressing on 3 lettuce leaves)
6 Melba Rounds
¾ cup Cauliflower Florets and 6 Red
   Bell Pepper Strips
1 small Apple
Coffee, Tea, or Mineral Water

DINNER

3 ounces Broiled Chicken Cutlet
   with Lemon-Honey Sauce
   (2 teaspoons lemon juice heated
   with 1 teaspoon honey)
½ cup *each* Cooked Sliced Carrot
   and Cut Green Beans with
   1 teaspoon Margarine
1 serving **Leek Salad**
½ cup Reduced-Calorie Chocolate
   Pudding
Iced Tea

SNACKS

2-inch wedge Honeydew Melon with
   Lemon Wedge

Total Optional Calories: 20

Leek Salad ◑

**2 cups sliced thoroughly washed leeks (white portion
   only), ½-inch slices**
½ cup boiling water
¼ teaspoon salt, divided
1 medium tomato, cut into thin wedges
1 egg, hard-cooked and diced
**1 tablespoon cider vinegar, mixed with 2¼ teaspoons
   water**
2 teaspoons olive oil
1½ teaspoons chopped fresh parsley
**⅛ teaspoon <u>each</u> Worchestershire sauce, minced fresh
   garlic, and crushed tarragon leaves**
Dash pepper

In 1-quart saucepan combine leeks, water, and ⅛ teaspoon
salt and cook for 5 minutes; drain and let cool.

   In salad bowl (not aluminum*) combine leeks, tomato, and
egg. In small bowl combine remaining ingredients; pour
over salad and toss to coat. Cover and refrigerate at least
1 hour.

MAKES 2 SERVINGS

Each serving provides: ½ Protein Exchange; 3 Vegetable Exchanges;
   1 Fat Exchange
Per serving: 157 calories; 5 g protein; 8 g fat; 18 g carbohydrate;
   84 mg calcium; 203 mg sodium; 137 mg cholesterol

*It's best to marinate in glass or stainless-steel containers; acidic ingredients
   such as vinegar may react with aluminum, causing color and flavor changes
   in foods.

TIP: Leeks should be washed thoroughly before cooking to ensure that
they are free of sand.

Tomato-Cream Sauce

Fabulous with Swiss Chard Gnocchi (see page 70).
Or try this creamy sauce on cooked pasta or rice.

**3 cups canned Italian tomatoes (with liquid); drain,
    seed, and dice tomatoes, reserving liquid, divided
2 teaspoons olive <u>or</u> vegetable oil
½ cup chopped onion
1 garlic clove, minced
2 teaspoons <u>each</u> minced fresh parsley and basil
¼ teaspoon salt
Dash pepper
¾ cup half-and-half (blend of milk and cream)**

In blender container process 2 cups tomatoes with the
reserved liquid until pureed; set aside.

In 3-quart saucepan heat oil over medium-high heat; add
onion and garlic and sauté until softened, 1 to 2 minutes.
Add pureed and diced tomatoes along with the parsley,
basil, salt, and pepper and stir to combine. Reduce heat to
low and let simmer, stirring frequently, until mixture is
reduced and slightly thickened, 25 to 30 minutes. Gradually
stir in half-and-half and cook until thoroughly heated and
flavors blend, 10 to 15 minutes longer (<u>do not boil</u>).

MAKES 4 SERVINGS

Each serving provides: 1¾ Vegetable Exchanges; ½ Fat Exchange;
    75 Optional Calories
Per serving: 123 calories; 3 g protein; 8 g fat; 12 g carbohydrate;
    106 mg calcium; 448 mg sodium; 17 mg cholesterol

BREAKFAST

1 medium Kiwi Fruit, sliced
Lox 'n' Bagel (½ small bagel topped
    with 1 tablespoon whipped cream
    cheese and 1 ounce smoked
    salmon)
½ cup Skim Milk
Coffee or Tea

LUNCH

Egg Salad in a Pita (2 hard-cooked
    eggs, chopped, with ¼ cup alfalfa
    sprouts, 2 lettuce leaves,
    1 teaspoon mustard, and
    2 teaspoons reduced-calorie
    mayonnaise in 1-ounce pita bread)
6 *each* Carrot and Celery Sticks
Coffee, Tea, or Mineral Water

DINNER

2 tablespoons **Guacamole** with
    6 Melba Rounds
3 ounces Roast Turkey
1 cup Cooked Artichoke Hearts with
    1 tablespoon Reduced-Calorie
    Italian Dressing
½ cup Cooked Sliced Beets
1½ cups Tossed Salad with
    1 tablespoon Buttermilk Dressing
1 small Apple, baked
½ cup Skim Milk
Coffee or Tea

SNACKS

½ cup Reduced-Calorie Chocolate
    Pudding sprinkled with 1 teaspoon
    Shredded Coconut; ⅛ medium
    Pineapple

Total Optional Calories: 110

Guacamole ◑

Serve as a dip with assorted vegetable sticks
or as a spread on warm tortillas or crackers.

**½ avocado, pitted (about 4 ounces), pared and cut into
    quarters
2 tablespoons seeded and chopped tomato
1 tablespoon <u>each</u> diced onion and sour cream
1 small garlic clove, minced
1 teaspoon freshly squeezed lime juice*
½ teaspoon minced fresh cilantro (Chinese parsley)
⅛ teaspoon <u>each</u> chili powder and salt
Dash hot sauce, or to taste**

In blender container combine all ingredients and process
until smooth. Transfer to small bowl (not aluminum†); cover
with plastic wrap and refrigerate until flavors are blended, at
least 30 minutes.

YIELDS ½ CUP

Each 2-tablespoon serving provides: ⅛ Vegetable Exchange; 60 Optional
    Calories
Per serving: 48 calories; 0.7 g protein; 4 g fat; 3 g carbohydrate;
    9 mg calcium; 77 mg sodium; 2 mg cholesterol

* If fresh limes are not available, bottled lime juice (no sugar added) may be
    used.
† It's best to marinate in glass or stainless-steel containers; acidic ingredients
    such as lime juice may react with aluminum, causing color and flavor
    changes in foods.

½ medium Grapefruit
1 Sunny-Side-Up Egg
½ English Muffin, toasted, with
   1 teaspoon Margarine
½ cup Skim Milk
Coffee or Tea

LUNCH

Tuna Sandwich (2 ounces tuna with
   2 tablespoons chopped onion and
   1 teaspoon mayonnaise on 2 slices
   reduced-calorie rye bread)
6 *each* Broccoli Florets and Carrot
   Sticks
¾ ounce Mixed Dried Fruit
Coffee, Tea, or Mineral Water

DINNER

3 ounces Roast Chicken basted with
   1 tablespoon Barbecue Sauce
1 cup Cooked Wax Beans
½ cup Coleslaw
1 serving **Jelly 'n' Nut-Topped Muffins**
½ cup Skim Milk
Coffee or Tea

SNACKS

½ cup Applesauce; 1 cup Skim Milk

Total Optional Calories: 170

Jelly 'n' Nut-Topped Muffins

Great for dessert or snack. Prepare a batch and freeze in resealable freezer bags. To serve, thaw at room temperature.

2 ¼ cups all-purpose flour
¼ cup granulated sugar
1 tablespoon double-acting baking powder
1 cup skim milk
¼ cup vegetable oil
1 egg, beaten
2 tablespoons reduced-calorie raspberry or strawberry spread (16 calories per 2 teaspoons)
1 ounce finely chopped almonds
1 tablespoon firmly packed dark brown sugar

Preheat oven to 400°F. Spray twelve 2½-inch-diameter muffin-pan cups with nonstick cooking spray and set aside.

In medium mixing bowl combine flour, granulated sugar, and baking powder; add milk, oil, and egg and stir just until combined (do not overmix; batter should be lumpy). Fill each muffin-pan cup with an equal amount of batter (each cup will be about ⅔ full). Using back of ½-teaspoon measure, press center of each portion of batter, making an indentation. Spoon ½ teaspoon spread into each indentation, then sprinkle each with an equal amount of almonds and ¼ teaspoon brown sugar. Bake in middle of center oven rack for about 20 minutes (until golden brown). Remove muffins to wire rack to cool.

MAKES 12 SERVINGS, 1 MUFFIN EACH

Each serving provides: 1 Bread Exchange; 1 Fat Exchange; 55 Optional
   Calories
Per serving: 178 calories; 4 g protein; 6 g fat; 26 g carbohydrate;
   91 mg calcium; 124 mg sodium; 23 mg cholesterol

Orange-Pecan Waffles ◑

½ cup all-purpose flour
½ teaspoon double-acting baking powder
¼ teaspoon <u>each</u> baking soda, ground cinnamon, and ground nutmeg
⅓ cup buttermilk
¼ cup orange juice (no sugar added)
1 egg, separated
1 teaspoon grated orange peel
½ ounce chopped pecans
2 tablespoons low-calorie pancake syrup (14 calories per tablespoon)

In medium mixing bowl combine flour, baking powder, baking soda, cinnamon, and nutmeg; set aside.

In small bowl combine buttermilk, orange juice, egg yolk, and orange peel; add to flour mixture and mix well.

Spray nonstick waffle baker with nonstick cooking spray and preheat according to manufacturer's directions. In separate small mixing bowl, using electric mixer at high speed, beat egg white until stiff but not dry; fold beaten white and pecans into batter. Following manufacturer's directions, prepare 4 waffles. Serve 2 waffles per portion; top each portion with 1 tablespoon syrup.

MAKES 2 SERVINGS, 2 WAFFLES EACH

Each serving provides: ½ Protein Exchange; 1 Bread Exchange;
    125 Optional Calories
Per serving: 249 calories; 8 g protein; 8 g fat; 35 g carbohydrate;
    130 mg calcium; 285 mg sodium; 139 mg cholesterol

TIP: Are waffles too much to fuss with in the morning? Here's a suggestion — prepare them in advance, wrap individually, and freeze. Then just pop them in the microwave or toaster-oven to enjoy!

BREAKFAST

¾ cup Grapefruit Juice
1 Scrambled Egg
1 slice Rye Bread, toasted, with
   1 teaspoon Reduced-Calorie
   Margarine
½ cup Skim Milk
Coffee or Tea

LUNCH

Chicken Salad (2 ounces julienne-cut
   chicken with ½ cup *each* sliced
   asparagus and carrot and
   2 teaspoons reduced-calorie
   mayonnaise)
6 Melba Rounds
Coffee, Tea, or Mineral Water

DINNER

3 ounces Broiled Flounder Fillet
6 Cooked Broccoli Spears
2 cups Tossed Salad with
   1 teaspoon Vegetable Oil mixed
   with 2 teaspoons Red Wine
   Vinegar plus Seasonings
1 serving **Orange-Banana Broil**
Herb Tea

SNACKS

½ cup Reduced-Calorie Chocolate
   Pudding; ½ cup Skim Milk

Total Optional Calories: 25

Orange-Banana Broil ◐◑

¾ cup orange juice (no sugar added)
2 teaspoons margarine
¼ ounce (about 1 teaspoon) uncooked quick farina
2 medium bananas (about 6 ounces each)
1 teaspoon lemon juice
1 small orange (about 6 ounces), peeled and sliced crosswise
1 teaspoon each firmly packed light brown sugar and granulated sugar

In small saucepan combine orange juice and margarine and cook over medium-high heat until mixture comes to a boil; stir in farina and cook, stirring constantly, until mixture thickens, 3 to 4 minutes. Remove saucepan from heat and set aside.

Peel bananas and cut in half lengthwise, then cut each half in half crosswise; sprinkle with lemon juice to prevent discoloring. In 8-inch pie pan or shallow 1½-quart flameproof casserole arrange banana pieces and orange slices, alternating fruits; top with orange juice mixture. In small cup combine sugars; sprinkle over fruit mixture and broil 6 to 8 inches from heat source until lightly browned, 5 to 7 minutes. Serve warm.

MAKES 4 SERVINGS

Each serving provides: ½ Fat Exchange; 1½ Fruit Exchanges; 25 Optional Calories
Per serving: 120 calories; 1 g protein; 2 g fat; 26 g carbohydrate; 23 mg calcium; 24 mg sodium; 0 mg cholesterol

Variations: Orange-Banana Sundae (Week 8) — Serve each portion of Orange-Banana Broil over ½ cup vanilla ice milk. Increase Optional Calories to 145.
Per serving: 212 calories; 4 g protein; 5 g fat; 40 g carbohydrate; 111 mg calcium; 76 mg sodium; 9 mg cholesterol

Orange-Banana Sherbet (Week 5) — Serve each portion of Orange-Banana Broil over ½ cup fruit-flavored sherbet. Increase Optional Calories to 175.
Per serving: 255 calories; 2 g protein; 4 g fat; 55 g carbohydrate; 75 mg calcium; 68 mg sodium; 7 mg cholesterol

BREAKFAST

½ cup Orange Sections
2-ounce Corn Muffin, toasted, with
    1 tablespoon Grape Jelly
1 cup Skim Milk

LUNCH

Tuna-Cheese Delight (1 ounce *each*
    tuna and sliced Muenster cheese
    with 2 tomato slices, 2 lettuce
    leaves, 5 dill pickle slices, and
    1 teaspoon mayonnaise on 2 slices
    reduced-calorie whole wheat bread)
1 small Apple
Coffee, Tea, or Mineral Water

DINNER

3 ounces Broiled Beef Sausage
3 ounces Cooked Potato mashed
    with 1 teaspoon Margarine
½ cup *each* Cooked Mushrooms and
    Chinese Pea Pods
1½ cups Tossed Salad with Lemon
    Juice and Herbs
1 serving **Irish Coffee**

SNACKS

½ cup Canned Pineapple Chunks;
    1 serving Reduced-Calorie Vanilla
    Dairy Drink

Total Optional Calories: 140

Irish Coffee ◑

1 tablespoon <u>each</u> granulated sugar and lemon juice
¼ cup Irish whiskey
2 tablespoons Scotch-flavored <u>or</u> coffee liqueur
1½ cups strong coffee (hot)
¼ cup thawed frozen dairy whipped topping

Sprinkle sugar onto small paper plate; pour lemon juice into small shallow dish. Dip rims of four 4-ounce flameproof goblets into lemon juice and then into sugar so that sugar adheres to rims of goblets; set goblets aside.

In small saucepan combine whiskey and liqueur and cook over medium heat until mixture is heated through (<u>do not boil</u>). Pour ¼ of mixture into each prepared goblet; add ¼ of the coffee to each portion and top each with 1 tablespoon whipped topping. Serve immediately.

MAKES 4 SERVINGS

Each serving provides: 90 Optional Calories
Per serving with Scotch-flavored liqueur: 58 calories; trace protein; 1 g fat;
    4 g carbohydrate; 2 mg calcium; 7 mg sodium; 0 mg cholesterol
With coffee liqueur: 83 calories; trace protein; 1 g fat; 14 g carbohydrate;
    2 mg calcium; 7 mg sodium; 0 mg cholesterol

TIP: Combine whiskey and liqueur in goblet and heat in microwave oven. No saucepan to wash!

April

Lamb Steaks with Creamy Mint Sauce

APRIL'S BEST BUYS FOR FRUITS AND VEGETABLES

alfalfa sprouts	broccoli	kumquats	potatoes
artichokes	cabbage	lettuce	radishes
asparagus	carrots	mushrooms	rhubarb
avocados	cauliflower	new potatoes	scallions (green onions)
bananas	celery	okra	spinach
bean sprouts	Chinese pea pods	onions	strawberries
beets	eggplants	papayas	summer squash
Belgian endives	green beans	peas	turnips
bell peppers	kiwi fruit	pineapples	zucchini

BREAKFAST

1 cup Strawberries, sliced
¾ ounce Cold Cereal
1 cup Skim Milk
Coffee or Tea

LUNCH

Roast Beef Sandwich (2 ounces
    sliced roast beef with 2 lettuce
    leaves, 4 tomato slices, and
    1 teaspoon *each* mayonnaise and
    mustard on 2 slices reduced-
    calorie wheat bread)
6 *each* Celery and Carrot Sticks
Coffee, Tea, or Mineral Water

DINNER

3 ounces Roast Turkey
¾ cup Cooked Chinese Pea Pods
    with ¼ cup Pimiento Strips
Chick-Pea Salad (1 ounce canned
    chick-peas with 1½ cups torn
    lettuce, 6 cucumber slices, ½ cup
    shredded red cabbage, and
    1 tablespoon Italian dressing)
Apple Yogurt (½ cup plain low-fat
    yogurt mixed with ½ cup
    applesauce)
White Wine Spritzer (¼ cup dry white
    wine with ½ cup club soda)
Coffee or Tea

SNACKS

1 tablespoon **Vegetable Cream Cheese**
    with ¾ ounce Breadsticks

Total Optional Calories: 100

Vegetable Cream Cheese Ⓒ ◑

Can be stored tightly covered in refrigerator for up to
2 weeks. Delicious on bagels, crackers, or breadsticks.

½ cup cream cheese, softened
**2 tablespoons <u>each</u> chopped celery, chopped scallion
    (green onion), diced green bell pepper, and diced
    carrot**

In work bowl of food processor* process cream cheese
until light and fluffy. Transfer to small bowl; add remaining
ingredients and stir to combine. Cover with plastic wrap
and refrigerate until flavors blend, at least 30 minutes.

YIELDS ½ CUP

Each 1-tablespoon serving provides: ⅛ Vegetable Exchange; 50 Optional
    Calories
Per serving: 51 calories; 1 g protein; 5 g fat; 1 g carbohydrate;
    13 mg calcium; 44 mg sodium; 16 mg cholesterol

*If food processor is not available, use electric mixer at medium speed
  and proceed as directed.

BREAKFAST

1 medium Kiwi Fruit, sliced
½ small Bagel, toasted, with
    1 serving **Walnut-Raisin Spread**
1 cup Skim Milk

LUNCH

Chicken "Reuben" Sandwich
    (2 ounces sliced chicken with
    ¼ cup sauerkraut and
    1½ teaspoons Russian dressing
    on 2 slices reduced-calorie
    rye bread)
6 *each* Carrot Sticks and Radishes
Coffee, Tea, or Mineral Water

DINNER

4 ounces Broiled Flounder sprinkled
    with Paprika
3 ounces Baked Sweet Potato
6 Cooked Asparagus Spears with
    1 teaspoon Margarine
Artichoke Salad (½ cup chilled cooked
    artichoke hearts with 1½ teaspoons
    Caesar dressing mixed with
    2 teaspoons lemon juice and
    ½ teaspoon mustard on 2 lettuce
    leaves)
½ cup Applesauce
½ cup Skim Milk
Coffee or Tea

SNACKS

Banana Yogurt (¼ cup plain low-fat
    yogurt mixed with ½ medium
    banana, sliced)

Total Optional Calories: 125

Walnut-Raisin Spread ◐

The flavor of this sweet and crunchy spread improves with time, so prepare it in advance. It will keep in the refrigerator, covered, for up to 2 weeks.

½ cup cream cheese, softened
½ ounce chopped walnuts
¼ cup dark raisins
⅛ teaspoon ground cinnamon
Dash ground nutmeg

In work bowl of food processor* process cream cheese until light and fluffy. Transfer to small bowl; add remaining ingredients and stir to combine. Cover with plastic wrap and refrigerate until flavors blend, at least 30 minutes.

MAKES 4 SERVINGS, ABOUT 2 TABLESPOONS EACH

Each serving provides: ½ Fruit Exchange; 125 Optional Calories
Per serving: 149 calories; 3 g protein; 12 g fat; 9 g carbohydrate;
    31 mg calcium; 85 mg sodium; 31 mg cholesterol

* If food processor is not available, use electric mixer at medium speed
  and proceed as directed.

Cauliflower-Rice Torte ⓒ

2 teaspoons margarine
2 tablespoons minced shallots
1 small garlic clove, minced
2 cups cooked long-grain rice
¾ cup part-skim ricotta cheese
1 ounce grated Parmesan cheese, divided
1 egg
2 tablespoons chopped fresh parsley
Dash <u>each</u> ground nutmeg and white pepper
1½ cups cooked cauliflower, finely chopped
1½ ounces <u>each</u> Fontina and mozzarella cheese,
  shredded

Preheat oven to 350°F. In 8-inch nonstick skillet heat margarine over medium heat until bubbly and hot; add shallots and garlic and sauté, stirring frequently, until softened, about 1 minute. Transfer to medium mixing bowl; add rice, ricotta cheese, ¾ ounce Parmesan cheese, and the egg, parsley, nutmeg, and pepper and mix well.

Spray 2-quart casserole with nonstick cooking spray; spread half of the rice mixture in casserole, top evenly with cauliflower, and sprinkle with half of the remaining Parmesan cheese. Spread remaining rice mixture over Parmesan cheese; sprinkle with Fontina, mozzarella, and remaining Parmesan cheese. Bake until torte is lightly browned and bubbly, about 20 minutes. Transfer casserole to wire rack and let cool for 5 minutes before cutting.

MAKES 4 SERVINGS

Each serving provides: 2 Protein Exchanges; 1 Bread Exchange;
   ¾ Vegetable Exchange; ½ Fat Exchange
Per serving: 332 calories; 18 g protein; 15 g fat; 31 g carbohydrate;
   372 mg calcium; 273 mg sodium; 109 mg cholesterol

Variation: 3 ounces Fontina <u>or</u> 3 ounces mozzarella cheese may be used instead of 1½ ounces each.

Per serving with Fontina cheese: 344 calories; 18 g protein; 16 g fat;
   31 g carbohydrate; 376 mg calcium; 233 mg sodium; 113 mg cholesterol
With mozzarella cheese: 321 calories; 17 g protein; 14 g fat;
   31 g carbohydrate; 369 mg calcium; 313 mg sodium; 105 mg cholesterol

BREAKFAST

BREAKFAST

½ cup Orange Sections
1 Hard-Cooked Egg
½ Matzo Board with 1 teaspoon
 Margarine
1 cup Skim Milk

LUNCH

1 serving **Gefilte Fish Loaf**
Carrot-Onion Salad (1 cup shredded
 lettuce with ½ cup shredded carrot,
 3 red onion slices, and 1 teaspoon
 vegetable oil mixed with 2
 teaspoons red wine vinegar)
½ cup Fruit Salad
Coffee, Tea, or Mineral Water

DINNER

¾ cup Chicken Bouillon
3 ounces Roast Turkey Breast
½ cup *each* Cooked Broccoli and
 Cauliflower Florets
2 cups Mixed Green Salad with
 1½ teaspoons French Dressing
 mixed with 2 teaspoons Lemon
 Juice and ¼ teaspoon Mustard
1 small Apple, baked
Coffee or Tea

SNACKS

½ Matzo Board with 2 teaspoons
 Strawberry Preserves; 1 cup Skim
 Milk

Total Optional Calories: 70

Gefilte Fish Loaf ©

A variation on a classic Passover specialty that makes a wonderful weekend lunch. This keeps well and is equally as good chilled. Just wrap any leftovers in plastic wrap and refrigerate for up to 1 week.

**1 pound 2 ounces whitefish, pike, _or_ carp fillets
 (or a mixture of all 3)
2 cups chopped onions
2 eggs
2 tablespoons _each_ lemon juice and cold water
1 tablespoon coarse salt
½ teaspoon white pepper
1 cup _each_ diced green bell peppers and shredded
 carrots
⅓ cup plus 2 teaspoons matzo meal
3 tablespoons chopped fresh dill
2 tablespoons prepared horseradish, thoroughly dried
 in paper towels
¼ teaspoon grated lemon peel
Garnish: dill sprigs _or_ lemon slices**

Preheat oven to 350°F. In work bowl of food processor, using an on-off motion, process fish until ground (<u>do not puree</u>); add onions, eggs, lemon juice, water, salt, and pepper and, continuing to use an on-off motion, process until combined, about 30 seconds. Transfer mixture to large mixing bowl; add remaining ingredients except garnish and mix well.

 Spray 9 x 5 x 3-inch loaf pan with nonstick cooking spray; line bottom and sides of pan with wax paper. Transfer fish mixture to prepared pan, spreading evenly and smoothing top; rap pan on counter top a few times to release any air bubbles. Set loaf pan in larger baking pan and pour hot water into baking pan to reach halfway up the sides of loaf pan; bake until center of fish loaf is firm to the touch, about 40 minutes. Remove baking pan from oven and loaf pan from water bath; let stand for 5 minutes. Invert fish loaf onto serving platter and remove wax paper; cut into 8 equal slices, and serve garnished with dill or lemon.

MAKES 8 SERVINGS, 1 SLICE EACH

Each serving provides: 2 Protein Exchanges; 1 Vegetable Exchange;
 25 Optional Calories
Per serving: 168 calories; 15 g protein; 7 g fat; 11 g carbohydrate;
 48 mg calcium; 885 mg sodium; 104 mg cholesterol

BREAKFAST

1 medium Kiwi Fruit, sliced
¾ ounce Cold Cereal
½ cup Skim Milk
Coffee or Tea

LUNCH

Chicken Salad in a Pita (2 ounces
    diced chicken with 2 tablespoons
    each chopped celery and onion,
    1 tablespoon minced pickle, and
    2 teaspoons reduced-calorie
    mayonnaise in 1-ounce pita bread)
½ cup Broccoli Florets and 6 Cherry
    Tomatoes
Coffee, Tea, or Mineral Water

DINNER

1 cup Mixed Vegetable Juice with
    Celery Stick
1 serving **Red Snapper with Anchovy
    Butter**
3 ounces Baked Potato topped with
    1 tablespoon Sour Cream and
    Chopped Chives
½ cup Cooked Chinese Pea Pods
½ cup *each* Shredded Red and Green
    Cabbage with 1 tablespoon
    French Dressing
½ cup Peaches
½ cup Skim Milk
Cinnamon Coffee

SNACKS

½ medium Papaya; Honey-Nutmeg
    Yogurt (½ cup plain low-fat
    yogurt mixed with 1 teaspoon
    honey and nutmeg)

Total Optional Calories: 80

Red Snapper with Anchovy Butter ◑

The skin of the red snapper fillets will make this dish extremely attractive so be sure to purchase fillets with the skin left on.

2 red snapper fillets (¼ pound each)
1 tablespoon chopped shallots
2 teaspoons <u>each</u> chopped fresh parsley, dry vermouth, and lightly salted whipped butter
1 teaspoon <u>each</u> mashed drained canned anchovies, lemon juice, and chopped chives
¼ teaspoon Dijon-style mustard

Using sharp knife, lightly score skin side of each fillet to prevent curling. Spray broiler pan with nonstick cooking spray; set fish in pan skin-side down and set aside.

Preheat broiler. In small bowl combine remaining ingredients, mixing well. Spread half of mixture onto each fillet; broil 6 to 8 inches from heat source until fish is opaque and flakes easily when tested with a fork, 4 to 5 minutes. Transfer fish to serving platter and top with any remaining pan juices.

MAKES 2 SERVINGS, I FILLET EACH

Each serving provides: 3 Protein Exchanges; 25 Optional Calories
Per serving: 140 calories; 23 g protein; 3 g fat; 2 g carbohydrate;
    28 mg calcium; 140 mg sodium; 69 mg cholesterol

BREAKFAST

1 cup Strawberries
½ small Bagel, toasted, with
   1 teaspoon Reduced-Calorie
   Margarine
¾ cup Skim Milk

LUNCH

Egg Salad Sandwich (2 hard-cooked
   eggs, chopped, with 2 *each* lettuce
   leaves and tomato slices,
   2 tablespoons chopped celery and
   2 teaspoons reduced-calorie
   mayonnaise on 2 slices reduced-
   calorie wheat bread)
6 *each* Red and Green Bell Pepper
   Strips
1 small Apple
Coffee, Tea, or Mineral Water

DINNER

1 serving **Angel Hair Pasta with Scallop
   Sauté**
1 cup Cooked Sliced Carrots
Tomato-Cucumber Salad (1½ cups
   torn lettuce with 3 tomato slices,
   6 cucumber slices, and
   1½ teaspoons Italian dressing
   mixed with 2 teaspoons red wine
   vinegar)
½ cup Reduced-Calorie Vanilla
   Pudding
Coffee or Tea

SNACKS

⅛ medium Pineapple

Total Optional Calories: 105

Angel Hair Pasta with Scallop Sauté ◑

Angel hair pasta cooks very quickly and the strands will stick together if prepared in advance. Therefore, prepare the sauce first, then cook the pasta.

1 teaspoon margarine
2 tablespoons minced shallots
1 small garlic clove, minced
7 ounces bay scallops (or sea scallops, cut into 1-inch pieces)
6 medium asparagus spears, diagonally cut into 1-inch pieces, blanched
½ cup low-fat milk (1% milk fat)
¼ cup half-and-half (blend of milk and cream)
1 ounce grated Parmesan cheese
2 tablespoons cream cheese
⅛ teaspoon white pepper
1 cup cooked angel hair pasta (cappelli d'angelo), hot*

In 10-inch nonstick skillet heat margarine over medium heat until bubbly and hot; add shallots and garlic and sauté until tender, about 1 minute. Add scallops to skillet and sauté until scallops begin to turn opaque, about 5 minutes; add asparagus and cook, stirring occasionally, for 2 minutes longer. Stir in remaining ingredients except pasta and cook, stirring constantly, until mixture comes just to a boil.

   To serve, arrange pasta in serving bowl; top with scallop mixture and toss to combine.

MAKES 2 SERVINGS

Each serving provides: 3 Protein Exchanges; 1 Bread Exchange;
   ½ Vegetable Exchange; ½ Fat Exchange; ¼ Milk Exchange; 105 Optional
   Calories
Per serving: 382 calories; 31 g protein; 16 g fat; 27 g carbohydrate;
   352 mg calcium; 534 mg sodium; 77 mg cholesterol

* Thin spaghetti or linguini may be substituted for the angel hair pasta.

Shrimp and Vegetable Pita Pizza ◖

2 teaspoons olive oil, divided
**3 medium asparagus spears, cut lengthwise into halves,
   then diagonally cut into 1-inch pieces and blanched**
¼ cup each sliced onion and thinly sliced mushrooms
1 small garlic clove, minced
3 ounces shelled and deveined shrimp, cut into pieces
**½ cup canned Italian tomatoes (with liquid), pureed and
   strained (discard seeds)**
**½ teaspoon each fresh basil leaves and minced fresh
   parsley**
2 pita breads (2 ounces each)
¼ pound mozzarella cheese, shredded
1 teaspoon grated Parmesan cheese

In 10-inch skillet heat 1 teaspoon oil over medium-high heat;
add asparagus, onion, mushrooms, and garlic and sauté until
vegetables are softened, 2 to 3 minutes. Add shrimp to
skillet and sauté until shrimp begin to turn pink, about 1
minute; stir in tomatoes, basil, and parsley. Reduce heat to
low and let simmer until flavors blend, 3 to 4 minutes.

Set pita breads on baking sheet and, using pastry brush,
brush top side of each with ¼ teaspoon oil. Broil 6 to 8
inches from heat source until lightly browned, 1 to 2
minutes; turn breads over, brush each with ¼ teaspoon oil,
and broil until lightly browned, 1 to 2 minutes longer.

Turn oven control to 450°F. Spread each pita with half of
the shrimp mixture; sprinkle each with 2 ounces mozzarella
cheese and ½ teaspoon Parmesan cheese. Bake until
cheese is melted and lightly browned, 5 to 7 minutes; serve
immediately.

MAKES 2 SERVINGS

Each serving provides: 3 Protein Exchanges; 2 Bread Exchanges;
   1¼ Vegetable Exchanges; 1 Fat Exchange; 5 Optional Calories
Per serving: 449 calories; 27 g protein; 18 g fat; 44 g carbohydrate;
   369 mg calcium; 778 mg sodium; 105 mg cholesterol

BREAKFAST

BREAKFAST

½ medium Grapefruit
½ cup Cooked Cereal with
    1 teaspoon Margarine
¾ cup Skim Milk
Coffee or Tea

LUNCH

Cheese Sandwich (2 ounces sliced
    Cheddar cheese with 3 tomato
    slices, ½ cup shredded lettuce,
    and 2 teaspoons mustard on
    2 slices reduced-calorie white
    bread)
6 *each* Green and Red Bell Pepper
    Strips
Coffee, Tea, or Mineral Water

DINNER

Special Bouillon (¾ cup chicken
    bouillon mixed with 1½ ounces
    diced tofu)
1 serving **Chicken-Asparagus Sauté**
¾ cup Cooked Baby Carrots with
    Mint Leaves
1½ cups Mixed Green Salad with
    1½ teaspoons Thousand Island
    Dressing mixed with 2 tablespoons
    Plain Low-Fat Yogurt and
    ¼ teaspoon Mustard
½ cup Fruit Salad
Coffee or Tea

SNACKS

Banana Yogurt (½ cup plain low-fat
    yogurt mixed with ½ medium
    banana, sliced)

Total Optional Calories: 45

Chicken-Asparagus Sauté

Balsamic vinegar, with its deep brown color and spicy sour-sweet flavor, is a unique addition to roasts, vegetables, salads, and dishes such as this.

2 teaspoons olive _or_ vegetable oil
½ pound chicken cutlets, cut into 3 x 1-inch strips
4 large plum tomatoes (about 2 ounces each), blanched, peeled, seeded, and chopped
1 cup diagonally sliced asparagus spears
2 garlic cloves, minced
¼ cup canned ready-to-serve chicken broth
2 tablespoons grated Parmesan cheese
1 tablespoon _each_ chopped fresh basil and balsamic _or_ red wine vinegar
1 teaspoon chopped fresh parsley
Dash pepper

In 12-inch nonstick skillet heat oil over medium-high heat; add chicken and cook, turning frequently, until lightly browned, 4 to 5 minutes. Transfer chicken to plate; set aside.

In same skillet combine tomatoes, asparagus, and garlic and sauté, stirring occasionally, until asparagus is just tender, 2 to 3 minutes; add chicken broth, cheese, basil, vinegar, parsley, and pepper. Reduce heat to low and let simmer, stirring frequently, until flavors blend, 5 to 6 minutes. Return chicken to skillet and cook, stirring occasionally, until tender, 2 to 3 minutes.

MAKES 2 SERVINGS

Each serving provides: 3 Protein Exchanges; 3 Vegetable Exchanges;
    1 Fat Exchange; 35 Optional Calories
Per serving: 234 calories; 32 g protein; 8 g fat; 9 g carbohydrate;
    123 mg calcium; 305 mg sodium; 70 mg cholesterol

Variation: Chicken-Asparagus Sauté with Rice or Pasta (Week 2) — Serve Chicken-Asparagus Sauté over 2 cups cooked long-grain rice or pasta. Add 2 Bread Exchanges to Exchange Information.

Per serving: 458 calories; 36 g protein; 8 g fat; 59 g carbohydrate;
    144 mg calcium; 305 mg sodium; 70 mg cholesterol

Oriental Chicken and Green Beans

1 tablespoon plus 1 teaspoon soy sauce,* divided
1 teaspoon cornstarch
½ pound chicken cutlets, cut into thin strips
1 tablespoon peanut oil, divided
½ cup diced onion
2 garlic cloves, minced
2½ cups cut green beans, blanched
1 cup sliced mushrooms
½ cup water
1 packet instant chicken broth and seasoning mix
⅛ teaspoon <u>each</u> ground ginger and pepper
2 teaspoons sesame seed, toasted

In small bowl combine 2 teaspoons soy sauce with the cornstarch, stirring to dissolve cornstarch; add chicken and toss to coat.

In 10-inch skillet heat 1½ teaspoons oil over medium-high heat; add chicken mixture and sauté until lightly browned, about 3 minutes. Remove chicken to a plate and set aside.

To same skillet add remaining 1½ teaspoons oil and heat; add onion and garlic and sauté until softened. Add green beans and mushrooms to skillet and sauté for 3 minutes; add water, broth mix, ginger, pepper, and remaining 2 teaspoons soy sauce and let simmer for 5 minutes. Return chicken to skillet and cook, stirring occasionally, until vegetables are tender-crisp and chicken is tender, about 3 minutes. Serve sprinkled with sesame seed.

MAKES 2 SERVINGS

Each serving provides: 3 Protein Exchanges; 4 Vegetable Exchanges;
    1½ Fat Exchanges; 30 Optional Calories
Per serving: 288 calories; 32 g protein; 10 g fat; 19 g carbohydrate;
    113 mg calcium; 1,265 mg sodium; 66 mg cholesterol

* Reduced-sodium soy sauce may be substituted. Reduce calories to 287,
    calcium to 111 mg, and sodium to 984 mg.

BREAKFAST

½ medium Pink Grapefruit
¾ ounce Cold Cereal
½ cup Skim Milk
Coffee or Tea

LUNCH

Tofu Salad (3 ounces diced tofu with
   ½ cup *each* broccoli florets and
   sliced zucchini, 6 red bell pepper
   strips, ¼ cup sliced radishes, and
   1 teaspoon *each* reduced-sodium
   soy sauce, Chinese sesame oil,
   and rice vinegar)
1 small Apple
Coffee, Tea, or Mineral Water

DINNER

1 serving **Lamb Steaks with Creamy
   Mint Sauce**
3 ounces Boiled New Potatoes with
   1 teaspoon Margarine and
   Chopped Parsley
1 cup Cooked Sliced Beets
1½ cups Mixed Green Salad with
   1½ teaspoons French Dressing
   mixed with 2 teaspoons Lemon
   Juice and ¼ teaspoon Mustard
Strawberry Yogurt (¼ cup plain
   low-fat yogurt mixed with 1 cup
   strawberries, sliced)
Coffee or Tea

SNACKS

½ cup Reduced-Calorie Chocolate
   Pudding; Peanut Butter Grahams
   (1 tablespoon peanut butter on
   2 honey graham crackers)

Total Optional Calories: 140

Lamb Steaks with Creamy Mint Sauce ◑

2 lamb steaks (5 ounces each)
⅛ teaspoon <u>each</u> salt and pepper
¼ cup cream cheese, softened
1 tablespoon lemon juice
1 teaspoon water
1 small garlic clove, minced
¼ cup chopped fresh mint

Sprinkle both sides of each lamb steak evenly with salt and pepper; set on rack in broiling pan and broil 6 inches from heat source until rare, 3 to 4 minutes on each side (timing will depend upon thickness of lamb steaks).

While lamb is broiling, in small mixing bowl, using electric mixer at medium speed, beat together cream cheese, lemon juice, water, and garlic until mixture is fluffy; stir in mint. Spread 1 side of each lamb steak with half the cream cheese mixture and broil until mixture is heated through and lightly browned, 2 to 3 minutes.

MAKES 2 SERVINGS, 1 LAMB STEAK EACH

Each serving provides: 3 Protein Exchanges; 100 Optional Calories
Per serving: 278 calories; 25 g protein; 18 g fat; 2 g carbohydrate;
   41 mg calcium; 281 mg sodium; 116 mg cholesterol

½ medium Banana, sliced
⅓ cup Cottage Cheese sprinkled
  with Nutmeg
½ cup Skim Milk
Coffee or Tea

LUNCH

Whitefish Salad in a Pita (2 ounces
  whitefish with 2 tablespoons *each*
  chopped celery and red bell pepper,
  2 lettuce leaves, and 1 tablespoon
  reduced-calorie mayonnaise in
  1-ounce pita bread)
¾ cup Cauliflower Florets and
  6 Carrot Sticks
Coffee, Tea, or Mineral Water

DINNER

1 serving **Lamb Steaks with Yogurt-Mustard Sauce**
6 Cooked Asparagus Spears
Scallion-Mushroom Salad (1½ cups
  torn lettuce with ¼ cup *each* sliced
  scallions and mushrooms and
  1½ teaspoons French dressing
  mixed with 2 teaspoons lemon
  juice and ¼ teaspoon mustard)
1-ounce Roll
½ cup Fruit Salad
Coffee or Tea

SNACKS

1 small Orange; 1 serving Reduced-
  Calorie Chocolate Dairy Drink

Total Optional Calories: 3

Lamb Steaks with Yogurt-Mustard Sauce ◐

2 lamb steaks (5 ounces each)
1 teaspoon margarine
2 tablespoons <u>each</u> sliced scallion (green onion) and mushrooms
½ small garlic clove, minced
2 tablespoons canned ready-to-serve beef broth
1½ teaspoons <u>each</u> Dijon-style mustard and chopped fresh dill
Dash white pepper
½ cup plain low-fat yogurt

On rack in broiling pan broil lamb 6 inches from heat source until rare, 3 to 4 minutes on each side (timing will depend upon thickness of steaks).

While lamb is broiling, in small saucepan heat margarine over medium heat until bubbly and hot; add scallion, mushrooms, and garlic and sauté until browned, 1 to 2 minutes. Add broth, mustard, dill, and pepper, stirring to combine; remove from heat and stir in yogurt. Return saucepan to low heat and let simmer, stirring frequently, until sauce is heated through, 5 to 10 minutes (<u>do not boil</u>). Serve lamb steaks topped with sauce.

MAKES 2 SERVINGS

Each serving provides: 3 Protein Exchanges; ¼ Vegetable Exchange;
  ½ Fat Exchange; ½ Milk Exchange; 3 Optional Calories
Per serving: 237 calories; 26 g protein; 12 g fat; 5 g carbohydrate;
  123 mg calcium; 289 mg sodium; 88 mg cholesterol

TIP: To help make cleanup easier, line broiling pan with foil and spray rack with nonstick cooking spray before broiling lamb steaks.

BREAKFAST

1 cup Strawberries, sliced
½ cup Cooked Cereal
1 cup Skim Milk
Coffee or Tea

LUNCH

Turkey Sandwich (2 ounces sliced
    turkey with 2 *each* tomato slices
    and lettuce leaves and 2 teaspoons
    reduced-calorie mayonnaise on
    2 slices whole wheat bread)
½ cup Broccoli Florets and 6 Celery
    Sticks
1 small Apple
Coffee, Tea, or Mineral Water

DINNER

1 serving **Ham and Pineapple Tidbits**
Shrimp Salad (2 ounces tiny shrimp
    with 1½ cups shredded lettuce,
    6 *each* cucumber slices and cherry
    tomatoes, ¼ cup alfalfa sprouts,
    and 1 tablespoon Thousand Island
    dressing)
½ cup *each* Cooked Diced Red and
    Green Bell Pepper
½ cup Low-Calorie Lemon-Flavored
    Gelatin
Coffee or Tea

SNACKS

Raspberry Yogurt (½ cup plain low-fat
    yogurt mixed with 1 tablespoon
    reduced-calorie raspberry spread);
    ⅛ medium pineapple

Total Optional Calories: 90

Ham and Pineapple Tidbits

Preparing for a crowd? Simply double or triple this recipe for an outstanding party-pleaser.

7 ounces cooked ham
1 egg
¼ cup chopped scallions (green onions)
3 tablespoons plain dried bread crumbs
2 teaspoons Dijon-style mustard, divided
⅛ teaspoon Worcestershire sauce
½ cup canned pineapple chunks (no sugar added),
    drained, reserving liquid (10 chunks)
1 tablespoon firmly packed brown sugar
1½ teaspoons <u>each</u> cornstarch and honey
1 teaspoon cider vinegar

In work bowl of food processor, using on-off motion, process ham until finely chopped; add egg, scallions, bread crumbs, ½ teaspoon mustard, and the Worcestershire sauce and process until combined (<u>do not puree</u>).

Preheat oven to 400°F. Cut each pineapple chunk in half and set aside. Divide ham mixture into 20 equal portions, about 1 tablespoon each, and roll each portion into a ball. Press 1 pineapple chunk half into each ham ball and roll ham mixture around pineapple to enclose. Place ham balls on nonstick baking sheet and bake, turning once, until browned, about 10 minutes on each side. Transfer to serving platter; set aside and keep warm.

In 1-cup liquid measure combine reserved pineapple liquid with enough water to measure ½ cup. Pour liquid into small saucepan; add sugar, cornstarch, honey, vinegar, and remaining 1½ teaspoons mustard, stirring to dissolve cornstarch. Cook, stirring frequently, until mixture comes to a boil. Reduce heat and let simmer until mixture thickens; pour into small bowl and serve as a dipping sauce for ham balls.

MAKES 4 SERVINGS, 5 TIDBITS EACH

Each serving provides: 2 Protein Exchanges; ⅛ Vegetable Exchange;
    60 Optional Calories
Per serving: 158 calories; 13 g protein; 5 g fat; 16 g carbohydrate;
    28 mg calcium; 726 mg sodium; 95 mg cholesterol

Peach-Glazed Ham Steak ◑

1 teaspoon margarine
6-ounce "fully cooked" boneless ham steak
2 tablespoons reduced-calorie apricot spread
(16 calories per 2 teaspoons)
1 tablespoon orange juice (no sugar added)
1½ teaspoons dry Madeira wine
½ teaspoon Dijon-style mustard
½ small garlic clove, minced
½ cup drained canned peach slices (no sugar added)

In 8-inch nonstick skillet heat margarine over medium-high heat until bubbly and hot; add ham and cook, turning once, until lightly browned, 2 to 3 minutes on each side. Transfer to plate; set aside and keep warm.

In same skillet combine remaining ingredients except peach slices; cook over medium heat, stirring with a wooden spoon and scraping up particles from sides and bottom of pan, until mixture is slightly thickened, 3 to 4 minutes. Add peach slices and cook, stirring occasionally, until heated through, 3 to 4 minutes longer. Return ham to skillet and turn once to coat with glaze; transfer ham to serving platter, cut in half, and top with remaining peach mixture.

MAKES 2 SERVINGS, ½ HAM STEAK EACH

Each serving provides: 3 Protein Exchanges; ½ Fat Exchange;
½ Fruit Exchange; 30 Optional Calories
Per serving: 190 calories; 18 g protein; 7 g fat; 12 g carbohydrate;
11 mg calcium; 1,085 mg sodium; 45 mg cholesterol

Variation: Apricot-Glazed Ham Steak (Week 5) — Substitute 4 dried apricot halves for the peach slices.

Per serving: 192 calories; 18 g protein; 7 g fat; 13 g carbohydrate;
13 mg calcium; 1,083 mg sodium; 45 mg cholesterol

BREAKFAST

⅓ cup Apple Juice
1 Soft-Cooked Egg
½ Matzo Board
1 cup Skim Milk

LUNCH

Tuna Salad (2 ounces tuna with
   ¼ cup *each* chopped celery and
   diced red and green bell pepper
   and 1 teaspoon mayonnaise on
   2 lettuce leaves)
½ Matzo Board
½ medium Banana
Coffee, Tea, or Mineral Water

DINNER

3 ounces Roast Chicken
¾ cup Cooked Baby Carrots drizzled
   with ½ teaspoon Honey
1 serving **Charoses (Chopped Fruit
   'n' Nut Medley)**
Spinach Salad (1½ cups torn spinach
   with 6 cherry tomatoes, ¼ cup
   sliced mushrooms, and 1 tablespoon French dressing)
½ Matzo Board
1 medium Kiwi Fruit, sliced
4 fluid ounces Dry Red Wine
Coffee or Tea

SNACKS

½ cup Plain Low-Fat Yogurt

Total Optional Calories: 145

Charoses (Chopped Fruit 'n' Nut Medley) ◐

This traditional Passover dish is delicious as a sweet side dish at any time of the year. The recipe can be doubled to serve more.

1 small Golden Delicious apple (about ¼ pound), cored, pared, and diced
3 tablespoons dark <u>or</u> golden raisins
3 pitted dates, chopped
¼ cup dry red table wine
1½ teaspoons granulated sugar
¼ teaspoon ground cinnamon
¼ ounce crushed <u>or</u> finely chopped walnuts

In small saucepan combine all ingredients except walnuts; cook over medium heat until apples are softened, about 10 minutes. Transfer to small bowl (not aluminum*) and stir in walnuts; cover with plastic wrap and refrigerate overnight to allow flavors to blend.

MAKES 4 SERVINGS

Each serving provides: 1 Fruit Exchange; 35 Optional Calories
Per serving: 81 calories; 0.6 g protein; 1 g fat; 16 g carbohydrate;
   11 mg calcium; 2 mg sodium; 0 mg cholesterol

*It's best to marinate in glass or stainless-steel containers; ingredients
   such as wine may react with aluminum, causing color and flavor changes
   in foods.

Gratin of Broccoli Ⓒ

A delightful vegetable casserole.

1 tablespoon lemon juice
2 teaspoons potato starch
1 teaspoon instant chicken bouillon or 1 chicken
** bouillon cube**
Dash each salt, pepper, and ground nutmeg
1 cup water
1 tablespoon plus 1 teaspoon margarine
1 cup diced onions
1 egg, beaten
1 ounce (about ½ cup) matzo farfel
2 medium bunches broccoli (about 2 pounds),
** trimmed, cut into spears, and cooked (hot)**
Garnish: lemon twists or wedges

In small saucepan combine lemon juice, potato starch, instant bouillon (or bouillon cube), and seasonings; add water and bring to a boil. Cook, stirring constantly, until mixture just thickens; set aside.

In 1-quart saucepan heat margarine over high heat until bubbly and hot; add onions and sauté until translucent, 1 to 2 minutes. Add bouillon mixture to saucepan; stir to combine. Reduce heat to low; remove 2 tablespoons broth mixture and stir into beaten egg. Slowly pour egg mixture into remaining sauce, stirring rapidly to prevent lumping; cook, stirring constantly, until thickened, about 1 minute (do not boil). Stir matzo farfel into sauce; remove saucepan from heat and let stand until farfel is evenly moistened, at least 5 minutes.

Spray 3-quart flameproof casserole with nonstick cooking spray and arrange broccoli in a single layer in casserole; top with farfel mixture and broil until thoroughly heated and topping is lightly browned, 1 to 2 minutes. Serve garnished with lemon.

MAKES 4 SERVINGS

Each serving provides: ½ Bread Exchange; 4½ Vegetable Exchanges;
  1 Fat Exchange; 25 Optional Calories
Per serving: 196 calories; 12 g protein; 6 g fat; 28 g carbohydrate;
  379 mg calcium; 410 mg sodium; 69 mg cholesterol

BREAKFAST

½ cup Orange Sections
⅓ cup Cottage Cheese
1 slice Whole Wheat Bread, toasted,
  with 1 teaspoon Margarine
½ cup Skim Milk
Coffee or Tea

LUNCH

Roast Beef Sandwich (2 ounces sliced
  roast beef with 3 tomato slices,
  ¼ cup sliced mushrooms, and
  1 teaspoon *each* mustard and
  reduced-calorie mayonnaise on
  2 slices reduced-calorie rye bread)
6 *each* Cucumber Spears and Green
  Bell Pepper Strips
Coffee, Tea, or Mineral Water

DINNER

3 ounces Poached Shrimp sprinkled
  with Chopped Parsley
1 serving **Lemon-Caper Cauliflower**
Carrot and Lettuce Salad (½ cup
  shredded carrot with 1 tablespoon
  reduced-calorie French dressing
  on 4 lettuce leaves)
½ cup Canned Peach Slices
½ cup Skim Milk
Coffee or Tea

SNACKS

1 small Apple; 1 serving Reduced-
  Calorie Chocolate Dairy Drink

Total Optional Calories: 30

Lemon-Caper Cauliflower ⓒ ◑

A wonderful way to serve any of your favorite leftover cooked vegetables. For a more attractive side dish, prepare it with a medley of colorful vegetables such as red and green bell pepper strips, sliced carrots, zucchini, and yellow squash.

2 cups cooked cauliflower florets (hot)
1 tablespoon <u>each</u> margarine, melted, drained capers, rinsed, and lemon juice
1½ teaspoons <u>each</u> chopped fresh Italian (flat-leaf) parsley and chives

In medium bowl combine all ingredients and toss to mix; serve immediately.

MAKES 2 SERVINGS

Each serving provides: 2 Vegetable Exchanges; 1½ Fat Exchanges
Per serving: 83 calories; 2 g protein; 6 g fat; 6 g carbohydrate;
    38 mg calcium; 186 mg sodium; 0 mg cholesterol

Hot Vinaigrette Vegetables ◑

For a colorful vegetable salad, prepare in advance and serve chilled.

2 cups <u>each</u> broccoli and cauliflower florets
1 cup thinly sliced onions
6 cherry tomatoes
½ cup red bell pepper strips
1 tablespoon vegetable oil
1½ teaspoons <u>each</u> lemon juice and raspberry vinegar
1 teaspoon walnut oil*
½ teaspoon <u>each</u> granulated sugar and salt
1 small garlic clove, mashed
¼ teaspoon oregano leaves
⅛ teaspoon pepper
1 teaspoon chopped fresh basil

In 2-quart saucepan bring 1 quart water to a boil; add broccoli and cauliflower and cook, stirring once, for 30 seconds to 1 minute (just to parboil). Drain vegetables and transfer to serving platter; add onions, tomatoes, and bell pepper and set aside.

In small metal measuring cup or other small flameproof container combine remaining ingredients except basil and cook over low heat until mixture comes just to a boil; pour over vegetables and toss until vegetables are thoroughly coated. Sprinkle with basil and serve immediately.

MAKES 4 SERVINGS

Each serving provides: 3 Vegetable Exchanges; 1 Fat Exchange;
   3 Optional Calories
Per serving: 97 calories; 4 g protein; 5 g fat; 12 g carbohydrate;
   71 mg calcium; 299 mg sodium; 0 mg cholesterol

*Walnut oil gives this salad a light, nutty flavor. If unavailable, substitute
   peanut oil or Chinese sesame oil.

New Potato Salad ©

6 ounces small red new potatoes
¼ cup plain low-fat yogurt
2 teaspoons mayonnaise
½ teaspoon <u>each</u> white vinegar and lemon juice
¼ teaspoon salt
Dash to ⅛ teaspoon white pepper
¼ cup diced onion
2 tablespoons chopped fresh dill
Garnish: dill sprig

In 1-quart saucepan combine potatoes with enough water to cover; bring water to a boil. Reduce heat and let simmer until potatoes are fork-tender, about 25 minutes; drain well. Transfer potatoes to salad bowl and set aside.

In small bowl combine yogurt, mayonnaise, vinegar, lemon juice, salt, and pepper; add onion and chopped dill and mix well. Pour dressing over potatoes and stir gently to combine. Serve warm or cover and refrigerate until chilled; stir again just before serving.

MAKES 2 SERVINGS

Each serving provides: 1 Bread Exchange; ¼ Vegetable Exchange;
  1 Fat Exchange; ¼ Milk Exchange
Per serving: 128 calories; 4 g protein; 4 g fat; 20 g carbohydrate;
  80 mg calcium; 323 mg sodium; 4 mg cholesterol

Variation: Potato Salad with Sour Cream Dressing (Week 4) —
Substitute 3 tablespoons sour cream for the yogurt. Omit
Milk Exchange from Exchange Information and add 50
Optional Calories.

Per serving: 156 calories; 3 g protein; 8 g fat; 18 g carbohydrate;
  53 mg calcium; 315 mg sodium; 12 mg cholesterol

BREAKFAST

1 serving **Banana-Farfel Custard**
¾ cup Skim Milk

LUNCH

Turkey Platter (2 ounces sliced turkey
    with 6 *each* tomato wedges,
    cucumber spears, and celery sticks,
    ¼ cup shredded carrot, and 3 radish
    roses on 3 lettuce leaves with
    1 teaspoon vegetable oil mixed
    with 2 teaspoons red wine vinegar)
1 small Orange
Coffee, Tea, or Mineral Water

DINNER

3 ounces Broiled Haddock Fillet
    with Chopped Fresh Parsley
½ cup Cooked Chopped Spinach
½ cup Cooked Red Cabbage
1½ cups Tossed Salad with
    1½ teaspoons Italian Dressing
    mixed with 2 teaspoons Red Wine
    Vinegar
⅛ medium Pineapple
Coffee or Tea

SNACKS

1 cup Skim Milk; ½ Matzo Board
    with 1 teaspoon Margarine

Total Optional Calories: 30

Banana-Farfel Custard ⓒ

Matzo farfel, the special ingredient in this delicious
custard, is actually matzo boards that have been broken
into little pieces. Prepare the custard ahead and serve
chilled for a fast breakfast or try it warm to top off
a dinner during the Passover holiday.

**1 medium banana (about 6 ounces), peeled and
    cut in half**
2 eggs
½ cup skim milk
1 teaspoon granulated sugar
¼ teaspoon ground cinnamon
1 ounce (about ½ cup) matzo farfel
2 teaspoons pancake syrup

Preheat oven to 350°F. Spray two 10-ounce custard cups
with nonstick cooking spray; set aside.

In blender container combine 1 banana half with the eggs,
milk, sugar, and cinnamon and process until smooth, about
1 minute; stir in matzo farfel. Dice remaining banana half;
add to farfel mixture and stir to combine. Pour half of
mixture into each prepared custard cup; place cups on
baking sheet and bake 20 to 25 minutes (until a knife,
inserted in center of custard, comes out clean). Serve each
portion topped with 1 teaspoon syrup.

MAKES 2 SERVINGS, 1 CUSTARD EACH

Each serving provides: 1 Protein Exchange; 1 Bread Exchange;
    1 Fruit Exchange; ¼ Milk Exchange; 30 Optional Calories
Per serving: 234 calories; 11 g protein; 6 g fat; 35 g carbohydrate;
    114 mg calcium; 102 mg sodium; 275 mg cholesterol

25th Anniversary Cheesecake ⊙⊙

Prepare this fast 'n' fancy dessert the night before serving.

1 tablespoon plus 1 teaspoon reduced-calorie margarine (tub)
8 graham crackers (2½-inch squares), made into fine crumbs
1 envelope unflavored gelatin
½ cup skim milk
2 cups <u>each</u> canned crushed pineapple (no sugar added), divided, and part-skim ricotta cheese
¼ cup granulated sugar
2 tablespoons reduced-calorie strawberry spread (16 calories per 2 teaspoons)

In small saucepan melt margarine; remove from heat and stir in graham cracker crumbs. Transfer to 8-inch springform pan and, using the back of a spoon, press mixture over bottom of pan. Cover pan with plastic wrap and freeze until firm, at least 10 minutes.

In small saucepan sprinkle gelatin over milk and let stand to soften, about 5 minutes; cook over low heat, stirring constantly, until gelatin is completely dissolved. Remove from heat and let cool slightly.

Drain pineapple, reserving liquid; transfer half of the solids and all of the liquid to work bowl of food processor or blender container. Cover and refrigerate remaining pineapple for later use. Add ricotta cheese, gelatin mixture, and sugar to food processor (or blender container) and process until smooth. Pour gelatin mixture over graham cracker crust; cover and refrigerate until firm, overnight or at least 4 hours.

In small bowl combine reserved pineapple and the strawberry spread. To serve, carefully remove sides of springform pan and spread top of cake with pineapple mixture.

MAKES 8 SERVINGS

Each serving provides: 1 Protein Exchange; ½ Bread Exchange;
    ½ Fruit Exchange; 50 Optional Calories
Per serving: 196 calories; 7 g protein; 9 g fat; 27 g carbohydrate;
    198 mg calcium; 154 mg sodium; 19 mg cholesterol

BREAKFAST

1 cup Strawberries
1 Scrambled Egg
1 slice Rye Bread, toasted, with
    1 teaspoon Margarine
1 cup Skim Milk

LUNCH

Muffin Pizza (½ English muffin,
    toasted, topped with 3 tablespoons
    tomato sauce, 1 ounce mozzarella
    cheese, and Italian seasonings,
    and broiled)
1½ cups Mixed Green Salad with
    1½ teaspoons Italian Dressing
    mixed with 2 teaspoons Red Wine
    Vinegar
1 medium Kiwi Fruit, sliced
Diet Soda

DINNER

Shrimp Cocktail (2 ounces shrimp
    with 1 tablespoon cocktail sauce)
3 ounces Broiled Steak
3 ounces Baked Potato topped with
    1 tablespoon Sour Cream
¾ cup Cooked Artichoke Hearts
½ cup Chilled Cooked Chinese Pea
    Pods on 2 Red Leaf Lettuce
    Leaves with 1½ teaspoons French
    Dressing mixed with 2 teaspoons
    Lemon Juice and ¼ teaspoon
    Mustard
1 serving **Gala Petit Fours**
Coffee or Tea

SNACKS

Banana Shake (1 cup skim milk,
    ½ medium banana, and ½ teaspoon
    vanilla extract processed in
    blender)

Total Optional Calories: 170

Gala Petit Fours

Petit fours can be prepared in advance and stored, covered, in the refrigerator or freezer. Thaw at room temperature. They are a simple, yet spectacular dessert to serve for weekend entertaining.

3 ounces semisweet chocolate chips
2 tablespoons plus 2 teaspoons sweet butter
5 ounces pound cake, cut into thirty-six 1-inch squares
¼ ounce crushed pistachio nuts

In double boiler combine chocolate and butter and cook over hot (<u>not boiling</u>) water, stirring frequently, until chocolate is melted and mixture is smooth;* transfer to small bowl and set aside.

    Place sheet of wax paper under a wire rack. Insert tines of fork into 1 cake cube and dip cube into chocolate mixture, coating all sides. Using another fork, gently push cake cube off first fork onto wire rack; scrape up any chocolate mixture that drips onto wax paper and return it to double boiler. Repeat procedure with remaining cake cubes. Sprinkle top of each petit four with an equal amount of pistachio nuts. Transfer petit fours to serving platter, cover loosely with plastic wrap, and refrigerate until chocolate hardens, about 5 minutes.

MAKES 12 SERVINGS, 3 CAKES EACH

Each serving provides: 120 Optional Calories
Per serving: 118 calories; 1 g protein; 9 g fat; 10 g carbohydrate;
    6 mg calcium; 14 mg sodium; 24 mg cholesterol

*When melting chocolate, it should not come in contact with water or steam; moisture will cause it to harden. Chocolate and butter can be melted in a microwave oven, if desired. Combine them in 1-cup heat-resistant glass liquid measure and microwave on High until ingredients begin to melt, 1 to 2 minutes; stir to combine. Microwave on High until mixture is completely melted and smooth, about 1 minute longer (<u>be care-ful not to burn</u>). Since cooking time may be different in your microwave oven, to help ensure good results be sure to check for doneness while cooking.

BREAKFAST

½ medium Papaya
¼ cup Part-Skim Ricotta Cheese
½ small Bagel, toasted
1 cup Skim Milk

LUNCH

Bologna Sandwich (2 ounces sliced
    bologna with 2 tomato slices,
    2 lettuce leaves, and 1 teaspoon
    each mustard and mayonnaise on
    2 slices reduced-calorie whole
    wheat bread)
6 *each* Celery Sticks and Red Bell
    Pepper Strips
2 tablespoons Raisins
Coffee, Tea, or Mineral Water

DINNER

3 ounces Broiled Fillet of Sole with
    Lemon Wedge
½ cup Cooked Peas with Minced
    Pimiento
Cabbage Salad (1½ cups torn
    lettuce with ½ cup shredded red
    cabbage and 1 tablespoon
    creamy Italian dressing)
½ cup Cooked Baby Carrots with
    ½ teaspoon Honey
1 serving **Quick Cakes** with ¾ cup
    Sliced Strawberries
Coffee or Tea

SNACKS

Apple-Cinnamon Yogurt (½ cup plain
    low-fat yogurt mixed with ¼ cup
    applesauce, plus cinnamon and
    nutmeg)

Total Optional Calories: 105

Quick Cakes ◐

Don't hassle with a time-consuming dessert for your next party. These elegant little cakes are easy to prepare and sure to please you and your guests. Serve as an accompaniment to fresh strawberries or melon balls.

12 ladyfingers (¼ ounce each), split lengthwise into halves
1 tablespoon strawberry, red raspberry, <u>or</u> apricot preserves, melted
½ ounce semisweet chocolate chips
1 teaspoon sweet butter

Spread the split side of 12 ladyfinger halves with ¼ teaspoon preserves each; top each with a remaining ladyfinger half, making 12 sandwiches. Arrange sandwiches on serving platter.

In small saucepan combine chocolate and butter and cook over low heat, stirring frequently, until chocolate is melted and mixture is combined. Drizzle an equal amount of chocolate mixture over each ladyfinger sandwich; refrigerate until chocolate hardens, about 5 minutes.

MAKES 6 SERVINGS, 2 CAKES EACH

Each serving provides: 95 Optional Calories
Per serving: 78 calories; 1 g protein; 3 g fat; 13 g carbohydrate;
    7 mg calcium; 11 mg sodium; 52 mg cholesterol

TIP: For colorful cakes use 1 teaspoon of each flavor of preserves.

May

MAY'S BEST BUYS FOR FRUITS AND VEGETABLES

alfalfa sprouts	cabbage	lettuce	potatoes
artichokes	carrots	mangoes	radishes
arugula	celery	mushrooms	rhubarb
asparagus	Chinese pea pods	new potatoes	scallions (green onions)
avocados	cucumbers	okra	spinach
bananas	eggplants	onions	strawberries
bean sprouts	green beans	papayas	summer squash
beets	kiwi fruit	peas	turnips
broccoli	kumquats	pineapples	zucchini

BREAKFAST

½ medium Banana, sliced
¾ ounce Cold Cereal
½ cup Skim Milk
Coffee or Tea

LUNCH

Chicken Salad in a Pita (2 ounces
    julienne-cut chicken with 2 lettuce
    leaves and 1 teaspoon *each* diced
    onion, red bell pepper, and
    mayonnaise in 1-ounce whole
    wheat pita bread)
½ cup Broccoli Florets and 6 Celery
    Sticks
1 medium Kiwi Fruit, sliced
Coffee, Tea, or Mineral Water

DINNER

1 serving **Crab-Filled Pods**
4 ounces Broiled Lemon Sole with
    Paprika and Lemon Wedges
3 ounces Baked Potato topped with
    2 tablespoons Sour Cream and
    Chopped Chives
½ cup Cooked Baby Carrots
1½ cups Mixed Green Salad with
    1 tablespoon Thousand Island
    Dressing
½ cup Skim Milk
Coffee or Tea

SNACKS

Strawberry Shake (1 serving reduced-
    calorie vanilla dairy drink and 1 cup
    strawberries processed in blender)

Total Optional Calories: 100

Crab-Filled Pods

An excellent filling for celery ribs or cherry tomatoes,
or use it as a spread for crackers.

2 ounces thawed and drained frozen crabmeat
2 tablespoons cream cheese
1 tablespoon <u>each</u> minced scallion (green onion) and
    sour cream
2 teaspoons chili sauce <u>or</u> seafood cocktail sauce
1 teaspoon <u>each</u> prepared horseradish and lemon juice
20 Chinese pea pods (stem ends and strings removed),
    blanched (about 3 ounces)
Garnish: 8 scallion (green onion) brushes

In small bowl combine all ingredients except pea pods,
mixing well. Split each pea pod in half lengthwise along
string side and, using a pastry bag fitted with a wide tube, or
a small measuring spoon, fill each pea pod with an equal
amount of the crab mixture. Arrange stuffed pea pods on
serving platter, cover with plastic wrap, and refrigerate until
chilled, at least 30 minutes. Garnish with scallion brushes
before serving.

MAKES 4 SERVINGS, 5 FILLED PODS EACH

Each serving provides: ½ Protein Exchange; ¾ Vegetable Exchange;
    35 Optional Calories
Per serving with chili sauce: 59 calories; 4 g protein; 4 g fat;
    3 g carbohydrate; 27 mg calcium; 93 mg sodium; 24 mg cholesterol
With seafood cocktail sauce: 59 calories; 4 g protein; 4 g fat;
    3 g carbohydrate; 27 mg calcium; 87 mg sodium; 24 mg cholesterol

Eggs in Biscuits ⓒ ◑

Try this recipe for a special Sunday breakfast.

**2 ready-to-bake refrigerated buttermilk flaky biscuits
    (1 ounce each)***
2 eggs
Salt and pepper
2 tomato slices
1 teaspoon margarine, melted
2 teaspoons grated Parmesan cheese
Garnish: parsley sprigs

Preheat oven to 400° F. Spray two flameproof 6-ounce
custard cups with nonstick cooking spray; set aside.

Roll each biscuit between 2 sheets of wax paper, forming
two 5-inch circles; carefully remove paper. Set each circle
into a sprayed custard cup and, using fingers, press dough
over bottom and up sides of cup. Break 1 egg into small
dish, then carefully slide egg into one of the cups; repeat
with remaining egg and the other cup. Sprinkle each
portion evenly with dash each salt and pepper and bake
until dough is browned and the egg is just set, about 10
minutes.

Remove cups from oven and turn oven control to broil.
Top each egg with 1 tomato slice, then brush each tomato
slice with half of the melted margarine; sprinkle each portion
with 1 teaspoon cheese and broil until cheese is browned,
1 to 2 minutes. Serve garnished with parsley.

MAKES 2 SERVINGS

Each serving provides: 1 Protein Exchange; 1 Bread Exchange;
    ¼ Vegetable Exchange; ½ Fat Exchange; 10 Optional Calories
Per serving: 190 calories; 8 g protein; 11 g fat; 14 g carbohydrate;
    54 mg calcium; 555 mg sodium; 275 mg cholesterol

* Refrigerated biscuits come in packages containing 5 or 10 biscuits. Bake
    those that you don't use in this recipe, then freeze in resealable plastic
    bags. Thaw at room temperature or reheat in microwave oven and enjoy
    warm.

Shrimp and Vegetable Sauté

Scallop Chowder
Sausage, Chicken, and Rice Soup
Creamed Onion Soup
Garlic Toast

Ham 'n' Cheese Muffins
Jelly 'n' Nut-Topped Muffins
Birthday Blueberry Muffins

Raspberry Crème Omelet

Salmon with Creamy Lime Sauce

BRUNCH

Pineapple Mimosa (⅓ cup pineapple-orange juice with ½ cup champagne)
1 serving **Potato and Bacon Frittata**
1 cup Mixed Green Salad with 1 tablespoon Reduced-Calorie French Dressing
1-ounce slice Italian Bread, toasted
Strawberries 'n' Yogurt (1 cup strawberries, sliced, topped with ¼ cup plain low-fat yogurt)
½ cup Skim Milk
Coffee, Tea, or Mineral Water

DINNER

4 ounces Broiled Chicken
½ cup *each* Cooked Peas and Diced Carrot
Special Eggplant (3 broiled eggplant slices sprinkled with seasonings and 1 teaspoon grated Parmesan cheese)
1½ cups Tossed Salad with 1 tablespoon Italian Dressing
Herb Tea or Cinnamon-Spiced Coffee

SNACKS

½ medium Papaya; 1 cup Skim Milk

Total Optional Calories: 260

Potato and Bacon Frittata

This dish can be prepared in advance and refrigerated, then just reheated when ready to serve.

1 teaspoon <u>each</u> olive <u>or</u> vegetable oil and margarine
6 ounces potato, scrubbed, thinly sliced, and thoroughly dried with paper towels
½ cup thinly sliced onion
4 eggs
¼ cup half-and-half (blend of milk and cream)
1 tablespoon chopped fresh Italian (flat-leaf) parsley
¼ teaspoon salt
3 slices crisp bacon, crumbled
1 medium tomato, thinly sliced

In 8-inch nonstick skillet that has an oven-safe or removable handle heat oil and margarine together until margarine is melted; remove from heat. Spread potato slices in a single layer over bottom and 1 inch up sides of skillet; top with onion slices and any remaining potato slices. Set another 8-inch skillet bottom-side down over potato and onion to weight them down and cook over medium heat until potato slices are tender, about 10 minutes.

Preheat oven to 450°F. In large mixing bowl lightly beat eggs; stir in remaining ingredients except tomato. Remove weight from potato and onion slices and add egg mixture evenly; top with tomato slices. Transfer skillet to oven and bake until eggs are set and golden brown, 15 to 20 minutes. Remove from oven and let stand for 5 minutes before serving.

MAKES 2 SERVINGS

Each serving provides: 2 Protein Exchanges; 1 Bread Exchange; 1½ Vegetable Exchanges; 1 Fat Exchange; 120 Optional Calories
Per serving: 377 calories; 19 g protein; 24 g fat; 22 g carbohydrate; 119 mg calcium; 607 mg sodium; 567 mg cholesterol

Vegetarian Pita Melt ◐◑

A fast lunch on a busy weekend.

½ cup small broccoli florets, blanched
¼ cup <u>each</u> small cauliflower florets and sliced carrot, blanched
2 tablespoons <u>each</u> chopped red onion and green bell pepper
1 tablespoon <u>each</u> red wine vinegar and lemon juice
2 teaspoons olive oil <u>or</u> vegetable oil
½ teaspoon <u>each</u> minced fresh parsley and minced fresh dill
Dash pepper
4 pita breads (1 ounce each)
2 ounces Monterey Jack cheese, shredded
½ cup bean sprouts

In small bowl combine broccoli, cauliflower, carrot, onion, and bell pepper, tossing to combine; in separate small bowl combine vinegar, lemon juice, oil, parsley, dill, and pepper, mixing well.

Using a sharp knife, cut each pita in half crosswise; carefully open each half to form a pocket. Fill each pocket with ⅛ of the vegetable mixture, then drizzle each portion of vegetables with ⅛ of the dressing. In 1-quart flameproof casserole stand pita halves cut-side up; sprinkle each with ¼ ounce cheese. Broil 6 inches from heat source until cheese is melted, 2 to 3 minutes; top each pita half with ⅛ of the bean sprouts and serve immediately.

MAKES 2 SERVINGS, 4 PITA POCKETS EACH

Each serving provides: 1 Protein Exchange; 2 Bread Exchanges;
    1¾ Vegetable Exchanges; 1 Fat Exchange
Per serving: 356 calories; 15 g protein; 14 g fat; 44 g carbohydrate;
    253 mg calcium; 536 mg sodium; 25 mg cholesterol

Variation: Creamy Pita Melt (Week 4) — Omit vinegar, lemon juice, oil, herbs, and pepper. In small bowl combine ¼ cup whipped cream cheese, 1 tablespoon <u>each</u> chopped fresh parsley, chopped fresh dill, and chopped scallion (green onion), and 1 small garlic clove, minced; spread inside of each pita pocket with ⅛ (about 1½ teaspoons) cream cheese mixture, then fill each with ⅛ of vegetable mixture. Proceed as directed. Omit Fat Exchange from Exchange Information and add 65 Optional Calories.

Per serving: 380 calories; 16 g protein; 16 g fat; 45 g carbohydrate;
    273 mg calcium; 604 mg sodium; 44 mg cholesterol

BREAKFAST

Applesauce-Yogurt Delight (½ cup applesauce mixed with ¼ cup plain low-fat yogurt and 2 teaspoons reduced-calorie orange marmalade)
1 slice Raisin Bread, toasted
½ cup Skim Milk
Coffee or Tea

LUNCH

Roast Beef Sandwich (2 ounces sliced roast beef with 2 lettuce leaves and 1 teaspoon *each* reduced-calorie mayonnaise and horseradish on 2 slices reduced-calorie wheat bread)
3 Pickle Spears and 6 Cherry Tomatoes
1 small Orange
Coffee, Tea, or Mineral Water

DINNER

1 serving **Silver Jubilee Salmon**
1 cup Cooked Rice
½ cup Cooked Sliced Beets with Grated Lemon Peel
6 Cooked Asparagus Spears
1½ cups Tossed Green Salad with 1 tablespoon Buttermilk Dressing
⅛ medium Pineapple
Coffee or Tea

SNACKS

1 serving Reduced-Calorie Chocolate Dairy Drink

Total Optional Calories: 165

Silver Jubilee Salmon ◖

¼ **cup diced onion**
½ **lemon**
3 to 4 black peppercorns
2 parsley sprigs
1 bay leaf
1 quart water
2 salmon steaks (5 ounces each)
1 teaspoon margarine
¼ **cup finely chopped seeded pared cucumber**
2 teaspoons minced shallots
¼ **cup sour cream**
2 teaspoons dry vermouth
½ **teaspoon each chopped fresh dill and Dijon-style mustard**
⅛ **teaspoon salt**
Dash white pepper

In 10-inch skillet combine onion, lemon, peppercorns, parsley, and bay leaf; add water and cook over high heat until mixture comes to a boil. Reduce heat to medium-low and let simmer for 5 minutes. Add salmon steaks to skillet and let simmer until fish flakes easily when tested with a fork, 8 to 10 minutes. Using a spatula, carefully transfer salmon to serving platter; cover and keep warm. Reserve 2 tablespoons poaching liquid.

In 8-inch nonstick skillet heat margarine over medium-high heat until bubbly and hot; add cucumber and shallots and sauté, stirring frequently, until softened, 1 to 2 minutes. Add sour cream, reserved poaching liquid, vermouth, dill, mustard, salt, and white pepper and cook, stirring frequently, until mixture is heated through, 2 to 3 minutes; pour sauce over salmon and serve immediately.

MAKES 2 SERVINGS

Each serving provides: 3 Protein Exchanges; ¼ Vegetable Exchange; ½ Fat Exchange; 70 Optional Calories
Per serving: 338 calories; 27 g protein; 23 g fat; 3 g carbohydrate; 130 mg calcium; 299 mg sodium; 57 mg cholesterol

BREAKFAST

½ medium Papaya with Lemon
    Wedge
1 Scrambled Egg
1 slice Reduced-Calorie Wheat
    Bread, toasted
½ cup Skim Milk
Coffee or Tea

LUNCH

Turkey in a Pita (2 ounces sliced
    turkey with 3 tomato slices, ¼ cup
    alfalfa sprouts, 2 lettuce leaves,
    and 2 teaspoons mustard in 1-ounce
    pita bread)
6 *each* Carrot and Celery Sticks
1 small Apple
Coffee, Tea, or Mineral Water

DINNER

1 cup Tomato Juice with Lime
    Wedge
1 serving **Festive Fettuccine with
    Shrimp and Walnut Sauce**
1 cup Cooked Chinese Pea Pods
Spinach-Mushroom Salad (1½ cups
    torn spinach with ¼ cup *each*
    sliced mushrooms, radishes, and
    red onion, 1 teaspoon imitation
    bacon bits, and 1 tablespoon
    reduced-calorie mayonnaise mixed
    with 2 teaspoons rice vinegar and
    1 teaspoon pickle relish)
1 medium Kiwi Fruit, sliced
Coffee or Tea

SNACKS

½ cup Reduced-Calorie Butterscotch
    Pudding

Total Optional Calories: 170

Festive Fettuccine with Shrimp and Walnut Sauce ◐

Purchase walnut oil in a gourmet food shop or in the gourmet section of the supermarket.

2 teaspoons margarine
1 teaspoon walnut oil*
½ ounce walnut halves
½ pound shelled and deveined medium shrimp
1 small garlic clove, minced
1 cup low-fat milk (2% milk fat)
¼ cup half-and-half (blend of milk and cream)
1½ cups cooked fettuccine (hot)
2 tablespoons <u>each</u> grated Parmesan cheese and
    diagonally sliced scallion (green onion)
1 tablespoon chopped fresh Italian (flat-leaf) parsley

In 10-inch skillet heat margarine and oil together until margarine is bubbly and mixture is hot; add walnut halves and sauté over medium heat until lightly browned (<u>be careful not to burn</u>). Using slotted spoon, transfer walnuts to plate; set aside.

In same pan combine shrimp and garlic and sauté until shrimp just turn pink. Reduce heat to low; stir in milk and half-and-half and let simmer, stirring frequently, for 1 minute. Add fettuccine, cheese, sautéed walnuts, and scallion and, using 2 forks, toss well until pasta is thoroughly coated with sauce; continue cooking until mixture thickens slightly, 1 to 2 minutes longer. Transfer fettuccine mixture to serving platter and serve sprinkled with parsley.

MAKES 2 SERVINGS

Each serving provides: 3 Protein Exchanges; 1½ Bread Exchanges;
    ⅛ Vegetable Exchange; 1½ Fat Exchanges; ½ Milk Exchange;
    150 Optional Calories
Per serving: 460 calories; 36 g protein; 20 g fat; 34 g carbohydrate;
    338 mg calcium; 451 mg sodium; 186 mg cholesterol

*1 teaspoon margarine may be substituted for the walnut oil.

Per serving: 457 calories; 36 g protein; 20 g fat; 34 g carbohydrate;
    339 mg calcium; 473 mg sodium; 186 mg cholesterol

Crunchy Oven-Fried Chicken

To pound chicken cutlets, place them between
2 sheets of plastic wrap, then pound with a meat mallet,
bottom of a saucepan, or a heavy can. The plastic wrap
will help make cleaning up easier and faster.

3 tablespoons buttermilk
1 1/2 teaspoons freshly squeezed lime juice*
1/4 teaspoon Dijon-style mustard
Dash each garlic powder, white pepper, and salt
2 chicken cutlets (1/4 pound each), pounded to 1/4-inch
  thickness
1 1/2 ounces (1/2 cup plus 2 tablespoons) cornflake crumbs
2 teaspoons vegetable oil, divided

Preheat oven to 450°F. In small mixing bowl combine
buttermilk, lime juice, mustard, and seasonings, stirring to
combine. Dip chicken into buttermilk mixture, coating both
sides and using entire mixture; on sheet of wax paper or a
paper plate dip chicken into cornflake crumbs, turning to
coat both sides with crumbs. Arrange chicken on nonstick
baking sheet. Drizzle 1/2 teaspoon oil over each cutlet and
bake until lightly browned, 8 to 10 minutes; turn chicken
over, drizzle each cutlet with 1/2 teaspoon oil and continue
baking until chicken is tender and coating is crisp, about 10
minutes longer.

MAKES 2 SERVINGS, 1 CHICKEN CUTLET EACH

Each serving provides: 3 Protein Exchanges; 1 Bread Exchange;
  1 Fat Exchange; 10 Optional Calories
Per serving: 322 calories; 42 g protein; 7 g fat; 20 g carbohydrate;
  47 mg calcium; 482 mg sodium; 100 mg cholesterol

*If fresh limes are not available, bottled lime juice (no sugar added)
  may be used.

BREAKFAST

½ medium Banana, sliced
¾ ounce Cold Cereal
½ cup Skim Milk
Coffee or Tea

LUNCH

Ham Sandwich (2 ounces baked ham
   with 3 tomato slices, 2 lettuce
   leaves, and 2 teaspoons mustard
   on 2 slices reduced-calorie rye
   bread)
6 *each* Red and Green Bell Pepper
   Strips
Coffee, Tea, or Mineral Water

DINNER

1 serving **Chicken à la King**
¾ cup Cooked Baby Carrots with
   1 teaspoon Reduced-Calorie
   Mayonnaise
¾ cup Cooked Broccoli Florets
Chicory-Sprout Salad (¾ cup *each*
   torn chicory and lettuce with
   ¼ cup *each* alfalfa sprouts and
   sliced radishes and 1 tablespoon
   Italian dressing)
½ medium Grapefruit
Coffee or Tea

SNACKS

1 small Apple; 1 cup Skim Milk

Total Optional Calories: 25

Chicken à la King ◖◗

A delicious way to use up leftover chicken.

1 teaspoon margarine
2 tablespoons chopped onion
1 tablespoon all-purpose flour
¼ teaspoon salt
Dash pepper
1 cup low-fat milk (1% milk fat)
6 ounces skinned and boned cooked chicken, cut into
   1-inch pieces
1 egg, hard-cooked and sliced
1 cup cooked spinach noodles (hot)
Garnish: paprika

In 1-quart saucepan heat margarine until bubbly and hot; add
onion and cook until softened, about 1 minute. Sprinkle
onion with flour, salt, and pepper and stir quickly to
combine. Continuing to stir, gradually add milk and bring
just to a boil. Reduce heat and cook, stirring constantly, until
mixture thickens. Stir in chicken and cook until heated
through; stir in egg. Serve over noodles and sprinkle with
paprika.

MAKES 2 SERVINGS

Each serving provides: 3½ Protein Exchanges; 1 Bread Exchange;
   ⅛ Vegetable Exchange; ½ Fat Exchange; ½ Milk Exchange; 25 Optional
   Calories
Per serving: 370 calories; 35 g protein; 13 g fat; 25 g carbohydrate;
   190 mg calcium; 462 mg sodium; 238 mg cholesterol

Greek-Style Lamb Chops ◖

1 garlic clove, mashed
½ teaspoon salt
1 tablespoon lemon juice
2 teaspoons olive oil
1 teaspoon rosemary leaves, crushed
¼ teaspoon <u>each</u> pepper and grated lemon peel
2 lamb shoulder chops (5 ounces each)
1 small plum tomato (about 1 ounce), cut crosswise into
   4 equal slices
1 ounce feta cheese, crumbled

Using a mortar and pestle, mash together garlic and salt to form a paste; add lemon juice, oil, rosemary, pepper, and lemon peel and continue to mash until well combined; set aside.

On rack in broiling pan broil lamb chops until browned on top, about 5 minutes. Turn chops over and spread each chop with ¼ of the rosemary mixture; broil until browned, 4 to 5 minutes longer. Set 2 tomato slices on each chop, then top each with ½ ounce feta cheese and half of the remaining rosemary mixture. Broil until cheese softens and is glazed, about 2 minutes.

MAKES 2 SERVINGS, 1 CHOP EACH

Each serving provides: 3½ Protein Exchanges; ¼ Vegetable Exchange;
   40 Optional Calories
Per serving: 261 calories; 25 g protein; 16 g fat; 3 g carbohydrate;
   96 mg calcium; 765 mg sodium; 98 mg cholesterol

Variation: Olive-Topped Chops (Week 5) — After topping chops with cheese, top each with 2 sliced pitted Greek olives, then remaining rosemary mixture; proceed as directed. Increase Optional Calories to 50.

Per serving: 277 calories; 25 g protein; 18 g fat; 3 g carbohydrate;
   100 mg calcium; 923 mg sodium; 98 mg cholesterol

TIP: If you don't have a mortar and pestle, mash garlic on cutting board using a knife, working salt into garlic to form a paste. Transfer to small bowl or cup and add lemon juice, oil, rosemary, salt, and lemon peel and, using a fork, mix well.

BREAKFAST

Apple-Cereal Breakfast (½ cup cooked cereal mixed with 1 small apple, chopped, and 1 teaspoon *each* brown sugar and margarine)
½ cup Skim Milk
Coffee or Tea

LUNCH

Turkey-Cheese Sandwich (1 ounce *each* sliced turkey and Muenster cheese with 1½ teaspoons Russian dressing on 2 slices reduced-calorie wheat bread)
½ cup Broccoli Florets and 6 Cucumber Spears
1 small Orange
Coffee, Tea, or Mineral Water

DINNER

1 serving **Pork Chops in Savory Sauce**
½ cup *each* Stewed Tomatoes and Cooked Sliced Celery
Cabbage Salad (¾ cup *each* shredded red and green cabbage with 1 tablespoon reduced-calorie Italian dressing)
½ cup Low-Calorie Strawberry-Flavored Gelatin topped with ¼ cup Plain Low-Fat Yogurt
Coffee or Tea

SNACKS

½ cup Fruit Salad; 1 serving Reduced-Calorie Vanilla Dairy Drink

Total Optional Calories: 55

Pork Chops in Savory Sauce

1½ teaspoons vegetable oil
½ cup sliced onion
½ small garlic clove, minced
½ cup quartered mushrooms
¼ cup water
1 tablespoon <u>each</u> soy sauce,* ketchup, and reduced-calorie orange marmalade (16 calories per 2 teaspoons)
½ teaspoon Chinese sesame oil
⅛ teaspoon powdered mustard
2 pork loin chops (5 ounces each), broiled until rare

In 8-inch nonstick skillet heat vegetable oil; add onion and garlic and sauté until translucent, about 2 minutes. Add mushrooms and sauté for 2 minutes. Add remaining ingredients except pork chops and stir to combine; bring mixture just to a boil. Reduce heat to low and add pork chops to skillet, spooning sauce over chops. Cover and let simmer, stirring occasionally, until chops are tender, 35 to 40 minutes.

MAKES 2 SERVINGS, 1 CHOP AND ABOUT ¼ CUP SAUCE EACH

Each serving provides: 3 Protein Exchanges; 1 Vegetable Exchange; 1 Fat Exchange; 20 Optional Calories
Per serving: 283 calories; 29 g protein; 14 g fat; 10 g carbohydrate; 26 mg calcium; 821 mg sodium; 83 mg cholesterol

* Reduced-sodium soy sauce may be substituted. Reduce calories to 282, calcium to 18 mg, and sodium to 460 mg.

BREAKFAST

1 cup Melon Balls
⅓ cup Cottage Cheese
1 slice Raisin Bread, toasted
½ cup Skim Milk
Coffee or Tea

LUNCH

Salmon in a Pita (2 ounces salmon
   with ¼ cup *each* diced green
   bell pepper and red onion and
   2 teaspoons reduced-calorie
   mayonnaise in 1-ounce whole
   wheat pita bread)
6 *each* Carrot and Celery Sticks
Coffee, Tea, or Mineral Water

DINNER

1 serving **Apple-Glazed Ham Steak**
3 ounces Baked Potato with
   2 teaspoons Reduced-Calorie
   Margarine
6 Cooked Asparagus Spears
1½ cups Tossed Salad with
   1½ teaspoons Blue Cheese
   Dressing mixed with 2 tablespoons
   Plain Low-Fat Yogurt plus Garlic
   Powder
⅛ medium Pineapple
Coffee or Tea

SNACKS

Banana with Spiced Yogurt
   (½ medium banana, sliced, topped
   with 2 tablespoons plain low-fat
   yogurt mixed with 1 teaspoon
   vanilla extract and nutmeg);
   ½ cup Reduced-Calorie Chocolate
   Pudding

Total Optional Calories: 25

Apple-Glazed Ham Steak ◑

Also wonderful with currant jelly, apricot preserves, or orange marmalade.

1 tablespoon apple jelly
1½ teaspoons Dijon-style mustard
⅛ to ¼ teaspoon grated orange peel
Dash ground allspice <u>or</u> ground cinnamon
6-ounce "fully cooked" boneless ham steak

In small metal measuring cup or other small flameproof container combine jelly, mustard, orange peel, and allspice (or cinnamon); cook over low heat, stirring occasionally, until jelly is melted (<u>do not boil</u>).

   Score both sides of ham steak in a crisscross pattern; transfer to nonstick baking sheet. Brush steak with half of the jelly mixture and broil until glazed, about 3 minutes. Turn steak over, brush with remaining jelly mixture, and broil for 3 minutes longer.

MAKES 2 SERVINGS

Each serving provides: 3 Protein Exchanges; 25 Optional Calories
Per serving: 154 calories; 18 g protein; 5 g fat; 9 g carbohydrate;
   9 mg calcium; 1,136 mg sodium; 45 mg cholesterol

BREAKFAST

½ cup Orange Sections
Open-Face Peanut Butter and Jelly
    Sandwich (1 tablespoon peanut
    butter with 2 teaspoons reduced-
    calorie raspberry spread on 1 slice
    reduced-calorie whole wheat bread,
    toasted)
1 cup Skim Milk
Coffee or Tea

LUNCH

Chicken "Reuben" (2 ounces sliced
    chicken with ¼ cup sauerkraut and
    1½ teaspoons Russian dressing on
    2 slices reduced-calorie rye bread)
¾ cup Cauliflower Florets and
    6 Cherry Tomatoes
1 small Apple
Coffee, Tea, or Mineral Water

DINNER

3 ounces Broiled Steak
1 serving **Creamy Broccoli-Topped Pasta**
Spinach Salad (2 cups torn spinach
    with ¼ cup *each* sliced radishes
    and mushrooms and 1½ teaspoons
    French dressing mixed with
    2 teaspoons lemon juice and
    ¼ teaspoon mustard)
½ cup Low-Calorie Cherry-Flavored
    Gelatin topped with 1 tablespoon
    Whipped Topping
Coffee or Tea

SNACKS

1 small Pear, ¾ cup Skim Milk

Total Optional Calories: 180

Creamy Broccoli-Topped Pasta

Any shape macaroni may be used in this dish.
For variety, try combining different shapes.

1 tablespoon plus 1 teaspoon margarine
1 cup <u>each</u> diced onions and red bell pepper
1 small garlic clove, minced
1 tablespoon all-purpose flour
1 packet instant chicken broth and seasoning mix
1 cup skim milk
¼ pound Gorgonzola <u>or</u> blue cheese
3 tablespoons whipped cream cheese
4 cups broccoli florets, blanched and chopped
3 cups cooked macaroni (hot)

In 12-inch nonstick skillet or 4-quart saucepan heat
margarine until bubbly and hot; add onions, pepper, and
garlic and sauté until onions are translucent, 2 to 3
minutes. Sprinkle flour and broth mix over vegetables
and stir quickly to combine; cook, stirring constantly, for
1 minute. Continuing to stir, gradually add milk and bring
just to a boil. Reduce heat to low; add cheeses and cook,
stirring constantly, until cheeses are melted. Stir in
broccoli and cook until heated through; serve over
macaroni.

MAKES 4 SERVINGS

Each serving provides: 1 Protein Exchange; 1½ Bread Exchanges;
    3 Vegetable Exchanges; 1 Fat Exchange; ¼ Milk Exchange;
    35 Optional Calories
Per serving: 366 calories; 19 g protein; 15 g fat; 42 g carbohydrate;
    310 mg calcium; 538 mg sodium; 30 mg cholesterol

1 cup Strawberries, sliced
¾ ounce Cold Cereal
½ cup Skim Milk
Coffee or Tea

Cheese Sandwich (2 ounces Monterey
   Jack cheese with 2 tablespoons
   each alfalfa sprouts and chopped
   tomatoes, ½ cup shredded lettuce,
   and 1 teaspoon *each* mustard and
   mayonnaise on 2 slices reduced-
   calorie multi-grain bread)
6 *each* Carrot Sticks and Cucumber
   Spears
Coffee, Tea, or Mineral Water

4 ounces Broiled Swordfish with
   Lime Wedges
1 serving **Brown Rice and Vegetable
   Medley**
½ cup Cooked Cut Green Beans with
   1 teaspoon Margarine
1½ cups Mixed Green Salad with
   1 tablespoon Reduced-Calorie
   Italian Dressing
⅛ medium Pineapple
White Wine Spritzer (¼ cup dry white
   wine with ½ cup club soda)
Coffee or Tea

Banana Shake (½ cup skim milk,
   ½ medium banana, and 3 ice cubes
   processed in blender); ½ cup
   Reduced-Calorie Chocolate Pudding

Total Optional Calories: 55

Brown Rice and Vegetable Medley ⓒ

Speed up meal preparation by substituting regular
long-grain rice for the brown rice.

2 teaspoons olive or vegetable oil
½ cup chopped scallions (green onions)
1 small garlic clove, minced
½ cup each sliced mushrooms and zucchini
¼ cup diced red bell pepper
1 cup cooked brown rice
1 tablespoon soy sauce*
⅛ teaspoon pepper

In 9-inch skillet heat oil over medium heat; add scallions and
garlic and sauté until softened. Add mushrooms, zucchini,
and red pepper and sauté until pepper is tender-crisp, about
5 minutes. Add rice, soy sauce, and pepper and stir to
combine; cook, stirring frequently, until mixture is heated
through.

MAKES 2 SERVINGS

Each serving provides: 1 Bread Exchange; 1¾ Vegetable Exchanges;
   1 Fat Exchange
Per serving: 182 calories; 4 g protein; 5 g fat; 30 g carbohydrate;
   43 mg calcium; 667 mg sodium; 0 mg cholesterol

*Reduced-sodium soy sauce may be substituted. Reduce calories to 181,
   calcium to 36 mg, and sodium to 307 mg.

BREAKFAST

1 medium Kiwi Fruit, sliced
1 Poached Egg
½ English Muffin, toasted, with
   2 teaspoons Reduced-Calorie
   Orange Marmalade
½ cup Skim Milk
Coffee or Tea

LUNCH

Couscous–Chick-Pea Salad
   (1 serving chilled **Couscous Salad**
   mixed with 2 ounces canned
   chick-peas on 1 cup shredded
   lettuce)
½ cup Broccoli Florets and 6 Cherry
   Tomatoes
1 Rice Cake
Coffee, Tea, or Mineral Water

DINNER

4 ounces Baked Chicken Breast
   with Tarragon Leaves
½ cup Cooked Noodles with
   1½ teaspoons Margarine
½ cup Cooked Chinese Pea Pods
Artichoke Salad (½ cup artichoke
   hearts with 1 tablespoon reduced-
   calorie French dressing on
   4 red-leaf lettuce leaves)
1 small Nectarine
½ cup Skim Milk
Coffee or Tea

SNACKS

1 cup Plain Popcorn; Fruit Shake
   (1 cup strawberries, ¼ medium
   banana, 1 cup skim milk, and 3 ice
   cubes processed in blender)

Total Optional Calories: 210

Couscous Salad ◑

**1½ ounces uncooked couscous (dry precooked
semolina)**
2 tablespoons dried currants <u>or</u> golden raisins
1 cup boiling water
1 ounce pignolias (pine nuts), toasted
**2 tablespoons <u>each</u> thinly sliced scallion (green onion)
and lemon juice**
**1 tablespoon <u>each</u> chopped fresh cilantro (Chinese
parsley) and olive oil**
1 teaspoon salt
½ teaspoon <u>each</u> pepper and honey

In 1-quart heatproof bowl combine couscous and currants
(or raisins); add boiling water. Stir well, cover, and let stand
until fruit is plumped and liquid is absorbed, about 5
minutes. Add remaining ingredients and toss to combine.
Serve immediately or cover and refrigerate until chilled.

MAKES 2 SERVINGS, ABOUT ¾ CUP EACH

Each serving provides: 1 Bread Exchange; ⅛ Vegetable Exchange;
   1½ Fat Exchanges; ½ Fruit Exchange; 85 Optional Calories
Per serving with currants: 246 calories; 7 g protein; 14 g fat;
   24 g carbohydrate; 29 mg calcium; 1,106 mg sodium; 0 mg cholesterol
With raisins: 248 calories; 7 g protein; 14 g fat; 24 g carbohydrate;
   26 mg calcium; 1,106 mg sodium; 0 mg cholesterol

TIP: To toast pine nuts, spread on baking sheet of toaster-oven and toast
at 300°F. until golden. Watch them carefully and shake baking sheet
occasionally to help prevent burning. They can also be toasted in a skillet
over medium heat, shaking skillet constantly. When golden, remove the
nuts from baking sheet or skillet immediately or they will continue to brown.

BREAKFAST

Strawberries 'n' Yogurt (1 cup
    strawberries, sliced, topped with
    ¼ cup plain low-fat yogurt)
1 slice Raisin Bread, toasted
½ cup Skim Milk
Coffee or Herb Tea

LUNCH

Liverwurst Sandwich (2 ounces sliced
    liverwurst with 2 *each* red onion
    slices and lettuce leaves and
    2 teaspoons mustard on 2 slices
    reduced-calorie pumpernickel
    bread)
6 *each* Red and Green Bell Pepper
    Strips
¾ ounce Mixed Dried Fruit
Coffee, Tea, or Mineral Water

DINNER

4 ounces Roast Veal
6 ounces Cooked New Potatoes
    with 2 teaspoons Margarine
1 cup Cooked Chopped Spinach
1½ cups Torn Iceberg Lettuce and
    6 Cherry Tomatoes with 2 table-
    spoons **Celebration Salad Dressing**
White Wine Spritzer (½ cup *each*
    dry white wine and club soda)
Coffee or Tea

SNACKS

2 medium Apricots; 1 cup Skim Milk

Total Optional Calories: 125

Celebration Salad Dressing ◑

This dressing may be stored for up to 1 week
in the refrigerator.

1½ ounces pitted avocado, pared
2 tablespoons olive <u>or</u> vegetable oil
2 tablespoons sour cream
1 tablespoon <u>each</u> red wine vinegar and water
1½ teaspoons <u>each</u> chopped chives, chopped cilantro
   (Chinese parsley), and freshly squeezed lime juice*
½ small garlic clove
½ teaspoon salt
¼ teaspoon white pepper
½ medium tomato, finely chopped

In blender container combine all ingredients except tomato
and process until smooth, scraping down sides of container
as necessary. Transfer mixture to small bowl and stir in
tomato; cover with plastic wrap and refrigerate until chilled.

YIELDS ¾ CUP

Each 2-tablespoon serving provides: ⅛ Vegetable Exchange;
    1 Fat Exchange; 25 Optional Calories
Per serving: 63 calories; 0.4 g protein; 6 g fat; 1 g carbohydrate;
    9 mg calcium; 187 mg sodium; 2 mg cholesterol

*If fresh limes are not available, bottled lime juice (no sugar added)
 may be used.

BREAKFAST

½ medium Banana, sliced
½ cup Cooked Cereal
½ cup Skim Milk
Coffee or Tea

LUNCH

Garbanzo-Spinach Salad (2 ounces
    canned chick-peas with 1 ounce
    shredded Cheddar cheese, 1 cup
    torn spinach, ¼ cup sliced
    radishes, 1 teaspoon imitation
    bacon bits, and 1½ teaspoons
    olive oil mixed with 2 teaspoons
    red wine vinegar plus seasonings)
1-ounce Roll
Coffee, Tea, or Mineral Water

DINNER

2 tablespoons **Creamy Dill Dip** with
    3 *each* Zucchini and Carrot Sticks
4 ounces Roast Cornish Hen
½ cup Cooked Long-Grain and Wild
    Rice
6 Cooked Asparagus Spears with
    1 teaspoon Margarine
½ cup Orange and Grapefruit
    Sections
½ cup Skim Milk
Coffee or Tea

SNACKS

½ cup Fruit Salad; 1 serving
    Reduced-Calorie Chocolate Dairy
    Drink

Total Optional Calories: 55

Creamy Dill Dip ◑

Chunks of hearty bread are wonderful with this cool and creamy party dip. Vegetables also make delicious dippers; try an assortment such as cherry tomatoes, whole mushrooms, carrot and celery sticks, broccoli and cauliflower florets, and zucchini slices. Dip may be stored in covered container in refrigerator for up to 2 weeks.

½ cup plus 1 tablespoon whipped cream cheese
½ cup each diced onion and chopped fresh dill
1 tablespoon plus 2 teaspoons mayonnaise
1 tablespoon sour cream
½ teaspoon salt
½ small garlic clove, mashed
Dash white pepper

In blender container combine all ingredients and process until smooth, scraping down sides of container as necessary. Transfer mixture to small serving bowl; cover with plastic wrap and refrigerate until flavors blend, at least 30 minutes.

YIELDS 1 CUP

Each 2-tablespoon serving provides: ⅛ Vegetable Exchange;
    ½ Fat Exchange; 45 Optional Calories
Per serving: 67 calories; 1 g protein; 6 g fat; 2 g carbohydrate;
    29 mg calcium; 196 mg sodium; 13 mg cholesterol

BREAKFAST

½ cup Orange Sections
¼ cup Part-Skim Ricotta Cheese
  sprinkled with Cinnamon
1 serving Reduced-Calorie Vanilla
  Dairy Drink

LUNCH

Tuna Sandwich (2 ounces tuna with
  ¼ cup *each* chopped celery and
  scallion, 2 lettuce leaves, and
  1 teaspoon mayonnaise on 2 slices
  reduced-calorie rye bread)
½ cup Broccoli Florets and 6 Cherry
  Tomatoes
Coffee, Tea, or Mineral Water

DINNER

3 ounces Broiled Flank Steak
¾ cup *each* Cooked Sliced Yellow
  Squash and Zucchini
1½ cups Mixed Green Salad with
  1 tablespoon Buttermilk Dressing
2 Corn Tortillas with 2 tablespoons
  Salsa
½ cup Applesauce
12 fluid ounces Light Beer

SNACKS

½ medium Grapefruit; 1 cup Skim
  Milk

Total Optional Calories: 100

Salsa ☾◑

Serve with warm tortillas.

1 medium tomato, blanched, peeled, seeded, and finely chopped
¼ cup tomato juice
2 tablespoons <u>each</u> finely chopped scallion (green onion) and green bell pepper
½ small garlic clove, minced
1 teaspoon minced fresh cilantro (Chinese parsley)
⅛ teaspoon <u>each</u> ground cumin, chili powder, and hot sauce
⅛ teaspoon minced jalapeño pepper (optional)

In small bowl combine all ingredients, mixing well. Cover with plastic wrap and refrigerate until flavors are blended, at least 30 minutes.

YIELDS ¾ CUP

Each 2-tablespoon serving provides: ½ Vegetable Exchange; 2 Optional Calories
Per serving: 7 calories; 0.3 g protein; trace fat; 2 g carbohydrate; 5 mg calcium; 42 mg sodium; 0 mg cholesterol

Berries with Sweet Yogurt Sauce ◖◑

This sauce is wonderful as a topping for any variety
of berries.

½ cup plain low-fat yogurt
2 tablespoons reduced-calorie raspberry spread
 (16 calories per 2 teaspoons), melted
1 teaspoon confectioners' sugar
⅛ teaspoon grated orange peel
2 cups strawberries, cut into quarters

In blender container combine all ingredients except
strawberries and process until smooth.

 Into each of 4 dessert dishes spoon ¼ of the strawberries
and top each portion with ¼ of the yogurt mixture (about
2 tablespoons); serve immediately.

MAKES 4 SERVINGS

Each serving provides: ½ Fruit Exchange; ¼ Milk Exchange; 15 Optional
 Calories
Per serving: 55 calories; 2 g protein; 0.7 g fat; 11 g carbohydrate;
 63 mg calcium; 21 mg sodium; 2 mg cholesterol

BREAKFAST

¼ small Cantaloupe
⅓ cup Cottage Cheese
2 Graham Crackers
1 cup Skim Milk

LUNCH

Chef's Salad (1 ounce *each*
     julienne-cut turkey and Swiss
     cheese with 1 cup torn lettuce,
     8 tomato wedges, 6 green bell
     pepper strips, ½ cup sliced
     mushrooms, ¼ cup sliced radishes,
     and 1 tablespoon blue cheese
     dressing)
¾ ounce Breadsticks
Coffee, Tea, or Mineral Water

DINNER

3 ounces Broiled Fillet of Sole with
     2 teaspoons Tartar Sauce
½ cup Cooked Noodles
½ cup Cooked Broccoli Florets
Artichoke Salad (½ cup *each*
     artichoke hearts and sliced yellow
     squash with 1 teaspoon olive oil
     mixed with 2 teaspoons red wine
     vinegar plus herbs on 8 Boston
     lettuce leaves)
1 serving **Gala Strawberry Charlotte**
4 fluid ounces Dry White Wine

SNACKS

½ cup Reduced-Calorie Vanilla
     Pudding topped with 2 tablespoons
     Raisins

Total Optional Calories: 295

Gala Strawberry Charlotte

Store leftovers in the refrigerator for up to 2 days.

1 envelope (eight ½-cup servings) low-calorie strawberry-flavored gelatin (8 calories per ½ cup)
2 cups boiling water
½ cup cold water
24 champagne egg biscuits (¼ ounce each)*
1¼ cups thawed frozen dairy whipped topping, divided
4 cups strawberries, sliced (reserve 6 whole berries for garnish)
5 mint sprigs

In medium heatproof bowl sprinkle gelatin over boiling water and stir until dissolved; add cold water and stir until combined. Cover bowl with plastic wrap and refrigerate until mixture is the consistency of unbeaten egg whites, about 30 minutes.

Cut 1 inch off one narrow end of each biscuit, reserving ends. In 8-inch springform pan arrange reserved biscuit ends in a single layer over bottom of pan. Stand biscuits cut-end down around sides of pan; set aside.

Add about ⅓ cup whipped topping to gelatin mixture and, using wire whisk, mix until combined; fold in sliced strawberries. Carefully spoon mixture into prepared pan; cover with plastic wrap and refrigerate until gelatin is set, about 1 hour.

Using a pastry bag fitted with a star tip, pipe remaining whipped topping over gelatin. Thinly slice remaining berries, leaving 1 whole, and arrange over gelatin. Garnish with mint sprigs. To serve, carefully remove sides of pan and set base of pan on cake plate.

MAKES 8 SERVINGS

Each serving provides: ½ Fruit Exchange; 145 Optional Calories
Per serving: 155 calories; 2 g protein; 6 g fat; 24 g carbohydrate;
     20 mg calcium; 94 mg sodium; 8 mg cholesterol

*Champagne egg biscuits are light Italian cookies, similar in shape to
     ladyfingers.

BREAKFAST

½ medium Grapefruit
½ cup Cooked Cereal
½ cup Skim Milk
Coffee or Tea

LUNCH

Chicken Sandwich (2 ounces sliced
chicken with 3 *each* tomato slices
and lettuce leaves and 1 teaspoon
each mayonnaise and mustard on
2 slices reduced-calorie rye bread)
6 *each* Carrot and Zucchini Sticks
1 small Apple
Coffee, Tea, or Mineral Water

DINNER

4 ounces Broiled Flounder Fillet
½ cup Cooked Barley with Chopped
Parsley
½ cup *each* Cooked Sliced Beets and
Cut Green Beans
1½ cups Tossed Salad with
1 tablespoon Blue Cheese Dressing
½ cup Applesauce
½ cup Skim Milk
Coffee or Tea

SNACKS

1 serving **Lemon-Cream Cheese
Cookies**; 1 cup Skim Milk

Total Optional Calories: 135

Lemon-Cream Cheese Cookies

Celebrate our Silver Jubilee year with these mouth-watering cookies.

1 egg, beaten, divided
¹/₃ cup plus 2 teaspoons granulated sugar, divided
¼ cup _each_ cream cheese, divided, and sweet butter
1 teaspoon lemon juice
½ teaspoon grated lemon peel, divided
½ cup plus 2 tablespoons all-purpose flour
¼ teaspoon double-acting baking powder
2 graham crackers (2½-inch squares), made into crumbs
1 teaspoon sour cream

Measure out and reserve 1 tablespoon egg. In mixing bowl combine ¹/₃ cup sugar with 2 tablespoons cream cheese, the butter and lemon juice, ¼ teaspoon lemon peel, and all but reserved egg; using electric mixer at medium speed, beat until creamy. In small mixing bowl combine flour and baking powder; add to cream cheese mixture and stir until blended. Form dough into a ball, wrap in plastic wrap, and freeze for 30 minutes.

On paper plate spread graham cracker crumbs. Divide dough into 16 equal portions and, using hands, shape each portion into a ball, then roll in crumbs; arrange balls on nonstick cookie sheet, leaving a space of about 1½ inches between each. Using fingers, gently press center of each ball, making an indentation in each cookie; transfer to refrigerator.

Preheat oven to 350°F. In small bowl combine remaining 2 tablespoons cream cheese, reserved tablespoon egg, remaining ¼ teaspoon lemon peel, and the sour cream, mixing until smooth. Remove cookies from refrigerator and spoon an equal amount of cream cheese mixture into each indentation. Sprinkle ⅛ teaspoon sugar over each cookie and bake in middle of center oven rack until edges of cookies are lightly browned, 15 to 20 minutes. Transfer to wire rack and let cool.

MAKES 8 SERVINGS, 2 COOKIES EACH

Each serving provides: ½ Bread Exchange; 135 Optional Calories
Per serving: 171 calories; 3 g protein; 9 g fat; 20 g carbohydrate; 21 mg calcium; 56 mg sodium; 58 mg cholesterol

BREAKFAST

½ cup Orange Juice
¾ ounce Cold Cereal
¾ cup Skim Milk
Coffee or Tea

LUNCH

Egg and Garbanzo Salad (1 hard-
    cooked egg, sliced, with 1 ounce
    canned chick-peas, ¼ cup *each*
    alfalfa sprouts and shredded carrot,
    1½ cups shredded lettuce, and
    1½ teaspoons Thousand Island
    dressing mixed with 2 tablespoons
    plain low-fat yogurt and
    ¼ teaspoon mustard)
2 Pickle Spears
½ medium Banana
Coffee, Tea, or Mineral Water

DINNER

4 ounces Broiled Swordfish with
    Lime Wedge
3 ounces Boiled New Potatoes with
    Chopped Parsley
¾ cup Cooked Chinese Pea Pods
Salad Medley (¼ cup *each* sliced
    radishes, cucumber, and celery,
    3 tomato slices, and ¼ cup
    artichoke hearts on 1 cup shredded
    lettuce with 1½ teaspoons Italian
    dressing mixed with 2 teaspoons
    red wine vinegar)
1 serving **Anniversary Pecan Pie**
Coffee or Tea

SNACKS

1 serving Reduced-Calorie Chocolate
    Dairy Drink with 2 Honey Graham
    Crackers; ½ small Mango

Total Optional Calories: 145

Anniversary Pecan Pie

The crust can be prepared earlier in the week to help speed up preparation on the day you bake the pie. Refrigerate dough ball for up to 3 days, or freeze rolled-out dough in pie plate for up to a week.

Crust

¾ cup all-purpose flour
Dash salt
2 tablespoons plus 2 teaspoons margarine
¼ cup sour cream

Filling

¼ pound pecan halves
4 eggs
**¼ cup <u>each</u> firmly packed dark brown sugar and
    evaporated skimmed milk**

To Prepare Crust: In mixing bowl combine flour and salt; with pastry blender, or 2 knives used scissors-fashion, cut in margarine until mixture resembles coarse meal. Add sour cream and mix thoroughly; form dough into a ball, wrap in plastic wrap, and refrigerate for at least 1 hour.

Between 2 sheets of wax paper roll dough, forming a 10-inch circle, about ¼ inch thick. Fit dough into a 9-inch pie plate; fold under any dough that extends beyond edge of plate and flute edge.

To Prepare Filling and Bake: Preheat oven to 375°F. Arrange pecans over bottom of crust. In small mixing bowl, using electric mixer at medium speed, beat eggs until frothy; add sugar and milk and continue beating until well blended. Carefully pour mixture into crust and bake for 40 to 45 minutes (until a knife, inserted in center, comes out clean). Remove pie plate to wire rack and let cool.

MAKES 8 SERVINGS

Each serving provides: ½ Protein Exchange; ½ Bread Exchange;
    1 Fat Exchange; 145 Optional Calories
Per serving: 258 calories; 6 g protein; 18 g fat; 20 g carbohydrate;
    60 mg calcium; 111 mg sodium; 140 mg cholesterol

June

Marinated Shrimp and Cucumber Salad

JUNE'S BEST BUYS FOR FRUITS AND VEGETABLES

alfalfa sprouts	carrots	lemons	plums
apricots	celery	limes	potatoes
arugula	cherries	mangoes	radishes
bananas	Chinese pea pods	mushrooms	raspberries
bean sprouts	corn on the cob	new potatoes	scallions (green onions)
beets	cucumbers	okra	spinach
bell peppers	eggplants	onions	strawberries
blackberries	green beans	papayas	summer squash
blueberries	kiwi fruit	peaches	watermelon
cantaloupes	kumquats	pineapples	zucchini

BREAKFAST

1 cup Cantaloupe Chunks
2-ounce Corn Muffin, toasted, with
2 teaspoons Reduced-Calorie
Grape Spread
1 cup Skim Milk

LUNCH

Muenster 'n' Sprouts Sandwich
(2 ounces sliced Muenster cheese
with ¼ cup alfalfa sprouts,
3 tomato slices, and 1½ teaspoons
margarine on 2 slices pumpernickel
bread)
6 *each* Green Bell Pepper Strips and
Celery Sticks
10 large Cherries
Coffee, Tea, or Mineral Water

DINNER

1 serving **Shrimp-Stuffed Shells Appetizer**
3 ounces Baked Flounder Fillet
Roll-Ups sprinkled with Paprika
1 cup Cooked Spinach
1½ cups Tossed Salad with
2 Pimiento-Stuffed Green Olives,
1 teaspoon Imitation Bacon Bits,
and Red Wine Vinegar plus
Seasonings
Iced Tea with Lemon Twist

SNACKS

Blueberry Delight (½ cup blueberries
mixed with 3 tablespoons sour
cream and ½ teaspoon brown
sugar); 1 cup Skim Milk

Total Optional Calories: 200

Shrimp-Stuffed Shells Appetizer

For pasta-shrimp salad, substitute ½ cup cooked small shell or elbow macaroni for the jumbo shells and stir into shrimp mixture.

¼ pound shelled and deveined cooked medium shrimp
½ ounce pignolias (pine nuts), toasted
¼ cup finely diced celery
2 tablespoons _each_ sliced scallion (green onion) and sour cream
2 teaspoons mayonnaise
½ teaspoon _each_ salt, lemon juice, and prepared horseradish
Dash _each_ pepper and hot sauce
8 lettuce leaves
4 uncooked jumbo macaroni shells (¾ ounce), cooked according to package directions and chilled
½ medium tomato, cut into 4 wedges

In medium bowl (not aluminum*) combine all ingredients except lettuce, shells, and tomato, mixing well. Cover with plastic wrap and refrigerate until chilled, at least 30 minutes.

To serve, line serving platter with lettuce leaves. Stir shrimp mixture and spoon ¼ of mixture (about ¼ cup) into each shell; arrange shells open-side up on lettuce and top each with 1 tomato wedge.

MAKES 4 SERVINGS, 1 STUFFED SHELL EACH

Each serving provides: 1 Protein Exchange; 1 Vegetable Exchange;
½ Fat Exchange; 55 Optional Calories
Per serving: 112 calories; 9 g protein; 6 g fat; 7 g carbohydrate;
65 mg calcium; 343 mg sodium; 47 mg cholesterol

*It's best to marinate in glass or stainless-steel containers; acidic ingredients such as lemon juice may react with aluminum, causing color and flavor changes in foods.

BREAKFAST

1 cup Strawberries, sliced
⅓ cup Cottage Cheese
3 Melba Rounds
½ cup Skim Milk
Coffee or Tea

LUNCH

Turkey Toss (1 ounce diced turkey
  with 8 tomato wedges, 1 cup torn
  lettuce, ½ cup sliced zucchini,
  ¼ cup shredded carrot, and
  1 tablespoon reduced-calorie
  buttermilk dressing)
Coffee, Tea, or Mineral Water

DINNER

1 serving **Ham, Fruit, and Cheese
  Kabobs**
3 ounces Grilled Sirloin Steak
Pasta Salad (¾ cup chilled cooked
  spiral macaroni with ½ cup broccoli
  florets, 4 red bell pepper rings,
  ¼ cup sliced mushrooms, 2 tablespoons diced onion, and 1 tablespoon Italian dressing)
1 cup Honeydew Melon Balls
Iced Cappuccino (1 cup espresso with
  ½ cup skim milk and ice cubes)

SNACKS

Apricot Rice Cake (1 rice cake topped
  with 1 teaspoon reduced-calorie
  apricot spread); 1 cup Skim Milk

Total Optional Calories: 40

Ham, Fruit, and Cheese Kabobs ◑

To help keep wooden skewers from burning while kabobs are broiling, either soak them in water for a few minutes before using or cover ends with foil.

2 teaspoons <u>each</u> olive <u>or</u> vegetable oil and margarine
1 small garlic clove, thinly sliced
2 ounces <u>each</u> French bread, cut crosswise into 8 thin slices, Brie cheese (rind removed), cut into 8 equal slices, and sliced prosciutto (Italian-style ham), cut into 8 equal strips
2 cups cantaloupe chunks

In small saucepan heat oil and margarine together over medium heat until margarine is melted and mixture is hot; add garlic and cook until lightly browned, 1 to 2 minutes; using a slotted spoon, remove and discard garlic.

On nonstick baking sheet arrange bread slices and, using a pastry brush and half of the margarine mixture, brush each bread slice with an equal amount of mixture; broil 6 inches from heat source until lightly browned, 2 to 3 minutes. Cut each slice of bread in half crosswise and top 8 of the bread halves with 1 slice of cheese each; top each portion of cheese with a remaining bread half, forming 8 sandwiches. Roll one prosciutto strip around each sandwich.

Onto each of four 8- or 9-inch wooden or metal skewers, alternating ingredients, thread 2 sandwiches and ½ cup cantaloupe chunks. Transfer skewers to baking sheet and brush each sandwich with ⅛ of the remaining margarine mixture. Broil 6 inches from heat source, turning once, until cheese is melted, 2 to 3 minutes on each side.

MAKES 4 SERVINGS, 1 SKEWER EACH

Each serving provides: 1 Protein Exchange; ½ Bread Exchange;
  1 Fat Exchange; ½ Fruit Exchange
Per serving: 175 calories; 8 g protein; 9 g fat; 15 g carbohydrate;
  44 mg calcium; 372 mg sodium; 22 mg cholesterol

½ cup Grapefruit Sections
½ cup Cooked Cereal
½ cup Skim Milk
Coffee or Tea

LUNCH

Open-Face Turkey Sandwich
(2 ounces sliced turkey with
2 lettuce leaves and 1 teaspoon
reduced-calorie mayonnaise on
1 slice reduced-calorie wheat
bread)
½ cup Broccoli Florets and 6 Celery
Sticks
1 small Apple
Coffee, Tea, or Mineral Water

DINNER

1 serving **Spinach-Feta Bake**
Shrimp Salad (2 ounces tiny shrimp
with 1 cup torn lettuce, ½ cup
shredded red cabbage, and
1½ teaspoons Thousand Island
dressing mixed with 2 tablespoons
plain low-fat yogurt and
¼ teaspoon mustard)
½ cup Cooked Sliced Carrot with
1 teaspoon Honey
½ cup Stewed Tomatoes
Peach 'n' Yogurt (½ cup peach slices
topped with 2 tablespoons plain
low-fat yogurt)
Coffee or Tea

SNACKS

1 serving Reduced-Calorie Chocolate
Dairy Drink; ½ cup Low-Calorie
Orange-Flavored Gelatin

Total Optional Calories: 30

Spinach-Feta Bake ©

1 pound fresh spinach*
3 eggs
5 ounces feta cheese, crumbled
12 melba rounds, crushed, divided
2 teaspoons lemon juice
½ teaspoon oregano leaves
2 tablespoons margarine, melted
Garnish: lemon slices

Wash spinach thoroughly and drain; remove and discard stems. In 12-inch nonstick skillet, over high heat and using only the water that clings to spinach leaves after washing, cook spinach, covered, until wilted. Transfer spinach to colander and drain well; chop and set aside.

Preheat oven to 425°F. In medium bowl beat eggs. Add spinach, cheese, 2 tablespoons melba round crumbs, and the lemon juice and oregano leaves; stir to combine. Spray 2-quart casserole with nonstick cooking spray; spread spinach mixture in bottom of casserole. In small bowl combine remaining melba round crumbs and margarine; sprinkle over spinach mixture and bake until crumbs are golden brown, about 15 minutes. Serve garnished with lemon slices.

MAKES 4 SERVINGS

Each serving provides: 2 Protein Exchanges; ½ Bread Exchange;
1 Vegetable Exchange; 1½ Fat Exchanges
Per serving: 250 calories; 14 g protein; 18 g fat; 10 g carbohydrate;
314 mg calcium; 604 mg sodium; 237 mg cholesterol

*A 10-ounce package frozen chopped spinach, thawed and well drained, can be substituted for the fresh; omit cooking procedure for spinach. Combine thawed spinach with eggs and proceed as directed.

Per serving: 242 calories; 12 g protein; 18 g fat; 9 g carbohydrate;
280 mg calcium; 567 mg sodium; 237 mg cholesterol

TIP: Spinach is very sandy and must be washed well before using. To wash spinach, fill sink with cold water and add spinach. Change water several times until spinach is clean.

1 cup Strawberries, sliced and
   sprinkled with ½ teaspoon
   Confectioners' Sugar
¼ cup Part-Skim Ricotta Cheese
1 Rice Cake
1 cup Skim Milk

LUNCH

Peanut Butter and Marmalade
   Sandwich (1 tablespoon peanut
   butter with 2 teaspoons reduced-
   calorie orange marmalade on
   2 slices reduced-calorie wheat
   bread)
½ medium Banana
Coffee, Tea, or Mineral Water

DINNER

1 serving **Crabmeat-Stuffed Flounder**
1 cup Cooked Spinach
Arugula Salad (1 cup *each* torn Bibb
   lettuce and arugula with 2
   teaspoons olive oil mixed with
   2 teaspoons tarragon vinegar plus
   seasonings)
1-ounce slice French Bread with
   1 teaspoon Reduced-Calorie
   Margarine
Mineral Water with Lime Wedge

SNACKS

1 serving Reduced-Calorie Chocolate
   Dairy Drink; 2 medium Plums

Total Optional Calories: 115

Crabmeat-Stuffed Flounder

2 teaspoons margarine
¼ cup <u>each</u> finely chopped celery and scallions (green onions)
1 small garlic clove, minced
2 tablespoons <u>each</u> lemon juice, divided, and dry sherry
¼ pound thawed and drained frozen crabmeat
⅓ cup plus 2 teaspoons plain dried bread crumbs
3 tablespoons sour cream
1 tablespoon <u>each</u> Worcestershire sauce and minced fresh parsley
1 teaspoon Dijon-style mustard
⅛ teaspoon <u>each</u> salt and white pepper
4 flounder fillets (¼ pound each)
¼ cup <u>each</u> dry white table wine and water
Paprika

Preheat oven to 350°F. In 8-inch nonstick skillet heat margarine over medium-high heat until bubbly and hot; add celery, scallions, and garlic and sauté, stirring frequently, until vegetables are softened, 2 to 3 minutes. Add 1 tablespoon lemon juice and the sherry and cook, stirring frequently, for 1 minute. Transfer mixture to medium mixing bowl; add crabmeat, bread crumbs, sour cream, Worcester-shire sauce, parsley, mustard, salt, and pepper, mixing until thoroughly combined. Spoon ¼ of crabmeat mixture onto center of each fillet and roll fish to enclose filling. Transfer rolls seam-side down to 1½-quart casserole; pour wine, water, and remaining tablespoon lemon juice into casserole and sprinkle each roll with dash paprika. Cover and bake, basting occasionally with pan juices, until fish flakes easily when tested with a fork, 20 to 25 minutes. Serve with pan juices.

MAKES 4 SERVINGS, 1 STUFFED FILLET EACH

Each serving provides: 4 Protein Exchanges; ½ Bread Exchange;
   ¼ Vegetable Exchange; ½ Fat Exchange; 50 Optional Calories
Per serving: 225 calories; 25 g protein; 6 g fat; 11 g carbohydrate;
   56 mg calcium; 397 mg sodium; 86 mg cholesterol

TIP: Simplify this method by dividing stuffing into 4 individual casseroles, then topping each with 1 fillet. Pour ¼ of the wine, water, and remaining lemon juice into each casserole, sprinkle each with dash paprika, and proceed as directed.

BREAKFAST

¼ small Cantaloupe
¾ ounce Cold Cereal
1 cup Skim Milk
Coffee or Tea

LUNCH

Tuna-Stuffed Pocket (2 ounces tuna
    with 6 cucumber slices, ¼ cup
    shredded lettuce, 2 tablespoons
    shredded carrot, and 2 teaspoons
    mayonnaise in 1-ounce whole
    wheat pita bread)
6 each Red and Green Bell Pepper
    Strips
1 medium Peach
Coffee, Tea, or Mineral Water

DINNER

1 serving **Grilled Chicken Oriental**
Grilled Vegetable Kabobs (½ cup each
    zucchini chunks and mushroom
    caps, 6 cherry tomatoes, and
    ¼ cup onion wedges on skewers)
1½ cups Mixed Green Salad with
    Lemon Juice and Herbs
½ cup Low-Calorie Cherry-Flavored
    Gelatin
Iced Herb Tea

SNACKS

½ cup Fruit Salad; ½ cup Reduced-
    Calorie Butterscotch Pudding

Total Optional Calories: 50

Grilled Chicken Oriental ◑

¼ cup soy sauce*
2 tablespoons plus 2 teaspoons honey, divided
1 tablespoon plus 1 teaspoon Chinese sesame oil
1-inch piece ginger root, pared and mashed
1 small garlic clove, mashed
4 chicken cutlets (¼ pound each)

In ½-cup metal measure or other small flameproof container combine soy sauce with 2 tablespoons honey and the oil, ginger, and garlic and cook, stirring frequently, until mixture is warm, about 1 minute. Transfer to self-sealing plastic bag or medium bowl (not aluminum†); add chicken and turn to coat with marinade. Seal bag or cover bowl and let stand 10 minutes to marinate.

In small metal measuring cup heat remaining 2 teaspoons honey over low heat until melted; set aside. Spray grill or broiler rack with nonstick cooking spray. Transfer chicken to grill (or rack), reserving marinade; brush with half of the reserved marinade and cook over hot coals (or in broiler) until browned on 1 side, about 5 minutes. Turn chicken over, brush with remaining marinade, and cook until other side is browned, about 5 minutes longer. Brush 1 side of each cutlet with ¼ teaspoon heated honey and continue cooking until glazed, 1 to 2 minutes. Turn chicken over; brush each cutlet with an equal amount of remaining honey and cook until chicken is glazed and cooked throughout, 1 to 2 minutes longer.

MAKES 4 SERVINGS, 1 CHICKEN CUTLET EACH

Each serving provides: 3 Protein Exchanges; 80 Optional Calories
Per serving: 223 calories; 27 g protein; 6 g fat; 14 g carbohydrate;
    29 mg calcium; 1,403 mg sodium; 66 mg cholesterol

*Reduced-sodium soy sauce may be substituted. Reduce calories to 221, calcium to 15 mg, and sodium to 682 mg.
†It's best to marinate in glass or stainless-steel containers; ingredients such as soy sauce may react with aluminum, causing color and flavor changes in foods.

BREAKFAST

Strawberry Yogurt (½ cup plain low-fat yogurt mixed with 1 cup strawberries, sliced, and 1 teaspoon wheat germ)
1 slice Whole Wheat Bread, toasted, with 1 teaspoon Reduced-Calorie Apricot Spread
Coffee or Tea

LUNCH

Shrimp-Spinach Salad (2 ounces diced shrimp with 1 cup spinach leaves, ½ cup sliced celery, ¼ cup button mushrooms, 8 tomato wedges, 2 tablespoons shredded carrot, and 1 teaspoon vegetable oil mixed with 2 teaspoons red wine vinegar plus seasonings)
6 Cucumber Spears
2 slices Cocktail Rye Bread
Coffee, Tea, or Mineral Water

DINNER

1 serving **Orange-Mustard Glazed Lamb Chops**
1 cup Cooked Cut Green Beans
Cabbage-Squash Salad (1 cup *each* shredded red cabbage and sliced yellow squash with 1 tablespoon Russian dressing on 4 lettuce leaves)
⅛ medium Pineapple
Tea

SNACKS

1 medium Peach; 1 cup Skim Milk

Total Optional Calories: 50

Orange-Mustard Glazed Lamb Chops ◑

1 garlic clove, chopped
1 tablespoon lemon juice
¼ teaspoon rosemary leaves
⅛ teaspoon salt
Dash pepper
4 lamb loin chops (3 ounces each)
2 tablespoons reduced-calorie orange marmalade (16 calories per 2 teaspoons)
1 tablespoon each orange juice (no sugar added) and canned ready-to-serve chicken broth
1½ teaspoons Dijon-style mustard
⅛ teaspoon grated orange peel

Using a mortar and pestle, mash garlic to form paste; add lemon juice and seasonings and mix well. Spread each side of each lamb chop with ⅛ of the garlic mixture; set chops on rack in broiling pan and broil 5 to 6 inches from heat source, turning once, until medium-rare, about 5 minutes on each side.

While chops are broiling, in small saucepan combine marmalade, orange juice, broth, mustard, and orange peel and cook over medium heat, stirring frequently, until mixture is smooth and thoroughly heated, 3 to 4 minutes. Spoon ¼ of orange mixture (about 1 tablespoon) onto each lamb chop and broil until chops are glazed, about 1 minute longer.

MAKES 2 SERVINGS, 2 CHOPS EACH

Each serving provides: 4 Protein Exchanges; 30 Optional Calories
Per serving: 245 calories; 32 g protein; 9 g fat; 8 g carbohydrate; 37 mg calcium; 361 mg sodium; 113 mg cholesterol

TIP: For a more economical meal, substitute two 6-ounce lamb shoulder chops for the 4 loin chops.

BREAKFAST

½ cup Orange Sections
¾ ounce Cold Cereal
½ cup Skim Milk
Coffee or Tea

LUNCH

Turkey 'n' Tomato Sandwich
    (3 ounces sliced turkey with
    4 lettuce leaves, 4 tomato slices,
    and 2 teaspoons reduced-calorie
    mayonnaise on 2 slices reduced-
    calorie rye bread)
½ cup Broccoli Florets and 6 Celery
    Sticks
Coffee, Tea, or Mineral Water

DINNER

¾ cup Chicken Bouillon
1 serving **Garbanzo Salad**
¾ ounce Breadsticks with
    1 teaspoon Reduced-Calorie
    Margarine
½ cup Raspberries topped with
1 tablespoon Whipped Topping
White Wine Spritzer (½ cup *each*
    dry white wine and club soda)

SNACKS

Cinnamon Banana (½ medium
    banana, sliced, topped with ¼ cup
    plain low-fat yogurt and sprinkled
    with cinnamon); 1 serving
    Reduced-Calorie Chocolate Dairy
    Drink

Total Optional Calories: 125

Garbanzo Salad Ⓒ ◑

6 ounces drained canned chick-peas (garbanzo beans)
1 ounce Swiss <u>or</u> Cheddar cheese, shredded
1 medium tomato, diced
¼ cup diagonally sliced scallions (green onions)
1 tablespoon <u>each</u> chopped fresh Italian (flat-leaf)
    parsley, olive oil, and lemon juice
½ teaspoon salt
½ small garlic clove, mashed
Dash pepper
8 romaine lettuce leaves
1 egg, hard-cooked and cut into quarters

In medium bowl combine chick-peas, cheese, tomato, scallions, and parsley. In small bowl combine oil, lemon juice, salt, garlic, and pepper; pour over chick-pea mixture and toss to combine.

To serve, line serving platter with lettuce leaves, top with chick-pea mixture, and garnish with egg quarters.

MAKES 2 SERVINGS

Each serving provides: 2½ Protein Exchanges; 2¼ Vegetable Exchanges;
    1½ Fat Exchanges
Per serving with Swiss cheese: 292 calories; 15 g protein; 15 g fat;
    25 g carbohydrate; 232 mg calcium; 923 mg sodium;
    150 mg cholesterol
With Cheddar cheese: 295 calories; 15 g protein; 16 g fat;
    25 g carbohydrate; 198 mg calcium; 974 mg sodium; 152 mg cholesterol

TIP: When hard-cooking eggs, choose ones that are 7 to 10 days old. Fresher eggs will be difficult to shell. To shell a hard-cooked egg easily, crack all over. Under running cold water and starting at large end of egg, gently peel off pieces of shell.

BREAKFAST

1 cup Cantaloupe Chunks
1 Scrambled Egg sprinkled with
   1 teaspoon Grated Parmesan
   Cheese
½ cup Skim Milk
Coffee or Tea

LUNCH

Chicken Sandwich (2 ounces sliced
   chicken with 4 tomato slices,
   4 lettuce leaves, and 2 teaspoons
   mayonnaise on 2 slices reduced-
   calorie multi-grain bread)
6 *each* Red and Green Bell Pepper
   Strips
1 small Apple
Coffee or Tea

DINNER

¾ cup Chicken Bouillon
1 serving **Marinated Shrimp and
   Cucumber Salad**
12 *each* Carrot and Zucchini Sticks
1-ounce slice French Bread with
   1 teaspoon Margarine
½ cup Skim Milk
Coffee or Tea

SNACKS

½ cup Canned Fruit Cocktail; ½ cup
   Reduced-Calorie Vanilla Pudding

Total Optional Calories: 20

Marinated Shrimp and Cucumber Salad ◐

Try using seasoned rice vinegar for a
subtle flavor change.

6 ounces shelled and deveined cooked shrimp
½ cup thinly sliced pared cucumber
**1 tablespoon plus 1½ teaspoons <u>each</u> rice vinegar and
   teriyaki sauce**
⅛ teaspoon <u>each</u> salt and ground ginger
6 lettuce leaves
**¼ cup thinly sliced scallions (green onions), green
   portion only, divided**

In small shallow bowl (not aluminum*) combine all
ingredients except lettuce and scallions. Cover with plastic
wrap and refrigerate for about 1 hour.

   To serve, line 2 small salad bowls with 3 lettuce leaves
each. Toss salad again and, using a slotted spoon, spoon half
of salad mixture onto each portion of lettuce; sprinkle each
serving with 2 tablespoons scallions.

MAKES 2 SERVINGS

Each serving provides: 3 Protein Exchanges; 1½ Vegetable Exchanges
Per serving: 125 calories; 22 g protein; 1 g fat; 6 g carbohydrate;
   121 mg calcium; 713 mg sodium; 128 mg cholesterol

*It's best to marinate in glass or stainless-steel containers; acidic ingredients
   such as vinegar may react with aluminum, causing color and flavor changes
   in foods.

BREAKFAST

½ cup Orange Sections
¾ ounce Cold Cereal
1 cup Skim Milk
Coffee or Tea

LUNCH

1 serving **Smoked Fish Salad**
6 *each* Cherry Tomatoes and Celery
    Sticks
1 medium Peach
Coffee, Tea, or Mineral Water

DINNER

Burger in a Pita (3 ounces grilled
    hamburger with ¼ cup steamed
    sliced onion and 2 teaspoons
    ketchup in 1-ounce pita bread)
1 cup Cooked Wax Beans with
    1 teaspoon Reduced-Calorie
    Margarine
1½ cups Tossed Salad with
    2 teaspoons Olive Oil mixed with
    2 teaspoons Red Wine Vinegar
    plus Herbs
Diet Soda

SNACKS

Banana Yogurt (½ cup plain low-fat
    yogurt mixed with ½ medium
    banana, sliced, and ½ teaspoon
    honey)

Total Optional Calories: 35

Smoked Fish Salad ◑

A weekend luncheon is the perfect time to try this
attractive salad.

2 tablespoons plain low-fat yogurt
2 teaspoons reduced-calorie mayonnaise
½ teaspoon <u>each</u> granulated sugar and lemon juice
¼ teaspoon curry powder
¼ pound skinned and boned smoked herring or
    whitefish, flaked
½ medium cucumber, scored and thinly sliced
2 tablespoons chopped chives
Garnish: 6 radish roses

In small bowl combine yogurt, mayonnaise, sugar, lemon
juice, and curry powder; on each of 2 salad plates arrange
2 ounces fish and half of the cucumber slices. Spoon half of
the yogurt mixture over each portion, then sprinkle each
with 1 tablespoon chives and garnish with radish roses.

MAKES 2 SERVINGS

Each serving provides: 2 Protein Exchanges; ¾ Vegetable Exchange;
    ½ Fat Exchange; 15 Optional Calories
Per serving: 92 calories; 14 g protein; 2 g fat; 4 g carbohydrate;
    49 mg calcium; 3,585 mg sodium; 46 mg cholesterol

BREAKFAST

1 cup Strawberries, sliced
¼ cup Part-Skim Ricotta Cheese
2 Graham Crackers
1 cup Skim Milk

LUNCH

Roast Beef Sandwich (2 ounces sliced
  roast beef with ½ cup alfalfa
  sprouts, 4 lettuce leaves, and
  2 teaspoons mayonnaise on
  2 slices reduced-calorie wheat
  bread)
2 Pickle Spears
2 medium Apricots
Coffee, Tea, or Mineral Water

DINNER

¾ cup Chicken Bouillon
1 serving **Cobb Salad**
1½ ounces Breadsticks
½ cup Low-Calorie Cherry-Flavored
Gelatin topped with 2 tablespoons
Whipped Topping
4 fluid ounces Dry White Wine

SNACKS

2 medium Plums; 1 cup Skim Milk

Total Optional Calories: 195

Cobb Salad ◖

This delicious salad is traditional to sunny southern California. The original was created in the late 1930s by Robert Cobb, proprietor of Hollywood's famed Brown Derby Restaurant, and was prepared table-side.

2 cups chopped Boston lettuce leaves
1 cup chopped romaine lettuce leaves
1 medium tomato, cut into wedges
¼ avocado (about 2 ounces), pared and diced
2 ounces skinned and boned cooked turkey, chilled and diced
1 ounce blue cheese, crumbled
1 egg, hard-cooked and diced
1 tablespoon tarragon vinegar or red wine vinegar
2 teaspoons each olive oil and water
½ teaspoon each Dijon-style mustard and minced fresh parsley
Dash pepper

In chilled serving bowl combine Boston and romaine lettuce, tomato, avocado, turkey, cheese, and egg. In small bowl or measuring cup combine remaining ingredients, mixing well; pour over salad and toss well to coat.

MAKES 2 SERVINGS

Each serving provides: 2 Protein Exchanges; 4 Vegetable Exchanges;
   1 Fat Exchange; 50 Optional Calories
Per serving: 242 calories; 17 g protein; 17 g fat; 8 g carbohydrate;
   135 mg calcium; 305 mg sodium; 169 mg cholesterol

Variation: Cobb Salad with Bacon (Week 6) — Add 3 slices crisp bacon, crumbled, to avocado mixture. Increase Optional Calories to 120.

Per serving: 297 calories; 19 g protein; 21 g fat; 8 g carbohydrate;
   136 mg calcium; 456 mg sodium; 178 mg cholesterol

BREAKFAST

½ cup Fruit Salad
1 ounce Gouda Cheese
1 slice Rye Bread, toasted, with
  1 teaspoon Reduced-Calorie
  Margarine
1 cup Skim Milk

LUNCH

Chicken Salad (2 ounces diced
  chicken with ¼ cup chopped celery
  and 2 teaspoons mayonnaise)
½ cup Cauliflower Florets and
  6 Yellow Squash Sticks
Coffee, Tea, or Mineral Water

DINNER

1 cup Tomato Juice with Celery
  Stick
1 serving **California Party Sandwiches**
Macaroni Salad (½ cup chilled cooked
  small macaroni shells with 2½
  ounces diced boiled ham, ½ cup
  each broccoli florets and Chinese
  pea pods, 6 cherry tomatoes, and
  2 tablespoons reduced-calorie
  buttermilk dressing)
¼ small Cantaloupe
Coffee or Tea

SNACKS

Blueberry Delight (½ cup blueberries
  topped with 2 tablespoons sour
  cream and ½ teaspoon brown
  sugar); 1 cup Skim Milk

Total Optional Calories: 165

California Party Sandwiches ◑

⅛ very ripe avocado (about 1 ounce), pared
1 tablespoon plus 1½ teaspoons whipped cream cheese
1½ teaspoons _each_ sour cream and diced onion
½ small garlic clove
1 teaspoon lemon _or_ lime juice (no sugar added)
2 teaspoons _each_ margarine and Dijon-style mustard
8 slices thin-sliced party-style rye bread (¾ ounce per each 2 slices)
8 small Boston _or_ Bibb lettuce leaves
2 ounces shelled and deveined cooked medium shrimp, chilled
4 cherry tomatoes, cut into quarters
2 small pitted black olives, cut into quarters

In blender container combine avocado, cream cheese, sour cream, onion, garlic, and lemon (or lime) juice and process until pureed, scraping down sides of container as necessary.

In small bowl combine margarine and mustard. Spread ⅛ of mixture (about ½ teaspoon) on each slice of bread, then top each with 1 lettuce leaf and ¼ ounce shrimp. Using a pastry bag fitted with a star tip, or a spoon, top each sandwich with ⅛ of the avocado mixture (about 2 teaspoons). Decoratively arrange 2 tomato quarters and 1 olive quarter on each sandwich. Transfer sandwiches to serving platter; cover with plastic wrap and refrigerate for at least 30 minutes.

MAKES 4 SERVINGS, 2 OPEN-FACE SANDWICHES EACH

Each serving provides: ½ Protein Exchange; 1 Bread Exchange; ½ Vegetable Exchange; ½ Fat Exchange; 30 Optional Calories
Per serving: 122 calories; 6 g protein; 5 g fat; 13 g carbohydrate; 50 mg calcium; 267 mg sodium; 26 mg cholesterol

TIP: Sprinkle unused portion of avocado with lemon juice to help keep it from turning brown.

BREAKFAST

1 cup Low-Calorie Cranberry Juice
1 Poached Egg
1 slice White Bread, toasted, with
1 teaspoon Reduced-Calorie
Margarine
1 cup Skim Milk

LUNCH

Tuna-Stuffed Pocket (2 ounces tuna
with ¼ cup chopped onion,
2 lettuce leaves, 6 cucumber slices,
and 2 teaspoons mayonnaise in
1-ounce whole wheat pita bread)
6 Carrot Sticks and 3 Radishes
2 medium Plums
Coffee, Tea, or Mineral Water

DINNER

3 ounces Poached Chicken Breast
1 serving **Spaghetti Gratinée**
Parmesan Eggplant (1 cup cooked cubed
eggplant with ½ cup stewed
tomatoes and 1 teaspoon grated
Parmesan cheese)
1½ cups Mixed Green Salad with
1 tablespoon Reduced-Calorie
Italian Dressing
Mineral Water with Lime Twist

SNACKS

1 cup Cantaloupe Chunks; 1 serving
Reduced-Calorie Chocolate Dairy
Drink

Total Optional Calories: 150

Spaghetti Gratinée ◑

Reheat leftover spaghetti by steaming over boiling water or setting in strainer and immersing in boiling water for a few seconds.

2 teaspoons reduced-calorie margarine (tub)
2 ounces Gruyère or Swiss cheese, shredded, divided
¼ cup half-and-half (blend of milk and cream)
1 tablespoon sour cream
½ garlic clove, minced
¼ teaspoon salt
Dash each ground nutmeg and white pepper
1 cup cooked spaghetti (hot)

Preheat oven to 400°F. Spread margarine over bottom and sides of 1-quart casserole; set aside.

In medium bowl combine 1 ounce cheese with the half-and-half, sour cream, garlic, salt, nutmeg, and pepper; add spaghetti and toss to combine. Transfer to prepared casserole, sprinkle with remaining ounce cheese, and bake until top is golden, about 10 minutes.

MAKES 2 SERVINGS

Each serving provides: 1 Protein Exchange; 1 Bread Exchange;
½ Fat Exchange; 65 Optional Calories
Per serving with Gruyère cheese: 268 calories; 12 g protein; 16 g fat;
18 g carbohydrate; 335 mg calcium; 422 mg sodium; 45 mg cholesterol
With Swiss cheese: 257 calories; 12 g protein; 15 g fat; 19 g carbohydrate;
321 mg calcium; 401 mg sodium; 40 mg cholesterol

BREAKFAST

1 cup Strawberries, sliced
¾ ounce Cold Cereal
¾ cup Skim Milk
Coffee or Tea

LUNCH

Turkey-Spinach Salad (2 ounces
    sliced turkey with 1 cup torn
    spinach, ½ cup *each* sliced
    mushrooms and carrot, and
    1 tablespoon blue cheese dressing)
6 *each* Red and Green Bell Pepper
    Strips
1 small Orange
Coffee, Tea, or Mineral Water

DINNER

¾ cup Chicken Bouillon
3 ounces Poached Salmon Steak
    with Lime Wedges
½ cup *each* Cooked Pearl Onions
    and Shredded Red Cabbage
1 serving **Creamy Minted Green Bean
    Salad**
1-ounce slice French Bread with
    1 teaspoon Margarine
½ cup Skim Milk
Coffee or Tea

SNACKS

½ medium Banana; ½ cup Skim Milk

Total Optional Calories: 15

Creamy Minted Green Bean Salad ◑◐

May be served at room temperature or chilled.

¼ cup plain low-fat yogurt
1 tablespoon chopped fresh mint
1½ teaspoons freshly squeezed lime juice*
½ teaspoon granulated sugar
½ small garlic clove, minced
Dash white pepper
2 cups whole green beans, cooked
6 cherry tomatoes, cut into quarters
1 tablespoon minced scallion (green onion)

In small mixing bowl combine yogurt, mint, lime juice, sugar, garlic, and pepper, stirring until thoroughly blended.

In salad bowl combine green beans, tomatoes, and scallions; add yogurt mixture and toss to coat.

MAKES 2 SERVINGS

Each serving provides: 2½ Vegetable Exchanges; ¼ Milk Exchange;
    5 Optional Calories
Per serving: 65 calories; 4 g protein; 1 g fat; 13 g carbohydrate;
    99 mg calcium; 29 mg sodium; 2 mg cholesterol

*If fresh limes are not available, bottled lime juice (no sugar added)
 may be used.

BREAKFAST

1 medium Kiwi Fruit, sliced
⅓ cup Cottage Cheese
½ Whole Wheat English Muffin, toasted, with 1 teaspoon Margarine
1 cup Skim Milk

LUNCH

Salmon Salad (2 ounces salmon with ¼ cup chopped onion and 2 teaspoons reduced-calorie mayonnaise)
2 slices Cocktail Rye Bread
6 *each* Cherry Tomatoes and Celery Sticks
2 medium Apricots
Coffee, Tea, or Mineral Water

DINNER

3 ounces Broiled Veal Patty
½ cup Cooked Noodles sprinkled with 1 teaspoon Poppy Seed
6 Cooked Broccoli Spears
1 serving **Roasted Pepper, Nut, 'n' Olive Salad**
10 large Cherries
Tea with Lemon

SNACKS

1 serving Reduced-Calorie Chocolate Dairy Drink; 2 cups Plain Popcorn

Total Optional Calories: 65

Roasted Pepper, Nut, 'n' Olive Salad

3 medium red bell peppers
2 teaspoons olive oil
½ ounce pignolias (pine nuts)
½ to 1 garlic clove, thinly sliced
2 tablespoons fresh basil
1 tablespoon plus 2 teaspoons freshly squeezed lime juice*
2 large pitted black olives, sliced
½ teaspoon salt
Dash pepper

Preheat broiler. On baking sheet lined with heavy-duty foil broil peppers 3 inches from heat source, turning frequently, until charred on all sides; let stand until cool enough to handle, 15 to 20 minutes.

Fit strainer into medium bowl (not aluminum†); peel peppers over strainer, removing and discarding stem ends and seeds and allowing juice from peppers to drip into bowl. Cut peppers into thin strips and add to bowl with juice; set aside.

In small nonstick skillet heat oil over medium heat; add pignolias and garlic and sauté, stirring occasionally, until lightly browned (be careful not to burn). Add pignolia mixture and remaining ingredients to peppers and stir to combine. Cover bowl with plastic wrap and refrigerate overnight to allow flavors to blend.

MAKES 2 SERVINGS, ABOUT ¾ CUP EACH

Each serving provides: 3 Vegetable Exchanges; 1 Fat Exchange; 45 Optional Calories
Per serving: 119 calories; 3 g protein; 9 g fat; 9 g carbohydrate; 43 mg calcium; 582 mg sodium; 0 mg cholesterol

* If fresh limes are not available, bottled lime juice (no sugar added) may be used.
† It's best to marinate in glass or stainless-steel containers; acidic ingredients such as lime juice may react with aluminum, causing color and flavor changes in foods.

BREAKFAST

½ cup Grapefruit Sections
1 Sunny-Side-Up Egg
1 slice Raisin Bread, toasted, with
    1 teaspoon Reduced-Calorie
    Margarine
½ cup Skim Milk
Coffee or Tea

LUNCH

Chicken-Vegetable Salad (2 ounces
    diced chicken with ½ cup broccoli
    florets, ¼ cup chopped celery,
    2 tablespoons shredded carrot, and
    1 tablespoon reduced-calorie
    creamy bacon dressing)
6 Melba Rounds
1 medium Peach
Coffee, Tea, or Mineral Water

DINNER

3 ounces Baked Flounder Fillet with
    Lemon Wedge
½ cup Cooked Sliced Zucchini with
    2 teaspoons Reduced-Calorie
    Margarine
1 serving **Fiesta Pasta Salad**
2 x 3-inch wedge Watermelon
Iced Tea

SNACKS

½ cup Reduced-Calorie Butterscotch
    Pudding; ½ cup Skim Milk

Total Optional Calories: 30

Fiesta Pasta Salad ⊙ ◑

1 cup cooked small macaroni shells, chilled
½ cup each diced red or green bell pepper and thinly
    sliced scallions (green onions) or diced red onion
1 tablespoon each mayonnaise and minced fresh
    cilantro (Chinese parsley) or Italian (flat-leaf) parsley
1½ teaspoons seeded and minced jalapeño pepper
½ teaspoon each salt and red wine vinegar
Dash to ⅛ teaspoon chili powder
Garnish: cilantro (Chinese parsley) or Italian (flat-leaf)
    parsley sprig

In medium bowl combine all ingredients except garnish;
cover with plastic wrap and refrigerate until chilled. Toss
again just before serving and garnish with parsley.

MAKES 2 SERVINGS

Each serving provides: 1 Bread Exchange; 1 Vegetable Exchange;
    1½ Fat Exchanges
Per serving with scallions: 141 calories; 3 g protein; 6 g fat;
    19 g carbohydrate; 30 mg calcium; 622 mg sodium; 4 mg cholesterol
With red onion: 148 calories; 3 g protein; 6 g fat; 21 g carbohydrate;
    25 mg calcium; 621 mg sodium; 4 mg cholesterol

BREAKFAST

1 cup Strawberries, sliced
¾ ounce Cold Cereal
1 cup Skim Milk
Coffee or Tea

LUNCH

Turkey-Stuffed Pita (2 ounces sliced
    turkey with 4 lettuce leaves,
    2 green bell pepper rings, 2 red
    onion slices, and 1 tablespoon
    Russian dressing in 1-ounce whole
    wheat pita bread)
6 *each* Carrot and Celery Sticks
Coffee, Tea, or Mineral Water

DINNER

Shrimp Salad Platter (4 ounces
    poached shrimp with 1 cup broccoli
    florets, 8 tomato wedges, and
    4 radish roses on 8 Boston lettuce
    leaves) with 2 teaspoons **Cilantro
    Mayonnaise**
1 cup Cantaloupe Balls with Mint
    Sprig
Sparkling Mineral Water with Lemon
    Twist

SNACKS

½ medium Banana; 1 serving
    Reduced-Calorie Chocolate Dairy
    Drink

Total Optional Calories: 40

Cilantro Mayonnaise ◖◑

Wonderful on broiled fish.

½ **cup firmly packed fresh cilantro (Chinese parsley)**
1 **egg**
½ **small jalapeño pepper, seeded and chopped**
1 **tablespoon** <u>each</u> **lemon** <u>or</u> **lime juice (no sugar
    added) and red wine vinegar**
1 **teaspoon salt**
1 **small garlic clove**
1 **cup olive** <u>or</u> **vegetable oil**

In blender container combine all ingredients except oil
and process until smooth, scraping down sides of
container as necessary. Remove center of blender cover
and, with motor running at high speed, slowly add oil in a
thin stream. When oil is well combined, turn off motor.
Scrape down sides of container; process until blended,
about ½ second. Transfer to resealable plastic container,
cover, and refrigerate until ready to use.

YIELDS ABOUT 1 CUP

Each 1-teaspoon serving provides: 1 Fat Exchange
Per serving: 42 calories; 0.1 g protein; 5 g fat; 0.1 g carbohydrate;
    2 mg calcium; 49 mg sodium; 6 mg cholesterol

BREAKFAST

1 serving **Sweet Semolina and Peaches**
Coffee or Tea

LUNCH

Peanut Butter and Jelly Sandwich
(2 tablespoons peanut butter with
1 tablespoon reduced-calorie
strawberry spread on 2 slices
raisin bread)
1 cup Skim Milk

DINNER

3 ounces Grilled Chicken
Lentil-Onion Combo (2 ounces
cooked lentils with ¼ cup diced
onion and 1 tablespoon Italian
dressing)
½ cup Cooked Sliced Zucchini
1½ cups Mixed Green Salad with
1½ teaspoons Russian Dressing
mixed with 2 tablespoons Plain
Low-Fat Yogurt and ¼ teaspoon
Mustard
½ medium Grapefruit
Diet Soda

SNACKS

1 small Pear; ½ cup Skim Milk

Total Optional Calories: 175

Sweet Semolina and Peaches ⓒ ◐

Try this peach of a breakfast idea on a leisurely Saturday or Sunday morning.

½ cup whole milk
¾ ounce uncooked couscous (dry precooked semolina)
1 medium peach (about ¼ pound), blanched, peeled, pitted, and sliced or ½ cup canned peach slices (no sugar added)
1 teaspoon honey or firmly packed brown sugar or maple syrup

In small saucepan heat milk until hot (do not boil); add couscous and stir to combine. Cover and let stand for 5 minutes. Transfer mixture to serving bowl; stir in peach slices and top with honey (or brown sugar or maple syrup).

MAKES I SERVING, ABOUT I CUP

Each serving provides: 1 Bread Exchange; 1 Fruit Exchange;
½ Milk Exchange; 50 Optional Calories
Per serving: 209 calories; 7 g protein; 4 g fat; 33 g carbohydrate;
150 mg calcium; 60 mg sodium; 17 mg cholesterol

Variation: Buttered Semolina (Week 5) — Omit peach slices and stir 1 teaspoon sweet butter into couscous mixture. Omit Fruit Exchange from Exchange Information and increase Optional Calories to 85.

Per serving: 206 calories; 7 g protein; 8 g fat; 23 g carbohydrate;
147 mg calcium; 61 mg sodium; 27 mg cholesterol

BREAKFAST

½ cup Orange Juice
¾ ounce Cold Cereal
1 cup Skim Milk
Coffee or Tea

LUNCH

Tuna Salad in a Pita (2 ounces tuna
    with ¼ cup *each* alfalfa sprouts and
    chopped celery, 2 tablespoons
    shredded carrot, and 2 teaspoons
    reduced-calorie mayonnaise in
    1-ounce pita bread)
2 medium Apricots
Coffee, Tea, or Mineral Water

DINNER

4 ounces Grilled Marinated Steak
    (marinated in 2 tablespoons
    teriyaki sauce, minced garlic, and
    minced pared ginger root)
3 ounces Baked Potato sprinkled
    with 1 teaspoon Imitation Bacon
    Bits
½ cup Cooked Sliced Beets
Romaine Salad (1½ cups torn
    romaine lettuce with 6 cherry
    tomatoes and 1 tablespoon
    Russian dressing)
1 serving **Anniversary Sundae
    Spectacular**
Coffee or Tea

SNACKS

Blueberry Yogurt (½ cup plain low-fat
    yogurt mixed with ½ cup
    blueberries)

Total Optional Calories: 270

Anniversary Sundae Spectacular ◖

A truly luxurious dessert for that extra-special occasion.

2 ounces white chocolate
**1 tablespoon <u>each</u> chocolate-flavored liqueur and
    whipping cream**
⅛ teaspoon vanilla extract
2 cups strawberry, vanilla, <u>or</u> chocolate ice milk
1 cup strawberries, cut into halves
½ ounce chopped macadamia nuts, lightly toasted

In double boiler combine white chocolate, liqueur, cream,
and vanilla and cook over hot (<u>not boiling</u>) water, stirring
frequently, until chocolate is melted and mixture is smooth
and thick, 3 to 4 minutes;* keep warm.

Into each of 4 dessert dishes scoop ½ cup ice milk, then
top each portion with ¼ of the chocolate mixture and
surround each scoop with ¼ of the strawberry halves;
sprinkle each sundae with ¼ of the nuts and serve
immediately.

MAKES 4 SERVINGS

Each serving provides: 260 Optional Calories
Per serving: 245 calories; 4 g protein; 11 g fat; 29 g carbohydrate;
    98 mg calcium; 66 mg sodium; 17 mg cholesterol

Variation: Raspberry-Chocolate-Nut Sundae (Week 8) —
Substitute 1 cup raspberries for the strawberries. Add ½ Fruit
Exchange to Exchange Information and reduce Optional
Calories to 250.

Per serving: 249 calories; 4 g protein; 11 g fat; 30 g carbohydrate;
    99 mg calcium; 65 mg sodium; 17 mg cholesterol

*When melting chocolate, it should not come in contact with water or
    steam; moisture will cause it to harden.

Puddin' Parfait ◉ ◑

2 cups skim milk
1 envelope (four ½-cup servings) reduced-calorie vanilla
    pudding mix
2 cups strawberries, cut into quarters
2 tablespoons reduced-calorie raspberry or strawberry
    spread (16 calories per 2 teaspoons)

Using the skim milk, prepare pudding according to
package directions but do not chill. In 1-quart nonstick
saucepan combine strawberries and spread and cook
over medium heat, stirring frequently, until spread is
melted and mixture is warm, 3 to 4 minutes.

Into each of four 8-ounce parfait glasses spoon ⅛ of
the pudding, then top each with ⅛ of the strawberry
mixture; repeat layers with remaining pudding and
strawberry mixture. Refrigerate until pudding is set, about
15 minutes.

MAKES 4 SERVINGS, 1 PARFAIT EACH

Each serving provides: ½ Fruit Exchange; 1 Milk Exchange; 12 Optional
    Calories
Per serving: 117 calories; 6 g protein; 1 g fat; 24 g carbohydrate;
    161 mg calcium; 69 mg sodium; 2 mg cholesterol

Variations: Cream-Topped Parfait (Week 2)—Top each
parfait with 2 tablespoons thawed frozen dairy whipped
topping. Increase Optional Calories to 35.

Per serving: 141 calories; 6 g protein; 3 g fat; 26 g carbohydrate;
    161 mg calcium; 79 mg sodium; 2 mg cholesterol

Parfait with "Crème Fraiche" (Week 4)— In small bowl
combine 3 tablespoons sour cream and 3 tablespoons
thawed frozen dairy whipped topping; top each parfait
with ¼ of mixture. Increase Optional Calories to 45.

Per serving: 150 calories; 6 g protein; 4 g fat; 25 g carbohydrate;
    174 mg calcium; 79 mg sodium; 7 mg cholesterol

BREAKFAST

½ cup Orange Sections
"Bacon" Omelet (1-egg omelet with
    1 teaspoon imitation bacon bits)
½ English Muffin, toasted, with
    1 teaspoon Reduced-Calorie
    Strawberry Spread
1 cup Skim Milk

LUNCH

Tuna Sandwich (2 ounces tuna with
    4 lettuce leaves, 4 tomato slices,
    and 2 teaspoons reduced-calorie
    mayonnaise on 2 slices reduced-
    calorie wheat bread)
6 Carrot Sticks and ½ cup
    Cauliflower Florets
1 medium Peach
Coffee, Tea, or Mineral Water

DINNER

3 ounces Broiled Chicken
1 cup Cooked French-Style Green
    Beans with ¼ cup Cooked Sliced
    Mushrooms
½ cup Cooked Sliced Beets
Lettuce Wedge with 1 tablespoon
    Creamy Italian Dressing
1 cup Strawberries topped with
    ¼ cup Plain Low-Fat Yogurt
Iced Tea

SNACKS

2 Rice Cakes; 1 serving **Chocolate
    Egg Cream**

Total Optional Calories: 50

Chocolate Egg Cream

A New York tradition.

**1 cup whole milk
1 can (12 fluid ounces) diet chocolate soda (4 calories
    per 12 fluid ounces), chilled**

Into each of two 12-ounce glasses pour ½ cup milk; add
6 fluid ounces of chocolate soda to each glass and stir
to combine. Place a straw into each glass and serve
immediately.

MAKES 2 SERVINGS

Each serving provides: ½ Milk Exchange; 30 Optional Calories
Per serving: 76 calories; 4 g protein; 4 g fat; 6 g carbohydrate;
    145 mg calcium; 95 mg sodium; 17 mg cholesterol

July

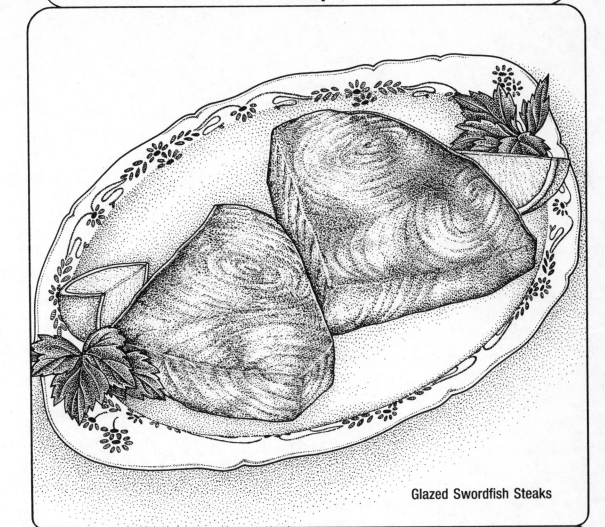

Glazed Swordfish Steaks

JULY'S BEST BUYS FOR FRUITS AND VEGETABLES

alfalfa sprouts	carrots	limes	plums
apricots	celery	mangoes	potatoes
arugula	cherries	mushrooms	radishes
bananas	Chinese pea pods	nectarines	raspberries
bean sprouts	corn on the cob	new potatoes	scallions (green onions)
beets	cucumbers	okra	strawberries
bell peppers	eggplants	onions	summer squash
blackberries	green beans	papayas	tomatoes
blueberries	kiwi fruit	peaches	watermelon
cantaloupes	lemons	pineapples	zucchini

BREAKFAST

1 cup Strawberries
1 Sunny-Side-Up Egg
1 slice Whole Wheat Bread, toasted, with 1 teaspoon Margarine
½ cup Skim Milk
Coffee or Tea

LUNCH

Salmon Sandwich (2 ounces salmon with 2 tomato slices, ¼ cup shredded lettuce, and 2 teaspoons reduced-calorie mayonnaise on 2 slices reduced-calorie rye bread)
¾ cup Broccoli Florets and 6 Radishes
1 medium Plum
Coffee, Tea, or Mineral Water

DINNER

1 serving **Papaya Delight**
3 ounces Roast Beef
½ cup Cooked Rice with 1 teaspoon Margarine
½ cup *each* Cooked Shredded Zucchini, Turnip, and Carrot
Raspberries 'n' Yogurt (½ cup raspberries topped with ¼ cup plain low-fat yogurt)
Coffee or Tea

SNACKS

1 serving Reduced-Calorie Chocolate Dairy Drink; 10 large Cherries

Total Optional Calories: 70

Papaya Delight ◑

1 cup shredded lettuce
½ medium papaya (about ½ pound), pared, seeded, and thinly sliced
½ ounce pignolias (pine nuts), toasted
1 tablespoon shredded coconut, toasted
2 tablespoons <u>each</u> lime juice (no sugar added) and lemon juice
1½ teaspoons honey

Line serving platter with lettuce and top with papaya; sprinkle with pignolias and coconut. In small bowl combine juices and honey; drizzle over salad.

MAKES 2 SERVINGS

Each serving provides: 1 Vegetable Exchange; ½ Fruit Exchange; 70 Optional Calories
Per serving: 178 calories; 3 g protein; 11 g fat; 22 g carbohydrate; 47 mg calcium; 16 mg sodium; 0 mg cholesterol

BREAKFAST

½ cup Low-Calorie Cranberry Juice
1 serving **Raspberry Crème Omelet**
½ English Muffin, toasted, with
    1 teaspoon Reduced-Calorie
    Margarine
1 cup Skim Milk

LUNCH

Tuna in a Pita (2 ounces tuna with
    1 tablespoon *each* diced onion and
    celery and 2 teaspoons reduced-
    calorie mayonnaise in 1-ounce
    whole wheat pita bread)
6 *each* Carrot and Celery Sticks
Coffee, Tea, or Mineral Water

DINNER

3 ounces Broiled Veal Chop
Spaghetti in Red Sauce (½ cup
    cooked spaghetti with ¼ cup
    tomato sauce and 1 teaspoon *each*
    Italian seasoning and grated
    Parmesan cheese)
½ cup *each* Cooked Diced Green Bell
    Pepper and Sliced Mushrooms
1½ cups Tossed Salad with
    1½ teaspoons Italian Dressing
    mixed with 2 teaspoons Red Wine
    Vinegar
½ cup Fruit Salad
Espresso

SNACKS

¼ small Cantaloupe; 1 serving
    Reduced-Calorie Vanilla Dairy
    Drink

Total Optional Calories: 105

Raspberry Crème Omelet

A colorful summertime weekend breakfast.

½ cup raspberries
1 teaspoon granulated sugar
¼ cup whipped cream cheese
1 tablespoon skim milk
1 teaspoon firmly packed light brown sugar
¾ teaspoon vanilla extract, divided
2 eggs, separated (at room temperature)
½ teaspoon confectioners' sugar
2 teaspoons reduced-calorie margarine (tub)
Garnish: mint sprig

In small bowl combine raspberries and granulated sugar, mixing well; let stand for 20 minutes.

Preheat oven to 325°F. In small mixing bowl combine cream cheese, milk, brown sugar, and ½ teaspoon vanilla and, using a wire whisk, beat until thoroughly combined; set aside.

In medium mixing bowl, using electric mixer at medium speed, beat egg yolks until thick and lemon-colored; set aside. In small mixing bowl, using clean beaters, beat egg whites until foamy; add confectioners' sugar and remaining ¼ teaspoon vanilla and continue beating until stiff peaks form. Fold beaten whites into yolks.

In 10-inch nonstick skillet that has an oven-safe or removable handle heat margarine over medium heat until bubbly and hot; tilt skillet to coat entire bottom with melted margarine. Pour in egg mixture and spread evenly over bottom of skillet; cook until underside is golden brown and top is firm, about 3 minutes. Spread cream cheese mixture over omelet; transfer skillet to oven and bake in middle of center rack for 5 to 6 minutes (until a knife, inserted in center, comes out clean). Spoon half of the raspberry mixture over half of the omelet. Using a spatula, loosen omelet around edges and, using a pancake turner, fold omelet in half; carefully slide onto warmed platter. Spoon remaining raspberry mixture over omelet and serve immediately, garnished with mint sprig.

MAKES 2 SERVINGS

Each serving provides: 1 Protein Exchange; ½ Fat Exchange;
    ½ Fruit Exchange; 95 Optional Calories
Per serving: 202 calories; 8 g protein; 14 g fat; 11 g carbohydrate;
    66 mg calcium; 184 mg sodium; 293 mg cholesterol

BRUNCH

Orange Fizz (½ cup *each* orange juice
  and club soda)
1 serving **Bacon Quiche Sans Crust**
1-ounce Roll
1½ cups Mixed Green Salad with
  1½ teaspoons Buttermilk Dressing
  mixed with 2 tablespoons Plain
  Low-Fat Yogurt and ¼ teaspoon
  Mustard
½ cup Blueberries
Coffee or Tea

DINNER

4 ounces Grilled Chicken Breast
  with 1 tablespoon Barbeque Sauce
1 small Ear Corn, cooked, with
  1 teaspoon Margarine
½ cup Cooked Cut Green Beans
Beet Salad (½ cup chilled sliced
  cooked beets with 1½ teaspoons
  French dressing on 2 lettuce
  leaves)
½ cup Reduced-Calorie Butterscotch
  Pudding
Iced Tea with Lemon Twist

SNACKS

2 cups Plain Popcorn; Strawberries
  'n' Yogurt (1 cup strawberries,
  sliced, topped with ¼ cup plain
  low-fat yogurt)

Total Optional Calories: 115

Bacon Quiche Sans Crust

This crustless treat, combined with a tossed green salad, is the perfect dish for Sunday brunch.

6 eggs
1 cup low-fat milk (2% milk fat)
6 ounces Swiss <u>or</u> Gruyère cheese, shredded
8 slices crisp bacon, crumbled
⅛ teaspoon ground nutmeg
Dash <u>each</u> salt and white pepper

Preheat oven to 375°F. Spray 9- or 10-inch quiche dish or pie pan with nonstick cooking spray; set aside.

  In medium mixing bowl, using a fork, beat together eggs and milk until blended; stir in remaining ingredients. Pour mixture into prepared dish (or pan) and bake in middle of center oven rack for 40 to 45 minutes (until a knife, inserted in center, comes out clean). Remove from oven and let stand for 5 minutes before cutting.

MAKES 4 SERVINGS

Each serving provides: 3 Protein Exchanges; ¼ Milk Exchange;
    100 Optional Calories
Per serving with Swiss cheese: 382 calories; 27 g protein; 27 g fat;
    5 g carbohydrate; 527 mg calcium; 480 mg sodium; 466 mg cholesterol
With Gruyère cheese: 398 calories; 28 g protein; 30 g fat;
    4 g carbohydrate; 548 mg calcium; 512 mg sodium; 473 mg cholesterol

BREAKFAST

½ cup Grapefruit Sections
⅓ cup Cottage Cheese
½ small Bagel, toasted
1 cup Skim Milk

LUNCH

Roast Beef Sandwich (2 ounces
    sliced roast beef with 2 lettuce
    leaves and 1 teaspoon *each*
    mustard and mayonnaise on
    2 slices reduced-calorie rye bread)
3 Dill Pickle Spears and 6 Carrot
    Sticks
1 medium Peach
Coffee, Tea, or Mineral Water

DINNER

1 serving **Cheese-Topped Shrimp**
1 cup Cooked Cauliflower Florets
½ cup Cooked Chinese Pea Pods
Lettuce and Tomato Salad (1 wedge
    iceberg lettuce with 2 tomato
    slices and 1 tablespoon Thousand
    Island dressing)
½ cup *each* Honeydew Melon and
    Cantaloupe Balls sprinkled with
    1 teaspoon Shredded Coconut
Coffee or Tea

SNACKS

½ cup Reduced-Calorie Chocolate
    Pudding; 2 Honey Graham
    Crackers

Total Optional Calories: 35

Cheese-Topped Shrimp

2 quarts water
2 dozen large (26–30s*) shrimp (about 1 pound)
3 tablespoons whipped cream cheese
1 tablespoon minced fresh cilantro (Chinese parsley)
½ teaspoon seeded and minced jalapeño pepper
1 garlic clove, minced

In 4-quart saucepan bring 2 quarts water to a boil; add shrimp, stir, and allow water to return to boil. Cook until shrimp turn pink, 3 to 5 minutes. Drain and chill.

Shell and devein shrimp, leaving last segment and tail in place. In small bowl combine cream cheese, cilantro, jalapeño pepper, and garlic, mixing thoroughly. Spoon an equal amount of cheese mixture (about ¼ teaspoon) into curl of each shrimp; insert a toothpick through tail of shrimp into base, securing cheese mixture. Arrange shrimp on serving platter and serve immediately or cover with plastic wrap and refrigerate until ready to serve.

MAKES 4 SERVINGS, 6 SHRIMP EACH

Each serving provides: 2 Protein Exchanges; 25 Optional Calories
Per serving: 91 calories; 14 g protein; 3 g fat; 1 g carbohydrate;
    73 mg calcium; 111 mg sodium; 92 mg cholesterol

*This indicates the approximate number of shrimp per pound before cooking, shelling, and deveining. Two dozen shrimp will yield about ½ pound cooked seafood.

Spaghetti with Garlic-Hazelnut Sauce

Peppers 'n' Potatoes

Flank Steak with Whiskey Sauce

Shrimp and Vegetable Pita Pizza

Crab-Filled Pods
Cheese 'n' Nut-Pepper Slices
Sushi for Cowards
California Party Sandwiches

Hot Buttered Rum
Lemon-Cream Cheese Cookies

BREAKFAST

1 cup Strawberries
1 Soft-Cooked Egg
1 slice Whole Wheat Bread, toasted
1 cup Skim Milk

LUNCH

Chicken in a Pita (2 ounces sliced
chicken with 2 tomato slices,
2 lettuce leaves, and 2 teaspoons
mayonnaise in 1-ounce pita bread)
6 *each* Zucchini and Yellow Squash
Sticks
½ medium Banana
Coffee, Tea, or Mineral Water

DINNER

1 serving **Glazed Swordfish Steaks**
½ cup *each* Cooked Chopped
Spinach and Sliced Carrot
1½ cups Mixed Green Salad with
1½ teaspoons French Dressing
mixed with 2 teaspoons Lemon
Juice and ¼ teaspoon Mustard
2 x 3-inch wedge Watermelon
Coffee or Tea

SNACKS

1 serving Reduced-Calorie Vanilla
Dairy Drink; ½ cup Low-Calorie
Lemon-Flavored Gelatin

Total Optional Calories: 25

Glazed Swordfish Steaks

2 boneless swordfish steaks (¼ pound each)
2 tablespoons <u>each</u> orange juice (no sugar added) and soy sauce*
1 tablespoon lemon juice
1½ teaspoons ketchup
½ teaspoon minced pared ginger root
½ small garlic clove, minced
¼ teaspoon cornstarch
2 lemon wedges

Set fish in single layer in shallow container (not aluminum†); set aside. In 1-cup liquid measure or small bowl combine orange juice, soy sauce, lemon juice, ketchup, ginger root, and garlic; pour over fish. Cover with plastic wrap and refrigerate for at least 30 minutes

Remove swordfish from marinade and set aside. Strain marinade into a small saucepan; discard ginger and garlic. Add cornstarch to marinade and stir to dissolve; cook over medium heat, stirring frequently, until mixture is smooth and thickened, 5 to 7 minutes.

Preheat grill or broiler. Set fish on grill or on rack in broiling pan; brush with half of the marinade and grill over hot coals (or broil) for 3 to 4 minutes. Carefully turn fish over; brush with remaining marinade and cook until fish flakes easily when tested with a fork and is lightly browned, 3 to 4 minutes longer. Serve each portion with a lemon wedge.

MAKES 2 SERVINGS

Each serving provides: 3 Protein Exchanges; 15 Optional Calories
Per serving: 161 calories; 23 g protein; 5 g fat; 5 g carbohydrate;
41 mg calcium; 1,435 mg sodium; 62 mg cholesterol

* Reduced-sodium soy sauce may be substituted. Reduce calories to 159, calcium to 26 mg, and sodium to 714 mg.
† It's best to marinate in glass or stainless-steel containers; acidic ingredients such as lemon juice may react with aluminum, causing color and flavor changes in foods.

BREAKFAST

1 medium Peach, sliced
¾ ounce Cold Cereal
1 cup Skim Milk
Coffee or Tea

LUNCH

Roast Beef Sandwich (2 ounces sliced
    roast beef with 3 *each* tomato and
    cucumber slices and 1 tablespoon
    reduced-calorie mayonnaise on
    2 slices reduced-calorie rye bread)
6 *each* Celery Sticks and Red Bell
    Pepper Strips
Coffee, Tea, or Mineral Water

DINNER

1 serving **Greek Shrimp and Feta Sauté**
¾ cup *each* Cooked Cut Green Beans
    and Cauliflower Florets
Spinach Salad (1¼ cups torn
    spinach with ¼ cup shredded
    carrot, 2 red onion rings, and
    1½ teaspoons Italian dressing
    mixed with 2 teaspoons red wine
    vinegar)
¼ small Cantaloupe
Coffee or Tea

SNACKS

Strawberry Yogurt (½ cup plain
    low-fat yogurt mixed with 1 cup
    strawberries, sliced, and
    1 teaspoon honey)

Total Optional Calories: 20

Greek Shrimp and Feta Sauté

2 teaspoons reduced-calorie margarine (tub), divided
¼ cup chopped scallions (green onions)
2 garlic cloves, minced
1 cup canned Italian tomatoes (with liquid); drain, seed, and dice tomatoes, reserving liquid
1 tablespoon minced fresh parsley
¼ teaspoon oregano leaves
Dash pepper
½ pound shelled and deveined large shrimp
2 ounces feta cheese, crumbled, divided

In 1-quart saucepan heat 1 teaspoon margarine over medium-high heat until bubbly and hot; add scallions and garlic and sauté until softened, about 1 minute. Add tomatoes, reserved liquid, parsley, and seasonings; mix well. Reduce heat to low and let simmer, stirring occasionally, until flavors blend, about 15 minutes. Set aside.

In 10-inch nonstick skillet heat remaining teaspoon margarine over high heat until bubbly and hot; add shrimp and cook, stirring frequently, until shrimp just turn pink, 2 to 3 minutes. Add tomato mixture and 1 ounce feta cheese; stir to combine and bring to a boil. Reduce heat to low and let simmer until cheese is melted and shrimp are cooked, 1 to 2 minutes (<u>do not overcook</u>). Transfer to serving platter and sprinkle with remaining ounce feta cheese.

MAKES 2 SERVINGS

Each serving provides: 4 Protein Exchanges; 1¼ Vegetable Exchanges; ½ Fat Exchange
Per serving: 241 calories; 29 g protein; 10 g fat; 8 g carbohydrate; 254 mg calcium; 791 mg sodium; 186 mg cholesterol

Variation: Greek Shrimp and Olive Sauté (Week 5) — Add 2 tablespoons dry sherry to sautéed scallions along with tomatoes. Add 8 Calamata or Gaeta olives to sautéed shrimp along with tomato mixture and 1 ounce feta cheese; proceed as directed. Add 35 Optional Calories to Exchange Information.

Per serving: 332 calories; 32 g protein; 17 g fat; 11 g carbohydrate; 333 mg calcium; 1,265 mg sodium; 199 mg cholesterol

BREAKFAST

½ cup Blueberries
1 Poached Egg
½ English Muffin, toasted, with
    1 teaspoon Margarine
1 cup Skim Milk

LUNCH

Tuna Salad in a Pita (2 ounces tuna
    with 2 tablespoons chopped celery
    and 2 teaspoons reduced-calorie
    mayonnaise in 1-ounce whole
    wheat pita bread)
6 *each* Carrot Sticks and Zucchini
    Spears
1 small Orange
Coffee, Tea, or Mineral Water

DINNER

1 serving **Chicken 'n' Broccoli-Topped
    Orzo**
1 cup Cooked Wax Beans
Cabbage-Scallion Salad (1 cup torn
    lettuce with ½ cup shredded red
    cabbage, 2 tablespoons sliced
    scallion, and 1 tablespoon
    reduced-calorie French dressing)
Gelatin 'n' Yogurt (½ cup low-calorie
    cherry-flavored gelatin topped
    with ¼ cup plain low-fat yogurt)
Coffee or Tea

SNACKS

1 small Apple; ½ cup Skim Milk

Total Optional Calories: 60

Chicken 'n' Broccoli-Topped Orzo ◑

2 teaspoons olive <u>or</u> vegetable oil
1 garlic clove, minced
½ pound chicken cutlets, cut into 1-inch cubes
1 cup broccoli florets, blanched
¼ cup canned ready-to-serve chicken broth
¼ teaspoon salt
⅛ teaspoon pepper
1½ ounces uncooked orzo (rice-shaped macaroni),
    cooked according to package directions and drained
1 tablespoon grated Parmesan cheese

In 10-inch skillet or a wok heat oil over high heat; add
garlic and sauté for 1 minute. Add chicken and cook,
stirring quickly and frequently, until chicken is no longer
pink, about 5 minutes. Add broccoli, broth, salt, and
pepper and let cook until chicken is tender and mixture is
heated through, 3 to 5 minutes. Serve over hot orzo and
sprinkle with Parmesan cheese.

MAKES 2 SERVINGS

Each serving provides: 3 Protein Exchanges; 1 Bread Exchange;
   1 Vegetable Exchange; 1 Fat Exchange; 20 Optional Calories
Per serving: 280 calories; 32 g protein; 7 g fat; 20 g carbohydrate;
   87 mg calcium; 532 mg sodium; 68 mg cholesterol

Seasoned Skillet Burgers ◖

15 ounces ground veal
1 egg
**2 tablespoons <u>each</u> drained capers, chopped, and
   minced onion <u>or</u> scallion (green onion)**
**1 tablespoon <u>each</u> chopped fresh Italian (flat-leaf)
   parsley and Worcestershire sauce**
½ teaspoon <u>each</u> salt and ground sage
Dash pepper
2 teaspoons <u>each</u> olive <u>or</u> vegetable oil and margarine
1 cup quartered mushrooms
**2 tablespoons <u>each</u> minced shallots and dry white table
   wine**

In medium mixing bowl combine veal, egg, capers, onion
(or scallion), parsley, Worcestershire sauce, and seasonings.
Shape into 4 equal patties.

In 10-inch skillet heat oil and margarine together until
margarine is bubbly and mixture is hot; add patties and
cook, turning once, until browned on both sides. Remove
burgers to plate; set aside.

In same skillet combine mushrooms and shallots and
sauté until lightly browned; add wine and bring to a boil.
Reduce heat to low; return burgers to skillet and let mixture
simmer until flavors blend and burgers are cooked
throughout, 2 to 3 minutes longer. Transfer burgers to
serving platter and top with mushroom mixture.

MAKES 4 SERVINGS, 1 BURGER EACH

Each serving provides: 3 Protein Exchanges; ¾ Vegetable Exchange;
   1 Fat Exchange; 25 Optional Calories
Per serving: 260 calories; 24 g protein; 16 g fat; 3 g carbohydrate;
   26 mg calcium; 504 mg sodium; 147 mg cholesterol

Open-Face Steakwiches ⓒ◑

Easy and economical.

1½ teaspoons <u>each</u> margarine and vegetable oil
2 slices rye bread, toasted
½ small Spanish <u>or</u> red onion (about 2 ounces), cut crosswise into 4 equal slices (about ¼-inch-thick slices)
1 tablespoon plus 1 teaspoon grated Parmesan cheese, divided
2 beef cubed steaks (¼ pound each), broiled until rare (hot)
½ medium tomato, cut crosswise into 4 slices (about ¼-inch-thick slices)
2 teaspoons chopped fresh Italian (flat-leaf) parsley

In small metal measuring cup or other small flameproof container melt margarine; remove from heat, add oil, and stir to combine.

Preheat broiler. Top each toast slice with 2 onion slices, then brush each with ½ teaspoon margarine mixture and sprinkle each with 1 teaspoon Parmesan cheese; broil until cheese is lightly browned, 1 to 2 minutes. Top each portion with 1 steak, then 2 tomato slices; brush each portion with half of the remaining margarine mixture. In small bowl combine remaining 2 teaspoons Parmesan cheese and the parsley; sprinkle evenly over each sandwich. Broil until cheese mixture is lightly browned, 1 to 2 minutes; serve immediately.

MAKES 2 SERVINGS, 1 OPEN-FACE SANDWICH EACH

Each serving provides: 3 Protein Exchanges; 1 Bread Exchange;
    1 Vegetable Exchange; 1½ Fat Exchanges; 20 Optional Calories
Per serving: 321 calories; 29 g protein; 15 g fat; 18 g carbohydrate;
    83 mg calcium; 311 mg sodium; 73 mg cholesterol

BREAKFAST

½ cup Orange Juice
1 Scrambled Egg
1 slice Rye Bread, toasted, with
   1 teaspoon Margarine
Café au Lait (½ cup *each* hot coffee
   and skim milk sprinkled with
   nutmeg)

LUNCH

Sardine-Stuffed Pocket (2 ounces
   sardines with 2 tablespoons diced
   onion, ¼ cup shredded lettuce, and
   1 tablespoon reduced-calorie
   mayonnaise in 1-ounce whole
   wheat pita bread)
6 *each* Carrot and Celery Sticks
½ cup Skim Milk
Coffee, Tea, or Mineral Water

DINNER

1 serving **Pineapple-Veal Kabobs**
1 cup Cooked Green Beans
Escarole and Tomato Salad (1½ cups
   escarole with 6 tomato wedges
   and 1 tablespoon reduced-calorie
   buttermilk dressing)
Sparkling Mineral Water

SNACKS

1 serving Reduced-Calorie Hot Cocoa;
   1 cup Strawberries

Total Optional Calories: 35

Pineapple-Veal Kabobs

2 tablespoons <u>each</u> teriyaki sauce and canned ready-to-serve beef broth
1 small garlic clove, minced
½ teaspoon <u>each</u> minced pared ginger root and vegetable oil
¼ teaspoon <u>each</u> chili oil and Chinese sesame oil
½ pound boneless veal loin, cut into 1-inch cubes
⅛ medium pineapple (about 4½ ounces), pared and cut into 12 chunks

In small saucepan combine teriyaki sauce, broth, garlic, ginger, and oils and cook over high heat until mixture comes to a boil. Transfer to small mixing bowl (not aluminum*); add veal and toss to coat. Cover with plastic wrap and refrigerate for 15 minutes.

Using a slotted spoon, remove veal from marinade, reserving marinade. Onto each of four 6- or 8-inch wooden skewers thread ¼ of the veal cubes and 3 pineapple chunks, starting and ending with a pineapple chunk; arrange kabobs in broiler pan. Pour reserved marinade evenly over kabobs and broil 6 to 8 inches from heat source, turning once, until veal is browned and cooked throughout, 3 to 4 minutes on each side (<u>do not overcook</u>). Transfer kabobs to serving platter and top with any remaining pan juices.

MAKES 2 SERVINGS, 2 KABOBS EACH

Each serving provides: 3 Protein Exchanges; ½ Fat Exchange;
   ½ Fruit Exchange; 3 Optional Calories
Per serving: 262 calories; 23 g protein; 15 g fat; 8 g carbohydrate;
   17 mg calcium; 734 mg sodium; 81 mg cholesterol

Variation: Kabobs with Rice (Week 2) — Serve each portion of Pineapple-Veal Kabobs with ½ cup cooked long-grain rice. Add 1 Bread Exchange to Exchange Information.

Per serving: 374 calories; 25 g protein; 15 g fat; 33 g carbohydrate;
   27 mg calcium; 734 mg sodium; 81 mg cholesterol

*It's best to marinate in glass or stainless-steel containers; ingredients such as teriyaki sauce may react with aluminum, causing color and flavor changes in foods.

BREAKFAST

BREAKFAST
1 medium Kiwi Fruit, sliced
¼ cup Part-Skim Ricotta Cheese
½ English Muffin, toasted
1 cup Skim Milk

LUNCH
Egg Salad (2 hard-cooked eggs with
    1 tablespoon *each* chopped celery
    and onion, 3 tomato slices, 2 green
    bell pepper rings, and 2 teaspoons
    reduced-calorie mayonnaise on
    4 lettuce leaves)
6 *each* Cucumber Spears and Yellow
    Squash Sticks
10 large Cherries
Coffee, Tea, or Mineral Water

DINNER
Knockwurst 'n' Sauerkraut (3 ounces
    grilled knockwurst with ½ cup
    sauerkraut and 2 teaspoons Dijon-
    style mustard on 2-ounce
    frankfurter roll)
1 serving **German Potato Salad**
Beet Salad (½ cup chilled cooked
    sliced beets with 1½ teaspoons
    French dressing on 2 lettuce
    leaves)
½ cup Blackberries
8 fluid ounces Beer

SNACKS
½ cup Reduced-Calorie Butterscotch
    Pudding topped with 1 tablespoon
    Whipped Topping

Total Optional Calories: 170

German Potato Salad Ⓒ ◐

**2 tablespoons <u>each</u> red wine vinegar and canned
    ready-to-serve beef broth**
½ teaspoon granulated sugar
2 teaspoons vegetable oil
2 tablespoons chopped onion
½ teaspoon all-purpose flour
2 slices crisp bacon, crumbled
Dash pepper
6 ounces cooked new red potatoes, sliced
½ teaspoon minced fresh parsley

In 1-cup liquid measure combine vinegar, broth, and sugar, stirring to dissolve sugar; set aside.

In 8-inch nonstick skillet heat oil over medium heat; add onion and sauté until softened, 1 to 2 minutes. Sprinkle flour over onion and stir quickly to combine; gradually stir in vinegar mixture. Add bacon and pepper and continue cooking, stirring frequently, until mixture thickens, 2 to 3 minutes. In salad bowl pour bacon mixture over potatoes; add parsley and toss well to coat. Serve immediately or let cool to room temperature.

MAKES 2 SERVINGS

Each serving provides: 1 Bread Exchange; ⅛ Vegetable Exchange;
    1 Fat Exchange; 55 Optional Calories
Per serving: 163 calories; 4 g protein; 8 g fat; 20 g carbohydrate;
    11 mg calcium; 166 mg sodium; 5 mg cholesterol

BREAKFAST

¼ small Cantaloupe
½ small Bagel, toasted, with
    2 tablespoons Whipped Cream
    Cheese
1 cup Skim Milk
Coffee or Tea

LUNCH

Chicken Salad (2 ounces diced
    chicken with ¼ cup *each* diced
    celery and tomato and
    1½ teaspoons Thousand Island
    dressing on 3 lettuce leaves)
6 *each* Cucumber Spears and Carrot
    Sticks
1 small Nectarine
Coffee, Tea, or Mineral Water

DINNER

3 ounces Broiled Scallops with
    ¼ cup **Roasted Red Pepper Sauce**
3 ounces Baked Potato sprinkled
    with 1 teaspoon Imitation Bacon
    Bits
1 cup Cooked Chinese Pea Pods
1½ cups Tossed Salad with
    1 tablespoon Italian Dressing
½ cup Applesauce sprinkled with
    dash Cinnamon
Coffee or Tea

SNACKS

1 cup Skim Milk; 2 Honey Graham
    Crackers

Total Optional Calories: 85

Roasted Red Pepper Sauce

Serve as an accompaniment to shrimp, scallops, clams, or oysters. Sauce can be stored in a covered container in refrigerator for up to 4 months.

2 medium red bell peppers
1 cup tomato juice
2 tablespoons chopped scallion (green onion)
1 tablespoon lime juice (no sugar added)
3 garlic cloves, minced
1½ teaspoons Worcestershire sauce
1 teaspoon chopped fresh basil
½ teaspoon salt
¼ teaspoon oregano leaves
⅛ to ¼ teaspoon hot sauce
⅛ teaspoon seeded chopped jalapeño pepper
Dash pepper

Preheat broiler. On baking sheet lined with heavy-duty foil broil bell peppers 3 inches from heat source, turning frequently, until charred on all sides; let stand until cool enough to handle, 15 to 20 minutes. Peel peppers; remove and discard stem ends and seeds and cut into strips.

In blender container or work bowl of food processor combine pepper strips and remaining ingredients and process until smooth. Transfer to small bowl (not aluminum*), cover with plastic wrap, and refrigerate until flavors blend, at least 30 minutes.

YIELDS ABOUT 1¾ CUPS

Each ¼-cup serving provides: ½ Vegetable Exchange; 10 Optional Calories
Per serving: 15 calories; 0.6 g protein; 0.1 g fat; 4 g carbohydrate;
    11 mg calcium; 299 mg sodium; 0 mg cholesterol

*It's best to marinate in glass or stainless-steel containers; acidic ingredients such as lime juice may react with aluminum, causing color and flavor changes in foods.

BREAKFAST
½ medium Banana, sliced
¾ ounce Cold Cereal
¾ cup Skim Milk
Coffee or Tea

LUNCH
Tuna Salad in a Pita (2 ounces tuna
   with ¼ cup alfalfa sprouts,
   2 tablespoons chopped celery, and
   2 teaspoons mayonnaise in 1-ounce
   pita bread)
6 *each* Red Bell Pepper Rings and
   Zucchini Sticks
Coffee, Tea, or Mineral Water

DINNER
3 ounces Broiled Lamb Chop
1 serving **Yogurt-Baked Eggplant**
½ cup Stewed Tomatoes
2 cups Mixed Green Salad with
   1 tablespoon Reduced-Calorie
   French Dressing mixed with
   2 teaspoons Lemon Juice and
   ¼ teaspoon Mustard
2-inch wedge Honeydew Melon
Coffee or Tea

SNACKS
Blueberry Yogurt (½ cup plain low-fat
   yogurt mixed with ½ cup
   blueberries)

Total Optional Calories: 30

Yogurt-Baked Eggplant ©

Select eggplants with fresh-looking green stems.
There should be no bruises or soft spots on the deep
purple skin.

1 medium eggplant (about 1 pound)
1½ teaspoons salt
1 tablespoon plus 1 teaspoon olive or vegetable oil
2 cups sliced onions
2 to 4 small garlic cloves, minced
½ cup plain low-fat yogurt
1 tablespoon chopped fresh mint
⅛ teaspoon each pepper and paprika

Trim off both ends of eggplant. Cut eggplant into ¼-inch-
thick slices and arrange slices, in single layer, on large
nonstick baking sheet. Sprinkle eggplant evenly with salt.
Broil until lightly browned, turning once, about 4 minutes on
each side.

Turn oven control to 375°F. In 12-inch nonstick skillet heat
oil; add onions and garlic and sauté until onions are
translucent. Transfer half of the onion mixture to shallow 2½-
or 3-quart casserole and spread over bottom of dish; top
with eggplant slices. In small bowl combine yogurt, mint,
and pepper; add remaining onion mixture and stir to
combine. Spread over eggplant slices, sprinkle with paprika,
and bake until bubbly and hot, about 15 minutes.

MAKES 4 SERVINGS

Each serving provides: 2½ Vegetable Exchanges; 1 Fat Exchange;
   ¼ Milk Exchange
Per serving: 117 calories; 4 g protein; 5 g fat; 16 g carbohydrate;
   122 mg calcium; 850 mg sodium; 2 mg cholesterol

BREAKFAST

1 cup Strawberries, sliced
⅓ cup Cottage Cheese
½ English Muffin, toasted, with
    2 teaspoons Reduced-Calorie
    Grape Spread
¾ cup Skim Milk

LUNCH

Turkey Sandwich (2 ounces sliced
    turkey with 3 *each* cucumber and
    tomato slices, 2 lettuce leaves,
    and 1 tablespoon reduced-calorie
    mayonnaise on 2 slices reduced-
    calorie rye bread)
6 *each* Carrot and Celery Sticks
Coffee, Tea, or Mineral Water

DINNER

3 ounces sliced Roast Beef
¾ cup Cooked Sliced Yellow Squash
    with ¼ cup Cooked Diced Green
    Bell Pepper
1 serving **Rice-Stuffed Tomatoes**
1½ cups Tossed Salad with
    1 teaspoon Imitation Bacon Bits
    and 1½ teaspoons Thousand
    Island Dressing mixed with
    2 tablespoons Plain Low-Fat
    Yogurt and ¼ teaspoon Mustard
½ cup Fruit Salad
Coffee or Tea

SNACKS

1 medium Peach; ½ cup Reduced-
    Calorie Vanilla Pudding

Total Optional Calories: 25

Rice-Stuffed Tomatoes

2 medium tomatoes
Salt
1 teaspoon olive oil
¼ cup <u>each</u> diced zucchini and mushrooms
2 tablespoons <u>each</u> diced carrot and chopped scallion
  (green onion)
½ garlic clove, minced
1 tablespoon red wine vinegar, divided
½ cup cooked brown rice, chilled
⅛ teaspoon pepper
2 teaspoons chopped fresh parsley
Garnish: parsley sprigs

Using sharp knife, cut each tomato into 8 equal wedges, being careful not to cut all the way through bottom. Scoop out pulp from tomatoes, discarding pulp and reserving shells. Sprinkle inside of each tomato shell with dash salt; set shells upside-down on wire rack and let drain.

In 8-inch skillet heat oil over medium heat; add zucchini, mushrooms, carrot, scallion, and garlic and sauté until vegetables are tender-crisp, about 5 minutes. Transfer to small bowl (not aluminum*); add 1 teaspoon vinegar and stir to combine. Cover and refrigerate until chilled, about 15 minutes.

In medium mixing bowl combine rice, remaining 2 teaspoons vinegar, and ⅛ teaspoon each salt and pepper; add vegetable mixture and chopped parsley and mix well. Spoon half of mixture into each reserved tomato shell; serve garnished with parsley sprigs.

MAKES 2 SERVINGS, 1 STUFFED TOMATO EACH

Each serving provides: ½ Bread Exchange; 1½ Vegetable Exchanges; ½ Fat Exchange
Per serving: 101 calories; 2 g protein; 3 g fat; 18 g carbohydrate; 23 mg calcium; 208 mg sodium; 0 mg cholesterol

*It's best to marinate in glass or stainless-steel containers; acidic ingredients such as vinegar may react with aluminum, causing color and flavor changes in foods.

BREAKFAST

BREAKFAST

½ cup Grapefruit Juice
1 ounce Broiled Canadian-Style
  Bacon
1 serving **Blueberry-Cornmeal
  Pancakes**
½ cup Skim Milk
Coffee or Tea

LUNCH

Fruit 'n' Cheese Platter (⅔ cup
  cottage cheese with ½ cup *each*
  honeydew, cantaloupe, and
  watermelon balls)
½ cup Cherry-Flavored Gelatin
Coffee, Tea, or Mineral Water

DINNER

3 ounces Broiled Halibut with
  Lemon Wedge
1 small Ear Corn, cooked, with
  1 teaspoon Margarine
1 cup Chinese Pea Pods
1½ cups Mixed Green Salad with
  1 tablespoon Blue Cheese Dressing
Raspberries 'n' Yogurt (½ cup
  raspberries topped with ¼ cup
  plain low-fat yogurt)
Club Soda with Lime Twist

SNACKS

1 serving Reduced-Calorie Chocolate
  Dairy Drink; 2 Graham Crackers
  with 2 teaspoons Reduced-Calorie
  Strawberry Spread

Total Optional Calories: 180

Blueberry-Cornmeal Pancakes ⒸⓄ

Fresh blueberries make this wonderful weekend breakfast special.

**2¼ ounces (⅓ cup plus 2 teaspoons) uncooked finely
  ground yellow cornmeal
3 tablespoons all-purpose flour
¼ teaspoon baking soda
½ cup buttermilk
¼ cup water
1 egg
1 cup blueberries
¼ cup reduced-calorie pancake syrup (60 calories per
  fluid ounce)**

In medium mixing bowl combine cornmeal, flour, and baking soda. In small mixing bowl beat together buttermilk, water, and egg; stir into dry ingredients, mixing well until thoroughly combined. Stir in blueberries.

Spray 10-inch nonstick skillet or griddle with nonstick cooking spray and heat over medium-high heat; using ⅓ of batter (about a scant ¼ cup), drop batter into skillet (or onto griddle), making 4 pancakes. Cook until browned on bottom and bubbles appear on surface, 2 to 3 minutes; using pancake turner, turn pancakes over and cook until other side is browned, 2 to 3 minutes longer. Remove to serving platter and keep warm. Using remaining batter, repeat procedure 2 more times, spraying pan (or griddle) each time and making 8 more pancakes. For each portion, serve 3 pancakes topped with 1 tablespoon syrup.

MAKES 4 SERVINGS, 3 PANCAKES EACH

Each serving provides: 1 Bread Exchange; ½ Fruit Exchange;
  65 Optional Calories
Per serving: 161 calories; 5 g protein; 2 g fat; 31 g carbohydrate;
  47 mg calcium; 102 mg sodium; 70 mg cholesterol

BREAKFAST

½ cup Orange Sections
1 Scrambled Egg
½ English Muffin, toasted, with
    1 teaspoon Reduced-Calorie
    Margarine
1 cup Skim Milk

LUNCH

Open-Face Fish Sandwich (2 ounces
    fish with 2 tablespoons *each*
    chopped green bell pepper and
    onion, 2 lettuce leaves, and
    2 teaspoons reduced-calorie
    mayonnaise on 1 slice
    pumpernickel bread)
6 *each* Cucumber Spears and Yellow
    Squash Sticks
1 medium Peach
Coffee, Tea, or Mineral Water

DINNER

3 ounces Roast Chicken
1 cup *each* Cooked Baby Carrots
    and Chopped Spinach
Arugula and Red Leaf Lettuce Salad
    (¾ cup *each* torn arugula and red
    leaf lettuce with 1½ teaspoons
    French dressing mixed with
    2 teaspoons lemon juice and
    ¼ teaspoon mustard)
1 cup Strawberries
Iced Tea with Lemon Twist

SNACKS

1 serving **Birthday Blueberry Muffins**;
    1 cup Skim Milk

Total Optional Calories: 85

Birthday Blueberry Muffins ©

Try these old-fashioned muffins warm from the oven.

Batter

2 cups all-purpose flour, divided
1½ teaspoons double-acting baking powder
¼ teaspoon <u>each</u> baking soda and ground cinnamon
⅛ teaspoon salt
⅓ cup granulated sugar
¾ cup <u>each</u> buttermilk and low-fat milk (1% milk fat)
1 egg
1 teaspoon grated lemon peel
1 cup blueberries

Topping

¼ cup <u>each</u> all-purpose flour and firmly packed dark brown sugar
2 tablespoons <u>each</u> margarine, melted, and granulated sugar
1 teaspoon ground cinnamon

To Prepare Batter: Preheat oven to 350°F. Into medium mixing bowl sift together 1¾ cups flour and the baking powder, baking soda, cinnamon, and salt; stir in sugar.

In small mixing bowl beat together buttermilk, low-fat milk, egg, and lemon peel; add to sifted dry ingredients and stir until combined. In small bowl combine blueberries with remaining ¼ cup flour; stir into batter. Spray twelve 2½-inch muffin-pan cups with nonstick cooking spray. Fill each with an equal amount of batter (each will be about ½ full).

To Prepare Topping and Bake: In small bowl combine all ingredients for topping, stirring until thoroughly combined; sprinkle an equal amount of topping over each muffin and bake in middle of center oven rack for 25 to 30 minutes (until muffins are lightly browned and a toothpick, inserted in center, comes out dry). Remove muffins to wire rack and let cool for 5 minutes.

MAKES 12 SERVINGS, 1 MUFFIN EACH

Each serving provides: 1 Bread Exchange; ½ Fat Exchange; 85 Optional Calories
Per serving: 176 calories; 4 g protein; 3 g fat; 33 g carbohydrate; 80 mg calcium; 148 mg sodium; 24 mg cholesterol

BREAKFAST

½ small Mango
⅓ cup Cottage Cheese
2 Zwieback
1 cup Skim Milk

LUNCH

Ham and Cheese Sandwich (1 ounce
    each sliced ham and Swiss cheese
    with 2 tomato slices, 2 lettuce
    leaves, and 2 teaspoons reduced-
    calorie mayonnaise on 2 slices
    reduced-calorie rye bread)
1 small Apple
Coffee, Tea, or Mineral Water

DINNER

3 ounces Broiled Veal Chop
1 cup Cooked Cut Green Beans
½ cup Cooked Pearl Onions
Pasta Salad (½ cup chilled cooked
    spiral macaroni with ½ cup *each*
    broccoli florets and diced red bell
    pepper and 1 tablespoon Italian
    dressing)
1 medium Kiwi Fruit, sliced, with
    2 tablespoons **Cherry-Cheese Dip**
Coffee or Tea

SNACKS

1 serving Reduced-Calorie Vanilla
    Dairy Drink

Total Optional Calories: 75

Cherry-Cheese Dip ◑

A wonderful dip for fresh fruit.

½ cup cream cheese, softened
20 large cherries, pitted*
1 tablespoon confectioners' sugar, sifted
1 teaspoon cherry liqueur

In blender container combine all ingredients and, using
an on-off motion, process until combined, scraping down
sides of container as necessary. Transfer mixture to
serving bowl; cover with plastic wrap and refrigerate
until chilled.

YIELDS ABOUT 1 CUP

Each ¼-cup serving provides: ½ Fruit Exchange; 120 Optional Calories
Per serving: 146 calories; 3 g protein; 10 g fat; 11 g carbohydrate;
    30 mg calcium; 84 mg sodium; 31 mg cholesterol
Each 2-tablespoon serving provides: 75 Optional Calories
Per serving: 73 calories; 1 g protein; 5 g fat; 6 g carbohydrate;
    15 mg calcium; 42 mg sodium; 16 mg cholesterol

*Thawed frozen pitted cherries (no sugar added) may be substituted.

BREAKFAST

2-inch wedge Honeydew Melon
½ English Muffin, toasted, with
    1 teaspoon Margarine and
    2 teaspoons Reduced-Calorie
    Strawberry Spread
1 cup Skim Milk

LUNCH

Beans 'n' Greens (2 ounces kidney
    beans with 1½ cups mixed green
    salad, 1 teaspoon imitation bacon
    bits, and 1 tablespoon reduced-
    calorie Italian dressing)
4 Melba Slices
1 medium Nectarine
Coffee, Tea, or Mineral Water

DINNER

4 ounces Roast Beef
½ cup Cooked Sliced Zucchini with
    ¼ cup Diced Pimientos
½ cup Cooked Sliced Beets
Iceberg Lettuce Wedge with
    1 tablespoon Caesar Dressing
½ cup Reduced-Calorie Vanilla
    Pudding
Coffee or Tea

SNACKS

1 serving **Festive Fruit and Cheese
    Fondue**

Total Optional Calories: 45

Festive Fruit and Cheese Fondue ◖◑

Sprinkling lemon juice over the apple and banana slices helps prevent them from turning brown.

Fondue

½ cup part-skim ricotta cheese
¼ cup plain low-fat yogurt
1 teaspoon confectioners' sugar, sifted
⅛ to ¼ teaspoon brandy extract

Fruit

**1 small apple (about ¼ pound), cored, sliced, and
    sprinkled with lemon juice**
**1 medium banana (about 6 ounces), peeled, sliced,
    and sprinkled with lemon juice**
1 cup strawberries, sliced

To Prepare Fondue: Force cheese through a sieve into small bowl; add yogurt, sugar, and extract and stir to combine. If desired, cover with plastic wrap and refrigerate until chilled, about 1 hour.

To Serve: Arrange fruit decoratively around edge of serving platter; transfer cheese mixture to small serving bowl and place in center of platter. Serve with toothpicks.

MAKES 4 SERVINGS

Each serving provides: ½ Protein Exchange; 1 Fruit Exchange; 15 Optional
    Calories
Per serving: 107 calories; 5 g protein; 3 g fat; 17 g carbohydrate; 118 mg
    calcium; 49 mg sodium; 10 mg cholesterol

BREAKFAST

1 cup Cantaloupe Balls
1/3 cup Cottage Cheese
1 slice Whole Wheat Bread, toasted
1 cup Skim Milk
Coffee or Tea

LUNCH

Salmon in a Pita (2 ounces salmon
  with 2 tablespoons *each* chopped
  celery and onion and 2 teaspoons
  reduced-calorie mayonnaise in
  1-ounce pita bread)
6 *each* Radishes and Yellow Squash
  Sticks
Coffee, Tea, or Mineral Water

DINNER

3 ounces Roast Chicken
1/2 cup *each* Cooked Sliced Onion,
  Carrot, and Green and Red Bell
  Pepper
Spinach Salad (1 1/2 cups torn spinach
  with 1/4 cup sliced mushrooms,
  6 tomato wedges, and 1 tablespoon
  Italian dressing)
1 small Apple
1 serving **Iced Orange Tea**

SNACKS

Strawberry Yogurt (1/2 cup plain
  low-fat yogurt mixed with 1/2 cup
  strawberries, sliced)

Total Optional Calories: 20

Iced Orange Tea ◐ ◑

1 1/2 cups brewed tea, chilled
1/2 cup orange juice (no sugar added)
2 teaspoons superfine sugar*
1 cup crushed ice <u>or</u> 8 ice cubes
Garnish: 2 <u>each</u> lemon slices and mint sprigs

Chill two 12-ounce glasses. In 2-cup liquid measure or small
pitcher combine tea, orange juice, and sugar, stirring to
dissolve sugar.

Fill each chilled glass with 1/2 cup crushed ice or 4 ice
cubes; pour half of the tea mixture into each glass and
garnish each with a lemon slice and mint sprig.

MAKES 2 SERVINGS, ABOUT 1 CUP EACH

Each serving provides: 1/2 Fruit Exchange; 20 Optional Calories
Per serving: 46 calories; 0.5 g protein; trace fat; 11 g carbohydrate;
    11 mg calcium; 0.7 mg sodium; 0 mg cholesterol

Variations: Iced Pineapple Tea (Week 5) — Substitute 1/3 cup
pineapple juice (no sugar added) for the orange juice.

Per serving: 41 calories; 0.2 g protein; trace fat; 10 g carbohydrate;
    12 mg calcium; 0.5 mg sodium; 0 mg cholesterol

Iced Pineapple-Orange Tea (Week 5) — Add 1/3 cup
pineapple juice (no sugar added) to tea mixture. Increase
Fruit Exchange to 1 Exchange.

Per serving: 69 calories; 0.6 g protein; 0.1 g fat; 17 g carbohydrate;
    18 mg calcium; 1 mg sodium; 0 mg cholesterol

* If superfine sugar is not available, process granulated sugar in blender until
  superfine.

BREAKFAST

½ medium Grapefruit sprinkled with
   ½ teaspoon Brown Sugar
1 Scrambled Egg
1 slice Whole Wheat Bread, toasted,
   with 1 teaspoon Margarine
½ cup Skim Milk
Coffee or Tea

LUNCH

Shrimp Salad (2 ounces tiny shrimp
   with ½ cup *each* alfalfa sprouts
   and shredded lettuce, ¼ cup *each*
   diced tomato and cucumber, and
   1 tablespoon reduced-calorie
   buttermilk dressing)
6 Saltines
¾ cup Broccoli Florets and
   6 Zucchini Sticks
20 small Grapes
Coffee, Tea, or Mineral Water

DINNER

3 ounces Roast Veal
Spaghetti in Red Sauce (½ cup
   cooked spaghetti with ¼ cup
   tomato sauce and 1 teaspoon
   grated Parmesan cheese)
1 cup Cooked Cut Green Beans
1½ cups Tossed Salad with
   1 tablespoon Creamy Italian
   Dressing
½ cup Low-Calorie Orange-Flavored
   Gelatin topped with 1 tablespoon
   Whipped Topping
1 serving **Orange-Cran Cooler**

SNACKS

Raspberry Yogurt (½ cup plain low-
   fat yogurt mixed with ¼ cup
   raspberries); ½ cup Skim Milk

Total Optional Calories: 70

Orange-Cran Cooler ◑◐

**½ cup low-calorie cranberry juice, chilled
1 tablespoon thawed frozen concentrated orange juice
   (no sugar added)
½ cup club soda or seltzer, chilled
1 cup crushed ice, divided
Garnish: 2 mint sprigs**

Chill two 8-ounce glasses. In blender container combine juices and process at high speed until combined and frothy, about 1 minute. Turn motor off and add club soda (or seltzer); process at low speed until combined, about 1 second.

   To serve, add ½ cup crushed ice to each chilled glass; pour juice mixture over ice and serve each portion garnished with a mint sprig. Serve immediately.

MAKES 2 SERVINGS

Each serving provides: ½ Fruit Exchange
Per serving: 26 calories; 0.2 g protein; 0.1 g fat; 6 g carbohydrate;
   7 mg calcium; 13 mg sodium; 0 mg cholesterol

TIP: If you don't have an ice crusher, place ice in resealable plastic bag and tap firmly with a meat mallet until ice is crushed.

August

Mexican Pasta Salad

AUGUST'S BEST BUYS FOR FRUITS AND VEGETABLES

alfalfa sprouts	cherries	lemons	pineapples
apricots	Chinese pea pods	limes	plums
arugula	corn on the cob	mangoes	potatoes
bananas	cucumbers	mushrooms	radishes
bean sprouts	eggplants	nectarines	scallions (green onions)
beets	figs	new potatoes	strawberries
bell peppers	grapes	okra	summer squash
cantaloupes	green beans	onions	tomatoes
carrots	honeydew	peaches	watermelon
celery	kiwi fruit		

BREAKFAST

½ cup Orange Juice
¾ ounce Cold Cereal
1 cup Skim Milk
Coffee or Tea

LUNCH

Egg Salad in a Pita (2 hard-cooked
    eggs, chopped, with 1 tablespoon
    chopped celery and 2 teaspoons
    reduced-calorie mayonnaise in
    1-ounce pita bread)
½ cup Broccoli Florets and
    6 Zucchini Sticks
2 medium Apricots
Coffee, Tea, or Mineral Water

DINNER

1 serving **Sushi for Cowards**
Chicken Stir-Fry (3 ounces julienne-
    cut chicken, 1½ ounces water
    chestnuts, sliced, and ¼ cup *each*
    sliced carrot and green bell pepper
    strips stir-fried in 1 teaspoon
    Chinese sesame oil and 1 table-
    spoon reduced-sodium soy sauce)
½ cup Cooked Rice
2 cups Mixed Green Salad with
    1½ teaspoons French Dressing
    mixed with 2 teaspoons Lemon
    Juice and ¼ teaspoon Mustard
½ cup Reduced-Calorie Chocolate
    Pudding topped with 1 tablespoon
    Whipped Topping
Coffee or Tea

SNACKS

1 Honey Graham Cracker; 1 cup
    Honeydew Melon Balls

Total Optional Calories: 55

Sushi for Cowards

Serve sushi with teriyaki or soy sauce for dipping.

1 tablespoon rice vinegar
1 teaspoon granulated sugar
½ cup cooked regular long-grain rice (hot)
2 ounces thinly sliced prosciutto (Italian-style ham) <u>or</u> boiled ham
1 medium kiwi fruit, pared and cut lengthwise into quarters
4 medium scallions (green onions), blanched and each cut lengthwise into 2 thin strips (green portion only)

In small bowl combine vinegar and sugar; add rice and stir to combine. Set aside.

On work surface form half the meat slices into a rectangle by slightly overlapping long side of slices; evenly spread meat with half of the rice mixture, then place 2 kiwi quarters end-to-end at one of the narrow ends of rectangle. Starting at kiwi-end, roll rectangle jelly-roll fashion to enclose filling. Repeat procedure using remaining meat, rice mixture, and kiwi fruit. Wrap each roll tightly in plastic wrap and refrigerate for about 1 hour or freeze for about 20 minutes (this will help make roll easier to cut).

Remove plastic wrap and set each roll on cutting board; cut each crosswise on the diagonal into 4 equal pieces. Wrap 1 scallion strip around each piece of sushi; secure each with a toothpick and arrange on serving platter.

MAKES 4 SERVINGS, 2 SUSHI EACH

Each serving provides: ½ Protein Exchange; ⅛ Vegetable Exchange;
    40 Optional Calories
Per serving: 64 calories; 4 g protein; 1 g fat; 11 g carbohydrate;
    11 mg calcium; 172 mg sodium; 8 mg cholesterol

BREAKFAST

¼ small Cantaloupe
½ small Bagel, toasted, with
   1 teaspoon Margarine
1 cup Skim Milk

LUNCH

Tuna Sandwich (2 ounces tuna with
   ¼ cup chopped celery, 2 lettuce
   leaves, and 2 teaspoons reduced-
   calorie mayonnaise on 2 slices
   reduced-calorie wheat bread)
6 *each* Cucumber Spears and Carrot
   Sticks
20 small Grapes
Coffee, Tea, or Mineral Water

DINNER

1 serving **Stuffed Cherry Tomatoes**
4 ounces Broiled Steak
3 ounces Baked Potato with
   1 teaspoon Margarine
1 cup Cooked Sliced Yellow Squash
1½ cups Tossed Green Salad with
   1 tablespoon Reduced-Calorie
   Italian Dressing
½ cup Low-Calorie Strawberry-
   Flavored Gelatin
Coffee or Tea

SNACKS

Peach Yogurt (½ cup plain low-fat
   yogurt mixed with ½ cup peach
   slices)

Total Optional Calories: 65

Stuffed Cherry Tomatoes ◑

6 cherry tomatoes
3 tablespoons whipped cream cheese
1½ teaspoons <u>each</u> minced onion <u>or</u> scallion (green onion) and drained canned pimiento

Cut a thin slice from top of each tomato, then scoop out pulp, discarding pulp and reserving shells; set shells upside-down on paper towels and let drain.

In small bowl combine remaining ingredients. Using a pastry bag fitted with a star tip, or a small spoon, fill each reserved tomato shell with ⅙ of the cheese mixture. Arrange stuffed tomatoes on serving plate; cover loosely with plastic wrap and refrigerate until chilled.

MAKES 2 SERVINGS, 3 TOMATOES EACH

Each serving provides: ¼ Vegetable Exchange; 50 Optional Calories
Per serving: 52 calories; 1 g protein; 5 g fat; 1 g carbohydrate;
   11 mg calcium; 55 mg sodium; 14 mg cholesterol

BRUNCH

Orange Fizz (½ cup *each* orange juice
  and club soda)
1 serving **Creole Omelets**
¾ cup Torn Arugula with
  1 tablespoon Reduced-Calorie
  Italian Dressing
1-ounce Buttermilk Flaky Biscuit
  with ½ teaspoon *each* Margarine
  and Honey
1 cup Skim Milk
Coffee or Tea

DINNER

¾ cup Chicken Bouillon
3 ounces Broiled Chicken Breast
½ cup Cooked Wax Beans with
  1 teaspoon Minced Pimiento
½ cup Cooked Red Bell Pepper Strips
2 cups Mixed Green Salad with
  1½ teaspoons French Dressing
  mixed with 2 teaspoons Lemon
  Juice and ¼ teaspoon Mustard
1-ounce Roll with 1 teaspoon
  Margarine
1 cup Watermelon Chunks
Coffee or Tea

SNACKS

Buttermilk-Banana Shake (¾ cup
  buttermilk, ½ medium banana,
  vanilla extract, and 3 ice cubes
  processed in blender)

Total Optional Calories: 25

Creole Omelets ©

Delicious for brunch or a light summertime dinner.

**1 cup canned Italian tomatoes (with liquid); drain and
seed tomatoes, reserving liquid, divided**
**2 tablespoons <u>each</u> chopped onion, celery, and green
bell pepper**
1 small garlic clove, minced
1 tablespoon Worcestershire sauce
¼ teaspoon hot sauce
4 eggs
**1 tablespoon seeded and diced mild <u>or</u> hot green chili
pepper, divided**
Pepper
2 teaspoons reduced-calorie margarine (tub), divided
2 ounces Muenster cheese, shredded, divided

In blender container process ½ cup tomatoes with
reserved liquid until smooth; dice remaining tomatoes
and set aside.

Spray 2-quart nonstick saucepan with nonstick
cooking spray and heat; add onion, celery, bell pepper,
and garlic and sauté over medium-high heat until
softened, 1 to 2 minutes. Add pureed and diced
tomatoes, Worcestershire sauce, and hot sauce, mixing
well. Reduce heat to low, cover, and let simmer, stirring
frequently, until flavors blend, 5 to 10 minutes.

In small bowl beat together 2 eggs, 1½ teaspoons chili
pepper, and dash pepper. In 8-inch skillet that has a
metal or removable handle heat 1 teaspoon margarine
until bubbly and hot; pour in egg mixture and cook until
bottom is set and lightly browned, 3 to 4 minutes.
Sprinkle 1 ounce cheese over eggs. Transfer pan to broiler
and broil until omelet is puffed and lightly browned.
Using spatula, loosen edges of omelet and fold in half;
carefully slide onto warmed plate and keep warm. Repeat
procedure, making 1 more omelet. Serve each omelet
topped with ½ of the tomato mixture.

MAKES 2 SERVINGS, 1 OMELET EACH

Each serving provides: 3 Protein Exchanges; 1½ Vegetable Exchanges;
  ½ Fat Exchange
Per serving: 320 calories; 21 g protein; 22 g fat; 10 g carbohydrate;
  299 mg calcium; 658 mg sodium; 575 mg cholesterol

BREAKFAST

½ cup Orange Juice
⅓ cup Cottage Cheese
1 slice Rye Bread, toasted, with
   1 teaspoon Reduced-Calorie
   Strawberry Spread
½ cup Skim Milk
Coffee or Tea

LUNCH

Roast Beef in a Pita (2 ounces sliced
   roast beef with 3 tomato slices
   and 1 teaspoon *each* mayonnaise
   and mustard in 1-ounce pita bread)
6 Cucumber Spears
1 small Nectarine
Coffee, Tea, or Mineral Water

DINNER

1 serving **Grilled Swordfish Baja Style**
½ cup Cooked Rice with ¼ cup
   Cooked Sliced Mushrooms
½ cup Cooked Chopped Spinach
   with 1 teaspoon Margarine
Beet Salad (½ cup chilled cooked
   sliced beets with 1½ teaspoons
   Italian dressing on 4 lettuce
   leaves)
1 medium Plum
Iced Tea with Lemon Wedge

SNACKS

Strawberry Yogurt (¼ cup plain
   low-fat yogurt mixed with ½ cup
   strawberries, sliced); ½ cup
   Reduced-Calorie Butterscotch
   Pudding

Total Optional Calories: 75

Grilled Swordfish Baja Style

2 boneless swordfish steaks (¼ pound each)
3 tablespoons freshly squeezed lime juice (or bottled lime juice, no sugar added), divided
1 tablespoon soy sauce*
1½ teaspoons chopped fresh cilantro (Chinese parsley), divided
½ teaspoon minced pared ginger root
¼ cup each sour cream and diced tomato
1 teaspoon chopped fresh parsley
½ teaspoon seeded and minced mild or hot green chili pepper
Garnish: 2 lime wedges

In shallow bowl large enough to hold swordfish steaks in a single layer (not aluminum†) combine 2 tablespoons lime juice with the soy sauce, ½ teaspoon cilantro, and the ginger; add swordfish and turn to coat with marinade. Cover with plastic wrap and refrigerate for at least 30 minutes, turning fish occasionally.

Preheat grill or broiler. Transfer fish to grill or broiling pan, discarding marinade; grill over hot coals (or broil 6 inches from heat source), turning once, until fish flakes easily when tested with a fork, 4 to 5 minutes on each side (exact timing will depend upon thickness of steaks).

While fish is cooking, in small saucepan combine sour cream, tomato, remaining tablespoon lime juice and teaspoon cilantro, parsley, and chili pepper and cook over medium heat, stirring occasionally, until thoroughly heated, 3 to 4 minutes (do not boil).

To serve, transfer swordfish to serving platter; top with sauce and garnish with lime wedges.

MAKES 2 SERVINGS

Each serving provides: 3 Protein Exchanges; ¼ Vegetable Exchange;
   65 Optional Calories
Per serving: 208 calories; 23 g protein; 11 g fat; 4 g carbohydrate;
   64 mg calcium; 411 mg sodium; 75 mg cholesterol

*Reduced-sodium soy sauce may be substituted. Reduce calories to 207, calcium to 60 mg, and sodium to 231 mg.
†It's best to marinate in glass or stainless-steel containers; acidic ingredients such as lime juice may react with aluminum, causing color and flavor changes in foods.

BREAKFAST

2-inch wedge Honeydew Melon
1 Poached Egg
½ English Muffin, toasted, with
    ½ teaspoon Margarine
½ cup Skim Milk
Coffee or Tea

LUNCH

Chicken Salad on a Roll (2 ounces
    diced chicken with 2 tablespoons
    chopped celery and 2 teaspoons
    reduced-calorie mayonnaise on
    1-ounce roll)
½ cup Cauliflower Florets and
    6 Cucumber Spears
1 small Apple
Coffee, Tea, or Mineral Water

DINNER

1 serving **Creamed Pasta and Shrimp**
½ cup *each* Cooked Sliced Zucchini
    and Red Bell Pepper Strips
1½ Cups Mixed Green Salad with
    1½ teaspoons French Dressing
    mixed with 2 teaspoons Lemon
    Juice and ¼ teaspoon Mustard
½ cup Reduced-Calorie Butterscotch
    Pudding
Coffee or Tea

SNACKS

Peach 'n' Yogurt (½ cup peach slices
    topped with ¼ cup plain low-fat
    yogurt)

Total Optional Calories: 50

Creamed Pasta and Shrimp

7 ounces medium <u>or</u> large shrimp
1 egg
¼ cup half-and-half (blend of milk and cream)
**½ ounce grated Parmesan cheese (about
    2 tablespoons)**
2 teaspoons reduced-calorie margarine (tub)
1 tablespoon minced shallots
1 garlic clove, minced
1 cup cooked linguine <u>or</u> fettuccine (hot)
1 tablespoon minced fresh Italian (flat-leaf) parsley
¼ teaspoon salt
Dash pepper

Shell and devein shrimp, leaving last segment and tail in place; set aside.

In small bowl combine egg and half-and-half and, using a fork or wire whisk, beat until thoroughly combined; stir in cheese and set aside.

In 9-inch nonstick skillet heat margarine until bubbly and hot; add shallots and garlic and sauté until shallots are soft. Add shrimp and cook, stirring frequently, until shrimp just turn pink, 1 to 2 minutes. Remove skillet from heat and pour in egg mixture, stirring to combine. Return to low heat and let simmer, stirring occasionally, until mixture thickens, 3 to 4 minutes. Add pasta, parsley, salt, and pepper; using 2 forks, toss well until pasta is thoroughly coated with sauce. Serve immediately.

MAKES 2 SERVINGS

Each serving provides: 3 Protein Exchanges; 1 Bread Exchange;
    ½ Fat Exchange; 50 Optional Calories
Per serving: 314 calories; 30 g protein; 12 g fat; 19 g carbohydrate;
    214 mg calcium; 698 mg sodium; 295 mg cholesterol

BREAKFAST

½ cup Orange Juice
1 Poached Egg
½ English Muffin, toasted, with
 1 teaspoon Reduced-Calorie
 Margarine
1 cup Skim Milk

LUNCH

Roast Beef on Rye (2 ounces sliced
 roast beef with 4 lettuce leaves,
 3 tomato slices, 4 dill pickle slices,
 and 1 teaspoon mustard on 2 slices
 reduced-calorie rye bread)
6 *each* Carrot and Celery Sticks
¾ ounce Mixed Dried Fruit
Coffee, Tea, or Mineral Water

DINNER

1 serving **Steamed Clams with Butter
 Broth**
1 small Ear Corn, cooked, with
 1 teaspoon Reduced-Calorie
 Margarine
½ cup Cooked Cut Green Beans
1½ cups Tossed Salad with
 1 tablespoon Blue Cheese Dressing
2 x 3-inch wedge Watermelon
12 fluid ounces Light Beer

SNACKS

2 Graham Crackers; Chocolate Milk
 (1 cup skim milk mixed with
 1 teaspoon chocolate syrup)

Total Optional Calories: 230

Steamed Clams with Butter Broth ⓒ

1½ dozen cherrystone clams*
**½ cup <u>each</u> carrot chunks, sliced celery (1-inch pieces),
 chopped onion, and dry white table wine**
2 parsley sprigs
1 small garlic clove
⅛ teaspoon salt
2 to 4 peppercorns, crushed
½ lemon
1 tablespoon lightly salted butter
Garnish: 2 lemon wedges

Using metal brush, scrub clams and rinse under running cold water. Transfer to large bowl; add cold water to cover and let stand for 10 minutes.

In 4-quart saucepan combine carrot, celery, onion, wine, parsley, garlic, salt, and peppercorns; squeeze juice from lemon half into mixture, then add squeezed lemon half to saucepan. Drain clams and arrange on vegetables; cover and cook over high heat until mixture comes to a full boil, about 5 minutes. Reduce heat to medium and cook until clams open, 8 to 10 minutes. Using a slotted spoon, spoon 9 clams into each of 2 bowls, reserving liquid. Set clams aside and keep warm.

Line sieve with cheesecloth and strain cooking liquid into small saucepan, discarding solids; add butter and cook, stirring frequently, until butter is melted and mixture comes to a boil. Divide liquid into 2 small bowls. Garnish each serving of clams with a lemon wedge and serve each portion with a bowl of dipping liquid. To eat, using small cocktail fork pull clam from shell, then dip into butter broth.

MAKES 2 SERVINGS

Each serving provides: 3 Protein Exchanges; 110 Optional Calories
Per serving: 196 calories; 15 g protein; 8 g fat; 9 g carbohydrate;
 107 mg calcium; 222 mg sodium; 72 mg cholesterol

*One and a half dozen cherrystone clams will yield about 6 ounces cooked
 seafood.

BREAKFAST

1 medium Kiwi Fruit, sliced
½ cup Cooked Cereal with
   1½ teaspoons Margarine
½ cup Skim Milk
Coffee or Tea

LUNCH

Peanut Butter and Jelly Sandwich
   (1 tablespoon peanut butter with
   2 teaspoons reduced-calorie grape
   spread on 2 slices reduced-calorie
   multi-grain bread)
2 medium Plums
Coffee, Tea, or Mineral Water

DINNER

1 cup Mixed Vegetable Juice with
   Celery Stick
2 ounces Cheddar Cheese with
   ¾ ounce Crispbread
1 serving **Seafood Salad**
1-ounce Roll with 1 teaspoon
   Margarine
½ cup Reduced-Calorie Chocolate
   Pudding
Coffee or Tea

SNACKS

Apricot Yogurt (½ cup plain low-fat
   yogurt mixed with 2 medium
   apricots, pitted and chopped)

Total Optional Calories: 225

Seafood Salad ◑

**1 medium head green cabbage (about 1½ pounds),
   shredded (about 10 cups)**
**¾ pound shelled and deveined cooked medium <u>or</u> large
   shrimp, chilled**
½ cup <u>each</u> diced onion and green bell pepper
**3 tablespoons <u>each</u> sour cream and chili sauce <u>or</u>
   seafood cocktail sauce**
**1 tablespoon plus 1 teaspoon reduced-calorie
   mayonnaise**
1 tablespoon prepared horseradish, drained
1 teaspoon granulated sugar
Dash to ⅛ teaspoon pepper
Garnish: 2 lemon wedges

In large salad bowl combine cabbage, shrimp, onion, and
bell pepper; cover with plastic wrap and refrigerate until
chilled. In small bowl combine remaining ingredients
except garnish; cover with plastic wrap and refrigerate
until chilled.

To serve, stir dressing and pour over salad; toss to
combine. Serve garnished with lemon wedges.

MAKES 4 SERVINGS

Each serving provides: 3 Protein Exchanges; 5½ Vegetable Exchanges;
   ½ Fat Exchange; 45 Optional Calories
Per serving with chili sauce: 205 calories; 24 g protein; 5 g fat;
   17 g carbohydrate; 201 mg calcium; 369 mg sodium;
   134 mg cholesterol
With seafood cocktail sauce: 205 calories; 24 g protein; 5 g fat;
   17 g carbohydrate; 199 mg calcium; 341 mg sodium;
   134 mg cholesterol

BREAKFAST

¼ small Cantaloupe
Lox 'n' Bagel (½ small bagel topped
   with 1 tablespoon whipped cream
   cheese and 1 ounce smoked
   salmon)
¾ cup Skim Milk

LUNCH

1 serving **Waldorf Chicken Salad**
6 *each* Carrot and Zucchini Sticks
Peach 'n' Yogurt (1 medium peach,
   sliced, topped with ¼ cup plain
   low-fat yogurt and sprinkled with
   nutmeg)
Club Soda with Mint Sprig

DINNER

3 ounces Broiled Steak
1 small Ear Corn, cooked, with
   ½ teaspoon Margarine
½ cup Cooked Chinese Pea Pods
1½ cups Mixed Green Salad with
   1½ teaspoons Thousand Island
   Dressing mixed with 2 tablespoons
   Plain Low-Fat Yogurt and
   ¼ teaspoon Mustard
2 medium Apricots
½ cup Skim Milk
Coffee or Tea

SNACKS

2 cups Plain Popcorn; Diet Soda

Total Optional Calories: 145

Waldorf Chicken Salad

An elegant weekend lunch.

**¼ pound skinned and boned cooked chicken, cut into
   cubes**
**1 small apple (about ¼ pound), cored and cut into
   ½-inch pieces**
1 ounce halved <u>or</u> chopped walnuts
¼ cup diagonally sliced celery
**2 tablespoons dark raisins, soaked in hot water until
   plumped, then drained**
**1 tablespoon <u>each</u> lemon juice, mayonnaise, and sour
   cream**
½ teaspoon salt
Dash white pepper
4 lettuce leaves

In medium mixing bowl combine chicken, apple, walnuts,
celery, raisins, and lemon juice.

In small cup or bowl combine mayonnaise, sour cream,
salt, and pepper; pour over chicken mixture and toss
thoroughly to combine. Line 2 salad plates with 2 lettuce
leaves each and top each portion with half of the chicken
mixture.

MAKES 2 SERVINGS

Each serving provides: 2 Protein Exchanges; ¾ Vegetable Exchange;
   1½ Fat Exchanges; 1 Fruit Exchange; 110 Optional Calories
Per serving: 329 calories; 19 g protein; 20 g fat; 20 g carbohydrate;
   63 mg calcium; 658 mg sodium; 58 mg cholesterol

Variation: Waldorf Salad with Yogurt Dressing (Week 8) —
Substitute ¼ cup plain low-fat yogurt for the sour cream.
Add ¼ Milk Exchange to Exchange Information and reduce
Optional Calories to 95.

Per serving: 332 calories; 21 g protein; 19 g fat; 22 g carbohydrate;
   107 mg calcium; 674 mg sodium; 56 mg cholesterol

BREAKFAST

BREAKFAST

Strawberries 'n' Yogurt (1 cup
strawberries, sliced, topped with
¼ cup plain low-fat yogurt)
1 slice Raisin Bread, toasted, with
1 teaspoon Reduced-Calorie
Margarine
½ cup Skim Milk
Coffee or Tea

LUNCH

Swiss Cheese Sandwich (2 ounces
sliced Swiss cheese with 3 lettuce
leaves and 2 teaspoons mustard
on 2 slices reduced-calorie wheat
bread)
½ cup Cauliflower Florets and
6 Cherry Tomatoes
½ medium Banana
Coffee, Tea, or Mineral Water

DINNER

1 serving **Parmesan Veal with
Mushroom-Wine Sauce**
½ cup Cooked Spaghetti with
2 teaspoons Reduced-Calorie
Margarine
½ cup *each* Cooked Sliced Zucchini
and Stewed Tomatoes
Celery-Carrot Salad (1 cup shredded
lettuce with ½ cup *each* sliced
celery and shredded carrot and
2 tablespoons reduced-calorie
Italian dressing)
1 small Apple, baked
Espresso

SNACKS

1 serving Reduced-Calorie Vanilla
Dairy Drink

Total Optional Calories: 55

Parmesan Veal with Mushroom-Wine Sauce ◖

**1 tablespoon <u>each</u> all-purpose flour and grated
Parmesan cheese**
¼ teaspoon salt, divided
⅛ teaspoon pepper
½ pound veal cutlets
1 tablespoon olive <u>or</u> vegetable oil, divided
1 cup diced onions
1 garlic clove, minced
1 cup sliced mushrooms
¼ teaspoon basil leaves
2 tablespoons <u>each</u> dry white table wine and water
1 tablespoon chopped fresh parsley

On sheet of wax paper or a paper plate combine flour,
Parmesan cheese, and ⅛ teaspoon each salt and pepper.
Dredge veal in flour mixture, coating both sides and
reserving any remaining flour mixture.

In 10-inch skillet heat 1½ teaspoons oil over medium-
high heat; add onions and garlic and sauté until onions are
softened. Add mushrooms, basil, and remaining ⅛ teaspoon
salt and sauté until mushrooms are tender, about 5 minutes.
Transfer mixture to a plate and set aside.

In same skillet heat remaining 1½ teaspoons oil; add veal
and cook, turning once, until lightly browned, 1 to 2 minutes
on each side. Stir in any reserved flour mixture; gradually
add wine and water and, continuing to stir, bring mixture
to a boil. Return mushroom mixture to pan and cook until
heated through. Serve sprinkled with parsley.

MAKES 2 SERVINGS

Each serving provides: 3 Protein Exchanges; 2 Vegetable Exchanges;
1½ Fat Exchanges; 45 Optional Calories
Per serving: 323 calories; 25 g protein; 18 g fat; 12 g carbohydrate;
82 mg calcium; 399 mg sodium; 83 mg cholesterol

Variation: Parmesan Chicken with Mushroom-Wine Sauce
(Week 2) — Substitute chicken cutlets for the veal.

Per serving: 262 calories; 29 g protein; 9 g fat; 12 g carbohydrate;
82 mg calcium; 395 mg sodium; 68 mg cholesterol

BREAKFAST

½ cup Grapefruit Sections
¾ ounce Cold Cereal
½ cup Skim Milk
Coffee or Tea

LUNCH

Tuna Sandwich (2 ounces tuna with
  2 tablespoons *each* chopped celery
  and red onion, 2 lettuce leaves, and
  1 tablespoon reduced-calorie
  mayonnaise on 2 slices reduced-
  calorie rye bread)
6 *each* Cucumber Spears and Red
  Bell Pepper Strips
10 small Grapes
Coffee, Tea, or Mineral Water

DINNER

Mushroom-Hamburger Special
  (3 ounces broiled hamburger with
  ½ cup sliced cooked mushrooms in
  1-ounce pita bread)
1 serving **Sweet and Sour Beets**
Lettuce and Tomato Salad (4 tomato
  slices with 1½ teaspoons French
  dressing mixed with 2 teaspoons
  lemon juice and ¼ teaspoon
  mustard on 4 lettuce leaves)
½ cup Cantaloupe Balls
Diet Soda

SNACKS

Apple Yogurt (¼ cup plain low-fat
  yogurt mixed with ½ small apple,
  diced); 1 serving Reduced-Calorie
  Chocolate Dairy Drink

Total Optional Calories: 30

Sweet and Sour Beets ⓒ

1¼ to 1½ pounds beets (with greens) or ¾ to 1 pound
  trimmed beets
1 cup water
¾ teaspoon salt, divided
2 tablespoons thawed frozen concentrated orange juice
  (no sugar added)
1 tablespoon each firmly packed dark brown sugar and
  lemon juice
2 teaspoons reduced-calorie margarine (tub)
½ cup diced onion
¼ teaspoon each grated orange peel, grated lemon peel,
  and pepper

Cut off all but 2 inches of beet tops (this will prevent beets
from "bleeding" during cooking). In 2½- or 3-quart
saucepan combine beets, water, and ½ teaspoon salt and
bring to a boil. Reduce heat to low, cover, and let simmer
until beets are tender, about 20 minutes; drain well. Cut off
beet tops and peel and slice beets (should yield about 2
cups); set aside.

In small bowl combine orange juice concentrate, sugar,
and lemon juice; set aside. In 2-quart saucepan heat
margarine until bubbly and hot; add onion and sauté until
golden. Add beets, juice mixture, orange and lemon peel,
pepper, and remaining ¼ teaspoon salt and, stirring
constantly, bring to a boil. Reduce heat and let simmer until
flavors blend, 3 to 4 minutes.

MAKES 2 SERVINGS

Each serving provides: 2½ Vegetable Exchanges; ½ Fat Exchange;
    ½ Fruit Exchange; 30 Optional Calories
Per serving: 140 calories; 3 g protein; 2 g fat; 28 g carbohydrate;
    45 mg calcium; 399 mg sodium; 0 mg cholesterol

BREAKFAST

2-inch wedge Honeydew Melon
½ English Muffin, toasted, with
   1 teaspoon Reduced-Calorie
   Margarine
1 cup Skim Milk

LUNCH

Turkey Sandwich (2 ounces sliced
   turkey with 2 lettuce leaves,
   3 tomato slices, and 2 teaspoons
   reduced-calorie mayonnaise on
   2 slices reduced-calorie wheat
   bread)
½ cup Cauliflower Florets and
   3 Radishes
1 medium Peach
Coffee, Tea, or Mineral Water

DINNER

1 serving **Greek Eggplant Salad**
4 ounces Broiled Lamb Chop
½ cup Cooked Noodles sprinkled
   with 1 teaspoon Grated Parmesan
   Cheese
½ cup Cooked Sliced Yellow Squash
1½ cups Tossed Salad with
   1 tablespoon Reduced-Calorie
   Italian Dressing
½ cup Low-Calorie Orange-Flavored
   Gelatin topped with 1 tablespoon
   Whipped Topping
Coffee or Tea

SNACKS

¾ cup Buttermilk; 1 cup
   Strawberries

Total Optional Calories: 35

Greek Eggplant Salad ©

Salad

1 large eggplant (about 1½ pounds)
1 medium tomato, diced
½ cup <u>each</u> diced onion and green bell pepper
2 tablespoons minced fresh Italian (flat-leaf) parsley
2 small garlic cloves, minced

Dressing

2 tablespoons <u>each</u> olive <u>or</u> vegetable oil and red wine vinegar
1 tablespoon lemon juice
1 teaspoon <u>each</u> oregano leaves and salt
½ teaspoon pepper

Garnish

1 lemon slice

To Prepare Salad: Preheat oven to 350°F. Using tines of fork, pierce eggplant; transfer to 8 x 8 x 2-inch baking pan and bake until eggplant is tender, about 30 minutes. Remove from oven and let cool.

   Cut eggplant in half lengthwise; remove pulp, discarding shell. Finely chop pulp and transfer to 1-quart salad bowl; add remaining ingredients for salad and stir to combine.

To Prepare Dressing and Serve: In small bowl combine all ingredients for dressing; pour over salad and stir to coat with dressing. Cover with plastic wrap and refrigerate until chilled. Just before serving, stir again and garnish with lemon slice.

MAKES 4 SERVINGS

Each serving provides: 3 Vegetable Exchanges; 1½ Fat Exchanges
Per serving: 125 calories; 3 g protein; 7 g fat; 15 g carbohydrate;
   85 mg calcium; 563 mg sodium; 0 mg cholesterol

BREAKFAST

½ cup Orange and Grapefruit
Sections
⅓ cup Cottage Cheese
½ cup Skim Milk
Coffee or Tea

LUNCH

Ham Sandwich (2 ounces boiled ham
with 2 *each* tomato slices and
lettuce leaves and 2 teaspoons
reduced-calorie mayonnaise on
2 slices pumpernickel bread)
6 *each* Celery Sticks and Cherry
Tomatoes
½ medium Banana
Coffee, Tea, or Mineral Water

DINNER

3 ounces Grilled Halibut Fillet with
Lemon Wedge
½ cup *each* Cooked Sliced Zucchini
and Carrot with 1 teaspoon
Reduced-Calorie Margarine
1 serving **Rice, Tomato, and Basil Salad**
½ cup Raspberries topped with ¼ cup
Plain Low-Fat Yogurt
Coffee or Tea

SNACKS

1 serving Reduced-Calorie Chocolate
Dairy Drink

Total Optional Calories: 5

Rice, Tomato, and Basil Salad ⊙◑

**1 cup cooked long-grain rice (hot) <u>or</u> 1 ½ ounces
uncooked orzo (rice-shaped macaroni), cooked
according to package directions and drained**
1 medium tomato, diced
¼ cup thinly sliced scallions (green onions)
1 tablespoon olive <u>or</u> vegetable oil
2 teaspoons dry white table wine
1 ½ teaspoons white wine vinegar
1 teaspoon lemon juice
½ teaspoon salt
½ small garlic clove
⅛ teaspoon pepper
2 tablespoons fresh basil leaves
1 tablespoon Italian (flat-leaf) parsley sprigs

In salad bowl combine rice, tomato, and scallions. In
blender container combine remaining ingredients except
basil and parsley and process until well blended; add basil
and parsley and, using an on-off motion, process until
chopped (<u>do not puree</u>). Pour dressing over salad and toss
to coat. Serve immediately or cover with plastic wrap and
refrigerate until chilled; toss again just before serving.

MAKES 2 SERVINGS, ABOUT 1 CUP EACH

Each serving provides: 1 Bread Exchange; 1¼ Vegetable Exchanges;
    1½ Fat Exchanges; 5 Optional Calories
Per serving with rice: 204 calories; 4 g protein; 7 g fat; 32 g carbohydrate;
    125 mg calcium; 556 mg sodium; 0 mg cholesterol
With macaroni: 171 calories; 4 g protein; 7 g fat; 23 g carbohydrate;
    121 mg calcium; 556 mg sodium; 0 mg cholesterol

Mexican Pasta Salad ⓒ ◑

For added flavor, set chili pepper on baking sheet lined with heavy-duty foil and broil 3 inches from heat source, turning frequently, until charred on all sides; let stand until cool enough to handle. Peel pepper; remove and discard stem ends and seeds. Chop pepper and proceed as directed.

1½ cups cooked small shell <u>or</u> elbow macaroni
1 medium tomato, chopped
¼ cup <u>each</u> diced onion and red <u>or</u> green bell pepper
1 medium mild <u>or</u> hot green chili pepper, seeded and chopped
1½ teaspoons chopped fresh cilantro (Chinese parsley)
½ small garlic clove, minced
1 tablespoon olive oil
1½ teaspoons <u>each</u> red wine vinegar and lime juice (no sugar added)
¼ teaspoon salt
⅛ teaspoon oregano leaves
Dash pepper

In large bowl (not aluminum*) combine macaroni, tomato, onion, bell pepper, chili pepper, cilantro, and garlic. In small bowl combine remaining ingredients; pour over salad and toss to coat. Cover and refrigerate until chilled. Toss again before serving.

MAKES 2 SERVINGS

Each serving provides: 1½ Bread Exchanges; 2 Vegetable Exchanges;
    1½ Fat Exchanges
Per serving: 204 calories; 5 g protein; 7 g fat; 30 g carbohydrate;
    25 mg calcium; 279 mg sodium; 0 mg cholesterol

*It's best to marinate in glass or stainless-steel containers; acidic ingredients such as vinegar and lime juice may react with aluminum, causing color and flavor changes in foods.

BREAKFAST

1 medium Peach, sliced
Honey-Cinnamon Yogurt (½ cup plain
    low-fat yogurt mixed with
    ½ teaspoon honey plus cinnamon)
1 slice Raisin Bread, toasted
Coffee or Tea

LUNCH

Tuna Salad Sandwich (2 ounces tuna
    with 2 tablespoons *each* diced
    celery and tomato and 2 teaspoons
    reduced-calorie mayonnaise on
    2 slices reduced-calorie rye bread)
½ cup Sliced Yellow Squash and
    6 Red Bell Pepper Strips
½ medium Banana
Coffee, Tea, or Mineral Water

DINNER

4 ounces Sliced Roast Veal
Vegetable Medley (½ cup *each*
    cooked cauliflower florets, sliced
    carrot, and sliced zucchini sprinkled
    with lemon juice)
Arugula Salad (1½ cups torn arugula
    with 6 tomato slices) with
    2 teaspoons **Basil Mayonnaise**
½ cup Reduced-Calorie Butterscotch
    Pudding
Coffee or Tea

SNACKS

1 cup Honeydew Melon Balls

Total Optional Calories: 10

Basil Mayonnaise ◖◑

This colorful dressing adds a delightful taste to chicken salad, pasta salad, or a crisp green salad.

½ cup firmly packed fresh basil leaves
1 egg
1 tablespoon freshly squeezed lemon juice
½ to 1 small garlic clove
½ teaspoon salt
1 cup olive <u>or</u> vegetable oil

In blender container combine all ingredients except oil and process until smooth, scraping down sides of container as necessary. Remove center of blender cover and, with motor running at high speed, slowly add oil in a thin stream. When oil is well combined, turn off motor. Scrape down sides of container; process until blended, about ½ second. Transfer to resealable plastic container, cover, and refrigerate until ready to use.

YIELDS ABOUT 1 CUP

Each 1-teaspoon serving provides: 1 Fat Exchange
Per serving: 34 calories; 0.1 g protein; 4 g fat; 0.1 g carbohydrate;
    4 mg calcium; 19 mg sodium; 5 mg cholesterol

BREAKFAST

½ cup Grapefruit Sections
¾ ounce Cold Cereal
¾ cup Skim Milk
Coffee or Tea

LUNCH

Egg Salad in a Pita (2 hard-cooked
   eggs, chopped, with 2 teaspoons
   each chopped celery and
   mayonnaise in 1-ounce whole
   wheat pita bread)
6 *each* Carrot Sticks and Cucumber
   Spears
1 small Apple
Coffee, Tea, or Mineral Water

DINNER

3 ounces Broiled Chicken
1 cup Cooked Wax Beans with
   1 teaspoon Margarine
½ cup Stewed Tomatoes
Spinach Salad (1½ cups torn spinach
   with ½ cup sliced mushrooms and
   4 red onion rings) with 2 tablespoons **Lemon Salad Dressing**
½ cup Fruit Salad
Iced Tea with Lemon Twist

SNACKS

1 serving Reduced-Calorie Vanilla
   Dairy Drink

Total Optional Calories: 10

Lemon Salad Dressing ©◑

This tangy dressing is excellent with a green salad or crisp cucumber slices.

¼ cup plain low-fat yogurt
1½ teaspoons freshly squeezed lemon juice*
¾ teaspoon granulated sugar
¼ teaspoon salt
Dash pepper

In small bowl combine all ingredients; cover with plastic wrap and refrigerate until chilled.

YIELDS ABOUT ¼ CUP

Each 2-tablespoon serving provides: ¼ Milk Exchange;
   10 Optional Calories
Per serving: 25 calories; 1 g protein; 0.4 g fat; 4 g carbohydrate;
   54 mg calcium; 290 mg sodium; 2 mg cholesterol

*For a more tart dressing, add up to an additional 2¼ teaspoons lemon juice.

BREAKFAST

BREAKFAST

¼ small Cantaloupe
Swiss Melt (1 ounce Swiss cheese
  melted on 1 slice rye bread)
¾ cup Skim Milk

LUNCH

Chicken Sandwich (2 ounces sliced
  chicken with 2 lettuce leaves and
  2 teaspoons reduced-calorie
  mayonnaise on 2 slices reduced-
  calorie wheat bread)
½ cup Broccoli Florets and 6 Yellow
  Squash Sticks
10 large Cherries
Coffee, Tea, or Mineral Water

DINNER

3 ounces Broiled Shrimp with
  Lemon Wedge
3 ounces Baked Potato topped with
  2 tablespoons Plain Low-Fat
  Yogurt plus Chopped Chives
1 cup Cooked Chinese Pea Pods
Cucumber-Radish Salad
  (12 cucumber slices, 6 sliced
  radishes, and 4 green bell pepper
  rings with 1 tablespoon buttermilk
  dressing on 4 lettuce leaves)
1 serving **Party Chocolate Chip-Filled
  Cones**
Coffee or Tea

SNACKS

1 small Nectarine; ½ cup Reduced-
  Calorie Vanilla Pudding sprinkled
  with 1 teaspoon Shredded Toasted
  Coconut

Total Optional Calories: 130

Party Chocolate Chip-Filled Cones ◑

Similar to Italian cannoli, but so much easier!

1 cup part-skim ricotta cheese
**1 ounce mini chocolate chips (reserve some of the chips
  for garnish)**
2 tablespoons confectioners' sugar
½ teaspoon grated orange peel, divided
4 sugar cones (½ ounce each)

In medium mixing bowl combine ricotta cheese, all except
reserved chocolate, the sugar, and ¼ teaspoon orange peel.
Cover and refrigerate until ready to use.

To serve, spoon ¼ of the cheese mixture into each cone,
or fit a pastry bag with a wide tip, fill bag with cheese
mixture, and pipe mixture into cones. Garnish cheese
mixture in each cone with ¼ of the reserved chocolate and
¼ of the remaining orange peel.

MAKES 4 SERVINGS, 1 CONE EACH

Each serving provides: 1 Protein Exchange; 120 Optional Calories
Per serving: 202 calories; 8 g protein; 9 g fat; 22 g carbohydrate;
  190 mg calcium; 119 mg sodium; 26 mg cholesterol

BREAKFAST

1 medium Kiwi Fruit, sliced
1/3 cup Cottage Cheese
1/2 English Muffin, toasted
1/4 cup Skim Milk
Coffee or Tea

LUNCH

Turkey Sandwich (2 ounces sliced
    turkey with 4 lettuce leaves,
    3 tomato slices, and 2 teaspoons
    reduced-calorie mayonnaise on
    2 slices reduced-calorie
    white bread)
6 *each* Red and Green Bell Pepper
    Strips
20 small Grapes
Coffee, Tea, or Mineral Water

DINNER

3 ounces Grilled Steak
1/2 cup Mushrooms sautéed in
    1 teaspoon Reduced-Calorie
    Margarine
1 small Ear Corn, cooked, with
    1 teaspoon Reduced-Calorie
    Margarine
1/2 cup Cooked Baby Carrots with
    Mint Leaves
1/2 cup Cooked Chopped Spinach
1 1/2 cups Tossed Salad with
    1 1/2 teaspoons Buttermilk Dressing
    mixed with 2 tablespoons Plain
    Low-Fat Yogurt and 1/4 teaspoon
    Mustard
1 serving **Silver Jubilee Sundae**
Coffee or Tea

SNACKS

1 serving Reduced-Calorie Chocolate
    Dairy Drink

Total Optional Calories: 200

Silver Jubilee Sundae ◑

A luscious vanilla sundae with banana sauce.

2 teaspoons margarine
1 medium banana (about 6 ounces), peeled and sliced
2 tablespoons vanilla- or banana-flavored liqueur
1 tablespoon firmly packed light brown sugar
1/8 teaspoon ground cinnamon
1 cup vanilla ice milk

In 10-inch nonstick skillet heat margarine over medium-high heat until bubbly and hot; add banana slices and sauté, stirring frequently, until banana is lightly browned, about 1 minute. Carefully stir in liqueur, sugar, and cinnamon, stirring to dissolve sugar; continue cooking, stirring frequently, until banana is cooked through and mixture thickens, 2 to 3 minutes.

To serve, into each of 2 dessert dishes scoop 1/2 cup ice milk and top each portion with half of the sauce.

MAKES 2 SERVINGS, 1 SUNDAE EACH

Each serving provides: 1 Fat Exchange; 1 Fruit Exchange; 200 Optional
    Calories
Per serving: 245 calories; 3 g protein; 7 g fat; 39 g carbohydrate; 100 mg
    calcium; 100 mg sodium; 9 mg cholesterol

Variation: Pecan-Topped Sundae (Week 8) — Add 1/2 ounce chopped pecans to skillet along with banana slices; proceed as directed. Increase Optional Calories to 250.

Per serving: 293 calories; 4 g protein; 12 g fat; 40 g carbohydrate;
    103 mg calcium; 100 mg sodium; 9 mg cholesterol

BREAKFAST

½ cup Orange Sections
1 Sunny-Side-Up Egg
1 slice Whole Wheat Bread, toasted
1 cup Skim Milk

LUNCH

Salmon in a Pita (2 ounces salmon
    with ¼ cup chopped celery and
    1 teaspoon mayonnaise in 1-ounce
    pita bread)
½ cup Broccoli Florets and
    6 Cucumber Spears
1 medium Peach
Coffee, Tea, or Mineral Water

DINNER

3 ounces Roast Chicken
½ cup *each* Cooked Cut Wax and
    Green Beans with Thyme Leaves
Spinach Salad (1 cup torn spinach
    with ½ cup shredded red cabbage,
    ¼ cup shredded carrot, and
    1 tablespoon French dressing)
1 cup **Watermelon Sorbet**
Coffee or Tea

SNACKS

½ cup Reduced-Calorie Chocolate
    Pudding

Total Optional Calories: 45

Watermelon Sorbet ⓒ ◑

4 cups pitted watermelon cubes
3 tablespoons confectioners' sugar
1 tablespoon lemon juice

In work bowl of food processor combine all ingredients and process until smooth;* transfer to large freezer-safe bowl, cover with plastic freezer wrap, and freeze until edges of mixture are firm, about 2 hours.

Remove sorbet from freezer and, using a fork, break into pieces. Using electric mixer, beat sorbet until fluffy but not melted; cover bowl and freeze until mixture is firm, at least 1 hour (may be frozen overnight).

When ready to serve, let sorbet stand at room temperature to soften slightly, about 10 minutes.

MAKES 4 SERVINGS, ABOUT 1 CUP EACH
<u>OR</u> 8 SERVINGS, ABOUT ½ CUP EACH

Each 1-cup serving provides: 1 Fruit Exchange; 45 Optional Calories
Per serving: 74 calories; 1 g protein; 0.7 g fat; 17 g carbohydrate;
    13 mg calcium; 4 mg sodium; 0 mg cholesterol
Each ½-cup serving provides: ½ Fruit Exchange; 25 Optional Calories
Per serving: 37 calories; 0.5 g protein; 0.4 g fat; 9 g carbohydrate;
    7 mg calcium; 2 mg sodium; 0 mg cholesterol

*If food processor is not available, blender may be used; combine all ingredients in bowl, then process 1 cup at a time.

TIP: Prepare this easy-to-toss-together treat the night before and let your freezer do its work while you sleep; the next day, enjoy a delicious dessert in 10 minutes.

BREAKFAST

½ medium Papaya
Ricotta 'n' Bagel (½ small bagel,
    toasted, topped with 2 tablespoons
    part-skim ricotta cheese and
    2 teaspoons reduced-calorie
    strawberry spread)
½ cup Skim Milk
Coffee or Tea

LUNCH

Roast Beef Sandwich (2 ounces roast
    beef with 2 *each* tomato slices and
    lettuce leaves and 2 teaspoons
    mustard on 2 slices reduced-calorie
    rye bread)
6 *each* Carrot and Celery Sticks
2 medium Plums
Coffee, Tea, or Mineral Water

DINNER

4 ounces Broiled Veal Chop
½ cup Cooked Spaghetti with
    1 teaspoon *each* Margarine and
    Grated Parmesan Cheese
½ cup *each* Cooked Sliced Zucchini
    and Yellow Squash
1½ cups Mixed Green Salad with
    1 tablespoon Russian Dressing
½ cup Reduced-Calorie Vanilla
    Pudding
Coffee or Tea

SNACKS

1 serving **Orange-Vanilla Froth**;
    Cinnamon-Raisin Yogurt (½ cup
    plain low-fat yogurt mixed with
    2 tablespoons raisins plus
    cinnamon)

Total Optional Calories: 145

Orange-Vanilla Froth ⓒ ◑

Low-calorie orange-flavored drink is an instant
beverage prepared from a powdered mix. It comes
in tubs that make 2 quarts each or in canisters for
preparing individual servings or pitcherfuls.

**1 cup <u>each</u> low-calorie orange-flavored drink (4 calories
    per 8 fluid ounces) and vanilla ice milk
3 ice cubes**

Chill two 10-ounce glasses. In blender container combine
orange drink and ice milk and process until combined; with
motor running add ice cubes, 1 at a time, processing after
each addition until all ice is dissolved and mixture is
smooth. Pour into chilled glasses and serve immediately.

MAKES 2 SERVINGS, ABOUT 1 CUP EACH

Each serving provides: 120 Optional Calories
Per serving: 94 calories; 3 g protein; 3 g fat; 14 g carbohydrate;
    88 mg calcium; 52 mg sodium; 9 mg cholesterol

BREAKFAST

½ cup Orange and Grapefruit
   Sections
¾ ounce Cold Cereal
½ cup Skim Milk
Coffee or Tea

LUNCH

Chicken Salad in a Pita (2 ounces
   diced chicken with ¼ cup chopped
   celery and 1 teaspoon mayonnaise
   in 1-ounce pita bread)
6 *each* Red and Green Bell Pepper
   Strips
½ medium Banana
Coffee, Tea, or Mineral Water

DINNER

3 ounces Broiled Flounder Fillet
   with Lemon Wedge
½ cup *each* Cooked Chopped
   Spinach and Stewed Tomatoes
2 cups Tossed Salad with
   1 tablespoon Italian Dressing
½ cup Reduced-Calorie Butterscotch
   Pudding
Coffee or Tea

SNACKS

1 serving **Peachy Buttermilk Shake**;
   ½ cup Low-Calorie Strawberry-
   Flavored Gelatin

Total Optional Calories: 55

Peachy Buttermilk Shake ⓒ ◐

**½ pound peaches, blanched,* peeled, pitted, and
   chopped**
½ cup skim milk
⅓ cup plus 2 teaspoons buttermilk
1 tablespoon plus 1 teaspoon granulated sugar
1 tablespoon orange juice (no sugar added)
1 teaspoon vanilla extract
5 to 6 ice cubes

Chill two 12-ounce glasses. In blender container combine all
ingredients except ice; process until smooth. With motor
running add ice cubes, 1 at a time, processing until mixture is
thick and frothy. Pour into chilled glasses and serve
immediately.

MAKES 2 SERVINGS, ABOUT 1¼ CUPS EACH

Each serving provides: 1 Fruit Exchange; ½ Milk Exchange; 45 Optional
   Calories
Per serving: 120 calories; 4 g protein; 0.6 g fat; 25 g carbohydrate;
   134 mg calcium; 80 mg sodium; 3 mg cholesterol

*To blanch peaches, cut an X through the skin at the bottom of each peach.
 Plunge peaches into boiling water for a few seconds until skin begins to
 peel at the X. Drain, let cool, then peel.

September

Apple Crisp

SEPTEMBER'S BEST BUYS FOR FRUITS AND VEGETABLES

alfalfa sprouts	celery	honeydew	pineapples
arugula	Chinese pea pods	kiwi fruit	plums
bananas	corn on the cob	lettuce	potatoes
bean sprouts	cucumbers	mangoes	radishes
beets	eggplants	mushrooms	scallions (green onions)
bell peppers	figs	onions	summer squash
cabbage	grapes	pears	tomatoes
carrots	green beans	persimmons	watermelon
cauliflower			

2-inch wedge Honeydew Melon
1 Sunny-Side-Up Egg
1 slice Whole Wheat Bread, toasted,
    with 1 teaspoon Reduced-Calorie
    Margarine
¾ cup Skim Milk

LUNCH

Turkey on a Bagel (2 ounces sliced
    turkey with 3 tomato slices,
    4 lettuce leaves, and 2 teaspoons
    mayonnaise on 1 small bagel)
6 *each* Celery and Carrot Sticks
1 small Apple
Coffee, Tea, or Mineral Water

DINNER

1 serving **Cream of Tomato Soup**
4 ounces Broiled Swordfish Steak
1 cup Cooked Cut Green Beans
Red and Green Cabbage Salad (¾ cup
    each shredded red and green
    cabbage with 4 green bell pepper
    rings and 1 tablespoon reduced-
    calorie Italian dressing on
    4 romaine lettuce leaves)
4 fluid ounces Dry White Wine

SNACKS

½ cup Reduced-Calorie Vanilla
    Pudding drizzled with 1 teaspoon
    Chocolate Syrup

Total Optional Calories: 165

Cream of Tomato Soup Ⓒ

2 teaspoons reduced-calorie margarine (tub)
2 tablespoons diced onion
½ garlic clove, minced
2 teaspoons all-purpose flour
3 medium tomatoes, blanched, peeled, seeded, and
    chopped
¼ cup dry white table wine
1 teaspoon chopped fresh basil, divided
¼ cup evaporated skimmed milk
¼ teaspoon salt
⅛ teaspoon pepper

In 1-quart saucepan heat margarine over medium heat
until bubbly and hot; add onion and garlic and sauté until
softened. Sprinkle with flour and stir quickly to combine;
cook, stirring constantly, for 2 minutes. Stir in tomatoes and
cook, stirring occasionally, for 5 minutes; add wine and
½ teaspoon basil and let simmer for 10 minutes. Remove
from heat and let cool slightly.

Pour soup into blender container and process at low
speed until smooth; pour soup back into saucepan. Add
milk, salt, and pepper; let simmer for 5 minutes (do not boil).
Serve sprinkled with remaining ½ teaspoon basil.

MAKES 2 SERVINGS, ABOUT ¾ CUP EACH

Each serving provides: 3⅛ Vegetable Exchanges; ½ Fat Exchange;
    ¼ Milk Exchange; 40 Optional Calories
Per serving: 105 calories; 4 g protein; 2 g fat; 13 g carbohydrate;
    137 mg calcium; 544 mg sodium; 1 mg cholesterol

TIP: Is creamed soup too much to fuss with when preparing dinner? Not if
you do most of the work in advance. Follow the recipe up until the point of
adding the milk, then refrigerate or freeze. When you want to enjoy this
delicious meal starter, just heat, add milk, salt, and pepper, and proceed
as directed.

BREAKFAST

½ medium Grapefruit sprinkled with
   ½ teaspoon Sugar
1 ounce Muenster Cheese
½ English Muffin, toasted, with
   1 teaspoon Reduced-Calorie
   Margarine
½ cup Skim Milk
Coffee or Tea

LUNCH

Peanut Butter and Jelly Sandwich
   (2 tablespoons peanut butter with
   2 teaspoons reduced-calorie apricot
   spread on 2 slices raisin bread)
20 small Grapes
Coffee, Tea, or Mineral Water

DINNER

1 serving **Eggplant Soup**
3 ounces Baked Veal Cutlet
1 cup *each* Cooked Sliced Zucchini
   and Carrots
1½ cups Mixed Green Salad with
   1 tablespoon Russian Dressing
½ cup Skim Milk
Coffee or Tea

SNACKS

Peach Yogurt (½ cup plain low-fat
   yogurt mixed with ½ cup canned
   peach slices)

Total Optional Calories: 130

Eggplant Soup ⊙

A great soup to have on hand. Double or triple the recipe and freeze extra in individual portions.

1 teaspoon olive <u>or</u> vegetable oil
¼ cup diced onion
½ garlic clove, minced
½ cup pared cubed eggplant
¼ cup <u>each</u> chopped green bell pepper, sliced celery, and sliced mushrooms
1½ cups water
1 medium tomato, blanched, peeled, seeded, and chopped
1 packet instant chicken broth and seasoning mix
¼ teaspoon basil leaves
⅛ teaspoon pepper
1 ounce drained canned white kidney (cannellini) beans

In 1-quart saucepan heat oil over medium heat; add onion and garlic and sauté until onion is softened, 2 to 3 minutes. Add eggplant, bell pepper, celery, and mushrooms and cook, stirring occasionally, for 5 minutes. Add water, tomato, broth mix, basil, and pepper and bring to a boil. Reduce heat, cover, and let simmer for 20 minutes; add beans and cook until vegetables are tender and beans are thoroughly heated, about 5 minutes longer.

MAKES 2 SERVINGS, ABOUT 1 CUP EACH

Each serving provides: 2½ Vegetable Exchanges; ½ Fat Exchange;
   25 Optional Calories
Per serving: 76 calories; 3 g protein; 3 g fat; 11 g carbohydrate;
   35 mg calcium; 552 mg sodium; 0 mg cholesterol

Rumaki-Style Date 'n' Cheese Bits ◐

For party fare, just double, triple, or quadruple this recipe and <u>voilà</u>, delicious and different quick-and-easy hors d'oeuvres.

4 pitted dates, split open lengthwise
**1 ounce Fontina, Swiss, <u>or</u> Gruyère cheese, cut into
    four ¹/₂-inch cubes**
2 slices crisp bacon, cut crosswise into quarters
2 tablespoons teriyaki sauce
2 teaspoons chopped chives

Preheat oven to 350°F. Into each date place a cheese cube. Arrange 1 piece of bacon on each long side of each stuffed date and secure with toothpicks. Transfer to shallow bowl (not aluminum*); sprinkle with teriyaki sauce and turn gently to coat. Let stand for 10 minutes, turning occasionally.

Transfer stuffed dates to nonstick baking sheet, reserving marinade. Bake until cheese begins to melt, about 5 minutes.

While dates are baking, in small serving bowl combine reserved marinade with chives.

To serve, transfer dates to serving platter and serve with teriyaki mixture for dipping.

MAKES 2 SERVINGS, 2 BITS EACH

Each serving provides: ½ Protein Exchange; 1 Fruit Exchange;
    45 Optional Calories
Per serving with Fontina cheese: 155 calories; 6 g protein; 8 g fat;
    16 g carbohydrate; 85 mg calcium; 700 mg sodium;
    22 mg cholesterol
With Swiss cheese: 153 calories; 7 g protein; 7 g fat; 16 g carbohydrate;
    143 mg calcium; 737 mg sodium; 18 mg cholesterol
With Gruyère cheese: 158 calories; 7 g protein; 8 g fat; 16 g carbohydrate;
    150 mg calcium; 748 mg sodium; 21 mg cholesterol

*It's best to marinate in glass or stainless-steel containers; ingredients
    such as teriyaki sauce may react with aluminum, causing color and
    flavor changes in foods.

Grape-Stuffed Cheese Balls

2 tablespoons cream cheese (at room temperature)
**1 ounce <u>each</u> Brie cheese (rind removed) and Roquefort
    cheese (at room temperature)**
6 large seedless grapes
1 tablespoon minced fresh parsley

In small mixing bowl combine cheeses and, using electric
mixer at medium speed, beat until thoroughly blended.
Cover with plastic wrap and refrigerate for at least 15
minutes (may be refrigerated overnight).

Line plate with sheet of wax paper and set aside. Using
palms of hands, flatten ¹/₆ of cheese mixture (about 1
tablespoon) into a small circle; place 1 grape in center of
circle and roll cheese to enclose. Roll cheese ball in minced
parsley and set on prepared plate. Repeat procedure 5
more times, making 5 more cheese balls; serve immediately
or cover and refrigerate until ready to use.

MAKES 2 SERVINGS, 3 BALLS EACH

Each serving provides: 1 Protein Exchange; 65 Optional Calories
Per serving: 161 calories; 7 g protein; 13 g fat; 4 g carbohydrate;
    135 mg calcium; 389 mg sodium; 43 mg cholesterol

Variation: Pecan-Cheese Balls (Week 8) — Omit parsley and roll cheese balls in ½ ounce chopped pecans. Increase Optional Calories to 115.

Per serving: 208 calories; 8 g protein; 18 g fat; 5 g carbohydrate;
    136 mg calcium; 388 mg sodium; 43 mg cholesterol

BRUNCH

Mimosa (½ cup *each* orange juice
and champagne with mint sprig)
1 serving **Italian Cheese and Egg Bake**
2 ounces Grilled Ham
1½ cups Tossed Salad with
1 teaspoon Olive Oil mixed with
2 teaspoons Red Wine Vinegar
plus Seasonings
Café au Lait (½ cup *each* hot coffee
and skim milk, sprinkled with
nutmeg)

DINNER

3 ounces Poached Salmon Fillet
with Lemon Wedge
1 cup Cooked Long-Grain and Wild
Rice with Chopped Chives
1 cup Cooked Cut Green Beans
Radish-Pepper Salad (¼ cup sliced
radishes with 4 green bell pepper
rings and 2 teaspoons reduced-
calorie mayonnaise on 8 Boston
lettuce leaves)
Peach 'n' Yogurt (½ cup canned
peach slices topped with ¼ cup
plain low-fat yogurt)
Coffee, Tea, or Mineral Water

SNACKS

12 large Grapes; ¾ cup Skim Milk

Total Optional Calories: 150

Italian Cheese and Egg Bake ©

This delicious cross between a quiche and French toast is ideal for one of those lazy weekend brunches. Prepare it the night before and, before baking, cover and refrigerate. Then, in the morning, just uncover and pop it in the oven (increase baking time to 40 to 45 minutes).

1 tablespoon plus 1 teaspoon margarine
½ small garlic clove
4 slices Italian bread (1 ounce each)
1 cup skim milk
2 eggs
½ cup part-skim ricotta cheese
2 tablespoons grated Parmesan cheese
⅛ teaspoon white pepper
1 ounce <u>each</u> Fontina and Monterey Jack cheeses, shredded

Preheat oven to 375°F. In small saucepan heat margarine over medium heat until bubbly and hot; add garlic and sauté, stirring frequently, until golden, about 1 minute. Remove and discard garlic. In 8 x 8 x 2-inch baking pan, using a pastry brush, brush margarine over bottom and up sides of pan; arrange bread slices in a single layer in bottom of pan and set aside.

In medium mixing bowl beat together milk, eggs, and ricotta cheese until thoroughly combined; stir in Parmesan cheese and pepper. Pour mixture over bread in baking pan and sprinkle with Fontina and Monterey Jack cheeses. Bake until mixture is set and lightly browned, 25 to 30 minutes; serve immediately.

MAKES 4 SERVINGS

Each serving provides: 1½ Protein Exchanges; 1 Bread Exchange;
1 Fat Exchange; ¼ Milk Exchange; 15 Optional Calories
Per serving: 281 calories; 16 g protein; 14 g fat; 21 g carbohydrate;
306 mg calcium; 400 mg sodium; 164 mg cholesterol

BREAKFAST

½ medium Grapefruit sprinkled with
½ teaspoon Confectioners' Sugar
1 Soft-Cooked Egg
1 slice Reduced-Calorie Wheat
Bread with 1 teaspoon Reduced-
Calorie Margarine
1 cup Skim Milk

LUNCH

Tuna Salad (2 ounces tuna with
¼ cup chopped celery and
2 teaspoons mayonnaise)
6 each Zucchini Sticks and Red Bell
Pepper Strips
3 Sesame Melba Rounds
1 small Orange
Coffee, Tea, or Mineral Water

DINNER

1 serving **Cottage Ham 'n' Apple Quiche**
6 Cooked Broccoli Spears
Spinach Salad (2 cups torn spinach
with 1 cup sliced mushrooms,
½ cup carrot strips, 1 teaspoon
imitation bacon bits, and
2 tablespoons reduced-calorie
Italian dressing)
Mint Tea

SNACKS

Fruited Yogurt (½ cup plain low-fat
yogurt mixed with ¼ cup canned
fruit cocktail); 2 Rice Cakes

Total Optional Calories: 35

Cottage Ham 'n' Apple Quiche ©

**4 ready-to-bake refrigerated buttermilk flaky biscuits
(1 ounce each)
2 teaspoons margarine
½ pound apples, cored, pared, and thinly sliced
2 ounces boiled ham, diced
½ cup chopped onion
2 ounces Cheddar cheese, shredded
⅔ cup cottage cheese
2 eggs
¼ cup skim milk
⅛ teaspoon ground nutmeg
Dash white pepper**

Preheat oven to 375°F. Carefully separate each biscuit into 4 thin layers of dough.* In 8-inch pie plate arrange biscuits with edges touching, in concentric circles, over bottom and up sides of plate; using fingers, spread to form crust, pressing edges of biscuits together to seal. Place sheet of foil over bottom of dough and fill with uncooked dry beans; bake for 5 minutes. Remove beans and foil; set crust aside.

In 10-inch nonstick skillet heat margarine over medium-high heat until bubbly and hot; add apples, ham, and onion and sauté until apples are tender, 2 to 3 minutes. Spoon apple mixture into crust and sprinkle with shredded cheese; set aside.

In blender container combine cottage cheese, eggs, milk, and seasonings and process until smooth, scraping down sides of container as necessary; pour into pie plate. Set pie plate on baking sheet and bake for 30 to 40 minutes (until top is puffed and lightly browned and a knife, inserted in center, comes out clean). Remove from oven and, keeping warm, let stand for 10 minutes.

MAKES 4 SERVINGS

Each serving provides: 2 Protein Exchanges; 1 Bread Exchange;
¼ Vegetable Exchange; ½ Fat Exchange; ½ Fruit Exchange;
5 Optional Calories
Per serving: 296 calories; 16 g protein; 15 g fat;
24 g carbohydrate; 165 mg calcium; 759 mg sodium;
165 mg cholesterol

*Separate dough into layers as soon as it is removed from the refrigerator; it will be difficult to work with if allowed to come to room temperature.

BREAKFAST

½ cup Canned Fruit Cocktail
½ cup Cooked Oatmeal
½ cup Skim Milk
Coffee or Tea

LUNCH

Roast Beef Sandwich (2 ounces sliced
    roast beef with 2 onion slices,
    4 lettuce leaves, 1 teaspoon
    mayonnaise, and 2 teaspoons
    ketchup on 1-ounce rye roll)
6 Celery Sticks and 4 Radishes
Coffee, Tea, or Mineral Water

DINNER

1 serving **Scallop 'n' Cheese Broil**
Parslied Tomato (½ medium tomato
    sprinkled with parsley and broiled)
1 cup Cooked Sliced Zucchini
1½ cups Tossed Salad with
    1½ teaspoons Olive Oil mixed with
    2 teaspoons Tarragon Vinegar plus
    Seasonings
½ cup Reduced-Calorie Chocolate
    Pudding
Coffee or Tea

SNACKS

½ cup Orange Sections; ½ cup Skim
    Milk

Total Optional Calories: 10

Scallop 'n' Cheese Broil ◑

Any firm white fish fillet, cut into bite-size pieces,
can be substituted for the scallops.

7 ounces sea <u>or</u> bay scallops
1 tablespoon lemon juice
1 teaspoon margarine, melted
Dash <u>each</u> salt and pepper
1 ounce Swiss, Monterey Jack, <u>or</u> Cheddar cheese,
    shredded

Preheat broiler. In broiler pan combine scallops, lemon
juice, and margarine, tossing to coat scallops. Spread
scallops in a single layer in pan and sprinkle with salt and
pepper; broil until golden, 2 to 3 minutes. Sprinkle with
cheese and broil until cheese is melted and browned,
1 to 2 minutes; serve immediately.

MAKES 2 SERVINGS

Each serving provides: 3 Protein Exchanges; ½ Fat Exchange
Per serving with Swiss cheese: 162 calories; 21 g protein; 7 g fat;
    3 g carbohydrate; 156 mg calcium; 286 mg sodium;
    50 mg cholesterol
With Monterey Jack cheese: 162 calories; 21 g protein; 7 g fat;
    3 g carbohydrate; 125 mg calcium; 326 mg sodium;
    49 mg cholesterol
With Cheddar cheese: 166 calories; 21 g protein; 7 g fat;
    3 g carbohydrate; 122 mg calcium; 337 mg sodium;
    51 mg cholesterol

Scallop and Bacon Sauté

¼ cup **each** dry white table wine and water
1 bay leaf
2 to 3 peppercorns
½ pound sea **or** bay scallops
2 teaspoons margarine
2 tablespoons chopped onion
1 tablespoon minced shallots
½ small garlic clove, minced
1 tablespoon all-purpose flour
3 slices crisp bacon, diced, divided
2 tablespoons half-and-half (blend of milk and
  cream)
1 teaspoon **each** prepared horseradish and grated
  Parmesan cheese

In 8-inch skillet combine wine, water, bay leaf, and
peppercorns and cook over medium heat until mixture
comes to a boil; add scallops. Reduce heat to low and let
simmer until scallops begin to turn opaque and are partially
cooked, 1 to 2 minutes. Using a slotted spoon, divide
scallops into 2 flameproof au gratin dishes, reserving
cooking liquid; set scallops aside.

Set sieve over small bowl and pour cooking liquid through
sieve; discard bay leaf and peppercorns and set liquid aside.

In 1-quart saucepan heat margarine over medium heat
until bubbly and hot; add onion, shallots, and garlic and
sauté until onion is softened, about 1 minute. Sprinkle with
flour and stir quickly to combine; continuing to stir, gradually
add reserved cooking liquid. Add half the bacon and the
half-and-half and horseradish and stir well to combine.
Reduce heat to low and let simmer, stirring frequently, until
slightly thickened, 5 to 7 minutes. Spoon half of mixture into
each au gratin dish, then top each portion with half of the
remaining bacon and ½ teaspoon Parmesan cheese. Broil 6
to 7 inches from heat source until sauce is bubbly and lightly
browned and scallops are cooked, about 5 minutes; serve
immediately.

MAKES 2 SERVINGS

Each serving provides: 3 Protein Exchanges; ⅛ Vegetable Exchange ;
  1 Fat Exchange; 145 Optional Calories
Per serving: 264 calories; 24 g protein; 11 g fat; 10 g carbohydrate;
  64 mg calcium; 406 mg sodium; 56 mg cholesterol

Pasta with Roasted Pepper Sauce

Pork Fajita Pitas
Chili Dogs
Party Popcorn Snack

Orange-Fennel Salad

Swiss Chard Gnocchi in Tomato-Cream Sauce

Baked Clams Iberian

September Salad

Brazilian Cocoa 'n' Crème
Party Chocolate Chip-Filled Cones

BREAKFAST

½ cup Orange Juice
¾ ounce Cold Cereal
½ cup Skim Milk
Coffee or Tea

LUNCH

Salmon Salad Sandwich (2 ounces salmon with ¼ cup *each* diced celery and onion, 4 lettuce leaves, and 1 tablespoon reduced-calorie mayonnaise on 2 slices reduced-calorie wheat bread)
6 *each* Red and Green Bell Pepper Strips
Coffee, Tea, or Mineral Water

DINNER

1 serving **Chicken Loaf with Tomato Sauce**
6 Cooked Broccoli Spears
Spinach-Mushroom Salad (½ cup *each* sliced mushrooms and cucumber, ¼ cup chopped scallions, 2 teaspoons imitation bacon bits, and 1½ teaspoons Italian dressing mixed with 2 teaspoons red wine vinegar on 1 cup spinach leaves)
Peach 'n' Yogurt (2 canned peach halves topped with ¼ cup plain low-fat yogurt)
Herb Tea

SNACKS

20 small Grapes; 1 cup Skim Milk

Total Optional Calories: 30

Chicken Loaf with Tomato Sauce ©

1 tablespoon plus 1 teaspoon reduced-calorie margarine (tub), divided
¾ cup diced onions, divided
¼ cup <u>each</u> diced celery and red <u>or</u> green bell pepper
2 small garlic cloves, minced, divided
1 packet instant chicken broth and seasoning mix
½ teaspoon <u>each</u> salt and thyme leaves
¼ teaspoon <u>each</u> oregano leaves and basil leaves
¾ pound skinned and boned chicken (white and dark meat), ground
¾ cup drained canned Italian tomatoes; chop ¼ cup tomatoes, reserving remaining whole tomatoes
½ cup part-skim ricotta cheese
⅓ cup plus 2 teaspoons seasoned dried bread crumbs
1 egg, lightly beaten
½ cup canned ready-to-serve chicken broth

Preheat oven to 350°F. In small nonstick skillet heat 2 teaspoons margarine until bubbly and hot; add ¼ cup onions along with the celery, bell pepper, half of the garlic, and the broth mix, salt, and herbs. Sauté, stirring occasionally, until vegetables are tender, 3 to 4 minutes; transfer to medium mixing bowl. Add chicken, ¼ cup chopped tomatoes, cheese, crumbs, and egg and mix until well combined. Transfer mixture to 8 x 8 x 2-inch nonstick baking pan and shape into a loaf; bake until golden brown and juices run clear, 30 to 35 minutes.

During last 10 minutes of baking time, prepare sauce. In 1-quart saucepan heat remaining 2 teaspoons margarine until bubbly and hot; add remaining ½ cup onions and the garlic and sauté until onions are tender, about 3 minutes. Add broth and remaining ½ cup tomatoes and, stirring occasionally, bring to a boil. Reduce heat to low and let simmer, stirring occasionally, until sauce is reduced slightly, about 3 minutes; transfer to blender container and process until smooth. Serve chicken loaf topped with sauce.

MAKES 4 SERVINGS

Each serving provides: 3 Protein Exchanges; ½ Bread Exchange;
  1 Vegetable Exchange; ½ Fat Exchange; 10 Optional Calories
Per serving: 250 calories; 26 g protein; 9 g fat; 15 g carbohydrate;
  145 mg calcium; 1,187 mg sodium; 138 mg cholesterol

BREAKFAST

½ cup Grapefruit Sections
Peanut Butter Grahams (1 tablespoon peanut butter on 2 graham crackers)
1 cup Skim Milk

LUNCH

Shrimp Salad Sandwich (2 ounces tiny shrimp with ¼ cup diced cucumber, 3 tomato slices, and 2 teaspoons reduced-calorie mayonnaise on 2 slices reduced-calorie wheat bread)
¼ cup *each* Broccoli and Cauliflower Florets
1 small Pear
Coffee, Tea, or Mineral Water

DINNER

1 serving **Sesame Chicken with Apricot Dipping Sauce**
Vegetable Stir-Fry (1 cup Chinese pea pods, ½ cup sliced mushrooms, ¼ cup diced onion, and 12 red bell pepper strips stir-fried in 1 teaspoon vegetable oil)
1½ cups Mixed Green Salad with 1 tablespoon Reduced-Calorie Buttermilk Dressing
Tea

SNACKS

2 x 3-inch wedge Watermelon; 1 cup Skim Milk

Total Optional Calories: 200

Sesame Chicken with Apricot Dipping Sauce ◑

½ cup plain dried bread crumbs
1 tablespoon sesame seed
2 tablespoons sour cream
1 teaspoon lemon juice
½ teaspoon Worcestershire sauce
1 garlic clove, minced, divided
⅛ teaspoon salt
Dash pepper
2 chicken cutlets (¼ pound each)
2 teaspoons vegetable oil
3 tablespoons reduced-calorie apricot spread (16 calories per 2 teaspoons)
2 teaspoons teriyaki sauce
¼ teaspoon <u>each</u> Dijon-style mustard and minced pared ginger root

Preheat oven to 425°F. On sheet of wax paper or a paper plate combine bread crumbs and sesame seed; in small bowl combine sour cream, lemon juice, Worcestershire sauce, half of the garlic, and the salt and pepper. Dip each cutlet into sour cream mixture, then into crumb mixture, turning to coat both sides and using all of the sour cream and crumb mixtures. Transfer chicken to nonstick baking sheet and drizzle each cutlet with 1 teaspoon oil; bake, turning once, until chicken is tender and golden brown, 12 to 15 minutes.

During last 5 minutes that chicken is baking, prepare sauce. In small saucepan combine apricot spread, teriyaki sauce, mustard, ginger, and remaining garlic; cook over medium heat, stirring frequently, until mixture is smooth and thoroughly heated, 3 to 4 minutes. To serve, cut chicken into bite-size pieces and serve with dipping sauce.

MAKES 2 SERVINGS

Each serving provides: 3 Protein Exchanges; 1 Bread Exchange; 1 Fat Exchange; 130 Optional Calories
Per serving: 366 calories; 31 g protein; 12 g fat; 31 g carbohydrate; 108 mg calcium; 637 mg sodium; 73 mg cholesterol

BREAKFAST

1 medium Kiwi Fruit, sliced
Lox 'n' Bagel (½ small bagel topped with 2 tablespoons whipped cream cheese and 1 ounce smoked salmon)
½ cup Skim Milk
Coffee or Tea

LUNCH

Liverwurst Sandwich (2 ounces sliced liverwurst with 3 tomato slices, 4 lettuce leaves, and 2 teaspoons mustard on 1-ounce roll)
3 Pickle Spears
12 large Grapes
Coffee, Tea, or Mineral Water

DINNER

½ cup Fruit Salad
1 serving **Chicken 'n' Noodles Amandine**
½ cup *each* Cooked Sliced Zucchini and Yellow Squash with 1 teaspoon Reduced-Calorie Margarine
1½ cups Tossed Salad with 2 Black Olives, sliced, and 1½ teaspoons French Dressing mixed with 2 teaspoons Lemon Juice and ¼ teaspoon Mustard
½ cup Skim Milk
Coffee or Tea

SNACKS

½ cup Reduced-Calorie Butterscotch Pudding; ½ medium Banana

Total Optional Calories: 135

Chicken 'n' Noodles Amandine

1 tablespoon margarine, divided
¼ ounce sliced <u>or</u> slivered almonds
2 chicken cutlets (¼ pound each)
½ cup <u>each</u> sliced mushrooms and diagonally sliced scallions (green onions)
½ teaspoon salt
Dash pepper
½ teaspoon all-purpose flour
½ cup water
2 tablespoons sour cream
½ packet (about ½ teaspoon) instant chicken broth and seasoning mix
1 cup cooked noodles (hot)

In 8- or 9-inch skillet heat 1 teaspoon margarine until bubbly and hot; stir in almonds and sauté, stirring constantly, until golden. Using slotted spoon, remove almonds to plate and set aside.

In same skillet heat remaining 2 teaspoons margarine until bubbly and hot; add chicken and cook, turning once, until browned on both sides, 2 to 3 minutes on each side. Remove from skillet and set aside.

In same skillet combine mushrooms, scallions, salt, and pepper and sauté until vegetables are tender-crisp; sprinkle flour over vegetables and stir quickly to combine. Gradually stir in water; add sour cream and broth mix and stir to blend. Reduce heat to low; return chicken to pan and let simmer until chicken is tender, about 5 minutes. Top noodles with chicken mixture and sprinkle with sautéed almonds.

MAKES 2 SERVINGS

Each serving provides: 3 Protein Exchanges; 1 Bread Exchange;
    1 Vegetable Exchange; 1½ Fat Exchanges; 60 Optional Calories
Per serving: 343 calories; 32 g protein; 13 g fat; 23 g carbohydrate;
    68 mg calcium; 946 mg sodium; 97 mg cholesterol

BREAKFAST

½ medium Banana, sliced
¾ ounce Cold Cereal
½ cup Skim Milk
Coffee or Tea

LUNCH

Sardine Sandwich (2 ounces sardines
  with ¼ cup diced onion, 3 tomato
  slices, and 1 teaspoon mayonnaise
  on 2 slices reduced-calorie rye
  bread)
6 *each* Celery Sticks and Red Bell
  Pepper Strips
1 small Orange
Coffee, Tea, or Mineral Water

DINNER

1 serving **Sliced Steak with Gorgonzola
  Sauce**
3 ounces Parslied Boiled Potatoes
1 cup Cooked Sliced Carrots with
  1 teaspoon Reduced-Calorie
  Margarine
1½ cups Mixed Green Salad with
  1 teaspoon Olive Oil mixed with
  2 teaspoons Red Wine Vinegar
  plus Seasonings
4 fluid ounces Dry Red Wine

SNACKS

Pineapple 'n' Yogurt (2 canned
  pineapple slices topped with ¼ cup
  plain low-fat yogurt and sprinkled
  with 1 teaspoon shredded
  coconut); 1 cup Skim Milk

Total Optional Calories: 150

Sliced Steak with Gorgonzola Sauce ◑

2 garlic cloves, minced, divided
1 teaspoon Worcestershire sauce
½ teaspoon Dijon-style mustard
¼ teaspoon salt, divided
Dash black pepper
**14 ounces boneless beef rib steak <u>or</u> beef top
  round steak**
2 teaspoons margarine
1 tablespoon minced shallots
½ teaspoon all-purpose flour
¼ cup low-fat milk (1% milk fat)
1 tablespoon plus 1 teaspoon dry vermouth
1 ounce Gorgonzola cheese, crumbled
3 tablespoons sour cream
1 tablespoon chopped fresh parsley
Dash <u>each</u> white pepper and ground nutmeg

Using mortar and pestle, mash half of the garlic to form
paste; add Worcestershire, mustard, ⅛ teaspoon salt, and
the black pepper, mixing well. Spread each side of steak
with half of garlic mixture and transfer to rack in broiling pan;
broil, turning once, until done to taste.

  While steak is broiling, prepare sauce. In small saucepan
heat margarine over medium heat until bubbly and hot; add
shallots and remaining garlic and sauté, stirring occasionally,
until shallots are softened, about 1 minute. Sprinkle with flour
and stir quickly to combine; continuing to stir, gradually add
milk. Reduce heat to low, add vermouth, and let simmer
until mixture thickens, 3 to 4 minutes. Add cheese, sour
cream, parsley, white pepper, nutmeg, and remaining ⅛
teaspoon salt, mixing well; cook until flavors blend, 3 to 4
minutes longer. Serve steak topped with cheese sauce.

MAKES 4 SERVINGS

Each serving provides: 3 Protein Exchanges; ½ Fat Exchange; 40 Optional
  Calories
Per serving with rib steak: 283 calories; 25 g protein; 18 g fat;
  3 g carbohydrate; 84 mg calcium; 362 mg sodium; 80 mg cholesterol
With top round steak: 249 calories; 30 g protein; 12 g fat;
  3 g carbohydrate; 81 mg calcium; 355 mg sodium; 82 mg cholesterol

BREAKFAST

1 cup Honeydew Melon Balls
⅓ cup Cottage Cheese
1 serving Reduced-Calorie Hot
    Cocoa

LUNCH

Chicken-Vegetable Salad (2 ounces
    diced chicken with ½ cup *each*
    broccoli florets and chopped celery,
    ¼ cup sliced carrot, and 1 table-
    spoon creamy Italian dressing)
3 Sesame Melba Rounds
Coffee, Tea, or Mineral Water

DINNER

¾ cup Beef Bouillon
1 serving **Roast Beef Melt**
1 cup Cooked Spinach Leaves
Iceberg Salad (iceberg lettuce wedge
    with 4 tomato slices plus lemon
    juice and herbs)
Sparkling Mineral Water with Lime
    Twist

SNACKS

1 cup Strawberries; 1 cup Skim Milk

Total Optional Calories: 20

Roast Beef Melt ⊙◑

A wonderful way to use up that leftover roast.

2 teaspoons margarine
1 small garlic clove, minced
3-ounce slice French bread (about 4 inches long), cut in
    half horizontally
¼ cup _each_ sliced mushrooms and onion
½ cup canned ready-to-serve beef broth
¼ pound thinly sliced roast beef
2 ounces Monterey Jack with jalapeño pepper cheese,*
    shredded

In 8-inch nonstick skillet heat margarine over medium-high heat until bubbly and hot; add garlic and sauté until golden, 1 to 2 minutes. Using pastry brush, brush cut side of each bread half with ½ teaspoon margarine mixture, leaving remaining mixture in skillet. Arrange bread halves margarine-side up on baking sheet and set aside.

Return skillet to medium-high heat; add mushrooms and onion and sauté, stirring occasionally, until lightly browned, 3 to 4 minutes. Set aside.

In 10-inch nonstick skillet cook broth over medium heat until liquid begins to simmer; add roast beef and cook until heated through, 2 to 3 minutes. Using slotted spoon, remove roast beef from broth, reserving broth; top each slice of bread with half of the beef slices, then top each portion with 1 ounce cheese. Broil 5 to 6 inches from heat source until cheese is melted and lightly browned, 2 to 3 minutes.

While sandwiches are broiling, add sautéed mushroom mixture to reserved broth and cook over low heat until heated through.

To serve, transfer sandwiches to 2 serving plates and top each with half of the mushroom mixture.

MAKES 2 SERVINGS, 1 OPEN-FACE SANDWICH EACH

Each serving provides: 3 Protein Exchanges; 1½ Bread Exchanges;
    ½ Vegetable Exchange; 1 Fat Exchange; 10 Optional Calories
Per serving: 389 calories; 28 g protein; 18 g fat; 26 g carbohydrate;
    241 mg calcium; 713 mg sodium; 72 mg cholesterol

*This peppered cheese adds a hot-and-spicy tang to this hearty open-face sandwich. For a milder flavor, regular Monterey Jack cheese may be substituted.

BREAKFAST

1 small Orange
Mushroom Omelet (1 egg with ¼ cup
   sliced mushrooms)
½ English Muffin, toasted, with
   1 teaspoon Reduced-Calorie
   Margarine
½ cup Skim Milk
Coffee or Tea

LUNCH

Tuna-Bean Salad (2 ounces tuna with
   ½ cup cooked cut green beans,
   chilled, 6 red bell pepper strips,
   and 1½ teaspoons Italian dressing)
3 Garlic Melba Rounds
1 small Apple
Coffee, Tea, or Mineral Water

DINNER

3 ounces Poached Chicken sprinkled
   with Chopped Parsley
1 serving **Skillet Eggplant and Pasta**
Sprout-Carrot Salad (½ cup *each*
   alfalfa sprouts and sliced carrot
   with lemon juice and herbs on
   4 Boston lettuce leaves)
½ cup Skim Milk
Coffee or Tea

SNACKS

½ cup Reduced-Calorie Vanilla
   Pudding; 1 cup Watermelon
   Chunks

Total Optional Calories: 30

Skillet Eggplant and Pasta ⊙

1 tablespoon olive _or_ vegetable oil
2 cups diced pared eggplant
½ cup _each_ diced onion, diced red _or_ green bell pepper,
   and quartered mushrooms
1 small garlic clove, minced
1 cup canned crushed tomatoes
2 teaspoons chopped fresh basil
½ teaspoon salt
⅛ teaspoon _each_ oregano leaves and pepper
1 cup cooked small macaroni shells (hot)
2 tablespoons grated Parmesan cheese

In 9- or 10-inch nonstick skillet heat oil over medium-high heat; add eggplant and cook, stirring occasionally, until slightly softened, about 5 minutes. Add onion, bell pepper, mushrooms, and garlic. Increase heat to high; cover and cook, stirring occasionally, until vegetables are tender-crisp, about 5 minutes. Stir in tomatoes and seasonings and bring to a boil; reduce heat to low and let simmer until flavors are blended, about 5 minutes. Add macaroni, stirring to combine; continue simmering for 5 minutes longer. Serve sprinkled with Parmesan cheese.

MAKES 2 SERVINGS

Each serving provides: 1 Bread Exchange; 4½ Vegetable Exchanges;
   1½ Fat Exchanges; 30 Optional Calories
Per serving: 228 calories; 7 g protein; 9 g fat; 31 g carbohydrate;
   162 mg calcium; 841 mg sodium; 4 mg cholesterol

TIP: Prepare this hearty side dish in advance, but don't add the macaroni until you're ready to serve it. You'll have extra-fast meal preparation with more time to sit and enjoy dinner.

BREAKFAST

½ medium Grapefruit
1 ounce Gouda Cheese
½ small Bagel, toasted
1 cup Skim Milk

LUNCH

Smoked Turkey Sandwich (2 ounces
    sliced smoked turkey with 4 lettuce
    leaves, 2 red onion slices, and
    2 teaspoons reduced-calorie
    mayonnaise on 2 slices reduced-
    calorie wheat bread)
6 Celery Sticks and ½ cup Broccoli
    Florets
½ medium Banana
Coffee, Tea, or Mineral Water

DINNER

3 ounces Broiled Lamb Chop with
    Chopped Mint
½ cup Cooked Rice
1 serving **Vegetable Hotchpotch**
Iceberg Lettuce Wedge with
    1½ teaspoons Buttermilk Dressing
    mixed with 2 tablespoons Plain
    Low-Fat Yogurt and ¼ teaspoon
    Mustard
4 fluid ounces Dry Red Wine

SNACKS

½ cup Fruit Salad; ¾ cup Skim Milk

Total Optional Calories: 100

Vegetable Hotchpotch ◑◐

This delicious medley can be the basis for many other
dishes. Besides serving it as is, try it as an omelet filling,
mixed with pasta or rice, sprinkled with cheese and
broiled, or flavored with wine vinegar or lemon juice
and served cold as an appetizer or side dish.

2 teaspoons olive <u>or</u> vegetable oil
½ cup diced onion
1 garlic clove, minced
1 cup cubed eggplant (1-inch cubes)
**½ cup <u>each</u> chopped celery, green bell pepper, and
    mushrooms**
**3 medium tomatoes, blanched, peeled, seeded, and
    chopped**
1 teaspoon chopped fresh basil
¼ teaspoon <u>each</u> salt and pepper

In 10-inch nonstick skillet heat oil over medium-high heat;
add onion and garlic and sauté until onion is softened, about
2 minutes. Add eggplant, celery, bell pepper, and mushrooms and sauté, stirring occasionally, for 3 minutes; add
tomatoes and seasonings and bring mixture to a boil.
Reduce heat to low, cover, and let simmer for 5 minutes;
remove cover and continue cooking, stirring occasionally,
until slightly thickened, about 5 minutes longer.

MAKES 2 SERVINGS

Each serving provides: 6 Vegetable Exchanges; 1 Fat Exchange
Per serving: 118 calories; 3 g protein; 5 g fat; 17 g carbohydrate;
    60 mg calcium; 316 mg sodium; 0 mg cholesterol

Kidney Bean Salad Olé ©◑

Cilantro (Chinese parsley) and Italian parsley look similar to the eye, but your taste buds will certainly notice the difference. Cilantro has a distinctive exotic flavor; Italian parsley has a milder taste, although it is more intense than curly parsley.

4 ounces drained canned red kidney beans
½ medium tomato, seeded and chopped
2 tablespoons each finely chopped celery and onion
1 tablespoon red wine vinegar
2 teaspoons olive oil
½ teaspoon each seeded and minced jalapeño pepper and minced fresh cilantro (Chinese parsley) or Italian (flat-leaf) parsley
½ small garlic clove, minced
Dash oregano leaves
1 cup shredded iceberg lettuce
1 ounce Cheddar cheese, shredded

In small mixing bowl combine beans, tomato, celery, onion, vinegar, oil, jalapeño pepper, cilantro (or Italian parsley), garlic, and oregano, mixing until thoroughly combined.

   Line serving platter with shredded lettuce; spoon bean mixture onto center of lettuce and sprinkle cheese around edges of lettuce.

MAKES 2 SERVINGS

Each serving provides: 1½ Protein Exchanges; 1¾ Vegetable
   Exchanges; 1 Fat Exchange
Per serving: 188 calories; 9 g protein; 10 g fat; 17 g carbohydrate;
   154 mg calcium; 294 mg sodium; 15 mg cholesterol

September Salad ⓒ ◑

With tomatoes, cucumbers, and green beans all fresh from the garden, September is the perfect month for this quick-and-easy combo.

8 Boston lettuce leaves
6 romaine lettuce leaves
1 medium tomato, cut into 8 wedges
**1 medium cucumber, scored and thinly sliced on the
    diagonal**
1 cup whole green beans, trimmed and blanched
¼ cup diagonally sliced scallions (green onions)
1 tablespoon <u>each</u> olive oil and red wine vinegar
½ teaspoon salt
Dash pepper
Garnish: basil leaves

Line serving platter with lettuce leaves; decoratively arrange tomato, cucumber, and green beans on lettuce. Top with scallions; cover and refrigerate until chilled.

To serve, in small bowl combine remaining ingredients except basil, mixing well; pour dressing over salad and garnish with basil leaves.

MAKES 2 SERVINGS

Each serving provides: 4½ Vegetable Exchanges; 1½ Fat Exchanges
Per serving: 113 calories; 3 g protein; 7 g fat; 12 g carbohydrate;
    74 mg calcium; 563 mg sodium; 0 mg cholesterol

TIP: Blanch the green beans the night before and it will be even quicker!

BREAKFAST

½ cup Orange Sections
½ cup Cooked Cereal
½ cup Skim Milk
Coffee or Tea

LUNCH

Roast Beef-Vegetable Pita (2 ounces
    sliced roast beef with ¼ cup bean
    sprouts, 6 cucumber slices,
    3 tomato slices, and 2 teaspoons
    reduced-calorie mayonnaise
    in 1-ounce pita bread)
6 Yellow Squash Sticks and
    3 Radishes
2 medium Plums
Coffee or Tea

DINNER

4 ounces Grilled Chicken with
    2 teaspoons Ketchup
1 cup Cooked Wax Beans
Cabbage-Carrot Salad (1 cup
    shredded green cabbage with
    ½ cup shredded carrot and
    1 tablespoon buttermilk dressing)
1-ounce Buttermilk Flaky Biscuit
    with 2 tablespoons **Pear Butter**
½ cup Skim Milk
Coffee or Tea

SNACKS

1 serving Reduced-Calorie
    Chocolate-Flavored Dairy Drink

Total Optional Calories: 30

Pear Butter ⓒ

This delicious spread can be stored in a covered
container in the refrigerator for up to 2 weeks.

1¾ pounds very ripe pears, cored, pared, and chopped
¼ cup orange juice (no sugar added)
2 tablespoons granulated sugar
1 teaspoon grated orange peel (optional)
Dash ground cloves

In 2-quart saucepan combine pears and orange juice and
bring to a boil. Reduce heat and let simmer, stirring
occasionally, until pears are softened, 15 to 20 minutes.
    Set food mill* over medium bowl; add pear mixture in
small batches to food mill and process. Return mixture to
saucepan; stir in remaining ingredients and bring to a boil.
Reduce heat and let simmer, stirring occasionally, until
mixture is thickened and reduced by half, 12 to 15 minutes.

YIELDS ¾ CUP

Each 2-tablespoon serving provides: 1 Fruit Exchange; 20 Optional
    Calories
Per serving: 93 calories; 0.5 g protein; 0.5 g fat; 24 g carbohydrate;
    14 mg calcium; 0.2 mg sodium; 0 mg cholesterol

*If food mill is not available, process pear mixture, in batches, in blender
container.

Spiced Carrot-Raisin Muffins ©

2¼ cups all-purpose flour
¾ cup firmly packed dark brown sugar
2 teaspoons double-acting baking powder
1 teaspoon <u>each</u> baking soda, ground cinnamon, and ground nutmeg
½ teaspoon <u>each</u> salt and ground ginger
2 eggs, beaten
⅓ cup plus 2 teaspoons vegetable oil
2 tablespoons thawed frozen concentrated orange juice (no sugar added) <u>or</u> 1 small orange (about 6 ounces), peeled, seeded, and chopped
1½ cups shredded carrots
½ cup plus 2 tablespoons dark raisins

Preheat oven to 350°F. Spray twelve 2½-inch muffin-pan cups with nonstick cooking spray; set aside.

In large mixing bowl combine flour, sugar, baking powder, baking soda, cinnamon, nutmeg, salt, and ginger, mixing thoroughly. In small bowl mix together eggs, oil, and juice concentrate (or chopped orange) until well blended; pour into dry ingredients and, using a fork, stir until mixture is moistened. Stir in carrots and raisins. Spoon an equal amount of batter into each sprayed cup (each will be about ⅔ full). Bake for 25 to 30 minutes (until muffins are browned and a toothpick, inserted in center, comes out clean). Remove muffins to wire rack and let cool.

MAKES 12 SERVINGS, 1 MUFFIN EACH

Each serving provides: 1 Bread Exchange; ¼ Vegetable Exchange; 1½ Fat Exchanges; ½ Fruit Exchange; 70 Optional Calories
Per serving with orange juice: 245 calories; 4 g protein; 8 g fat; 40 g carbohydrate; 67 mg calcium; 253 mg sodium; 46 mg cholesterol
With orange: 246 calories; 4 g protein; 8 g fat; 40 g carbohydrate; 71 mg calcium; 253 mg sodium; 46 mg cholesterol

TIP: No time to prepare breakfast in the morning? Make these spiced muffins in advance, wrap individually in plastic freezer wrap, and freeze. Remove from freezer the night before and let thaw at room temperature, or in the morning remove from freezer and thaw in microwave or toaster-oven.

BREAKFAST

2-inch wedge Honeydew Melon
1 ounce Swiss Cheese
½ Whole Wheat English Muffin,
   toasted, with 1 teaspoon
   Margarine
1 cup Skim Milk

LUNCH

Open-Face Egg Salad Sandwich
   (2 hard-cooked eggs, chopped,
   with ¼ cup *each* diced celery and
   onion, 2 lettuce leaves, and
   2 teaspoons reduced-calorie
   mayonnaise on 1 slice reduced-
   calorie rye bread)
6 *each* Cucumber Spears and Green
   Bell Pepper Strips
Coffee, Tea, or Mineral Water

DINNER

Special Bouillon (¾ cup chicken
   bouillon mixed with ¼ cup sliced
   bamboo shoots)
3 ounces Baked Chicken with
   Rosemary
3 ounces Baked Potato sprinkled
   with 1 teaspoon Imitation Bacon
   Bits
1 cup Cooked Spinach
1½ cups Tossed Salad with Lemon
   Juice and Herbs
1 serving **Apple Crisp**
½ cup Skim Milk
Coffee or Tea

SNACKS

1 large Tangerine; ½ cup Skim Milk

Total Optional Calories: 30

Apple Crisp Ⓒ

½ pound apples, cored, pared, and thinly sliced
1½ teaspoons lemon juice
1 tablespoon water
1 teaspoon honey
¼ teaspoon ground cinnamon
2 teaspoons margarine
2 graham crackers (2½-inch squares), made into crumbs

Preheat oven to 375°F. In small mixing bowl combine apples and lemon juice, tossing to coat; add water, honey, and cinnamon, mixing well. Transfer to 2-cup casserole; dot with margarine and sprinkle with graham cracker crumbs. Bake until apples are soft, 30 to 35 minutes.

MAKES 2 SERVINGS

Each serving provides: ½ Bread Exchange; 1 Fat Exchange;
   1 Fruit Exchange; 10 Optional Calories
Per serving: 129 calories; 0.8 g protein; 5 g fat; 23 g carbohydrate;
   12 mg calcium; 93 mg sodium; 0 mg cholesterol

Variations: Cream-Topped Crisp (Week 3) — Top each portion of Apple Crisp with 2 tablespoons whipped topping. Increase Optional Calories to 35.

Per serving: 153 calories; 0.8 g protein; 7 g fat; 25 g carbohydrate;
   12 mg calcium; 103 mg sodium; 0 mg cholesterol

Apple Crisp 'n' Ice Milk (Week 8) — Serve each portion of Apple Crisp with ½-cup scoop of ice milk. Increase Optional Calories to 130.

Per serving: 220 calories; 3 g protein; 8 g fat; 37 g carbohydrate;
   100 mg calcium; 146 mg sodium; 9 mg cholesterol

Prune-Cheese Delight (¼ cup part-skim ricotta cheese mixed with 3 medium prunes, pitted and chopped, and sprinkled with cinnamon)
1 slice Raisin Bread, toasted
1 cup Skim Milk

LUNCH

Turkey Sandwich (2 ounces sliced turkey with 4 lettuce leaves, 2 red onion slices, and 1½ teaspoons Thousand Island dressing on 2 slices reduced-calorie rye bread)
6 *each* Celery Sticks and Green Bell Pepper Strips
1 small Pear
Coffee, Tea, or Mineral Water

DINNER

3 ounces Broiled Scallops with Lemon Wedge and Parsley
Linguine in Red Sauce (¾ cup cooked linguine with ¼ cup tomato sauce and 1 teaspoon grated Romano cheese)
½ cup Cooked Chinese Pea Pods
1½ cups Romaine Lettuce with 1 tablespoon French Dressing
1 medium Kiwi Fruit, sliced
4 fluid ounces Dry White Wine

SNACKS

1 serving **Chocolate-Peanut Butter Cups**; ½ cup Plain Low-Fat Yogurt

Total Optional Calories: 170

Chocolate-Peanut Butter Cups ◑

A wonderful combination of two favorite treats.

2 tablespoons chunky peanut butter
1 ounce semisweet chocolate chips

In small heatproof bowl combine peanut butter and chocolate; place bowl in medium heatproof bowl and fill the medium bowl with boiling water. Let stand, stirring frequently, until mixture is melted and well combined.*

Set 8 fluted paper candy liners on serving platter; using a teaspoon, spoon ⅛ of chocolate mixture into each liner. Cover platter with plastic wrap and refrigerate until candies are firm.

MAKES 4 SERVINGS, 2 CANDIES EACH

Each serving provides: ½ Protein Exchange; 60 Optional Calories
Per serving: 84 calories; 3 g protein; 7 g fat; 5 g carbohydrate; 5 mg calcium; 38 mg sodium; 0 mg cholesterol

*When melting chocolate, it should not come in contact with water or steam; moisture will cause it to harden.

October

Veal Chops with Pears and Bacon

OCTOBER'S BEST BUYS FOR FRUITS AND VEGETABLES

alfalfa sprouts	carrots	kiwi fruit	pumpkins
apples	cauliflower	leeks	radishes
bananas	celery	lettuce	scallions (green onions)
bean sprouts	Chinese pea pods	mushrooms	spinach
beets	cranberries	onions	sweet potatoes
bell peppers	eggplants	pears	turnips
broccoli	escarole	persimmons	winter squash
brussels sprouts	figs	pineapples	yams
cabbage	grapes	potatoes	

BREAKFAST

½ medium Banana, sliced
¾ ounce Cold Cereal
1 cup Skim Milk
Coffee or Tea

LUNCH

Turkey on a Bagel (2 ounces sliced
turkey with 2 red onion slices,
4 lettuce leaves, and 1 teaspoon
mayonnaise on 1 small bagel)
½ cup Sliced Zucchini and
4 Radishes
1 small Apple
Coffee, Tea, or Mineral Water

DINNER

1 serving **Scallop Chowder** with
10 Oyster Crackers
Greek Salad (2 ounces crumbled feta
cheese with 2 cups torn romaine
lettuce, 2 pitted black olives,
2 anchovy fillets, ½ cup sliced
cherry tomatoes, and 1 teaspoon
olive oil mixed with 2 teaspoons
red wine vinegar plus herbs)
½ cup Low-Calorie Orange-Flavored
Gelatin sprinkled with 1 teaspoon
Shredded Coconut
Coffee or Tea

SNACKS

Pudding and Fruit (½ cup reduced-
calorie vanilla pudding topped with
1 medium kiwi fruit, sliced)

Total Optional Calories: 120

Scallop Chowder

½ cup **each** bottled clam juice and water
¼ cup dry white table wine
½ bay leaf
1 lime slice
1 to 2 peppercorns
5 ounces bay scallops (or sea scallops, cut into 1-inch
   pieces)
2 teaspoons olive **or** vegetable oil
¼ cup **each** diced leeks (white portion only), sliced carrot,
   and diced celery
1 tablespoon minced shallots
2 small garlic cloves, minced
1 tablespoon all-purpose flour
3 small plum tomatoes (about 1 ounce each), blanched,
   peeled, seeded, and chopped
3 ounces diced pared potato
1½ teaspoons minced fresh parsley
⅛ teaspoon thyme leaves
Dash pepper
2 tablespoons half-and-half (blend of milk and cream)

In 10-inch skillet combine clam juice, water, wine, bay leaf,
lime, and peppercorns and cook over medium-high heat
until mixture comes to a boil; add scallops, cover, and cook
until scallops are partially cooked and turn opaque, 2 to 3
minutes. Using slotted spoon, transfer scallops to medium
bowl. Strain liquid; discard solids and reserve liquid.

In 1½-quart saucepan heat oil over medium-high heat;
add leeks, carrot, celery, shallots, and garlic and sauté until
softened, 2 to 3 minutes. Sprinkle with flour, stirring quickly
to combine. Gradually stir in reserved liquid; add tomatoes,
potato, parsley, thyme, and pepper and stir to combine.
Reduce heat to low, cover, and let simmer, stirring
occasionally, until potato is tender, 15 to 20 minutes. Add
scallops and the half-and-half and cook until scallops are
heated through, 2 to 3 minutes (do not boil).

MAKES 2 SERVINGS, ABOUT 1 CUP EACH

Each serving provides: 2 Protein Exchanges; ½ Bread Exchange;
   1½ Vegetable Exchanges; 1 Fat Exchange; 80 Optional Calories
Per serving: 243 calories; 17 g protein; 7 g fat; 24 g carbohydrate;
   67 mg calcium; 391 mg sodium; 37 mg cholesterol

BREAKFAST

Peach Yogurt (½ cup plain low-fat
yogurt mixed with ½ cup canned
peach slices)
1 slice Raisin Bread, toasted, with
1 teaspoon Reduced-Calorie
Margarine
Coffee or Tea

LUNCH

Chef's Salad (1 ounce *each* julienne-
cut chicken and thinly sliced Swiss
cheese with 1 cup torn lettuce,
8 tomato wedges, ½ cup *each*
sliced cucumber and celery, ½ cup
shredded red cabbage, and
1½ teaspoons Thousand Island
dressing mixed with 2 tablespoons
plain low-fat yogurt and
¼ teaspoon mustard)
1-ounce Roll
1 small Orange
Coffee, Tea, or Mineral Water

DINNER

1 serving **Roquefort-Pear Salad**
4 ounces Broiled Pork Chop
3 ounces Parslied Boiled Potato
½ cup Cooked Sliced Carrot with
1 teaspoon Reduced-Calorie
Margarine
½ cup Canned Fruit Cocktail
Coffee or Tea

SNACKS

Banana Shake (¼ medium banana,
¾ cup skim milk, and 3 ice cubes
processed in blender)

Total Optional Calories: 110

Roquefort-Pear Salad ◑

An elegant yet easy first course.

**2 small Barlett pears (about 5 ounces each), cored,
pared, and thinly sliced**
1 teaspoon lemon juice
4 each Boston and red-leaf lettuce leaves
1 ounce Roquefort cheese, crumbled
½ ounce coarsely chopped walnuts
1 tablespoon raspberry vinegar
2 teaspoons water
1½ teaspoons olive oil
½ teaspoon walnut oil*
¼ teaspoon minced fresh parsley
Dash pepper

In small bowl combine pear slices and lemon juice, tossing
slices with juice to prevent browning.

Line serving platter with lettuce leaves and decoratively
arrange pear slices on platter; top with cheese and walnuts.

In small bowl combine remaining ingredients, mixing well;
pour over salad and serve immediately.

MAKES 2 SERVINGS

Each serving provides: ½ Protein Exchange; ¾ Vegetable Exchange;
1 Fat Exchange; 1 Fruit Exchange; 50 Optional Calories
Per serving: 229 calories; 5 g protein; 15 g fat; 22 g carbohydrate;
137 mg calcium; 261 mg sodium; 13 mg cholesterol

*If walnut oil is not available, increase olive oil to 2 teaspoons.

Chili-Cheese Fondue or Dip ◖◑

Serve with chunks of hearty bread such as pumpernickel, rye, or whole-grain bread or vegetable dippers such as celery and carrot sticks, red and green bell pepper strips, and cherry tomatoes.

1 tablespoon plus 1 teaspoon margarine
2 medium mild <u>or</u> hot green chili peppers, seeded and minced
1 small garlic clove, minced
1 tablespoon all-purpose flour
½ cup beer
¼ pound <u>each</u> Monterey Jack and extra-sharp Cheddar cheese, shredded
1 teaspoon Worcestershire sauce
2 to 4 drops hot sauce (optional)

In 1-quart saucepan heat margarine over medium heat until bubbly and hot; add chili peppers and garlic and sauté until peppers are softened and lightly browned (<u>be careful not to burn</u>). Sprinkle mixture with flour and stir quickly to combine; cook, stirring constantly, for 1 minute. Gradually stir in beer; bring to a boil. Reduce heat to low; stir in remaining ingredients and let simmer, stirring occasionally, until cheeses melt. Pour into small fondue pot or warm bowl.

MAKES 8 SERVINGS, ABOUT 6 TABLESPOONS EACH

Each serving provides: 1 Protein Exchange; ¼ Vegetable Exchange;
   ½ Fat Exchange; 10 Optional Calories
Per serving: 140 calories; 7 g protein; 11 g fat; 2 g carbohydrate;
   211 mg calcium; 196 mg sodium; 27 mg cholesterol

BREAKFAST

½ cup Orange Sections
⅓ cup Cottage Cheese
1 slice Reduced-Calorie Multi-
   Grain Bread, toasted
1 serving Reduced-Calorie Hot
   Cocoa

LUNCH

Salmon Salad Sandwich (1½ ounces
   salmon with 2 tablespoons *each*
   chopped celery and onion,
   2 lettuce leaves, and 2 teaspoons
   reduced-calorie mayonnaise on
   2 slices reduced-calorie wheat
   bread)
1 small Apple
Coffee, Tea, or Mineral Water

DINNER

1 serving **Swiss Pinwheels**
3 ounces Roast Chicken
3 ounces Baked Sweet Potato
   drizzled with 1 teaspoon Honey
1 cup Cooked Cut Green Beans
1½ cups Tossed Salad with
   1 tablespoon Russian Dressing
½ cup Low-Calorie Strawberry-
   Flavored Gelatin
½ cup Skim Milk
Coffee or Tea

SNACKS

½ cup Raspberries topped with ¼ cup
   Plain Low-Fat Yogurt

Total Optional Calories: 50

Swiss Pinwheels ©◑

2 slices reduced-calorie white bread (40 calories per slice)
1 teaspoon <u>each</u> honey and prepared mustard
1 ounce thinly sliced Swiss cheese (at room temperature)
2 teaspoons imitation bacon bits

Between 2 sheets of plastic wrap or wax paper, using a rolling pin, flatten each slice of bread; remove plastic wrap (or wax paper). In cup or small bowl combine honey and mustard; spread half of mixture on each slice of bread. Top each portion with ½ ounce cheese and sprinkle each with 1 teaspoon bacon bits. Roll each bread slice jelly-roll fashion and set seam-side down on baking sheet; broil until bread is lightly browned, about 1 minute. Cut each roll crosswise into 4 equal slices and secure each slice with a decorative toothpick.

MAKES 2 SERVINGS, 4 PINWHEELS EACH

Each serving provides: ½ Protein Exchange; ½ Bread Exchange;
   20 Optional Calories
Per serving: 115 calories; 7 g protein; 4 g fat; 13 g carbohydrate;
   163 mg calcium; 259 mg sodium; 13 mg cholesterol

Variation: Swiss and Bacon Pinwheels (Week 6) — Substitute 2 slices crisp bacon, crumbled, for the bacon bits. Increase Optional Calories to 55.

Per serving: 142 calories; 8 g protein; 7 g fat; 13 g carbohydrate;
   159 mg calcium; 266 mg sodium; 18 mg cholesterol

BRUNCH

BRUNCH

½ medium Grapefruit sprinkled with ½ teaspoon Sugar
1 serving **Mexican Eggs**
1 slice Whole Wheat Bread, toasted
½ cup Skim Milk
Coffee or Tea

DINNER

Special Bouillon (¾ cup chicken bouillon mixed with ¼ cup sliced bamboo shoots)
Chicken Stir-Fry (3 ounces julienne-cut chicken, ½ cup *each* sliced mushrooms and onion, 12 green bell pepper strips, and ½ cup broccoli florets stir-fried in 2 teaspoons vegetable oil and 1 tablespoon reduced-sodium soy sauce)
1 cup Cooked Rice
½ cup Canned Mandarin Orange Sections
Tea

SNACKS

1 serving Reduced-Calorie Vanilla Dairy Drink; Apple Yogurt (¼ cup plain low-fat yogurt mixed with ½ cup applesauce)

Total Optional Calories: 60

Mexican Eggs

½ cup <u>each</u> diced onion, green bell pepper, and tomato, divided
1 tablespoon chopped fresh cilantro (Chinese parsley) <u>or</u> Italian (flat-leaf) parsley, divided
1½ teaspoons lime juice (no sugar added) <u>or</u> lemon juice
½ small jalapeño pepper, seeded and minced, divided
¼ teaspoon salt
Dash pepper
3 eggs
1 tablespoon <u>each</u> half-and-half (blend of milk and cream) and whipped cream cheese
½ garlic clove, minced
1 teaspoon <u>each</u> margarine and olive <u>or</u> vegetable oil
1 ounce Monterey Jack <u>or</u> Cheddar cheese, shredded
2 teaspoons sour cream

In blender container combine ¼ cup each onion, bell pepper, and tomato, 1½ teaspoons cilantro (or parsley), the lime (or lemon) juice, half the jalapeño pepper, and the salt and pepper; using an on-off motion, process until finely chopped (<u>do not puree</u>). Set aside.

In medium mixing bowl, using electric mixer at medium speed, beat together eggs, half-and-half, and cream cheese until blended; stir in garlic and remaining onion, bell pepper, tomato, cilantro (or parsley), and jalapeño pepper.

In 8-inch nonstick skillet heat margarine and oil together until margarine is bubbly and mixture is hot; pour in egg mixture and sprinkle with cheese. Cook, stirring frequently with a wooden spoon to allow uncooked portions to flow to bottom of pan, until egg is set and forms large, soft curds. Transfer egg mixture to serving platter; top with chopped vegetable mixture and sour cream.

MAKES 2 SERVINGS

Each serving provides: 2 Protein Exchanges; 1½ Vegetable Exchanges; 1 Fat Exchange; 40 Optional Calories
Per serving with Monterey Jack cheese: 276 calories; 14 g protein; 21 g fat; 9 g carbohydrate; 187 mg calcium; 533 mg sodium; 433 mg cholesterol
With Cheddar cheese: 280 calories; 14 g protein; 21 g fat; 9 g carbohydrate; 183 mg calcium; 545 mg sodium; 436 mg cholesterol

BREAKFAST

½ medium Banana, sliced
Maple Oatmeal (½ cup cooked
    oatmeal drizzled with ½ teaspoon
    maple syrup)
½ cup Skim Milk
Coffee or Tea

LUNCH

1 serving **Greek Pizzas**
2 cups Mixed Green Salad with Red
    Wine Vinegar and Herbs
1 small Orange
Orange-Flavored Seltzer

DINNER

Italian Steak (3 ounces broiled steak
    with ½ cup cooked canned Italian
    tomatoes, garlic, basil, and
    1 teaspoon grated Parmesan
    cheese)
1 cup Cooked Sliced Zucchini with
    1 teaspoon Reduced-Calorie
    Margarine
Bibb Salad (¼ cup shredded carrot
    with 1 tablespoon creamy Italian
    dressing on 8 Bibb lettuce leaves)
Coffee or Tea

SNACKS

½ cup Reduced-Calorie Chocolate
    Pudding; ½ cup Skim Milk

Total Optional Calories: 20

Greek Pizzas ⊙ ◑

Spice up a weekend lunch with these tasty
pita bread pizzas.

2 pita breads (1 ounce each)
1 teaspoon olive <u>or</u> vegetable oil, divided
½ cup thawed frozen chopped spinach
2 tablespoons chopped scallion (green onion)
1 teaspoon chopped fresh dill
½ medium tomato, cut into 4 thin slices
¼ pound feta cheese, crumbled
⅛ teaspoon oregano leaves
Pepper

On baking sheet arrange pita breads and, using pastry brush,
brush top of each with ¼ teaspoon oil; broil 6 inches from
heat source until lightly browned, 1 to 2 minutes. Turn pitas
over, brush top of each with ¼ teaspoon oil, and broil until
lightly browned, 1 to 2 minutes; remove from oven.

Turn oven control to 450°F. In small bowl combine
spinach, scallion, and dill, mixing well; top each pita bread
with 2 tomato slices, then spread each with half of the
spinach mixture. Sprinkle each portion with 2 ounces feta
cheese, half of the oregano, and dash pepper; bake until
cheese is lightly browned, 5 to 7 minutes. Serve
immediately.

MAKES 2 SERVINGS, 1 PIZZA EACH

Each serving provides: 2 Protein Exchanges; 1 Bread Exchange;
    1⅛ Vegetable Exchanges; ½ Fat Exchange
Per serving: 275 calories; 13 g protein; 15 g fat; 25 g carbohydrate;
    354 mg calcium; 857 mg sodium; 51 mg cholesterol

Variation: Greek Pizzas with Olives (Week 5) — Slice 4 pitted
black <u>or</u> Calamata olives. After topping pitas with spinach
mixture, top each with half of the olive slices; proceed as
directed. Add 10 Optional Calories to Exchange Information.
Per serving: 291 calories; 13 g protein; 16 g fat; 25 g carbohydrate;
    361 mg calcium; 911 mg sodium; 51 mg cholesterol

BREAKFAST

½ cup Canned Crushed Pineapple
⅓ cup Cottage Cheese
½ cup Skim Milk
Coffee or Tea

LUNCH

Turkey Sandwich (1 ounce sliced
    turkey with ½ cup torn spinach,
    6 cucumber slices, and 2 teaspoons
    reduced-calorie mayonnaise on
    2 slices reduced-calorie wheat
    bread)
½ cup Cauliflower Florets and
    6 Celery Sticks
Coffee, Tea, or Mineral Water

DINNER

1 serving **Pan-Fried Swordfish with
    Tomatoes and Roasted Pepper**
6 Cooked Broccoli Spears
1-ounce Roll
2 cups Tossed Salad with
    1½ teaspoons Buttermilk Dressing
    mixed with 2 tablespoons Plain
    Low-Fat Yogurt and ¼ teaspoon
    Mustard
Peach "Melba" (2 canned peach
    halves filled with 2 teaspoons
    reduced-calorie raspberry spread)
Cappucino (½ cup *each* hot espresso
    and hot skim milk sprinkled with
    cinnamon)

SNACKS

1 small Orange; ¾ cup Skim Milk

Total Optional Calories: 16

Pan-Fried Swordfish with Tomatoes and Roasted Pepper

1 medium red bell pepper
2 teaspoons vegetable oil
½ pound boneless swordfish steak
¼ cup finely chopped onion
2 garlic cloves, minced
**4 small plum tomatoes (about 1 ounce each), blanched,
    peeled, seeded, and chopped**
1 tablespoon lemon juice
2 teaspoons each minced fresh parsley and mint
⅛ teaspoon salt
Dash crushed red pepper

Preheat broiler. On baking sheet lined with heavy-duty
foil broil bell pepper 3 inches from heat source, turning
frequently, until charred on all sides; let stand until cool
enough to handle, 15 to 20 minutes.

Fit strainer into small bowl and peel pepper over strainer,
removing and discarding stem ends and seeds and allowing
juice from pepper to drip into bowl; dice pepper and set
pepper and juice aside.

In 10-inch nonstick skillet heat oil over medium heat; add
swordfish and cook, turning once, until fish begins to brown,
3 to 4 minutes on each side. Transfer fish to plate; set aside.

In same skillet combine onion and garlic and sauté over
medium-high heat until onion is softened, 1 to 2 minutes;
add diced bell pepper, reserved juice, tomatoes, lemon
juice, parsley, mint, salt, and crushed red pepper, stirring to
combine. Reduce heat to low, cover, and let simmer, stirring
occasionally, until flavors blend, 5 to 7 minutes. Return
swordfish to skillet and cook, uncovered, until fish is heated
through and flakes easily when tested with a fork, 1 to 2
minutes.

MAKES 2 SERVINGS

Each serving provides: 3 Protein Exchanges; 2¼ Vegetable Exchanges;
    1 Fat Exchange
Per serving: 208 calories; 23 g protein; 9 g fat; 8 g carbohydrate;
    42 mg calcium; 208 mg sodium; 62 mg cholesterol

BREAKFAST

½ cup Orange and Grapefruit
    Sections
¾ ounce Cold Cereal
½ cup Skim Milk
Coffee or Tea

LUNCH

Chicken Salad-Stuffed Pita (2 ounces
    diced chicken with ¼ cup *each*
    diced celery and cucumber,
    4 lettuce leaves, and 1 teaspoon
    reduced-calorie mayonnaise in
    1-ounce whole wheat pita bread)
½ cup *each* Sliced Zucchini and
    Carrot
1 small Apple
Coffee, Tea, or Mineral Water

DINNER

1 serving **Deviled Lobster au Gratin**
½ cup Cooked Rice with ¼ cup
    Cooked Sliced Mushrooms
½ cup Cooked Chopped Spinach
Bibb Salad (2 cups torn Bibb lettuce
    with 1 cup alfalfa sprouts and
    1½ teaspoons blue cheese dressing
    mixed with 2 tablespoons plain
    low-fat yogurt plus garlic powder)
4 fluid ounces Champagne

SNACKS

½ cup Reduced-Calorie Butterscotch
    Pudding

Total Optional Calories: 160

Deviled Lobster au Gratin

1 tablespoon margarine
2 tablespoons minced shallots
1 tablespoon all-purpose flour
¼ cup dry white table wine
½ cup skim milk
1 teaspoon Dijon-style mustard
7 ounces cooked lobster meat,* shredded
1 ounce grated Parmesan cheese, divided
1 tablespoon <u>each</u> chopped fresh Italian (flat-leaf)
parsley and plain dried bread crumbs

In small nonstick skillet heat margarine over medium heat until bubbly and hot; add shallots and sauté until soft, about 1 minute. Sprinkle with flour and stir quickly to combine; cook, stirring constantly, for 1 minute. Gradually stir in wine; continuing to stir, bring mixture to a boil. Reduce heat to low; add milk and mustard and cook, stirring constantly, until mixture is thickened (<u>do not boil</u>). Add lobster meat and cook, stirring occasionally, until lobster is heated, about 5 minutes; stir in all but 2 tablespoons cheese and remove skillet from heat.

Divide mixture into 2 individual au gratin dishes or 1½-cup casseroles. In cup or small bowl combine parsley, bread crumbs, and remaining 2 tablespoons cheese and sprinkle half of mixture over each portion of deviled lobster; broil until topping is lightly browned and hot, 1 to 2 minutes.

MAKES 2 SERVINGS

Each serving provides: 4 Protein Exchanges; ⅛ Vegetable Exchange;
    1½ Fat Exchanges; ¼ Milk Exchange; 60 Optional Calories
Per serving: 293 calories; 28 g protein; 12 g fat; 12 g carbohydrate;
    350 mg calcium; 672 mg sodium; 97 mg cholesterol

* Cooked lobster meat can be purchased fresh or frozen; if frozen, allow to thaw before adding to sauce.

Variation: Deviled Tilefish au Gratin (Week 2) — Substitute cooked flaked tilefish for the lobster meat.
Per serving: 300 calories; 31 g protein; 11 g fat; 12 g carbohydrate;
    302 mg calcium; 532 mg sodium; 83 mg cholesterol

½ cup Grapefruit Sections
Cheddar Melt (1 ounce Cheddar
 cheese melted on 1 slice
 pumpernickel bread)
½ cup Skim Milk
Coffee or Tea

LUNCH

Salmon Salad (2 ounces salmon with
 ¼ cup *each* chopped onion and
 celery and 1 tablespoon reduced-
 calorie mayonnaise on 4 lettuce
 leaves)
6 Sesame Melba Rounds
6 Red Bell Pepper Strips and
 3 Radishes
Coffee, Tea, or Mineral Water

DINNER

¾ cup Chicken Bouillon
1 serving **Chicken Cacciatore with
 Green Beans**
1 cup Cooked Sliced Carrots
1½ cups Mixed Green Salad with
 1½ teaspoons Italian Dressing
 mixed with 2 teaspoons Red Wine
 Vinegar
½ cup Canned Peach Slices
Coffee or Tea

SNACKS

Cinnamon-Banana Yogurt (½ cup
 plain low-fat yogurt mixed with
 ½ medium banana, sliced, and
 sprinkled with cinnamon); ½ cup
 Skim Milk

Total Optional Calories: 10

Chicken Cacciatore with Green Beans ◑

Simply delicious and deliciously simple.

1 teaspoon vegetable oil
¼ cup <u>each</u> chopped onion and green bell pepper
1 garlic clove, minced
½ pound chicken cutlets, cut into 1-inch cubes
**½ cup <u>each</u> drained canned whole tomatoes, chopped,
 and frozen cut green beans**
¼ teaspoon oregano leaves
⅛ teaspoon salt

In 8- or 10-inch skillet heat oil over medium heat; add onion, green pepper, and garlic and sauté for 1 to 2 minutes. Add chicken to skillet and continue to sauté until chicken is no longer pink, about 5 minutes; stir in tomatoes, green beans, and seasonings. Reduce heat to low and let simmer, stirring occasionally, until chicken is cooked through and tender, 5 to 8 minutes.

MAKES 2 SERVINGS

Each serving provides: 3 Protein Exchanges; 1½ Vegetable Exchanges;
 ½ Fat Exchange
Per serving: 180 calories; 28 g protein; 4 g fat; 8 g carbohydrate;
 53 mg calcium; 312 mg sodium; 66 mg cholesterol

Veal Chops with Pears and Bacon ◑

1 teaspoon <u>each</u> margarine and olive oil
2 veal loin chops (6 ounces each)
1 small Bosc pear (about 5 ounces), cored, pared, and
thinly sliced (¼-inch-thick slices)
1 tablespoon minced shallots
½ small garlic clove, minced
1 teaspoon all-purpose flour
¼ cup canned ready-to-serve chicken broth
2 tablespoons pear brandy
2 slices crisp bacon, crumbled
½ teaspoon minced fresh parsley
Dash pepper

In 10-inch nonstick skillet heat margarine and oil together over medium-high heat until margarine is bubbly and mixture is hot; add veal and cook, turning once, until browned on both sides, 3 to 4 minutes on each side. Transfer veal to plate; set aside.

In same skillet combine pear slices, shallots, and garlic and sauté over medium heat, stirring frequently, until pear is lightly browned, 1 to 2 minutes. Sprinkle flour over mixture and stir quickly to combine; continuing to stir, gradually add broth and brandy. Stir in bacon, parsley, and pepper; return veal to skillet. Reduce heat to low, cover, and let simmer until veal is tender and sauce has thickened, 4 to 5 minutes.

MAKES 2 SERVINGS, 1 VEAL CHOP EACH

Each serving provides: 4 Protein Exchanges; 1 Fat Exchange;
½ Fruit Exchange; 95 Optional Calories
Per serving: 429 calories; 33 g protein; 23 g fat; 16 g carbohydrate;
26 mg calcium; 323 mg sodium; 120 mg cholesterol

BREAKFAST

BREAKFAST

½ medium Grapefruit drizzled with
  ½ teaspoon Honey
¾ ounce Cold Cereal
½ cup Skim Milk
Coffee or Tea

LUNCH

Turkey-Spinach Salad (2 ounces
  sliced turkey with ¾ cup *each* torn
  spinach and lettuce, 6 cherry
  tomatoes, ¼ cup shredded carrot,
  and 1 tablespoon Thousand Island
  dressing)
1 small Apple
Coffee, Tea, or Mineral Water

DINNER

1 serving **Braised Pork Chops in
  Tomato-Caper Sauce**
1 cup *each* Cooked Broccoli Florets
  and Sliced Yellow Squash
1-ounce Roll
Lettuce Wedge with 1 tablespoon
  Reduced-Calorie Blue Cheese
  Dressing
Mint Tea

SNACKS

1 cup Strawberries topped with ¼ cup
  Plain Low-Fat Yogurt

Total Optional Calories: 55

Braised Pork Chops in Tomato-Caper Sauce

2 center-cut pork chops (5 ounces each)
2 teaspoons olive oil
½ cup quartered mushrooms
2 tablespoons chopped shallots
½ garlic clove, minced
**2 small plum tomatoes (about 1 ounce each), blanched,
  peeled, seeded, and diced**
¼ cup canned ready-to-serve chicken broth
**1½ teaspoons <u>each</u> chopped drained capers and
  fresh basil**
Dash <u>each</u> thyme leaves and salt

On rack in broiling pan broil chops 6 inches from heat
source, turning once, until lightly browned and rare, 2 to 3
minutes on each side.

In 10-inch nonstick skillet heat oil over medium heat; add
mushrooms, shallots, and garlic and sauté, stirring
occasionally, until mushrooms are lightly browned, 2 to 3
minutes. Add tomatoes, broth, capers, and seasonings to
skillet and stir to combine; add pork chops. Reduce heat to
low and let simmer, stirring occasionally, until meat is tender,
15 to 20 minutes.

MAKES 2 SERVINGS, 1 PORK CHOP EACH

Each serving provides: 3 Protein Exchanges; 1⅛ Vegetable Exchanges;
  1 Fat Exchange; 5 Optional Calories
Per serving: 259 calories; 28 g protein; 14 g fat; 4 g carbohydrate;
  21 mg calcium; 317 mg sodium; 83 mg cholesterol

Variation: Braised Pork Chops in Wine Sauce (Week 2) —
Add 2 tablespoons dry red table wine along with the
tomatoes, broth, capers, and seasonings to skillet; proceed
as directed. Increase Optional Calories to 20.

Per serving: 271 calories; 28 g protein; 14 g fat; 5 g carbohydrate;
  22 mg calcium; 318 mg sodium; 83 mg cholesterol

Pasta with Crabmeat Fra Diavolo

1½ cups canned Italian tomatoes (with liquid); seed tomatoes, reserving liquid, divided
2 teaspoons olive <u>or</u> vegetable oil
¼ cup chopped onion
1½ garlic cloves, minced
⅛ teaspoon crushed red pepper, or to taste
2 tablespoons dry sherry
1 tablespoon chopped fresh basil
1½ teaspoons chopped fresh parsley
⅛ teaspoon salt
Dash pepper
2 ounces drained thawed frozen crabmeat, flaked
1 tablespoon half-and-half (blend of milk and cream)
1 cup cooked angel hair pasta (cappelli d'angelo), hot*

In blender container process ¾ cup tomatoes until smooth; dice remaining tomatoes and set aside.

In 2- or 3-quart saucepan heat oil over medium heat; add onion, garlic, and red pepper and sauté until onion is softened, 2 to 3 minutes. Add sherry and let mixture simmer for 1 minute; stir in processed and diced tomatoes, reserved tomato liquid, and seasonings and bring to a boil. Reduce heat to low, cover, and let simmer, stirring frequently, until flavors are blended, 20 to 25 minutes. Add crabmeat and half-and-half, stirring well to combine; cook, stirring occasionally, until crabmeat is heated through, 3 to 4 minutes (<u>do not boil</u>).

To serve, arrange pasta on serving platter and top with crabmeat mixture.

MAKES 2 SERVINGS

Each serving provides: 1 Protein Exchange; 1 Bread Exchange; 1¾ Vegetable Exchanges; 1 Fat Exchange; 30 Optional Calories
Per serving: 223 calories; 10 g protein; 7 g fat; 28 g carbohydrate; 97 mg calcium; 497 mg sodium; 31 mg cholesterol

*Thin spaghetti or linguine may be substituted for the angel hair pasta.

BREAKFAST

½ medium Grapefruit
1 Soft-Cooked Egg
½ Whole Wheat English Muffin,
    toasted, with 1 teaspoon Reduced-
    Calorie Margarine
1 cup Skim Milk

LUNCH

Turkey in a Pita (2 ounces sliced
    turkey with 3 tomato slices,
    4 lettuce leaves, and 2 teaspoons
    mustard in 1-ounce pita bread)
6 *each* Celery and Carrot Sticks
Coffee, Tea, or Mineral Water

DINNER

3 ounces Broiled Ground Veal Patty
    with 2 teaspoons Ketchup
1 serving **Parmesan-Sage Potato
    Wedges**
1 cup Cooked Shredded Red
    Cabbage
1½ cups Mixed Green Salad with
    1 tablespoon Creamy Italian
    Dressing
½ cup Canned Pineapple Chunks
Coffee or Tea

SNACKS

1 small Apple; 1 serving Reduced-
    Calorie Chocolate Dairy Drink

Total Optional Calories: 25

Parmesan-Sage Potato Wedges ☕◑

6 ounces potato, well scrubbed
2 cups cold water
1 teaspoon olive oil
1 tablespoon grated Parmesan cheese
⅛ teaspoon <u>each</u> salt and rubbed sage
Dash pepper

Using sharp knife, cut potato into ¼-inch-thick wedges. In 1½-quart saucepan combine potato wedges and cold water and bring to a boil; cook until potato wedges are tender-crisp, 4 to 5 minutes. Transfer potato wedges to a colander and set under running cold water until cool; pat dry with paper towels.

In 8- or 9-inch nonstick skillet heat oil over high heat; add potato wedges and cook, turning occasionally, until lightly browned, 2 to 3 minutes on each side. Sprinkle cheese and seasonings over potato wedges and mix until thoroughly combined.

MAKES 2 SERVINGS

Each serving provides: 1 Bread Exchange; ½ Fat Exchange; 15 Optional
    Calories
Per serving: 94 calories; 3 g protein; 3 g fat; 14 g carbohydrate;
    47 mg calcium; 191 mg sodium; 2 mg cholesterol

BREAKFAST

BREAKFAST

⅓ cup Pineapple Juice
½ cup Cooked Cereal
1 serving Reduced-Calorie Hot
   Cocoa

LUNCH

Tuna Salad Sandwich (2 ounces tuna
   with ¼ cup chopped celery,
   4 lettuce leaves, and 1½ teaspoons
   Russian dressing on 2 slices
   reduced-calorie wheat bread)
½ cup Cauliflower Florets and
   4 Green Bell Pepper Rings
Coffee, Tea, or Mineral Water

DINNER

3 ounces Baked Chicken Breast
   with Rosemary
1 serving **Potato, Bacon, and Fruit Sauté**
1 cup Cooked Chopped Spinach
1½ cups Tossed Salad with 2 Black
   Olives, pitted, and 1 teaspoon
   Olive Oil mixed with 2 teaspoons
   Red Wine Vinegar plus Herbs
½ cup Low-Calorie Raspberry-
   Flavored Gelatin topped with
   2 tablespoons Aerosol Instant
   Whipped Cream
Coffee or Tea

SNACKS

1 small Orange, cut into wedges
   and sprinkled with Cinnamon;
   Chocolate Milk (1 cup skim milk
   mixed with 1 teaspoon chocolate
   syrup)

Total Optional Calories: 120

Potato, Bacon, and Fruit Sauté ◑

2 teaspoons vegetable oil
6 ounces baked potato (with skin), sliced crosswise into
   ⅛-inch-thick slices
1½ ounces mixed dried fruit, diced
1 ounce julienne-cut Canadian-style bacon (thin strips)
½ cup canned ready-to-serve beef broth
Dash pepper
2 slices crisp bacon, crumbled

In 10-inch nonstick skillet heat oil over medium-high heat;
arrange potato slices in a single layer over bottom of skillet
and cook, turning once, until slices are lightly browned, 1 to
2 minutes on each side. Transfer potato slices to plate.

   In same skillet combine fruit and Canadian-style bacon
and sauté until fruit softens, 1 to 2 minutes; add potato,
broth, and pepper. Reduce heat to low, cover skillet, and
cook until fruit is plumped, 3 to 4 minutes. Uncover and
continue cooking until broth is absorbed, 2 to 3 minutes
longer; sprinkle with crumbled bacon.

MAKES 2 SERVINGS

Each serving provides: ½ Protein Exchange; 1 Bread Exchange;
   1 Fat Exchange; 55 Optional Calories
Per serving: 249 calories; 8 g protein; 9 g fat; 36 g carbohydrate;
   19 mg calcium; 543 mg sodium; 12 mg cholesterol

BREAKFAST

½ cup Grapefruit Sections
Lox 'n' Bagel (½ small bagel topped
with 2 tablespoons whipped cream
cheese and ½ ounce smoked
salmon)
½ cup Skim Milk
Coffee or Tea

LUNCH

Peanut Butter and Jelly Grahams
(2 tablespoons peanut butter with
2 teaspoons reduced-calorie grape
spread on 2 graham crackers)
1 small Apple
Coffee, Tea, or Mineral Water

DINNER

3 ounces Baked Bluefish Fillet with
Lemon Wedge
Parmesan Cheese Noodles (½ cup
cooked noodles with 1 teaspoon
each margarine and grated
Parmesan cheese)
1 cup Cooked Broccoli Florets with
1 teaspoon Margarine
2 cups Mixed Green Salad with
2 tablespoons **Creamy Blue Cheese
Dressing**
½ cup Skim Milk
Coffee or Tea

SNACKS

½ cup Applesauce; 1 serving
Reduced-Calorie Chocolate Dairy
Drink

Total Optional Calories: 200

Creamy Blue Cheese Dressing ◑

Keep a batch of this cool and creamy dressing in the refrigerator. It will keep in a covered container for up to 2 weeks. Stir before each use.

¼ pound blue cheese
⅓ cup plus 2 teaspoons sour cream
2 tablespoons plus 2 teaspoons vegetable oil <u>or</u> mayonnaise
2 tablespoons rice <u>or</u> cider vinegar
½ to 1 small garlic clove
½ teaspoon granulated sugar
⅛ teaspoon pepper

In blender container combine all ingredients and process until smooth, scraping down sides of container as necessary. Transfer mixture to 1-cup container with tight-fitting cover and refrigerate until ready to use.

YIELDS 1 CUP

Each 2-tablespoon serving provides: ½ Protein Exchange;
1 Fat Exchange; 25 Optional Calories
Per serving: 115 calories; 3 g protein; 11 g fat; 1 g carbohydrate;
88 mg calcium; 204 mg sodium; 15 mg cholesterol

Banana Pancakes ⓒ ◑

Serve these delicious pancakes topped with reduced-calorie pancake syrup or fruit-flavored spread for a special weekend breakfast.

**1 very ripe medium banana (about 6 ounces), peeled
  and cut into pieces**
1 egg
1 teaspoon margarine
½ teaspoon vanilla extract
3 tablespoons all-purpose flour
1 teaspoon double-acting baking powder

In blender container combine banana, egg, margarine, and vanilla and process until smooth, scraping down sides of container as necessary; add flour and baking powder and process to combine.

Spray 9-inch nonstick skillet with nonstick cooking spray and heat. Drop 4 heaping tablespoonfuls batter into hot skillet, making 4 pancakes; using back of spoon, spread each into a circle about 3 inches in diameter. Cook over medium-high heat until pancakes are browned on bottom and bubbles appear on surface; using pancake turner, turn pancakes over and brown other side. Remove pancakes to warm serving platter and keep warm. Repeat procedure, spraying skillet and making 4 more pancakes.

MAKES 2 SERVINGS, 4 PANCAKES EACH

Each serving provides: ½ Protein Exchange; ½ Bread Exchange;
  ½ Fat Exchange; 1 Fruit Exchange
Per serving: 157 calories; 5 g protein; 5 g fat; 23 g carbohydrate;
  126 mg calcium; 271 mg sodium; 137 mg cholesterol

BREAKFAST

½ cup Orange Sections
1 ounce Swiss Cheese
2 slices Cocktail Rye Bread with
    1 teaspoon Reduced-Calorie
    Margarine
½ cup Skim Milk
Coffee or Tea

LUNCH

Turkey on a Roll (2 ounces sliced
    turkey with 3 tomato slices, ¼ cup
    shredded lettuce, and 1½ teaspoons
    Russian dressing on 1-ounce roll)
6 Green Bell Pepper Strips and
    3 Radishes
Coffee, Tea, or Mineral Water

DINNER

3 ounces Baked Fillet of Sole
1 cup Cooked French-Style Green
    Beans
Mushroom Salad (1 cup sliced
    mushrooms with 6 red onion rings
    and 1 tablespoon reduced-calorie
    mayonnaise on 4 romaine lettuce
    leaves)
1 serving **Apples in Orange-Ginger
    Syrup**
Café au Lait (½ cup *each* hot coffee
    and skim milk sprinkled with
    nutmeg)

SNACKS

Pineapple 'n' Yogurt (2 canned
    pineapple slices topped with ½ cup
    plain low-fat yogurt)

Total Optional Calories: 55

Apples in Orange-Ginger Syrup ● ◐

2 small apples (about ¼ pound each), cored
¼ cup orange juice (no sugar added)
2 tablespoons water
1 tablespoon plus 1 teaspoon granulated sugar
1 teaspoon lemon juice
1 slice pared ginger root (about ½ inch thick)
⅛ teaspoon <u>each</u> grated orange peel and grated lemon peel

Starting at stem end, pare each apple half of the way down; set aside.

In 1½-quart saucepan combine remaining ingredients and cook over high heat, stirring occasionally, until sugar is dissolved and mixture comes to a boil. Reduce heat to medium; add apples, stem-end up. Cover saucepan and let cook, basting occasionally, until apples are fork-tender and liquid is syrupy, 7 to 10 minutes; remove and discard ginger root.

To serve, into each of 2 dessert dishes place 1 apple and top with half of the syrup; serve warm.

MAKES 2 SERVINGS, 1 APPLE EACH

Each serving provides: 1 Fruit Exchange; 55 Optional Calories
Per serving: 109 calories; 0.4 g protein; 0.4 g fat; 28 g carbohydrate;
    11 mg calcium; 1 mg sodium; 0 mg cholesterol

BREAKFAST

½ medium Banana, sliced
¾ ounce Cold Cereal
¾ cup Skim Milk
Coffee or Tea

LUNCH

Shrimp Salad (2 ounces tiny shrimp
    with ¼ cup chopped celery and
    2 teaspoons reduced-calorie
    mayonnaise on 4 lettuce leaves)
½ cup Broccoli Florets and 6 Yellow
    Squash Sticks
12 large Grapes
Coffee, Tea, or Mineral Water

DINNER

3 ounces Baked Ham
Candied Yam (3 ounces cooked yam
    with 1 teaspoon *each* reduced-
    calorie margarine and honey)
1 cup Cooked Chinese Pea Pods
1½ cups Mixed Green Salad with
    1½ teaspoons Thousand Island
    Dressing mixed with 2 tablespoons
    Plain Low-Fat Yogurt and
    ¼ teaspoon Mustard
½ cup Grapefruit Sections
Coffee or Tea

SNACKS

1 serving **Celebration Cheesecake
    Squares**; 1 serving Reduced-Calorie
    Hot Cocoa topped with 2 table-
    spoons Whipped Topping

Total Optional Calories: 155

Celebration Cheesecake Squares

24 graham crackers (2½-inch squares), made into fine crumbs
2 tablespoons margarine, melted
Dash ground cinnamon
1¾ cups less 1 tablespoon whipped cream cheese
2 eggs
¼ cup granulated sugar
2 tablespoons sour cream
Dash lemon juice

Preheat oven to 375°F. In medium bowl combine graham cracker crumbs, margarine, and cinnamon, mixing thoroughly. Transfer to 13 x 9 x 2-inch nonstick baking pan and, using the back of a spoon, press crumb mixture over bottom of pan; bake until lightly browned, 4 to 5 minutes. Remove baking pan to wire rack and let cool.

Reduce oven temperature to 350°F. In mixing bowl combine cream cheese, eggs, sugar, sour cream, and lemon juice and, using electric mixer at medium speed, beat until smooth. Carefully spread cheese mixture over cooled crust and bake in middle of center oven rack until set, 25 to 30 minutes (do not overbake). Transfer to wire rack and let cool completely. Cut into 24 squares; serve at room temperature or cover and refrigerate until chilled.

MAKES 12 SERVINGS, 2 SQUARES EACH

Each serving provides: 1 Bread Exchange; ½ Fat Exchange; 110 Optional Calories
Per serving: 178 calories; 4 g protein; 12 g fat; 15 g carbohydrate; 28 mg calcium; 209 mg sodium; 68 mg cholesterol

TIP: This cake freezes well, so wrap individual squares in resealable plastic freezer bags and store in freezer until ready to use; then, for a quick-and-easy dessert, just thaw at room temperature.

BREAKFAST

½ cup Orange Juice
1 serving **Cran-Raisin Muffins** with
　½ teaspoon Honey
1 cup Hot Skim Milk with 1 teaspoon
　Honey

LUNCH

Tuna-Vegetable Salad (2 ounces tuna
　with 1 cup torn lettuce, ½ cup
　alfalfa sprouts, ¼ cup *each* sliced
　zucchini and grated carrot, and
　1 teaspoon olive oil mixed with
　2 teaspoons red wine vinegar plus
　herbs)
2 slices Cocktail Rye Bread
1 small Pear
Coffee, Tea, or Mineral Water

DINNER

4 ounces Broiled Lamb Chop with
　1 tablespoon Mint Jelly
4 ounces Baked Butternut Squash
　sprinkled with ½ teaspoon Brown
　Sugar and Nutmeg
1 cup Cooked Broccoli Florets
Cucumber-Pepper Salad (8 *each*
　cucumber slices and red bell
　pepper rings with lemon juice and
　herbs on 8 Boston lettuce leaves)
½ cup Reduced-Calorie Vanilla
　Pudding sprinkled with 1 teaspoon
　Shredded Coconut
Coffee or Tea

SNACKS

½ cup Applesauce; 1 cup Skim Milk

Total Optional Calories: 165

Cran-Raisin Muffins

Prepare ahead and freeze, then just thaw at room temperature or heat in microwave or toaster-oven and serve warm.

1½ cups cranberries, chopped
½ cup margarine, melted, divided
¼ cup firmly packed dark brown sugar
2¼ cups all-purpose flour
2 tablespoons granulated sugar
1 tablespoon double-acting baking powder
½ teaspoon salt
1 cup skim milk
1 egg, beaten
⅓ cup plus 2 teaspoons golden raisins

Preheat oven to 350°F. Spray twelve 2½-inch-diameter muffin-pan cups with nonstick cooking spray. Spoon 1/12 of the cranberries into each cup, then top each portion with 1 teaspoon melted margarine and 1 teaspoon brown sugar; set aside.

　In large mixing bowl combine flour, granulated sugar, baking powder, and salt; add milk, egg, and remaining margarine and stir until mixture is moistened (do not beat or overmix). Add raisins to batter and stir to combine; spoon an equal amount of batter over cranberry mixture in each muffin-pan cup (each will be about ⅔ full). Bake in middle of center oven rack for 25 to 30 minutes (until muffins are golden brown and a toothpick, inserted in center, comes out clean). Invert muffins onto wire rack and let cool.

MAKES 12 SERVINGS, 1 MUFFIN EACH

Each serving provides:　1 Bread Exchange; 2 Fat Exchanges; 65 Optional
　Calories
Per serving:　213 calories; 4 g protein; 8 g fat; 31 g carbohydrate;
　95 mg calcium; 306 mg sodium; 23 mg cholesterol

BREAKFAST

½ medium Banana, sliced
¾ ounce Cold Cereal
1 cup Skim Milk
Coffee or Tea

LUNCH

Peanut Butter and Jelly Sandwich
 (2 tablespoons peanut butter with
 2 teaspoons reduced-calorie orange
 marmalade on 2 slices reduced-
 calorie raisin bread)
20 small Grapes
Coffee, Tea, or Mineral Water

DINNER

4 ounces Broiled Chicken with
 Lemon Juice and Herbs
½ cup Cooked Cracked Wheat with
 1 tablespoon Cooked Chopped
 Onion and 1 teaspoon Margarine
½ cup *each* Stewed Tomatoes and
 Cooked Sliced Yellow Squash
Artichoke Salad (½ cup artichoke
 hearts with 6 cherry tomatoes and
 1 tablespoon French dressing on
 4 lettuce leaves)
1 serving **Coconut-Spice Birthday
 Cupcakes**
Coffee or Tea

SNACKS

1 medium Kiwi Fruit; 1 serving
 Reduced-Calorie Chocolate Dairy
 Drink

Total Optional Calories: 175

Coconut-Spice Birthday Cupcakes

1 cup plus 2 tablespoons all-purpose flour
2 teaspoons double-acting baking powder
¼ teaspoon ground cinnamon
Dash <u>each</u> ground cloves and salt
½ cup whipped sweet butter
¼ cup granulated sugar
1 teaspoon vanilla extract
2 eggs
⅓ cup skim milk
¼ cup shredded coconut

In small bowl combine flour, baking powder, cinnamon, cloves, and salt; set aside.

  Preheat oven to 375°F. In medium mixing bowl, using electric mixer at medium speed, beat together butter and sugar until mixture is light and fluffy. Beat in vanilla, then eggs, 1 at a time, beating until well combined; add flour mixture alternately with milk, beating until batter is smooth. Stir in coconut.

  Spray twelve 2½-inch-diameter muffin-pan cups with nonstick cooking spray; fill each cup with an equal amount of batter (each cup will be about ½ full). Bake in middle of center oven rack for 20 to 25 minutes (until cupcakes are golden brown and a toothpick, inserted in center, comes out dry). Invert cupcakes onto wire rack and let cool.

MAKES 12 SERVINGS, 1 CUPCAKE EACH

Each serving provides: ½ Bread Exchange; 80 Optional Calories
Per serving: 117 calories; 3 g protein; 5 g fat; 14 g carbohydrate;
  52 mg calcium; 102 mg sodium; 56 mg cholesterol

TIP: To help make cleanup even easier, omit nonstick cooking spray and line muffin-pan cups with paper baking cups before filling.

BREAKFAST

Fruit 'n' Cheese Delight (⅓ cup cottage cheese mixed with ¾ ounce mixed dried fruit and 1 teaspoon shredded coconut on ½ small bagel)
1 cup Skim Milk

LUNCH

Chicken Sandwich (2 ounces sliced chicken with 4 tomato slices, 4 lettuce leaves, and 1½ teaspoons Thousand Island dressing on 2 slices pumpernickel bread)
6 *each* Celery and Carrot Sticks
1 small Pear
Coffee, Tea, or Mineral Water

DINNER

1 cup Chilled Mixed Vegetable Juice
3 ounces Baked Bluefish Fillet
Vegetable Sauté (1 cup Chinese pea pods and ½ cup *each* red bell pepper strips and sliced bamboo shoots sautéed in 2 teaspoons vegetable oil and sprinkled with ½ teaspoon sesame seed)
½ cup Coleslaw
1 medium Kiwi Fruit
½ cup Skim Milk
Coffee or Tea

SNACKS

1 serving **Cat's Tongue Cookies (Langues de Chat)**; ½ cup Skim Milk

Total Optional Calories: 210

Cat's Tongue Cookies (Langues de Chat)

This Halloween specialty gets its name from the cookie's shape and appearance. Children of all ages will love them.

¼ cup <u>each</u> granulated sugar and sweet butter
1 egg white
1 teaspoon vanilla extract
¼ cup all-purpose flour
2 ounces semisweet chocolate chips

Preheat oven to 400°F. In medium mixing bowl, using electric mixer at medium speed, beat together sugar and butter until mixture is fluffy; add egg white and vanilla and beat until combined. Gradually beat in flour, beating until smooth.

Fit a pastry bag with a No. 6 round or No. 30 star tip and spoon batter into bag; pipe out ⅓ of batter onto nonstick cookie sheet, forming 12 strips, each about 3 inches long and ¼ inch wide, and leaving a space of about 2 inches between each. Bake in middle of center oven rack until edges of cookies are lightly browned, 4 to 5 minutes. Using a spatula, remove cookies to wire rack and let cool. Using cooled cookie sheet, repeat procedure 2 more times, making 24 more cookies.

In double boiler heat chocolate over hot (<u>not boiling</u>) water until melted.* Dip both ends of each cookie into chocolate, coating about ½ inch of each end; arrange on wire rack and let stand until chocolate hardens.

MAKES 12 SERVINGS, 3 COOKIES EACH

Each serving provides: 90 Optional Calories
Per serving: 86 calories; 0.8 g protein; 6 g fat; 9 g carbohydrate;
    3 mg calcium; 5 mg sodium; 10 mg cholesterol

*When melting chocolate, it should not come in contact with water or steam; moisture will cause it to harden.

November

Whole Wheat–Banana Muffins

NOVEMBER'S BEST BUYS FOR FRUITS AND VEGETABLES

alfalfa sprouts	cauliflower	kohlrabi	pineapples
apples	celery	leeks	potatoes
bananas	Chinese pea pods	lettuce	radishes
bean sprouts	cranberries	mandarin oranges	scallions (green onions)
Belgian endives	eggplants	mushrooms	spinach
bell peppers	escarole	mustard greens	sweet potatoes
broccoli	fennel	onions	Swiss chard
brussels sprouts	figs	papayas	turnips
cabbage	kale	pears	winter squash
carrots	kiwi fruit	persimmons	yams

BREAKFAST

½ cup Orange-Grapefruit Juice
¾ ounce Cold Cereal
½ cup Skim Milk
Coffee or Tea

LUNCH

Tuna-Stuffed Pocket (2 ounces tuna
    with ¼ cup chopped celery,
    4 lettuce leaves, 3 tomato slices,
    and 1 teaspoon mayonnaise in
    1-ounce whole wheat pita bread)
6 *each* Carrot and Fennel Sticks
1 small Apple
Coffee, Tea, or Mineral Water

DINNER

1 serving **Tomato-Sausage Soup**
1-ounce slice Italian Bread topped
    with 2 ounces Provolone Cheese
2 cups Tossed Salad with 1 teaspoon
    Imitation Bacon Bits and
    1½ teaspoons Italian Dressing
    mixed with 2 teaspoons Red Wine
    Vinegar
½ cup Reduced-Calorie Chocolate
    Pudding topped with 2 tablespoons
    Whipped Topping
Orange-Flavored Seltzer

SNACKS

½ medium Banana; ½ cup Skim Milk
    with 1 Graham Cracker

Total Optional Calories: 155

Tomato-Sausage Soup

This hot and hearty soup is a meal in itself.
Keep it on hand to heat up when you want
something fast and filling.

1 tablespoon plus 1 teaspoon olive <u>or</u> vegetable oil
1½ cups diced eggplant
½ cup chopped onion
¼ cup chopped fennel
2 garlic cloves, minced
2 cups mixed vegetable juice
1 cup <u>each</u> tomato puree, canned ready-to-serve
    chicken broth, and canned Italian tomatoes (with
    liquid); drain, seed, and dice tomatoes, reserving
    liquid
1 bay leaf
1 tablespoon chopped fresh basil
¼ teaspoon <u>each</u> salt and pepper
½ pound cooked veal sausage, sliced
1 cup cooked small macaroni shells

In 4-quart saucepan heat oil over medium-high heat; add
eggplant, onion, fennel, and garlic and sauté, stirring
frequently, until vegetables are lightly browned, 3 to 4
minutes. Add juice, tomato puree, broth, tomatoes,
reserved liquid, bay leaf, basil, salt, and pepper; mix well.
Reduce heat to low, cover, and cook, stirring frequently,
until flavors are blended, about 30 minutes. Add sausage
and macaroni and cook until heated through, 5 to 10
minutes longer. Remove and discard bay leaf before serving.

MAKES 4 SERVINGS, ABOUT 1 CUP EACH

Each serving provides: 2 Protein Exchanges; ½ Bread Exchange;
    2½ Vegetable Exchanges; 1 Fat Exchange; 40 Optional Calories
Per serving: 299 calories; 21 g protein; 12 g fat; 27 g carbohydrate;
    82 mg calcium; 1,213 mg sodium; 57 mg cholesterol

BREAKFAST

½ cup Grapefruit Sections
1 slice Cinnamon-Raisin Bread,
    toasted, with 1 teaspoon Reduced-
    Calorie Apricot Spread
½ cup Skim Milk
Coffee or Tea

LUNCH

Turkey Salad (2 ounces diced turkey
    with ¼ cup *each* diced celery,
    mushrooms, cucumber, and
    scallions, ¼ cup cauliflower florets,
    ½ cup shredded lettuce, and
    1 tablespoon Italian dressing)
1 Rice Cake
Coffee, Tea, or Mineral Water

DINNER

1 serving **Wild Rice Soup**
Ham and Egg Salad (2½ ounces
    julienne-cut boiled ham with
    1 hard-cooked egg, sliced, 2 cups
    torn lettuce, ¼ cup shredded
    carrot, 8 tomato wedges, and
    1 tablespoon reduced-calorie blue
    cheese dressing)
1 slice Reduced-Calorie Rye Bread
½ cup Fruit Salad
½ cup Skim Milk
Coffee or Tea

SNACKS

1 cup Strawberries; ½ cup Skim Milk

Total Optional Calories: 95

Wild Rice Soup

A perfect recipe for using up leftover cooked wild rice.
If you don't have any left over, prepare the rice before
you begin sautéing the vegetables. It should be ready
when you need to add it to the soup.

1 tablespoon plus 1 teaspoon margarine
½ cup <u>each</u> chopped onion, chopped celery, and diced
  carrot
3 tablespoons all-purpose flour
2 cups low-fat milk (1% milk fat)
1 cup canned ready-to-serve chicken broth
2 ounces Cheddar cheese, shredded
1 cup cooked wild rice
2 teaspoons chopped fresh parsley
⅛ teaspoon <u>each</u> white pepper and salt

In 3-quart saucepan heat margarine over medium-high heat
until bubbly and hot; add onion, celery, and carrot and sauté
until onion is softened, 2 to 3 minutes. Sprinkle flour over
vegetables and stir quickly to combine. Continuing to stir,
gradually add milk; add broth and, stirring, bring just to a
boil. Reduce heat to low, cover, and let simmer, stirring
frequently, for 20 minutes. Add remaining ingredients to
saucepan and cook, stirring constantly, until cheese is
melted, 5 to 10 minutes (<u>do not boil</u>).

MAKES 4 SERVINGS, ABOUT ¾ CUP EACH

Each serving provides: ½ Protein Exchange; ½ Bread Exchange;
    ¾ Vegetable Exchange; 1 Fat Exchange; ½ Milk Exchange; 45 Optional
    Calories
Per serving: 238 calories; 11 g protein; 10 g fat; 25 g carbohydrate;
    276 mg calcium; 535 mg sodium; 20 mg cholesterol

Variations: Wild Rice Soup with Almonds (Week 8) — Add
1 ounce sliced almonds along with the cheese, rice, and
seasonings to soup. Increase Optional Calories to 85.

Per serving: 279 calories; 13 g protein; 14 g fat; 27 g carbohydrate;
    295 mg calcium; 536 mg sodium; 20 mg cholesterol

Rice Soup (Week 2) — Substitute regular long-grain white
rice for the wild rice.

Per serving: 243 calories; 10 g protein; 10 g fat; 27 g carbohydrate;
    279 mg calcium; 534 mg sodium; 20 mg cholesterol

BREAKFAST

1 small Orange
1 Scrambled Egg sprinkled with
   1 teaspoon Imitation Bacon Bits
½ small Bagel with 1 teaspoon
   Margarine
1 cup Skim Milk

LUNCH

Chicken-Stuffed Pocket (2 ounces
   sliced chicken with 4 lettuce
   leaves, 3 tomato slices, and
   2 teaspoons Dijon-style mustard in
   1-ounce whole wheat pita bread)
6 *each* Celery and Zucchini Sticks
1 small Pear
Coffee, Tea, or Mineral Water

DINNER

1 serving **Cheese 'n' Nut-Pepper Slices**
3 ounces Parslied Broiled Scallops
   with Lemon Wedge
1 cup Cooked Noodles
6 Cooked Broccoli Spears
Bibb Salad (2 cups torn Bibb lettuce
   with ½ cup shredded carrot and
   1 tablespoon Russian dressing)
Coffee or Tea

SNACKS

½ cup Applesauce sprinkled with
   Cinnamon; Cucumber Snack
   (½ cup plain low-fat yogurt mixed
   with ½ cup sliced cucumber plus
   dillweed)

Total Optional Calories: 110

Cheese 'n' Nut-Pepper Slices ◐

1 medium red, yellow, <u>or</u> green bell pepper
¼ pound Swiss <u>or</u> Gruyère cheese, shredded
¼ cup whipped cream cheese
2 ounces pecan halves (reserve 8 for garnish)

Remove and discard stem end, seeds, and membranes
from pepper; rinse pepper and thoroughly dry inside with
paper towel. Set aside.

In work bowl of food processor combine cheeses and
pecan halves; process until well blended. Spoon cheese
mixture into pepper; using back of spoon, pack mixture
firmly to remove air pockets. Wrap stuffed pepper in plastic
wrap and refrigerate until cheese mixture is firm, overnight
or at least 2 hours.

To serve, remove plastic wrap and cut pepper
crosswise into 8 equal slices. Garnish each stuffed pepper
slice with a reserved pecan half.

MAKES 8 SERVINGS, 1 SLICE EACH

Each serving provides: ½ Protein Exchange; ¼ Vegetable Exchange;
   65 Optional Calories
Per serving with Swiss cheese: 119 calories; 5 g protein; 10 g fat;
   2 g carbohydrate; 143 mg calcium; 55 mg sodium; 18 mg cholesterol
With Gruyère cheese: 124 calories; 5 g protein; 11 g fat; 2 g carbohydrate;
   150 mg calcium; 66 mg sodium; 20 mg cholesterol

Variation: Cheese 'n' Pepper Slices (Week 4) — Omit pecans
from recipe. Reduce Optional Calories to 15.

Per serving with Swiss cheese: 72 calories; 4 g protein; 6 g fat;
   1 g carbohydrate; 140 mg calcium; 55 mg sodium; 18 mg cholesterol
With Gruyère cheese: 77 calories; 5 g protein; 6 g fat; 0.7 g carbohydrate;
   147 mg calcium; 66 mg sodium; 20 mg cholesterol

TIP: For that big bash, try tripling this recipe and using 1 bell pepper of each
color.

Vegetable-Stuffed Fillet of Sole ◑

2 sole fillets (5 ounces each)
1 tablespoon lemon juice
Dash <u>each</u> salt, pepper, and onion powder
1 medium carrot, cut into matchstick pieces and blanched
½ medium red bell pepper, seeded, cut into 4 strips, and blanched
4 medium scallions (bulb and 2 inches of green portion), blanched
1 teaspoon <u>each</u> soy sauce,* Chinese sesame oil, and margarine, melted

Preheat oven to 450°F.† Sprinkle fillets evenly with lemon juice, salt, pepper, and onion powder. Crosswise along center of each fillet arrange half of the carrot sticks, 2 pepper strips, and 2 scallions; sprinkle each portion of vegetables with ½ teaspoon each soy sauce and sesame oil, then roll fillets to enclose filling. Set rolls seam-side down in 8 x 8 x 2-inch baking pan; brush each roll with half of the melted margarine and bake until fish flakes easily when tested with a fork, 15 to 20 minutes.

MAKES 2 SERVINGS, 1 FISH ROLL EACH

Each serving provides: 4 Protein Exchanges; 1¾ Vegetable Exchanges;
   1 Fat Exchange
Per serving: 184 calories; 24 g protein; 6 g fat; 8 g carbohydrate;
   46 mg calcium; 480 mg sodium; 67 mg cholesterol

* Reduced-sodium soy sauce may be substituted. Reduce calcium to 44 mg and sodium to 360 mg.
† This dish may be prepared in a microwave oven. Blanch vegetables in microwave oven rather than on top of stove; stuff and roll fillets as directed. Set rolls in 8-inch microwave-safe pie plate and microwave on High for 1 minute 45 seconds; rotate plate ¼ turn and microwave on High until fish flakes easily when tested with a fork, 1 minute 45 seconds longer. Let stand 1 minute before serving. Timing may be different in your microwave oven. To ensure good results, be sure to check for doneness while cooking.

BREAKFAST

½ cup Orange Juice
½ English Muffin, toasted, with
   1 tablespoon Peanut Butter and
   1 teaspoon Reduced-Calorie
   Orange Marmalade
1 cup Skim Milk ·

LUNCH

Egg Salad (1 hard-cooked egg,
   chopped, with ¼ cup diced celery
   and 2 teaspoons mayonnaise on
   4 lettuce leaves)
6 Fennel Sticks and ½ cup Broccoli
   Florets
6 Melba Rounds
1 large Tangerine
Coffee, Tea, or Mineral Water

DINNER

1 serving **Baked Crab Creole**
1 cup Cooked Spinach Leaves
   sprinkled with 1 teaspoon
   Imitation Bacon Bits
Carrot-Tomato Salad (½ cup
   shredded carrot with 6 tomato
   slices and 2 teaspoons reduced-
   calorie mayonnaise on 4 lettuce
   leaves)
½ cup Low-Calorie Cherry-Flavored
   Gelatin topped with 1 tablespoon
   Whipped Topping
Mint Tea

SNACKS

½ cup Applesauce; 1 cup Skim Milk

Total Optional Calories: 150

Baked Crab Creole ◑

2 teaspoons reduced-calorie margarine (tub)
½ cup <u>each</u> chopped celery, green bell pepper, and scallions (green onions)
6 ounces cooked fresh <u>or</u> thawed and drained frozen crabmeat
3 tablespoons sour cream
2 tablespoons chopped drained canned pimiento
1 tablespoon plus 1 teaspoon lemon juice
2 teaspoons <u>each</u> minced fresh parsley and Dijon-style mustard
½ teaspoon Worcestershire sauce
¼ teaspoon hot sauce
⅛ teaspoon ground red pepper
⅓ cup plus 2 teaspoons plain dried bread crumbs
Garnish: lemon wedges

Preheat oven to 400°F. In 8-inch nonstick skillet heat margarine over medium-high heat until bubbly and hot; add celery, bell pepper, and scallions and sauté until lightly browned, 2 to 3 minutes. Transfer to medium mixing bowl; add remaining ingredients except bread crumbs and garnish and stir to combine. Stir bread crumbs into mixture; divide into 2 large scallop shells or individual 1½-cup casseroles and bake until lightly browned and heated through, about 15 minutes. Serve garnished with lemon wedges.

MAKES 2 SERVINGS

Each serving provides: 3 Protein Exchanges; 1 Bread Exchange;
   1½ Vegetable Exchanges; ½ Fat Exchange; 50 Optional Calories
Per serving: 246 calories; 19 g protein; 10 g fat; 21 g carbohydrate;
   115 mg calcium; 580 mg sodium; 95 mg cholesterol

BREAKFAST

½ medium Grapefruit sprinkled with
  ½ teaspoon Confectioners' Sugar
1 Sunny-Side-Up Egg
½ small Bagel, toasted, with
  1 teaspoon Reduced-Calorie
  Raspberry Spread
1 serving Reduced-Calorie Hot Cocoa

LUNCH

Kidney Bean Salad (4 ounces canned
  kidney beans with ¼ cup *each*
  diced tomato and red onion, thyme
  leaves, and 2 teaspoons olive oil
  mixed with 2 teaspoons red wine
  vinegar)
6 *each* Cucumber Spears and Carrot
  Sticks
1 large Mandarin Orange
Coffee, Tea, or Mineral Water

DINNER

⅓ cup Apple Cider
1 serving **Turkey Cutlets with
  Cranberry-Orange Sauce**
6 ounces Baked Yam drizzled with
  1 teaspoon Maple Syrup
1 cup Cooked Brussels Sprouts
1½ cups Tossed Salad with Lemon
  Juice and Herbs
Coffee or Tea

SNACKS

1 Cinnamon Graham Cracker; 1 cup
  Skim Milk

Total Optional Calories: 105

Turkey Cutlets with Cranberry-Orange Sauce ◐

Serve this easy and elegant entrée for an intimate
Thanksgiving dinner for two.

½ **cup cranberries**
¼ **cup orange juice (no sugar added)**
2 **tablespoons canned ready-to-serve chicken broth**
1 **tablespoon orange liqueur**
2 **teaspoons firmly packed light brown sugar**
1½ **teaspoons lemon juice**
⅛ **teaspoon** <u>each</u> **grated orange peel and ground ginger**
½ **pound turkey cutlets, pounded to ¼-inch thickness**
1 **tablespoon all-purpose flour**
1 **teaspoon** <u>each</u> **vegetable oil and margarine**
Dash <u>each</u> **salt and pepper**

In 1- or 2-quart saucepan combine cranberries, orange juice,
broth, liqueur, sugar, lemon juice, orange peel, and ginger,
stirring to dissolve sugar; cook over medium heat, stirring
frequently, until cranberries burst and mixture thickens
slightly, 4 to 5 minutes. Remove saucepan from heat; set
aside.

On sheet of wax paper or a paper plate lightly dredge
turkey in flour, coating both sides of each cutlet. In 10-inch
skillet heat oil and margarine together until margarine is
bubbly and mixture is hot; add turkey and cook, turning
once, until lightly browned on both sides, 2 to 3 minutes on
each side. Transfer turkey to serving platter; set aside and
keep warm.

To same skillet add cranberry mixture and cook, scraping
particles from bottom and sides of pan, until mixture is
heated through, 1 to 2 minutes; sprinkle with salt and
pepper and stir to combine. Pour cranberry mixture over
turkey.

MAKES 2 SERVINGS

Each serving provides: 3 Protein Exchanges; 1 Fat Exchange;
  ½ Fruit Exchange; 65 Optional Calories
Per serving: 249 calories; 27 g protein; 6 g fat; 17 g carbohydrate;
  26 mg calcium; 230 mg sodium; 70 mg cholesterol

Skillet Ground Turkey Hash ⓒ◑

1 teaspoon <u>each</u> vegetable oil and margarine
¼ pound ground turkey
1 cup <u>each</u> diced onions and sliced mushrooms
½ cup <u>each</u> diced green bell pepper and drained canned
   Italian tomatoes, chopped
½ teaspoon <u>each</u> oregano leaves, salt, and pepper
½ small garlic clove, minced
2 eggs
1 ounce Cheddar cheese, shredded

In 8-inch skillet that has an oven-safe or removable handle
heat oil and margarine together until margarine is bubbly
and mixture is hot; add turkey and cook, breaking up large
pieces of turkey with back of a wooden spoon, until turkey
is crumbly and no longer pink, 3 to 4 minutes. Add onions,
mushrooms, bell pepper, tomatoes, seasonings, and garlic
and cook, stirring occasionally, until vegetables are soft,
about 5 minutes. Remove skillet from heat.

   Preheat oven to 400°F. Using back of large spoon, make
2 indentations in turkey mixture. Break 1 egg into small cup,
being careful not to break yolk; carefully slide egg into one
of the indentations. Repeat with remaining egg; sprinkle
evenly with cheese and bake until cheese is melted and
eggs are set, about 5 minutes.

MAKES 2 SERVINGS

Each serving provides: 3 Protein Exchanges; 3 Vegetable Exchanges;
   1 Fat Exchange
Per serving: 323 calories; 22 g protein; 21 g fat; 13 g carbohydrate;
   201 mg calcium; 881 mg sodium; 327 mg cholesterol

Variation: Turkey Hash From Leftover Turkey (Week 1) —
Substitute 3 ounces finely diced cooked turkey for the
ground turkey. Cook vegetables in oil-margarine mixture
until soft; add diced turkey and cook, stirring occasionally,
until heated through. Proceed as directed.

Per serving: 302 calories; 25 g protein; 17 g fat; 13 g carbohydrate;
   193 mg calcium; 859 mg sodium; 322 mg cholesterol

BREAKFAST

½ cup Canned Fruit Cocktail
⅓ cup Cottage Cheese
½ cup Skim Milk
Coffee or Tea

LUNCH

Salmon Sandwich (2 ounces salmon
    with 4 lettuce leaves, ¼ cup
    shredded carrot, 3 tomato slices,
    and 1 tablespoon reduced-calorie
    mayonnaise on 2 slices reduced-
    calorie wheat bread)
6 *each* Celery and Zucchini Sticks
½ cup Skim Milk
Coffee, Tea, or Mineral Water

DINNER

Beefy Spinach Soup (1½ cups beef
    bouillon with ¼ cup chopped
    spinach)
1 serving **Sloppy Joes**
2 cups Tossed Salad with
    1½ teaspoons Italian Dressing
    mixed with 2 teaspoons Red Wine
    Vinegar
½ cup Orange Sections
Diet Soda

SNACKS

¼ small Cantaloupe; 1 cup Skim Milk

Total Optional Calories: 30

Sloppy Joes ◐◑

1 teaspoon margarine
¼ cup <u>each</u> diced onion and red <u>or</u> green bell pepper
½ garlic clove, minced
¼ pound cooked ground beef, crumbled
**¼ cup canned Italian tomatoes (with liquid), pureed
    and strained (discard seeds)**
1 tablespoon ketchup
1½ teaspoons Worcestershire sauce
½ teaspoon chili powder
⅛ teaspoon powdered mustard
2 pita breads (1 ounce each)

In 8-inch nonstick skillet heat margarine over medium-
high heat until bubbly and hot; add onion, bell pepper,
and garlic and sauté until tender, 2 to 3 minutes. Add
ground beef, tomatoes, ketchup, Worcestershire sauce,
chili powder, and mustard to skillet, mixing well. Reduce
heat to low and cook, stirring frequently, until mixture
thickens and is heated through, 8 to 10 minutes.

To serve, using a sharp knife, cut ¼ of the way around
edge of each pita; open to form pocket. Fill each pita with
half of beef mixture.

MAKES 2 SERVINGS

Each serving provides: 2 Protein Exchanges; 1 Bread Exchange;
    ¾ Vegetable Exchange; ½ Fat Exchange; 10 Optional Calories
Per serving: 291 calories; 18 g protein; 13 g fat; 25 g carbohydrate;
    31 mg calcium; 434 mg sodium; 49 mg cholesterol

Variation: Veal Sloppy Joes (Week 1) — Substitute 5 ounces
raw ground veal for the ground beef. Add to skillet with
onion, bell pepper, and garlic and, using back of a wooden
spoon to crumble meat, sauté until veal is cooked
throughout, 4 to 5 minutes. Proceed as directed.

Per serving: 259 calories; 18 g protein; 10 g fat; 25 g carbohydrate;
    32 mg calcium; 438 mg sodium; 50 mg cholesterol

BREAKFAST

BREAKFAST

Apple-Yogurt Cereal (½ cup plain low-fat yogurt mixed with ¾ ounce cold cereal and 1 small apple, diced)

Café au Lait (½ cup *each* hot coffee and skim milk with cinnamon stick)

LUNCH

Chicken Salad (2 ounces diced chicken with ¼ cup *each* sliced celery and mushrooms, 8 tomato wedges, ¼ cup diced scallions, and 1 tablespoon Italian dressing)

2 slices Cocktail Rye Bread

Coffee, Tea, or Mineral Water

DINNER

¾ cup Chicken Bouillon

1 serving **Pork Chops with Apricot Glaze**

½ cup Cooked Brown Rice sprinkled with 1 teaspoon Imitation Bacon Bits

½ cup *each* Cooked Green Bell Pepper Strips and Sliced Carrot

1½ cups Mixed Green Salad with 1 teaspoon Olive Oil mixed with 2 teaspoons Tarragon Vinegar plus Seasonings

½ cup Grapefruit Sections

Coffee or Tea

SNACKS

½ medium Banana; ½ cup Skim Milk

Total Optional Calories: 60

Pork Chops with Apricot Glaze ◑

2 tablespoons reduced-calorie apricot spread (16 calories per 2 teaspoons)
1½ teaspoons dry Madeira wine
1 teaspoon <u>each</u> Dijon-style mustard and honey
⅛ teaspoon minced pared ginger root
2 pork loin chops (5 ounces each)
Dash <u>each</u> salt, pepper, and garlic powder

In small saucepan combine apricot spread, wine, mustard, honey, and ginger and cook over medium heat, stirring frequently, until mixture is smooth and thickened, 3 to 4 minutes. Remove from heat; cover and keep warm.

Season pork chops with salt, pepper, and garlic powder and arrange on rack in broiling pan; broil for 6 minutes. Turn chops over and, using a pastry brush, brush each with 1 teaspoon apricot mixture; broil until chops are thoroughly cooked, about 6 minutes longer. Transfer chops to serving platter and serve with remaining apricot mixture.

MAKES 2 SERVINGS, 1 PORK CHOP EACH

Each serving provides: 3 Protein Exchanges; 40 Optional Calories
Per serving: 238 calories; 27 g protein; 9 g fat; 10 g carbohydrate; 6 mg calcium; 207 mg sodium; 83 mg cholesterol

Variation: Pork Chops with Oriental Glaze (Week 5) — Add 1 teaspoon hoisin sauce along with the wine, mustard, honey, and ginger to apricot spread; proceed as directed. Increase Optional Calories to 45.

Per serving: 241 calories; 27 g protein; 9 g fat; 10 g carbohydrate; 6 mg calcium; 292 mg sodium; 83 mg cholesterol

BREAKFAST

BREAKFAST

½ cup Orange Sections
1 ounce Muenster Cheese
1 slice Pumpernickel Bread with
    1 teaspoon Reduced-Calorie
    Margarine
1 cup Skim Milk
Coffee or Tea

LUNCH

Turkey Sandwich (2 ounces sliced
    turkey with 3 tomato slices,
    4 lettuce leaves, and 2 teaspoons
    mustard on 2 slices reduced-calorie
    wheat bread)
6 Celery Sticks
Coffee, Tea, or Mineral Water

DINNER

3 ounces Baked Bluefish Fillet
1 serving **Creamed Mushrooms**
1 cup *each* Cooked Broccoli Florets
    and Sliced Carrots
1½ cups Mixed Green Salad with
    1 tablespoon Buttermilk Dressing
1 small Apple, baked
Tea with Lemon

SNACKS

1 medium Peach; ¾ cup Skim Milk

Total Optional Calories: 0

Creamed Mushrooms ⊂ ◑

Sautéing with mayonnaise adds a subtle richness to this delicious side dish.

2 teaspoons reduced-calorie mayonnaise
½ cup chopped scallions (green onions)
2 cups sliced mushrooms
¼ teaspoon <u>each</u> salt and marjoram leaves
⅛ teaspoon paprika
Dash pepper
¼ cup plain low-fat yogurt
1 tablespoon chopped fresh parsley

In 8- or 9-inch skillet heat mayonnaise until bubbly and hot; add scallions and sauté until softened, about 2 minutes. Add mushrooms to skillet and sauté for 5 minutes; cover and cook for 5 minutes longer. Sprinkle mixture with salt, marjoram, paprika, and pepper; stir in yogurt and heat (<u>do not boil</u>). Serve sprinkled with parsley.

MAKES 2 SERVINGS

Each serving provides: 2½ Vegetable Exchanges; ½ Fat Exchange;
    ¼ Milk Exchange
Per serving: 56 calories; 3 g protein; 2 g fat; 7 g carbohydrate;
    76 mg calcium; 332 mg sodium; 3 mg cholesterol

Sweet Potato Chips ©

For paper-thin potato slices in a flash,
use a food processor.

2 teaspoons vegetable oil
6 ounces thinly sliced sweet potato (⅛-inch-thick slices)
1 teaspoon firmly packed brown sugar
½ teaspoon salt
Dash to ⅛ teaspoon ground cinnamon

Preheat oven to 400°F. In small mixing bowl drizzle oil over potato slices and, using 2 forks, toss to coat. On nonstick baking sheet arrange slices in a single layer. In cup or small bowl combine remaining ingredients and sprinkle evenly over potatoes; bake for 10 minutes. Reduce oven temperature to 350°F.; turn potato slices over and continue baking until crisp, 15 to 20 minutes (<u>check for doneness frequently to prevent burning</u>). Transfer potato chips to small serving bowl; serve immediately or let cool to room temperature.

MAKES 2 SERVINGS

Each serving provides: 1 Bread Exchange; 1 Fat Exchange; 10 Optional
   Calories
Per serving: 138 calories; 1 g protein; 5 g fat; 23 g carbohydrate;
   25 mg calcium; 559 mg sodium; 0 mg cholesterol

Vegetable Stuffing ©

1 tablespoon plus 1 teaspoon reduced-calorie margarine (tub)
1 cup diced onions
½ pound apples, cored, pared, and diced
½ cup <u>each</u> diced carrot, celery, green bell pepper, and mushrooms
1 small garlic clove, minced
1 cup canned Italian tomatoes (with liquid); drain and chop tomatoes, reserving liquid
1 egg, beaten
4 slices stale white bread, cut into cubes
1 packet instant chicken broth and seasoning mix
¼ teaspoon poultry seasoning

Preheat oven to 375°F. Spray 8 x 8 x 2-inch baking pan with nonstick cooking spray; set aside.

In 10-inch nonstick skillet heat margarine until bubbly and hot; add onions, apples, carrot, celery, bell pepper, mushrooms, and garlic and sauté, stirring occasionally, until tender, 3 to 4 minutes. In medium bowl combine tomatoes, reserved liquid, and egg; stir in sautéed vegetable mixture, bread cubes, broth mix, and poultry seasoning. Transfer mixture to sprayed pan and bake until heated through, 15 to 20 minutes. For a crisper top, turn oven control to broil and broil for 1 to 2 minutes.

MAKES 4 SERVINGS

Each serving provides: 1 Bread Exchange; 2 Vegetable Exchanges;
   ½ Fat Exchange; ½ Fruit Exchange; 20 Optional Calories
Per serving: 173 calories; 6 g protein; 5 g fat; 29 g carbohydrate;
   68 mg calcium; 545 mg sodium; 69 mg cholesterol

BREAKFAST

1 cup sliced Papaya
1 Soft-Cooked Egg
½ English Muffin, toasted, with
    2 teaspoons Blueberry Jam
1 cup Skim Milk

LUNCH

Italian Cheese Salad (2 ounces sliced
    mozzarella cheese with 2 pitted
    black olives, sliced, ½ cup
    artichoke hearts, 4 tomato slices,
    and 1½ teaspoons olive oil mixed
    with 2 teaspoons red wine vinegar
    plus basil leaves)
6 Sesame Melba Rounds
Coffee, Tea, or Mineral Water

DINNER

⅓ cup Apple Cider
4 ounces Roast Turkey
1 serving Fruit-Walnut Stuffing
Mashed Cinnamon Turnips (1 cup
    cooked turnips mashed with
    2 teaspoons reduced-calorie
    margarine and sprinkled with
    cinnamon)
2 cups Tossed Salad with
    1 tablespoon Reduced-Calorie
    Buttermilk Dressing
½ cup Canned Fruit Cocktail
Coffee or Tea

SNACKS

1 serving Reduced-Calorie Vanilla
    Dairy Drink

Total Optional Calories: 165

Fruit-Walnut Stuffing

This filling and delicious stuffing will grace your Thanksgiving meal.

2 tablespoons plus 2 teaspoons reduced-calorie margarine (tub)
1 cup each diced onions, celery, and green bell peppers
1 small garlic clove, mashed
½ pound apples (Golden Delicious, McIntosh, or Granny Smith), cored and diced
¼ cup raisins, soaked in hot water until plumped, then drained
2 ounces chopped walnuts
1 teaspoon salt
½ teaspoon thyme leaves or poultry seasoning
¼ teaspoon each ground sage and pepper
8 slices stale white bread, cut into cubes
2 packets instant chicken broth and seasoning mix, dissolved in 2 cups hot water
1 egg, lightly beaten

Preheat oven to 350°F. Spray 2-quart casserole with nonstick cooking spray; set aside.

In 10-inch nonstick skillet heat margarine until bubbly and hot; add onions, celery, bell peppers, and garlic and sauté until onions are translucent. Add apples, raisins, walnuts, and seasonings to skillet; stir to combine. Reduce heat to low, cover, and let simmer until apples are soft, about 5 minutes. Transfer fruit mixture to large mixing bowl; add bread cubes and toss to combine. In medium bowl combine dissolved broth mix and egg; add to bread mixture and stir to combine. Transfer stuffing to sprayed casserole and bake until lightly browned, 20 to 25 minutes.

MAKES 8 SERVINGS, ABOUT 1 CUP EACH

Each serving provides: 1 Bread Exchange; ¾ Vegetable Exchange;
    ½ Fat Exchange; ½ Fruit Exchange; 60 Optional Calories
Per serving: 181 calories; 5 g protein; 8 g fat; 24 g carbohydrate;
    50 mg calcium; 708 mg sodium; 35 mg cholesterol

TIP: For a crisper top, after stuffing is baked turn oven control to broil; broil stuffing for 1 to 2 minutes. Be sure to use a flameproof casserole.

BREAKFAST

2 Canned Pineapple Slices
1/3 cup Cottage Cheese
Café au Lait (1/2 cup *each* hot coffee
    and skim milk sprinkled with
    cinnamon)

LUNCH

Tuna Salad Sandwich (2 ounces tuna
    with 1/4 cup *each* chopped celery
    and onion, 6 cucumber slices,
    4 lettuce leaves, and 2 teaspoons
    reduced-calorie mayonnaise on
    2 slices reduced-calorie rye bread)
6 Zucchini Sticks
Coffee, Tea, or Mineral Water

DINNER

3 ounces Roast Turkey
1 cup Cooked French-Style Green
    Beans with 1/4 cup Cooked Button
    Mushrooms
1 serving **Gruyère-Spinach Salad**
1-ounce slice French Bread with
    1 teaspoon Margarine
1/2 medium Grapefruit drizzled with
    1/2 teaspoon Honey
1/2 cup Skim Milk
Coffee or Tea

SNACKS

Peach Yogurt (1/2 cup plain low-fat
    yogurt mixed with 1/2 cup canned
    peach slices, diced)

Total Optional Calories: 65

Gruyère-Spinach Salad ⒸⓂ

1/4 cup buttermilk
2 teaspoons <u>each</u> lemon juice and olive oil
1/4 teaspoon granulated sugar
1/8 teaspoon salt
Dash white pepper
1 teaspoon chopped chives
3 cups spinach leaves
1/2 cup sliced red onion
1 ounce Gruyère cheese, shredded

In blender container combine buttermilk, lemon juice, oil, sugar, salt, and pepper and process until combined; stir in chives. Use immediately or refrigerate, covered, until ready to use (can be prepared up to a day in advance).

In small serving bowl combine spinach, onion, and cheese; pour buttermilk mixture over salad and serve immediately.

MAKES 2 SERVINGS

Each serving provides: 1/2 Protein Exchange; 3 1/2 Vegetable Exchanges;
    1 Fat Exchange; 20 Optional Calories
Per serving: 146 calories; 8 g protein; 10 g fat; 8 g carbohydrate;
    274 mg calcium; 286 mg sodium; 17 mg cholesterol

BREAKFAST

2 tablespoons Raisins
1/3 cup Cottage Cheese
1 slice Whole Grain Bread with
　2 teaspoons Reduced-Calorie
　Orange Marmalade
1 cup Skim Milk

LUNCH

Ham and Cheese Sandwich (1 ounce
　each baked ham and Brie cheese
　with 3 tomato slices and 2 tea-
　spoons mustard on 2 slices
　reduced-calorie white bread)
3/4 cup Cauliflower Florets and
　6 Green Bell Pepper Strips
Coffee, Tea, or Mineral Water

DINNER

3 ounces Broiled Cod sprinkled with
　Basil
1/2 cup Cooked Noodles with
　1 teaspoon Margarine
1 cup Cooked Kale with 1 teaspoon
　Margarine and Lemon Juice
1 serving **Orange-Fennel Salad**
1 medium Kiwi Fruit
White Wine Spritzer (1/2 cup *each* dry
　white wine and club soda)
Coffee or Tea

SNACKS

1 serving Reduced-Calorie Hot
　Cocoa; 1/2 cup Fruit Salad

Total Optional Calories: 165

Orange-Fennel Salad ◑

2 small navel oranges (about 6 ounces each)
1 small garlic clove, lightly crushed
2 cups julienne-cut fennel (thin strips)
1/2 cup thinly sliced red onion
8 red-leaf lettuce leaves
2 teaspoons <u>each</u> lemon juice and water
1/4 teaspoon <u>each</u> granulated sugar and Dijon-style
**　mustard**
Dash <u>each</u> salt and pepper
1 tablespoon plus 1 teaspoon olive oil, divided
1 ounce pignolias (pine nuts)
2 tablespoons dry white table wine
Garnish: dill sprigs

Over small bowl to catch juice, remove skin and membranes from oranges; cut each orange crosswise into slices and add to bowl with juice.

Using small mixing bowl, rub garlic clove over surface of bowl; discard garlic. Add fennel and onion to bowl and toss to combine.

Line serving platter with lettuce; spoon fennel mixture onto center of platter. Using a slotted spoon, remove orange slices from juice, reserving juice; arrange slices decoratively on lettuce leaves. Set aside.

Add lemon juice, water, sugar, mustard, salt, and pepper to reserved orange juice, stirring to dissolve sugar. Using a wire whisk, gradually beat in 1 tablespoon oil and continue beating until mixture thickens; set aside.

In small nonstick skillet heat remaining teaspoon oil over medium heat; add pignolias and cook, stirring frequently, until lightly browned, 1 to 2 minutes. Add wine and cook, stirring constantly, until liquid evaporates, 1 to 2 minutes; add to orange juice mixture, stir to combine, and pour over salad. Serve immediately or cover and refrigerate until chilled. Serve garnished with dill sprigs.

MAKES 4 SERVINGS

Each serving provides:　1 3/4 Vegetable Exchanges; 1 Fat Exchange;
　1/2 Fruit Exchange; 50 Optional Calories
Per serving:　134 calories; 3 g protein; 8 g fat; 13 g carbohydrate;
　73 mg calcium; 106 mg sodium; 0 mg cholesterol

Creamy Parsley Dip ◖◗

This fresh parsley dip can be prepared a day or two
in advance. Serve with assorted fresh vegetables for
dipping or use as a sandwich spread.

1 cup fresh parsley leaves
¼ cup <u>each</u> mayonnaise, cream cheese, and chopped
    onion <u>or</u> scallions (green onions)
1 tablespoon lemon juice
1 small garlic clove, crushed
½ teaspoon salt
Dash white pepper

In blender container combine all ingredients and process
until smooth, scraping down sides of container as
necessary. Transfer to small serving bowl; serve
immediately or cover with plastic wrap and refrigerate
until ready to serve.

YIELDS 1 CUP

Each 2-tablespoon serving provides: 1½ Fat Exchanges; 25 Optional
    Calories
Per serving: 79 calories; 0.8 g protein; 8 g fat; 1 g carbohydrate;
    19 mg calcium; 200 mg sodium; 12 mg cholesterol

BREAKFAST

BREAKFAST

1 small Pear, cut into wedges
1 serving **Whole Wheat-Banana Muffins**
1 cup Skim Milk

LUNCH

Turkey on a Bagel (2 ounces sliced
    turkey with 4 lettuce leaves,
    4 green bell pepper rings, and
    2 teaspoons reduced-calorie
    mayonnaise on 1 small bagel)
6 Cherry Tomatoes
Coffee, Tea, or Mineral Water

DINNER

4 ounces Broiled Scallops with
    Lemon Wedge
½ cup Cooked Noodles
Vegetable Stir-Fry (½ cup *each*
    Chinese pea pods, sliced
    mushrooms, and red bell pepper
    strips stir-fried in 1 teaspoon
    vegetable oil)
1½ cups Mixed Green Salad with Red
    Wine Vinegar and Herbs
4 fluid ounces Dry White Wine

SNACKS

1 small Orange; Cucumber Snack
    (½ cup plain low-fat yogurt mixed
    with ½ cup sliced cucumber plus
    dillweed)

Total Optional Calories: 140

Whole Wheat-Banana Muffins

A perfect prepare-ahead breakfast. Wrap individually in plastic freezer wrap and freeze. Then just thaw overnight at room temperature or heat in microwave oven and enjoy warm.

¾ cup plus 2 tablespoons all-purpose flour
¼ cup whole wheat flour
1½ ounces ready-to-eat bran flakes cereal
1 teaspoon double-acting baking powder
¼ teaspoon baking soda
⅛ teaspoon ground allspice
1½ very ripe medium bananas (9 ounces), peeled*
½ cup buttermilk
1 egg
2 tablespoons firmly packed brown sugar
2 tablespoons plus 2 teaspoons vegetable oil
1 teaspoon vanilla extract
4 pitted dates, chopped

Preheat oven to 375°F. In medium mixing bowl combine flours, cereal, baking powder, baking soda, and allspice; set aside.

In work bowl of food processor combine bananas, buttermilk, egg, sugar, oil, and vanilla and process until smooth; add to dry ingredients along with dates and stir until combined (do not overmix; mixture will be lumpy).

Spray eight 2½-inch diameter muffin-pan cups with nonstick cooking spray; spoon ⅛ of batter (about ¼ cup) into each sprayed cup (each will be about ⅔ full) and partially fill remaining cups with water (this will prevent pan from warping and/or burning). Bake in middle of center oven rack for 20 minutes (until muffins are lightly browned and a toothpick, inserted in center, comes out clean). Remove pan from oven and carefully drain off water (remember, it will be boiling hot); remove muffins to wire rack and let cool.

MAKES 8 SERVINGS, 1 MUFFIN EACH

Each serving provides: 1 Bread Exchange; 1 Fat Exchange; ½ Fruit
    Exchange; 40 Optional Calories
Per serving: 185 calories; 4 g protein; 6 g fat; 30 g carbohydrate;
    60 mg calcium; 155 mg sodium; 35 mg cholesterol

*Very ripe bananas are perfect to use for baking. To have them on hand
    when you need them, peel and sprinkle with lemon juice, pack in
    resealable plastic freezer bags, and freeze for up to 1 month.

Anniversary Apples with Spiced "Ice Cream" Ⓒ

**2 teaspoons reduced-calorie pancake syrup (60 calories
    per fluid ounce)**
½ teaspoon ground cinnamon, divided
**2 small Red _or_ Golden Delicious apples (about
    ¼ pound each)**
½ cup vanilla ice milk
**⅛ teaspoon _each_ ground ginger, ground mace, ground
    allspice, and ground nutmeg**

Preheat oven to 375°F. In small bowl combine syrup and ¼
teaspoon cinnamon; set aside. Core apples, leaving bottoms
intact; set apples upright in 8 x 8 x 2-inch baking pan. Spoon
half of syrup mixture (about 1 teaspoon) into each apple.
Pour water into baking pan to a depth of about 1 inch and
bake until apples are tender, 20 to 30 minutes. Using slotted
spoon, transfer apples to serving plate; let cool for 10
minutes.

Spoon ice milk into a small mixing bowl and let stand a
few minutes to soften; add remaining ¼ teaspoon cinnamon
and the ginger, mace, allspice, and nutmeg and mix
thoroughly. Spoon half of the spiced "ice cream" onto each
apple and serve immediately.

MAKES 2 SERVINGS, 1 BAKED APPLE EACH

Each serving provides: 1 Fruit Exchange; 70 Optional Calories
Per serving: 121 calories; 2 g protein; 2 g fat; 26 g carbohydrate;
    60 mg calcium; 27 mg sodium; 5 mg cholesterol

BREAKFAST

½ cup Grapefruit Sections
½ cup Cooked Cereal with 1 teaspoon
   Margarine
½ cup Skim Milk
Coffee or Tea

LUNCH

Tuna-Vegetable Salad (2 ounces tuna
   with 1 cup torn lettuce, 6 cherry
   tomatoes, ½ cup sliced zucchini,
   2 red onion slices, and 1 tablespoon
   reduced-calorie buttermilk dressing)
6 *each* Carrot and Celery Sticks
6 Melba Rounds
Coffee, Tea, or Mineral Water

DINNER

4 ounces Broiled Chicken sprinkled
   with Oregano Leaves
1 cup *each* Cooked Cauliflower
   Florets and Diced Red Bell
   Peppers
Cucumber-Mushroom Salad (½ cup
   each sliced cucumber and
   mushrooms with 1 tablespoon
   Russian dressing on 8 Bibb lettuce
   leaves)
1 serving **Broiled Banana-Chocolate
   Pudding**
Orange-Flavored Club Soda

SNACKS

Onion Dip (¼ cup plain low-fat
   yogurt mixed with ½ teaspoon
   instant onion broth and seasoning
   mix) with 6 Assorted Vegetable
   Sticks; 1 small Apple

Total Optional Calories: 45

Broiled Banana-Chocolate Pudding Ⓒ◐

Serve warm or chilled.

2 cups skim milk
**1 envelope (four ½-cup servings) reduced-calorie instant
   chocolate pudding mix**
**1 medium banana (about 6 ounces), peeled and thinly
   sliced**
2 teaspoons firmly packed light _or_ dark brown sugar

In medium mixing bowl combine milk and pudding mix
and, using electric mixer at low speed, beat until well
blended, 1 to 2 minutes. Into each of 4 flameproof
6-ounce custard cups pour ¼ of the pudding; cover and
refrigerate for at least 10 minutes (can be prepared up to
a day in advance).

Arrange ¼ of the banana slices over each portion of
pudding; sprinkle each with ½ teaspoon sugar. Place
custard cups on baking sheet; broil until sugar melts and
is bubbly, about 1 minute (be careful not to burn).

MAKES 4 SERVINGS

Each serving provides: ½ Fruit Exchange; 1 Milk Exchange; 10 Optional
   Calories
Per serving: 122 calories; 5 g protein; 0.7 g fat; 26 g carbohydrate;
   157 mg calcium; 65 mg sodium; 2 mg cholesterol

Pound Cake Pudding

2 ounces pound cake, cut into ½-inch cubes
2 tablespoons golden raisins
1 cup low-fat milk (1% milk fat)
½ cup orange juice (no sugar added)
2 eggs
2 teaspoons granulated sugar
½ teaspoon grated orange peel
1 teaspoon confectioners' sugar

Preheat oven to 350°F. Spray two 10-ounce custard cups
with nonstick cooking spray; fill each with 1 ounce cake
cubes and 1 tablespoon raisins. Set aside.

In medium mixing bowl, using wire whisk, beat together
milk, orange juice, eggs, granulated sugar, and orange peel;
pour half of mixture into each custard cup. Place cups in
8 x 8 x 2-inch baking pan and fill pan with water to a depth
of about 1 inch; bake for 40 to 45 minutes (until a knife,
inserted in center, comes out clean). Remove baking pan
from oven and cups from water bath; set cups on wire rack
and let cool.

When ready to serve, using a small tea strainer, sift half
of the confectioners' sugar onto each pudding.

MAKES 2 SERVINGS

Each serving provides: 1 Protein Exchange; 1 Fruit Exchange;
    ½ Milk Exchange; 170 Optional Calories
Per serving: 341 calories; 12 g protein; 15 g fat; 39 g carbohydrate;
    195 mg calcium; 163 mg sodium; 321 mg cholesterol

Festive Coffee Ring

An easy-to-prepare pumpkin cake that will surely impress your guests! Leftovers freeze well; thaw at room temperature.

1 cup canned <u>or</u> cooked and pureed pumpkin
¼ cup firmly packed brown sugar
1 egg
2 graham crackers (2½-inch squares), made into fine crumbs
½ teaspoon pumpkin pie spice
1 loaf frozen bread dough (1 pound), thawed
16 large prunes, pitted and finely chopped
¼ cup confectioners' sugar
1 tablespoon hot water
¼ to ½ teaspoon grated lemon peel

Preheat oven to 375°F. In small bowl combine pumpkin, brown sugar, egg, graham cracker crumbs, and pumpkin pie spice; set aside.

On work surface, using your hands, press and gently stretch dough into a 20 x 8-inch rectangle. Spread dough with pumpkin mixture to about 1 inch from edge; sprinkle evenly with prunes. Starting from one long side, roll dough jelly-roll fashion to enclose filling; place seam-side down on nonstick baking sheet. Shape dough into a ring, pinching ends together to seal; bake in middle of center oven rack until golden brown, about 30 minutes. Remove ring from baking sheet and set on wire rack to cool.

In small bowl combine confectioners' sugar, water, and lemon peel and stir until mixture is smooth and thoroughly combined. Drizzle sugar mixture over cooled coffee ring and let stand until mixture hardens. To serve, cut into 16 equal slices.

MAKES 16 SERVINGS, 1 SLICE EACH

Each serving provides: 1 Bread Exchange; ⅛ Vegetable Exchange;
  ½ Fruit Exchange; 40 Optional Calories
Per serving: 134 calories; 3 g protein; 2 g fat; 27 g carbohydrate;
  24 mg calcium; 149 mg sodium; 19 mg cholesterol

Variation: Pumpkin-Walnut Coffee Ring (Week 8) —
Sprinkle 1 ounce chopped walnuts <u>or</u> pecans along with the prunes over pumpkin mixture; proceed as directed. Increase Optional Calories to 50.

Per serving with walnuts: 145 calories; 3 g protein; 3 g fat;
  27 g carbohydrate; 26 mg calcium; 149 mg sodium; 19 mg cholesterol
With pecans: 146 calories; 3 g protein; 3 g fat; 27 g carbohydrate;
  25 mg calcium; 149 mg sodium; 19 mg cholesterol

December

Greek-Style Spinach Salad

DECEMBER'S BEST BUYS FOR FRUITS AND VEGETABLES

alfalfa sprouts	celery	leeks	potatoes
bananas	Chinese pea pods	mandarin oranges	radishes
bean sprouts	cranberries	mushrooms	scallions (green onions)
beet greens	eggplants	mustard greens	spinach
Belgian endives	escarole	onions	sweet potatoes
broccoli	fennel	oranges	Swiss chard
brussels sprouts	grapefruit	parsnips	tangerines
cabbage	kale	pears	turnips
carrots	kiwi fruit	persimmons	winter squash
cauliflower	kohlrabi	pineapples	yams

BREAKFAST

½ cup Canned Peach Slices
¾ ounce Cold Cereal
1 cup Skim Milk

LUNCH

Swiss Cheese Sandwich (2 ounces sliced Swiss cheese with 3 tomato slices, 2 teaspoons reduced-calorie mayonnaise, and 1 teaspoon mustard on 2 slices reduced-calorie multi-grain bread)
½ cup Broccoli Florets and 6 Celery Sticks
1 small Orange
Coffee, Tea, or Mineral Water

DINNER

1 serving **Curried Cream of Carrot Soup**
3 ounces Broiled Chicken Breast sprinkled with Lemon Juice and Chopped Parsley
1 cup Cooked Cut Green Beans with 1 teaspoon Margarine
1½ cups Tossed Salad with 1 tablespoon Reduced-Calorie French Dressing
½ cup Fruit Salad
Coffee or Tea

SNACKS

Chocolate Milk (¾ cup skim milk mixed with ½ teaspoon chocolate syrup)

Total Optional Calories: 55

Curried Cream of Carrot Soup ⓒ

When processing a hot mixture in the blender always let it cool slightly, then process no more than 2 cups of mixture at a time. Always start at low speed.

2 teaspoons margarine
¼ cup chopped scallions (green onions)
½ small garlic clove, minced
2 teaspoons all-purpose flour
1 cup water
1¼ cups sliced carrots
1 packet instant chicken broth and seasoning mix
½ teaspoon curry powder
½ cup skim milk
⅛ teaspoon salt
Dash white pepper

In 1½-quart saucepan heat margarine until bubbly and hot; add scallions and garlic and sauté until soft, about 2 minutes. Sprinkle with flour and stir quickly to combine; cook, stirring constantly, for 1 minute. Continuing to stir, gradually add water; add carrots, broth mix, and curry powder and bring mixture to a boil. Reduce heat to low, cover, and cook until carrots are very soft, about 20 minutes. Remove from heat and let cool slightly.

Pour soup into blender container and process until smooth. Pour soup back into saucepan; stir in milk, salt, and pepper and heat (do not boil). Pour into 2 soup bowls; serve hot.

MAKES 2 SERVINGS, ABOUT 1 CUP EACH

Each serving provides: 1½ Vegetable Exchanges; 1 Fat Exchange; ¼ Milk Exchange; 15 Optional Calories
Per serving: 113 calories; 4 g protein; 4 g fat; 16 g carbohydrate; 113 mg calcium; 742 mg sodium; 1 mg cholesterol

BREAKFAST
BREAKFAST

½ cup Orange Sections
½ English Muffin, toasted, with
    2 teaspoons Reduced-Calorie
    Strawberry Spread
1 cup Skim Milk

LUNCH

Open-Face Tuna Salad Sandwich
    (2 ounces tuna with 1 tablespoon
    shredded carrot, 2 lettuce leaves,
    and 2 teaspoons mayonnaise on
    1 slice rye bread)
6 Cucumber Spears and ½ cup
    Cauliflower Florets
½ medium Banana
Coffee, Tea, or Mineral Water

DINNER

1 serving **Tomato Florentine-Noodle
    Soup**
4 ounces Broiled Veal Chop
1 cup Cooked Sliced Zucchini
Seasoned Eggplant (3 broiled eggplant
    slices seasoned with salt, pepper,
    and minced garlic)
1 small Apple, cut into wedges,
    sprinkled with Cinnamon
Coffee or Tea

SNACKS

½ cup Reduced-Calorie Butterscotch
    Pudding topped with 1 tablespoon
    Whipped Topping

Total Optional Calories: 65

Tomato Florentine-Noodle Soup ℂ

1 teaspoon <u>each</u> olive <u>or</u> vegetable oil and margarine
½ cup <u>each</u> diced onion and green bell pepper
1 garlic clove, minced
1½ cups water
**1 cup <u>each</u> spinach leaves, chopped, and canned Italian
    tomatoes (with liquid); drain and chop tomatoes,
    reserving liquid**
1 tablespoon chopped fresh basil
1 packet instant chicken broth and seasoning mix
¾ ounce uncooked noodles (medium width)
¼ teaspoon <u>each</u> salt and pepper
2 tablespoons grated Parmesan cheese

In 2-quart saucepan heat oil and margarine together until
margarine is bubbly and mixture is hot; add onion, bell
pepper, and garlic and sauté until onion is golden, 2 to 3
minutes. Add water, spinach, tomatoes, reserved liquid,
basil, and broth mix and bring mixture to a boil. Reduce heat
and let simmer until flavors blend, about 10 minutes; stir in
noodles, salt, and pepper and cook, stirring occasionally,
until noodles are tender, 10 to 15 minutes longer.

    To serve, ladle soup into 2 bowls and sprinkle each
portion with 1 tablespoon cheese.

MAKES 2 SERVINGS

Each serving provides: ½ Bread Exchange; 3 Vegetable Exchanges;
    1 Fat Exchange; 35 Optional Calories
Per serving: 159 calories; 7 g protein; 7 g fat; 20 g carbohydrate;
    161 mg calcium; 1,101 mg sodium; 14 mg cholesterol

TIP: To save time and effort, substitute frozen chopped spinach for the
fresh.

BREAKFAST

BREAKFAST

½ cup Orange Juice
1 Poached Egg
1 slice Whole Wheat Bread, toasted
½ cup Skim Milk
Coffee or Tea

LUNCH

Peanut Butter and Jelly Sandwich
 (1 tablespoon *each* peanut butter
 and grape jelly on 2 slices reduced-
 calorie white bread)
6 *each* Carrot and Celery Sticks
1 large Tangerine
Coffee, Tea, or Mineral Water

DINNER

¾ cup Chicken Bouillon
Stir-Fried Chicken and Vegetables
 (3 ounces julienne-cut chicken
 with ½ cup *each* broccoli florets,
 Chinese pea pods, and sliced red
 bell pepper stir-fried in 2 teaspoons
 vegetable oil and 1 tablespoon
 reduced-sodium soy sauce)
½ cup Cooked Rice
Spinach Salad (1½ cups torn spinach
 with ½ cup sliced mushrooms and
 1½ teaspoons Italian dressing
 mixed with 2 teaspoons red wine
 vinegar)
Sweet Yogurt (¾ cup plain low-fat
 yogurt mixed with 1 teaspoon *each*
 brown sugar and vanilla extract)
Coffee or Tea

SNACKS

1 serving **Herbed Cheese Dip** with
 3 *each* Green Bell Pepper Strips
 and Cucumber Slices; 2 Canned
 Peach Halves

Total Optional Calories: 170

Herbed Cheese Dip ⓒ ◑

Serve with assorted fresh vegetables or melba rounds.

½ cup part-skim ricotta cheese
⅓ cup plus 2 teaspoons whipped cream cheese
2 tablespoons <u>each</u> chopped scallion (green onion) and fresh parsley
1 tablespoon lemon juice
1½ teaspoons chopped fresh dill
½ teaspoon salt
½ garlic clove, minced
¼ teaspoon <u>each</u> powdered mustard and Worcestershire sauce

In work bowl of food processor or blender container combine ricotta cheese and cream cheese and process until smooth, scraping down sides of container as necessary. Transfer mixture to small mixing bowl; add remaining ingredients and mix well until thoroughly combined. Cover with plastic wrap and refrigerate until chilled and flavors blend, at least 30 minutes.

MAKES 4 SERVINGS

Each serving provides: ½ Protein Exchange; 50 Optional Calories
Per serving: 94 calories; 5 g protein; 7 g fat; 3 g carbohydrate;
  102 mg calcium; 370 mg sodium; 24 mg cholesterol

Variation: Herb 'n' Olive Cheese Dip (Week 5) — Add 4 large pitted black olives, finely chopped, along with remaining ingredients. Increase Optional Calories to 55.

Per serving: 102 calories; 5 g protein; 8 g fat; 3 g carbohydrate;
  107 mg calcium; 401 mg sodium; 24 mg cholesterol

BREAKFAST

½ medium Grapefruit
½ cup Cooked Oatmeal drizzled with
  ½ teaspoon Honey
1 cup Skim Milk

LUNCH

Chicken Salad-Vegetable Combo
  (2 ounces julienne-cut chicken with
  4 torn lettuce leaves, 1 tablespoon
  sliced scallion, 6 cucumber slices,
  6 tomato wedges, and 1 tablespoon
  blue cheese dressing)
1 slice Reduced-Calorie Wheat
  Bread
½ medium Banana
Coffee, Tea, or Mineral Water

DINNER

1 serving **Cheese and Egg Triangle Bites**
3 ounces Baked Fillet of Sole with
  Lemon Wedge
Minted Carrots (1 cup cooked baby
  carrots with 1 teaspoon reduced-
  calorie margarine and mint leaves)
1½ cups Mixed Green Salad with
  1 tablespoon Reduced-Calorie
  French Dressing
½ cup Low-Calorie Strawberry-
  Flavored Gelatin
Coffee or Tea

SNACKS

Pineapple Yogurt (½ cup plain low-fat
  yogurt mixed with ½ cup canned
  crushed pineapple)

Total Optional Calories: 50

Cheese and Egg Triangle Bites ◖◑

1 ounce Cheddar or Monterey Jack cheese, shredded
2 teaspoons reduced-calorie margarine (tub)
½ teaspoon prepared spicy brown mustard
¼ teaspoon Worcestershire sauce
**1 whole wheat pita bread (1 ounce), cut in half
  horizontally**
1 egg, hard-cooked and sliced
2 tablespoons diagonally sliced scallion (green onion)

In small bowl combine cheese, margarine, mustard,
and Worcestershire sauce, mixing until blended.

On nonstick baking sheet set pita halves cut-side up;
arrange half of the egg slices on each pita half and top
each portion of egg with half of the cheese mixture. Broil
2 inches from heat source until cheese is melted and
bubbly, 2 to 3 minutes. Sprinkle each portion with 1
tablespoon scallion, then cut each into quarters; serve
immediately.

MAKES 2 SERVINGS, 4 TRIANGLES EACH

Each serving provides: 1 Protein Exchange; ½ Bread Exchange;
  ⅛ Vegetable Exchange; ½ Fat Exchange
Per serving with Cheddar cheese: 158 calories; 8 g protein; 10 g fat;
  10 g carbohydrate; 124 mg calcium; 273 mg sodium;
  152 mg cholesterol
With Monterey Jack cheese: 154 calories; 8 g protein; 9 g fat;
  10 g carbohydrate; 127 mg calcium; 261 mg sodium;
  149 mg cholesterol

TIP: To hard-cook an egg, place in saucepan with cold water to cover
by about 1 inch. Bring water to a boil. Remove from heat, cover, and let
stand for 17 minutes. Drain and plunge into cold water for several
seconds to cool.

BREAKFAST

½ cup Orange Juice
1 serving **Buttermilk Pancakes**
Spiced Café au Lait (1 cup hot coffee
with ¼ cup skim milk and dash
allspice)

LUNCH

Vegetable-Beef Soup (1 cup canned
beef broth with 1 ounce diced roast
beef and ¼ cup *each* sliced onion,
sliced celery, and diced carrot)
6 Melba Rounds
Red Cabbage Salad (½ cup *each*
shredded red cabbage and romaine
lettuce with 1 teaspoon reduced-
calorie mayonnaise)
1 small Apple, baked
Coffee, Tea, or Mineral Water

DINNER

3 ounces Roast Turkey
½ cup *each* Cooked Mushrooms and
Green Beans
1½ cups Tossed Salad with
1 tablespoon Russian Dressing
½ cup Reduced-Calorie Chocolate
Pudding
Coffee or Tea

SNACKS

½ cup Fruit Salad; ½ cup Skim Milk

Total Optional Calories: 100

Buttermilk Pancakes ⊕ ◑

A spark of orange wakes up this weekend breakfast
specialty.

¹/₃ cup plus 2 teaspoons buttermilk
2 eggs
¹/₃ cup plus 2 teaspoons all-purpose flour
1 tablespoon granulated sugar
½ teaspoon baking soda
¼ teaspoon grated orange peel
2 teaspoons reduced-calorie margarine (tub)
1 tablespoon maple syrup

In blender container combine buttermilk and eggs and
process until well combined, about 1 minute; add flour, sugar,
baking soda, and orange peel and process until batter is
smooth, scraping down sides of container as necessary.

Spray 8-inch skillet or a griddle with nonstick cooking
spray and heat. Using half of batter for 3 pancakes (scant 3
tablespoons per pancake), drop batter into hot skillet (or
onto griddle), making 3 pancakes, each 3 to 4 inches in
diameter. Cook until bubbles appear on surface and bottom
is browned; using pancake turner, turn pancakes over and
cook until the other side is browned. Remove pancakes to
plate and keep warm. Repeat procedure, spraying pan and
making 3 more pancakes. Serve each portion of pancakes
topped with 1 teaspoon margarine and 1½ teaspoons syrup.

MAKES 2 SERVINGS, 3 PANCAKES EACH

Each serving provides: 1 Protein Exchange; 1 Bread Exchange;
½ Fat Exchange; ¼ Milk Exchange; 60 Optional Calories
Per serving: 249 calories; 10 g protein; 8 g fat; 33 g carbohydrate;
96 mg calcium; 363 mg sodium; 276 mg cholesterol

Baked Clams Iberian

1 tablespoon plus 1 teaspoon olive <u>or</u> vegetable oil
¼ cup <u>each</u> diced red bell pepper and finely chopped onion
3 garlic cloves, minced
2 ounces cooked smoked ham, chopped
½ cup dry sherry
¼ cup chopped fresh parsley
2 tablespoons lemon juice
¼ teaspoon thyme leaves
⅛ teaspoon ground red pepper
3 dozen littleneck clams;* shuck, drain, and finely chop clams, reserving liquid
¾ cup plain dried bread crumbs

Preheat oven to 400°F. In 12-inch nonstick skillet heat oil over medium-high heat; add bell pepper, onion, and garlic and sauté until vegetables are softened, 1 to 2 minutes. Add ham, sherry, parsley, lemon juice, and seasonings and cook, stirring occasionally, until flavors blend, 1 to 2 minutes. Transfer to large mixing bowl; add clams and mix well to combine.

Line fine sieve with cheesecloth and set over mixing bowl containing clam mixture; pour reserved clam liquid through sieve so that liquid flows into bowl. Add bread crumbs and mix well.

Into each of 4 large scallop shells spoon ¼ of clam mixture; transfer shells to baking sheet and bake until mixture is thoroughly heated and lightly browned, 10 to 15 minutes.

MAKES 4 SERVINGS

Each serving provides: 2 Protein Exchanges; 1 Bread Exchange; ¼ Vegetable Exchange; 1 Fat Exchange; 30 Optional Calories
Per serving: 229 calories; 13 g protein; 7 g fat; 20 g carbohydrate; 81 mg calcium; 414 mg sodium; 36 mg cholesterol

*3 dozen littleneck clams will yield about 6 ounces cooked seafood.

TIP: Shucking clams can slow down meal preparation. To help make the most of your time, call the fish store in advance and let them know you'll need shucked clams. They may be able to shuck them for you before you arrive.

BREAKFAST

½ medium Pink Grapefruit
¾ ounce Cold Cereal
½ cup Skim Milk
Coffee or Tea

LUNCH

Chicken Salad (2 ounces diced
    chicken with 2 tablespoons
    chopped celery and 2 teaspoons
    reduced-calorie mayonnaise on
    4 lettuce leaves)
1 small Apple
Coffee, Tea, or Mineral Water

DINNER

1 serving **Shrimp in Spicy Mustard
    Sauce**
½ cup Cooked Rice
¾ cup Cooked Sliced Zucchini with
    ¼ cup Chopped Pimientos
Spinach Salad (1 cup torn spinach
    with 2 red onion slices and
    1½ teaspoons buttermilk dressing
    mixed with 2 tablespoons plain
    low-fat yogurt and ¼ teaspoon
    mustard)
1 small Nectarine
½ cup Skim Milk
Coffee or Tea

SNACKS

Cinnamon Toast (1 slice raisin bread,
    toasted, with 1 teaspoon reduced-
    calorie margarine, sprinkled with
    ½ teaspoon *each* cinnamon and
    sugar); ¾ cup Skim Milk

Total Optional Calories: 60

Shrimp in Spicy Mustard Sauce

9 ounces medium shrimp
¼ cup half-and-half (blend of milk and cream)
1 tablespoon Dijon-style mustard*
⅛ teaspoon _each_ ground cumin and curry powder
1 teaspoon olive _or_ vegetable oil
1 small garlic clove, minced
Garnish: chopped fresh Italian (flat-leaf) parsley

Shell and devein shrimp, leaving last segment and tail in place; set aside.

In 1-cup liquid measure combine half-and-half, mustard, and seasonings; set aside.

In 8-inch skillet heat oil over high heat; add shrimp and garlic and cook, stirring constantly, until shrimp just turn pink, 2 to 3 minutes. Pour half-and-half mixture into skillet and cook, stirring constantly, until mixture comes just to a boil. Reduce heat to low and let simmer until slightly thickened, 1 to 2 minutes. Using a slotted spoon, remove shrimp to serving platter; set aside. Increase heat to medium-high and continue cooking sauce until mixture is reduced by half, about 5 minutes. Pour sauce over shrimp and sprinkle with parsley.

MAKES 2 SERVINGS

Each serving provides: 3 Protein Exchanges; ½ Fat Exchange;
    50 Optional Calories
Per serving: 187 calories; 25 g protein; 8 g fat; 3 g carbohydrate;
    100 mg calcium; 472 mg sodium; 172 mg cholesterol

*Coarse-grain mustard can be substituted for the Dijon-style mustard.

BREAKFAST

½ medium Banana
¼ cup Part-Skim Ricotta Cheese
mixed with ½ teaspoon Caraway
Seed
¾ cup Skim Milk

LUNCH

Open-Face Tuna Salad Sandwich
(2 ounces tuna with 2 tablespoons
chopped celery, 2 lettuce leaves,
and 2 teaspoons reduced-calorie
mayonnaise on 1 slice rye bread)
½ cup Broccoli Florets and 6 Red
Bell Pepper Strips
1 small Orange
Coffee, Tea, or Mineral Water

DINNER

1 serving **Broiled Chicken Breasts with
Red Pepper Sauce**
½ cup Cooked Broad Noodles with
1 teaspoon Reduced-Calorie
Margarine
1 cup Cooked Cut Green Beans
Iceberg-Romaine Salad (1 cup *each*
torn iceberg and romaine lettuce
with 3 cherry tomatoes and
1½ teaspoons Thousand Island
dressing mixed with 2 tablespoons
plain low-fat yogurt and
¼ teaspoon mustard)
½ cup Reduced-Calorie Chocolate
Pudding topped with 1 tablespoon
Whipped Topping
Coffee or Tea

SNACKS

2 cups Plain Popcorn; ½ cup
Applesauce

Total Optional Calories: 60

Broiled Chicken Breasts with Red Pepper Sauce ◑

For an attractive presentation, after cooking pepper set aside a few strips to be used for garnish.

2 chicken breasts (6 ounces each)
2 teaspoons reduced-calorie margarine (tub)
¼ cup diced onion
½ small garlic clove, minced
½ medium red bell pepper, seeded and cut into thin strips
1 tablespoon plus 1½ teaspoons whipped cream cheese
1½ teaspoons sour cream
1 teaspoon dry white table wine
1 tablespoon chopped fresh parsley

On rack in broiling pan broil chicken breasts skin-side up for 5 minutes; turn chicken over and broil until cooked throughout, about 5 minutes longer.

While chicken is broiling, in small saucepan heat margarine until bubbly and hot; add onion and garlic and sauté until onion is translucent, about 2 minutes. Add pepper strips and cook, stirring occasionally, until tender-crisp, about 5 minutes. Transfer pepper mixture to blender container; add cream cheese, sour cream, and wine and process until smooth, scraping down sides of container as necessary. Return sauce to saucepan and cook over low heat until heated through (do not boil).

To serve, remove and discard skin from chicken; transfer chicken to serving platter, top with sauce, and sprinkle with parsley.

MAKES 2 SERVINGS

Each serving provides: 3 Protein Exchanges; ¾ Vegetable Exchange; ½ Fat Exchange; 35 Optional Calories
Per serving: 250 calories; 40 g protein; 7 g fat; 3 g carbohydrate; 37 mg calcium; 181 mg sodium; 107 mg cholesterol

BREAKFAST

½ cup Orange Sections
¾ ounce Cold Cereal
1 cup Skim Milk

LUNCH

Cheddar Cheese Sandwich (2 ounces
    sliced Cheddar cheese with
    2 tomato slices, 3 red onion slices,
    2 lettuce leaves, and 2 teaspoons
    reduced-calorie mayonnaise on
    2 slices reduced-calorie rye bread)
6 *each* Carrot and Celery Sticks
Coffee, Tea, or Mineral Water

DINNER

1 serving **Grapefruit Chicken**
½ cup *each* Cooked Broccoli and
    Cauliflower Florets
1½ cups Tossed Salad with
    1 tablespoon French Dressing
Gelatin 'n' Fruit (½ cup low-calorie
    strawberry-flavored gelatin topped
    with ¼ cup canned crushed
    pineapple)
Coffee or Tea

SNACKS

1 small Apple; 1 serving Reduced-
    Calorie Hot Cocoa

Total Optional Calories: 45

Grapefruit Chicken ☻

Fruit and honey — a winning combination with chicken.

1 medium grapefruit (about ½ pound)
2¼ pounds chicken parts (legs with thighs attached),
    skinned
2 tablespoons honey
1 tablespoon soy sauce*
2 teaspoons cornstarch

Over bowl to catch juice, peel and section grapefruit, setting
grapefruit sections aside and reserving juice. Arrange
chicken parts in 13 x 9 x 2-inch baking pan and set aside.

In small saucepan combine honey, soy sauce, and 1
tablespoon of the reserved juice; heat over high heat,
stirring constantly, just until honey is melted. Brush half of
honey mixture evenly over chicken parts and broil 8 inches
from heat source for 10 minutes; turn chicken over, brush
with remaining honey mixture, and broil until juices run clear
when chicken is pierced with a fork, about 25 minutes.
Transfer chicken to serving platter, reserving pan drippings;
keep chicken warm.

In small saucepan combine remaining grapefruit juice with
cornstarch, stirring to dissolve cornstarch; add grapefruit
sections and pan drippings and cook over medium heat just
until mixture is slightly thickened, about 1 minute. Pour over
chicken and serve immediately.

MAKES 4 SERVINGS

Each serving provides: 3 Protein Exchanges; ½ Fruit Exchange;
    35 Optional Calories
Per serving: 184 calories; 25 g protein; 4 g fat; 13 g carbohydrate;
    21 mg calcium; 420 mg sodium; 79 mg cholesterol

*Reduced-sodium soy sauce may be substituted. Reduce calories to 181,
    calcium to 18 mg, and sodium to 88 mg.

BREAKFAST

1 medium Kiwi Fruit, sliced
½ English Muffin, toasted, with
  2 teaspoons Reduced-Calorie
  Margarine
½ cup Skim Milk
Coffee or Tea

LUNCH

Fish Salad (2 ounces fish with ¼ cup
  alfalfa sprouts, 2 tablespoons *each*
  chopped celery and red onion, and
  1 tablespoon reduced-calorie
  buttermilk dressing on 4 lettuce
  leaves)
2 Pickle Spears
1-ounce Roll
Coffee, Tea, or Mineral Water

DINNER

1 serving **Flank Steak with Whiskey
  Sauce**
½ cup Cooked Barley with ¼ cup
  Cooked Sliced Mushrooms
1 cup Cooked Chopped Kale
  sprinkled with Lemon Juice
Artichoke Salad (3 chilled cooked
  artichoke hearts with 1 tablespoon
  diced pimiento and 1½ teaspoons
  Italian dressing mixed with
  2 teaspoons red wine vinegar on
  2 lettuce leaves)
½ cup Fruit Salad
Coffee or Tea

SNACKS

Banana Shake (1 cup skim milk,
  ½ medium banana, ½ teaspoon
  vanilla extract, and 3 ice cubes
  processed in blender); 2 Zwieback
  with Café au Lait (½ cup *each* hot
  coffee and skim milk)

Total Optional Calories: 100

Flank Steak with Whiskey Sauce

¼ **cup teriyaki sauce**
4 **garlic cloves, minced, divided**
2 **teaspoons** <u>each</u> **red wine vinegar and Worcestershire
  sauce**
⅛ **teaspoon hot sauce**
15 **ounces beef flank steak**
1 **tablespoon plus 1 teaspoon margarine**
¼ **cup minced onion**
⅓ **cup plus 2 teaspoons whiskey**
2 **teaspoons** <u>each</u> **Dijon-style mustard and cornstarch**
1 **cup canned ready-to-serve beef broth**
2 **teaspoons chopped fresh parsley**
⅛ **teaspoon pepper**
Garnish: watercress sprigs

In medium glass or stainless-steel bowl combine teriyaki
sauce, 1½ teaspoons garlic, and the vinegar, Worcestershire
sauce, and hot sauce; add steak and turn several times to
coat. Cover with plastic wrap and refrigerate overnight or
at least 30 minutes.

  In small saucepan heat margarine over medium heat until
bubbly and hot; add onion and remaining garlic and sauté
until onion is softened, 1 to 2 minutes. Carefully add whiskey
to pan, then add mustard and mix well; cook, stirring
occasionally, until mixture is reduced by half and forms a thin
glaze, 2 to 3 minutes. Sprinkle cornstarch over broth and stir
to dissolve; add to whiskey mixture along with parsley
and pepper and stir to combine. Reduce heat to low and let
simmer, stirring occasionally, until mixture thickens, 4 to 5
minutes; keep warm.

  Transfer steak to rack in broiling pan, discarding marinade;
broil, turning once, until steak is rare, about 4 minutes on
each side. Slice steak across the grain, top with sauce, and
garnish with watercress.

MAKES 4 SERVINGS

Each serving provides: 3 Protein Exchanges; ⅛ Vegetable Exchange;
  1 Fat Exchange; 70 Optional Calories
Per serving: 319 calories; 23 g protein; 17 g fat; 5 g carbohydrate;
  16 mg calcium; 783 mg sodium; 60 mg cholesterol

TIP: Be very careful when adding whiskey, or any liquor, to a cooking
mixture; if the pan is too hot, the whiskey may ignite.

BRUNCH

Screwdriver (½ cup orange juice
 mixed with 2 tablespoons vodka)
1 serving **Ham and Cheese Custard**
1-ounce Buttermilk Flaky Biscuit
 with 1 teaspoon *each* Margarine
 and Reduced-Calorie Strawberry
 Spread
2 Canned Pear Halves drizzled with
 ½ teaspoon Chocolate Syrup
½ cup Skim Milk
Coffee or Tea

DINNER

4 ounces Baked Veal Chop
Spaghetti 'n' Sauce (½ cup cooked
 spaghetti with ¼ cup tomato
 sauce, 1 teaspoon grated Parmesan
 cheese, plus Italian seasoning)
1 cup Cooked Spinach Leaves
1½ cups Tossed Salad with
 1 tablespoon Italian Dressing
1-ounce slice Italian Bread
½ cup Low-Calorie Orange-Flavored
 Gelatin topped with 1 tablespoon
 Whipped Topping
Coffee or Tea

SNACKS

1 small Apple; 1 serving Reduced-
 Calorie Hot Cocoa

Total Optional Calories: 125

Ham and Cheese Custard

Makes a delightful brunch for Christmas day. Cover and refrigerate any leftovers, then just reheat to serve.

1 cup diagonally sliced thoroughly washed leeks (white and green portion)
1 medium tomato, thinly sliced
¼ pound <u>each</u> Gruyère <u>or</u> Muenster cheese, shredded, and diced boiled ham
4 eggs
1 cup skim milk
½ cup evaporated skimmed milk
1 tablespoon chopped fresh Italian (flat-leaf) parsley
1 teaspoon Dijon-style mustard
½ teaspoon ground nutmeg

Preheat oven to 350°F. Spray 8 x 8 x 2-inch baking pan with nonstick cooking spray and arrange leeks in bottom of pan. Arrange tomato slices over leeks, then sprinkle with cheese and ham; set aside.

In medium mixing bowl, using a fork or wire whisk, beat eggs; add remaining ingredients, beating until combined. Carefully pour egg mixture over mixture in baking pan; bake for 35 to 40 minutes (until a knife, inserted in center, comes out clean). Transfer pan to wire rack and let stand for 10 minutes before cutting.

MAKES 4 SERVINGS

Each serving provides: 3 Protein Exchanges; 1 Vegetable Exchange;
 ½ Milk Exchange
Per serving with Gruyère cheese: 309 calories; 26 g protein; 17 g fat;
 13 g carbohydrate; 504 mg calcium; 619 mg sodium;
 323 mg cholesterol
With Muenster cheese: 296 calories; 24 g protein; 16 g fat;
 13 g carbohydrate; 421 mg calcium; 702 mg sodium;
 319 mg cholesterol

BREAKFAST

Cheese and Peach Breakfast (1/3 cup
cottage cheese mixed with 1/2 cup
canned peach slices)
1/2 small Bagel, toasted, with
1 teaspoon Raspberry Preserves
1/2 cup Skim Milk
Coffee or Tea

LUNCH

Open-Face Turkey Sandwich
(2 ounces sliced turkey with
2 tomato slices, 2 lettuce leaves,
and 1 teaspoon mayonnaise on
1 slice rye bread)
6 *each* Carrot and Celery Sticks
1 small Orange
Coffee, Tea, or Mineral Water

DINNER

3 ounces Broiled Fillet of Sole
1 serving **Sour Cream Latkes
(Pancakes)** topped with 1/2 cup
Applesauce
1/2 cup Cooked Green Beans
1 1/2 cups Mixed Green Salad with
1 tablespoon French Dressing
1/2 cup Skim Milk
Coffee or Tea

SNACKS

Spicy Honey Yogurt (1/2 cup plain
low-fat yogurt mixed with
1 teaspoon honey and dash *each*
cinnamon and nutmeg)

Total Optional Calories: 95

Sour Cream Latkes (Pancakes) ⓒ

Latkes are delicious topped with sour cream, yogurt, or applesauce.

3/4 cup skim milk
3 tablespoons sour cream
1 egg
3/4 cup all-purpose flour
1/2 teaspoon each baking soda and salt
1 cup finely diced onions
1/4 cup chopped fresh dill

In blender container combine milk, sour cream, and egg and process until combined; with motor running at low speed, gradually add flour, baking soda, and salt, processing until combined, about 1 minute. Turn motor off and scrape down sides of container; add onions and dill and process just until combined.

Spray 10-inch skillet or a griddle with nonstick cooking spray and heat. Using 1 heaping tablespoon batter for each pancake, drop 4 heaping tablespoonfuls into hot skillet (or onto griddle), making 4 pancakes; using the back of a spoon, spread each pancake into a circle about 3 inches in diameter. Cook until bubbles appear on surface and latkes are browned on bottom; using pancake turner, turn pancakes over and cook until other side is browned. Remove pancakes to plate and keep warm. Repeat procedure 3 more times, spraying pan each time and making 12 more pancakes.

MAKES 4 SERVINGS, 4 LATKES EACH

Each serving provides: 1 Bread Exchange; 1/2 Vegetable Exchange;
60 Optional Calories
Per serving: 160 calories; 6 g protein; 4 g fat; 24 g carbohydrate;
105 mg calcium; 425 mg sodium; 74 mg cholesterol

Variation: Yogurt Latkes (Week 1) — Substitute 1/4 cup plain low-fat yogurt for the sour cream. Add 1/4 Milk Exchange and reduce Optional Calories to 25.

Per serving: 146 calories; 7 g protein; 2 g fat; 25 g carbohydrate;
119 mg calcium; 430 mg sodium; 70 mg cholesterol

½ medium Banana, sliced
¾ ounce Cold Cereal
1 cup Skim Milk

LUNCH

Tuna-Stuffed Pita (2 ounces tuna
    with ½ cup shredded lettuce,
    1 tablespoon chopped celery, and
    2 teaspoons mayonnaise in 1-ounce
    whole wheat pita bread)
½ cup *each* Broccoli and Cauliflower
    Florets
Coffee, Tea, or Mineral Water

DINNER

4 ounces Broiled Pork Chop
½ cup Cooked Brown Rice
1 serving **Eggplant-Tomato Medley**
1½ cups Tossed Salad with
    1 tablespoon Reduced-Calorie
    Creamy Cucumber Dressing
½ cup Orange and Grapefruit
    Sections
Coffee or Tea

SNACKS

½ cup Canned Pineapple Chunks;
    ½ cup Reduced-Calorie Chocolate
    Pudding

Total Optional Calories: 60

Eggplant-Tomato Medley

Freeze extra portions so you'll always have this delicious side dish on hand. Then just thaw and reheat.

1 tablespoon plus 1 teaspoon olive oil
4 cups cubed eggplant (1-inch cubes)
½ cup diced onion
2 garlic cloves, minced
2 cups canned Italian tomatoes (with liquid); drain and chop tomatoes, reserving liquid
1 cup chopped mushrooms
½ cup dry red table wine
1 tablespoon chopped fresh parsley
2 teaspoons chopped fresh basil
½ teaspoon salt
¼ teaspoon pepper

In 3-quart saucepan heat oil; add eggplant, onion, and garlic and sauté for 5 minutes. Add remaining ingredients and, stirring occasionally, bring mixture to a boil. Reduce heat to low, cover, and let simmer, stirring occasionally, for 30 minutes.

MAKES 4 SERVINGS, ABOUT 1 CUP EACH.

Each serving provides: 3¾ Vegetable Exchanges; 1 Fat Exchange;
    30 Optional Calories
Per serving: 124 calories; 3 g protein; 5 g fat; 14 g carbohydrate;
    79 mg calcium; 476 mg sodium; 0 mg cholesterol

Variation: Eggplant, Tomato, and Tofu Medley (Week 2) — Add ¾ pound firm-style tofu (soybean curd), cut into cubes, to Eggplant-Tomato Medley during last 15 minutes of cooking time. Add 1 Protein Exchange to Exchange Information.

Per serving: 185 calories; 9 g protein; 9 g fat; 17 g carbohydrate;
    188 mg calcium; 482 mg sodium; 0 mg cholesterol

BREAKFAST

1 medium Kiwi Fruit, sliced
½ English Muffin, toasted, with
   1 teaspoon *each* Reduced-Calorie
   Margarine and Honey
1 cup Skim Milk

LUNCH

Bologna Sandwich (2 ounces sliced
   bologna with ¼ cup *each* alfalfa
   sprouts and shredded lettuce and
   2 teaspoons Dijon-style mustard
   on 2 slices reduced-calorie wheat
   bread)
1 large Tangerine
Coffee, Tea, or Mineral Water

DINNER

4 ounces Roast Chicken
1 serving **Bulgur Pilaf**
½ cup Cooked Chinese Pea Pods
Escarole-Romaine Salad (½ cup *each*
   torn escarole and romaine lettuce
   with ½ cup sliced fennel and
   1 tablespoon French dressing)
½ cup Low-Calorie Cherry-Flavored
   Gelatin topped with 1 tablespoon
   Whipped Topping
Coffee or Tea

SNACKS

Strawberry-Flavored Yogurt (½ cup
   plain low-fat yogurt mixed with
   2 teaspoons reduced-calorie
   strawberry spread); 2 Graham
   Crackers

Total Optional Calories: 75

Bulgur Pilaf

Cracked wheat comes in fine, medium, and coarse grain — all are appropriate for this recipe.

1 teaspoon margarine
1 tablespoon minced shallots
½ garlic clove, minced
1 cup canned ready-to-serve chicken broth
4 dried apricot halves, diced
2 tablespoons dark <u>or</u> golden raisins
1 teaspoon minced fresh parsley
Dash <u>each</u> ground cinnamon, salt, and pepper
2 ounces uncooked cracked wheat (bulgur)

In 1-quart saucepan heat margarine over medium heat until bubbly and hot; add shallots and garlic and sauté until shallots are softened, 1 to 2 minutes. Stir in broth, apricots, raisins, parsley, and seasonings; cover and bring to a boil. Add cracked wheat and stir well. Reduce heat to low, cover, and let simmer until liquid is completely absorbed and cracked wheat is tender, 30 to 40 minutes.

MAKES 2 SERVINGS

Each serving provides: 1 Bread Exchange; ½ Fat Exchange;
   1 Fruit Exchange; 20 Optional Calories
Per serving: 181 calories; 4 g protein; 2 g fat; 35 g carbohydrate;
   27 mg calcium; 594 mg sodium; 0 mg cholesterol

Variation: Rice Pilaf (Week 5) — Substitute uncooked regular long-grain rice for the cracked wheat.

Per serving: 183 calories; 4 g protein; 2 g fat; 36 g carbohydrate;
   25 mg calcium; 595 mg sodium; 0 mg cholesterol

Peppers 'n' Potatoes ©

2 tablespoons margarine
1 cup <u>each</u> julienne-cut red and green bell peppers
   (3 x ¼-inch strips) and diced onions
½ to 1 small garlic clove, minced
1½ cups water
2 packets instant chicken broth and seasoning mix
⅛ teaspoon pepper
1 pound 2 ounces scrubbed red new potatoes, thinly
   sliced
Garnish: Italian (flat-leaf) parsley sprigs

In 12-inch nonstick skillet heat margarine until bubbly and
hot; add bell peppers, onions, and garlic and sauté until
vegetables are softened, about 5 minutes. Stir in water,
broth mix, and pepper; bring to a boil. Reduce heat to low;
add potatoes, cover, and let simmer, stirring occasionally,
until potatoes are tender, about 15 minutes (if necessary,
add more water to prevent sticking). Transfer to serving
platter; serve garnished with parsley sprigs.

MAKES 4 SERVINGS

Each serving provides: 1½ Bread Exchanges; 1½ Vegetable Exchanges;
   1½ Fat Exchanges; 5 Optional Calories
Per serving: 178 calories; 4 g protein; 6 g fat; 28 g carbohydrate;
   27 mg calcium; 572 mg sodium; 0 mg cholesterol

BREAKFAST

½ medium Grapefruit
1 Egg scrambled in 1 teaspoon
    Margarine
½ English Muffin, toasted, with
    2 teaspoons Peach Preserves
¾ cup Skim Milk

LUNCH

Chicken Sandwich (2 ounces sliced
    chicken with ¼ cup shredded
    lettuce, 2 tablespoons alfalfa
    sprouts, and 2 teaspoons reduced-
    calorie mayonnaise on 2 slices
    reduced-calorie rye bread)
6 Cherry Tomatoes and ½ cup
    Broccoli Florets
Coffee, Tea, or Mineral Water

DINNER

3 ounces Baked Cod sprinkled with
    Paprika
3 ounces Baked Potato topped with
    2 tablespoons Plain Low-Fat
    Yogurt plus Chopped Chives
1 cup Cooked Brussels Sprouts
1 serving **Fennel Salad**
½ cup Canned Peach Slices
Coffee or Tea

SNACKS

½ cup Fruit Salad; ½ cup Plain
    Low-Fat Yogurt

Total Optional Calories: 35

Fennel Salad ◑

Fennel has a crunchy texture similar to celery and a mild licorice-like flavor. It's delicious raw in salads or steamed as a side dish.

1 large fennel bulb (leaves and stalks removed), cut lengthwise into thin slices (about 2 cups)
1 tablespoon plus 1½ teaspoons freshly squeezed lemon juice
1 tablespoon chopped fresh parsley
2 teaspoons olive oil
1½ teaspoons chopped onion
½ garlic clove, minced
¼ teaspoon salt
Dash freshly ground pepper, or to taste

In salad bowl combine all ingredients, tossing well; cover with plastic wrap and refrigerate for at least 30 minutes.

MAKES 2 SERVINGS

Each serving provides: 2 Vegetable Exchanges; 1 Fat Exchange
Per serving: 63 calories; 1 g protein; 5 g fat; 5g carbohydrate;
    60 mg calcium; 379 mg sodium; 0 mg cholesterol

BREAKFAST

½ medium Banana, sliced
¾ ounce Cold Cereal
½ cup Skim Milk
Coffee or Tea

LUNCH

Shrimp-Stuffed Pita (1 ounce tiny
   shrimp with ½ cup shredded
   lettuce, 2 tablespoons chopped
   cucumber, and 2 teaspoons
   mayonnaise in 1-ounce pita bread)
6 *each* Carrot and Celery Sticks
1 small Orange
Coffee, Tea, or Mineral Water

DINNER

¾ cup Chicken Bouillon
4 ounces Broiled Lamb Chop
Pimiento Cauliflower (¾ cup cooked
   cauliflower florets with ¼ cup
   pimiento strips and 1 teaspoon
   margarine)
1 serving **Greek-Style Spinach Salad**
¾ cup Sliced Strawberries topped
   with ¼ cup Plain Low-Fat Yogurt
Coffee or Tea

SNACKS

Chocolate Milk (¾ cup skim milk
   mixed with 1 teaspoon chocolate
   syrup)

Total Optional Calories: 40

Greek-Style Spinach Salad ⓒ ◑

¼ **cup plain low-fat yogurt**
1½ **teaspoons <u>each</u> lemon juice and chopped fresh dill**
¾ **teaspoon granulated sugar**
Dash white pepper
2 **cups spinach leaves, washed well and torn into
   bite-size pieces**
1 **ounce feta cheese, crumbled**
6 **cherry tomatoes, cut into halves**
½ **medium cucumber, pared, seeded, and sliced**
2 **tablespoons sliced scallion (green onion)**

In small bowl combine yogurt, lemon juice, dill, sugar, and
pepper, mixing well.

   In large salad bowl combine spinach, feta cheese, cherry
tomatoes, cucumber, and scallion; pour dressing over salad
and toss well until thoroughly combined. Serve immediately.

MAKES 2 SERVINGS

Each serving provides: ½ Protein Exchange; 3⅛ Vegetable Exchanges;
   ¼ Milk Exchange; 10 Optional Calories
Per serving: 88 calories; 6 g protein; 4 g fat; 9 g carbohydrate;
   194 mg calcium; 229 mg sodium; 14 mg cholesterol

BREAKFAST

½ medium Grapefruit
1 Scrambled Egg
1 slice Whole Wheat Bread, toasted,
    with 1 teaspoon Margarine
1 cup Skim Milk

LUNCH

Tuna-Vegetable Sandwich (1 ounce
    tuna with 2 tomato slices, 3 green
    bell pepper strips, 2 lettuce leaves,
    and 1 teaspoon mayonnaise on
    2 slices reduced-calorie multi-grain
    bread)
6 *each* Zucchini Sticks and Radishes
Coffee, Tea, or Mineral Water

DINNER

4 ounces Broiled Chicken
1 cup Cooked Chopped Broccoli
Cucumber-Mushroom Salad
    (6 cucumber slices with ½ cup
    sliced mushrooms and
    1½ teaspoons Thousand Island
    dressing mixed with 2 tablespoons
    plain low-fat yogurt and
    ¼ teaspoon mustard on 4 lettuce
    leaves)
Gelatin 'n' Fruit (½ cup low-calorie
    strawberry-flavored gelatin topped
    with ¼ cup canned crushed
    pineapple)
Coffee or Tea

SNACKS

½ cup **Cinnamon-Sweet Applesauce**;
    ¾ cup Skim Milk

Total Optional Calories: 35

Cinnamon-Sweet Applesauce ©

May be served warm or chilled.

3 pounds Granny Smith apples, cored, pared, and chopped
½ cup water
2 cinnamon sticks (2 inches each)
½ teaspoon lemon juice
3 tablespoons firmly packed light brown sugar

In 4-quart saucepan combine all ingredients except sugar; bring to a boil. Reduce heat to low, cover, and let simmer, stirring occasionally, until apples soften, about 10 minutes; stir in sugar and cook for about 5 minutes longer.* Remove and discard cinnamon sticks.

YIELDS 1 QUART

Each ½-cup serving provides: 1½ Fruit Exchanges; 25 Optional Calories
Per serving: 103 calories; 0.2 g protein; 0.4 g fat; 27 g carbohydrate;
    14 mg calcium; 2 mg sodium; 0 mg cholesterol

*Applesauce will be slightly chunky; for a smooth applesauce, puree mixture in work bowl of food processor or blender container.

BREAKFAST

½ cup Orange Sections
¾ ounce Cold Cereal
½ cup Skim Milk
Coffee or Tea

LUNCH

Open-Face Pimiento 'n' Cheese
    Sandwich (2 ounces sliced
    Cheddar cheese with 2 tablespoons
    pimiento strips, 2 lettuce leaves,
    and 2 teaspoons *each* mustard and
    reduced-calorie mayonnaise on
    1 slice reduced-calorie multi-grain
    bread)
6 *each* Cucumber Spears and Carrot
    Sticks
1 serving **Almond Cookies**
Coffee, Tea, or Mineral Water

DINNER

4 ounces Baked Flounder
1 cup Cooked Chopped Spinach
    with 1 teaspoon Reduced-Calorie
    Margarine
½ cup Cooked Sliced Leeks
1½ cups Mixed Green Salad with
    1 tablespoon Reduced-Calorie
    Onion and Chive Dressing
½ cup Reduced-Calorie Butterscotch
    Pudding
Coffee or Tea

SNACKS

1 small Apple; ½ cup Skim Milk

Total Optional Calories: 65

Almond Cookies Ⓒ

Store leftover cookies in an airtight container
for up to 2 weeks or freeze for up to 1 month.

½ cup unsalted margarine (at room temperature)
⅓ cup plus 2 teaspoons granulated sugar, divided
1 egg, separated
1 teaspoon almond extract
1½ cups all-purpose flour, sifted

In mixing bowl, using electric mixer at medium speed, beat
together margarine and all but 1 tablespoon sugar until light
and fluffy. Add egg yolk, half of the egg white, and the
almond extract and continue beating until combined. Add
flour and mix to form an elastic dough. Divide dough into 4
equal portions, forming each into a ball; wrap each ball in
plastic wrap and refrigerate for at least 30 minutes.

Using palms of hands, on flat surface roll 1 portion of
dough into a 12-inch-long rope. Cut rope into eight 1½-inch
pieces and arrange on a nonstick cookie sheet, leaving a
space of about 1 inch between each. Using the tines of a fork,
flatten each cookie slightly. Repeat procedure with another
portion of dough and arrange on cookie sheet.

Preheat oven to 375°F. Using pastry brush, brush top of
cookies with half of the remaining egg white and sprinkle
with 1½ teaspoons sugar. Bake in middle of center oven rack
until edges of cookies are lightly browned, 8 to 10 minutes
(do not overbake). Using a spatula, remove cookies to wire
rack to cool. Repeat procedure with remaining 2 portions
of dough, brushing cookies with remaining egg white and
sprinkling evenly with remaining sugar, making 16 more
cookies.

MAKES 16 SERVINGS, 2 COOKIES EACH

Each serving provides: ½ Bread Exchange; 1½ Fat Exchanges; 25 Optional
    Calories
Per serving: 117 calories; 2 g protein; 6 g fat; 14 g carbohydrate;
    5 mg calcium; 5 mg sodium; 17 mg cholesterol

BREAKFAST

½ medium Pink Grapefruit
⅓ cup Cottage Cheese
1½-ounce Plain Croissant with
  1 teaspoon *each* Margarine and
  Red Raspberry Preserves
1 cup Skim Milk

LUNCH

Chicken-Stuffed Pita (2 ounces sliced
  chicken with ¼ cup shredded
  lettuce, 2 tomato slices, and
  2 teaspoons *each* Dijon-style
  mustard and reduced-calorie
  mayonnaise in 1-ounce whole
  wheat pita bread)
½ cup *each* Broccoli and Cauliflower
  Florets
Coffee, Tea, or Mineral Water

DINNER

1 cup Mixed Vegetable Juice with
  Celery Stick
3 ounces Broiled Steak
3 ounces Baked Potato topped with
  2 tablespoons Sour Cream
½ cup Cooked Chinese Pea Pods
  with ¼ cup Cooked Sliced
  Mushrooms
1½ cups Mixed Green Salad with
  1 tablespoon Reduced-Calorie
  Russian Dressing
1 serving **Gala Fruit and Nut Cookies**
Coffee or Tea

SNACKS

1 serving Reduced-Calorie Vanilla
  Dairy Drink

Total Optional Calories: 260

Gala Fruit and Nut Cookies

1½ **cups all-purpose flour**
½ **teaspoon <u>each</u> cream of tartar and baking soda**
⅛ **teaspoon ground cinnamon**
8 <u>each</u> **pitted dates and dried apricot halves, finely chopped**
¼ **cup dark raisins, finely chopped**
½ **ounce chopped walnuts**
⅓ **cup reduced-calorie margarine (tub)**
¼ **cup firmly packed dark brown sugar**
1 **egg**
½ **teaspoon vanilla extract**

On sheet of wax paper or a paper plate sift together flour, cream of tartar, baking soda, and cinnamon; set aside.

In small bowl combine dates, apricots, raisins, and walnuts; add 1 tablespoon flour mixture and toss to combine. Set aside.

In medium bowl, using electric mixer at medium speed, cream margarine with sugar; add egg and vanilla and beat until light and fluffy. Gradually beat in sifted dry ingredients; stir in fruit mixture. Cover bowl with plastic wrap and refrigerate for 15 minutes.

Preheat oven to 350°F. Spray cookie sheet with nonstick cooking spray. Using hands, shape dough into sixteen 1-inch balls; arrange on cookie sheet, leaving about 2 inches between each. Using tines of fork, lightly press each ball down to flatten, then press down lightly in opposite direction to create a checkerboard pattern.

Bake in middle of center oven rack until cookies are lightly browned, about 15 minutes; using a spatula, remove cookies to wire rack to cool.

Repeat procedure with remaining dough, spraying cookie sheet with nonstick cooking spray and making 16 more cookies.

MAKES 8 SERVINGS, 4 COOKIES EACH

Each serving provides: 1 Bread Exchange; 1 Fat Exchange; 1 Fruit Exchange;
  50 Optional Calories
Per serving: 211 calories; 4 g protein; 6 g fat; 37 g carbohydrate;
  22 mg calcium; 143 mg sodium; 34 mg cholesterol

TIP: To keep dried fruit from sticking to the knife while chopping, spray knife with nonstick cooking spray before starting; or fruit can be chopped in the food processor. Add the 1 tablespoon flour mixture to processor along with the fruit and it will help to keep the fruit from sticking.

BREAKFAST

1 medium Kiwi Fruit, sliced
1 Poached Egg
1 slice Rye Bread, toasted, with
    1 teaspoon Reduced-Calorie
    Margarine
1 cup Skim Milk

LUNCH

Turkey Sandwich (2 ounces sliced
    turkey with 3 tomato slices,
    2 lettuce leaves, and 1½ teaspoons
    mayonnaise on 2 slices reduced-
    calorie wheat bread)
6 *each* Carrot and Celery Sticks
¾ ounce Mixed Dried Fruit
Coffee, Tea, or Mineral Water

DINNER

Garlic Shrimp (3 ounces broiled
    shrimp with 2 teaspoons reduced-
    calorie margarine and ½ teaspoon
    minced garlic)
½ cup Mashed Baked Acorn Squash
Special Zucchini (½ cup *each* cooked
    sliced zucchini and diced red bell
    pepper sprinkled with oregano)
1½ cups Tossed Salad with
    1 tablespoon Reduced-Calorie
    Creamy Cucumber Dressing
1 serving **Hot Buttered Rum**

SNACKS

2 Canned Pear Halves; ½ cup
    Reduced-Calorie Chocolate
    Pudding

Total Optional Calories: 150

Hot Buttered Rum ◐

1 tablespoon firmly packed dark brown sugar
2 teaspoons whipped sweet butter
Dash ground cloves
Zest of 1 small orange,* removed in 1 long piece, then cut in half
1 cinnamon stick (10 inches), broken in half†
6 whole cloves
1 cup brewed tea (hot)
²/₃ cup unfermented apple cider or apple juice (no sugar added)
¼ cup dark rum

In small bowl combine sugar, butter, and ground cloves, mixing until well blended; set aside. Wrap each strip of orange zest around each cinnamon stick and insert 3 whole cloves into each strip of zest. Trim zest if necessary.

Into each of two 8-ounce mugs place 1 prepared cinnamon stick and any remaining orange zest; add ½ cup tea, ¹/₃ cup apple cider (or juice), and 2 tablespoons rum and stir to combine. Top each portion with half of the sugar-butter mixture; serve immediately.

MAKES 2 SERVINGS

Each serving provides: 1 Fruit Exchange; 120 Optional Calories
Per serving: 166 calories; 0.3 g protein; 2 g fat; 20 g carbohydrate;
    54 mg calcium; 6 mg sodium; 5 mg cholesterol

*The zest of the orange is the peel without any of the pith (white membrane). To remove zest from orange, use a zester or vegetable peeler; wrap orange in plastic wrap and refrigerate for use at another time.
†If 10-inch cinnamon stick is not available, substitute two 2-inch cinnamon sticks.

BREAKFAST

½ cup Orange Sections
½ small Bagel, toasted, with
    Cinnamon-Cream Cheese
    (2 tablespoons whipped cream
    cheese mixed with ¼ teaspoon
    cinnamon)
1 cup Skim Milk

LUNCH

Kidney Bean Salad (4 ounces canned
    kidney beans with 2 tablespoons
    each diced tomato and onion and
    2 teaspoons olive oil mixed with
    2 teaspoons red wine vinegar plus
    thyme on 2 lettuce leaves)
1 small Apple
Coffee, Tea, or Mineral Water

DINNER

4 ounces Roast Cornish Hen
Parslied Noodles (½ cup cooked broad
    noodles with 1 teaspoon margarine,
    sprinkled with chopped parsley)
½ cup Cooked Artichoke Hearts
½ cup Cooked Chopped Kale with
    Lemon Juice
Iceberg-Romaine Salad (1 cup *each*
    torn iceberg and romaine lettuce
    with ¼ cup alfalfa sprouts and
    1 tablespoon reduced-calorie blue
    cheese dressing)
4 Canned Apricot Halves
¾ cup **Silver Jubilee Sparkling Punch**

SNACKS

2 Honey Graham Crackers; 1 serving
    Reduced-Calorie Hot Cocoa

Total Optional Calories: 150

Silver Jubilee Sparkling Punch ◑

Try this with any fruit-flavored liqueur.

**½ tub (about 2 teaspoons) low-calorie fruit punch-
    flavored drink mix (4 calories per 8 fluid ounces)***
1 quart cold water
**1 cup <u>each</u> dry champagne and dry white table wine,
    chilled**
¼ cup raspberry liqueur
1½ quarts club soda, chilled
5 scored lemon slices
1 cup raspberries, divided

In punch bowl sprinkle drink mix over water and stir well
to dissolve; add champagne, wine, and liqueur. Pour in club
soda, then add lemon slices and top each with 1 raspberry.
Serve each portion of punch with an equal amount of
raspberries.

YIELDS 3 QUARTS

Each ¾-cup serving provides: 45 Optional Calories
Per serving: 40 calories; 0 g protein; 0 g fat; 3 g carbohydrate;
    4 mg calcium; 1 mg sodium; 0 mg cholesterol

Variation: Sweet Sparkling Punch (Week 2) — Substitute
raspberry syrup for the liqueur. Increase Optional Calories
to 50.

Per serving: 42 calories; 0 g protein; 0 g fat; 6 g carbohydrate;
    4 mg calcium; 1 mg sodium; 0 mg cholesterol

*1 tub low-calorie fruit punch-flavored drink mix makes eight 8-fluid-
    ounce servings.

Six Weeks
of Menus

Our <u>Quick and Easy Menu Cookbook</u> contains a wealth of 1-day menu ideas to go with each of the more than 250 recipes. But if you'd rather plan your menus for an entire week at a time, you'll love these 7-day Menu Planners. Here we present six of them, corresponding to Weeks 1, 2, 3, 4, 5, and 8 of the Quick Success Program, so you can see at a glance exactly what you're going to have. The recipes have been selected from throughout the book. Whether you're shopping and cooking for yourself or for a family, our Menu Planners will certainly make your life easier. We hope you'll use and enjoy them.

Week 1

You're ready to begin following the Food Plan, full of high hopes and motivation, and we're going to help you with our Week 1 Menu Planner. Nutritious meals don't have to be dull. Just look at the exciting things you can do with vegetables, for instance. Day 1 features Creamy Minted Green Bean Salad at lunch, while lunch on Day 6 includes a serving of Hot Vinaigrette Vegetables. On Day 7, Creamed Mushrooms accompany a dinner of Glazed Swordfish Steaks.

Our main course dishes are just as varied and interesting. Try chicken two ways: Crunchy Oven-Fried Chicken on Day 2, and Sweet 'n' Sour Chicken on Day 4. Pork Fajita Pitas introduce a bit of Mexican cuisine into our Day 5 menu, while our Day 6 dinner features Hawaiian-style Pineapple-Veal Kabobs.

DAY 1

BREAKFAST
½ cup Orange Sections
¾ ounce Cold Cereal
¾ cup Skim Milk
Coffee or Tea

LUNCH
Roast Beef in a Pita (2 ounces roast beef with 2 *each* tomato slices, red onion slices, and lettuce leaves, and 1 teaspoon *each* mustard and mayonnaise in 1-ounce pita bread)
1 serving **Creamy Minted Green Bean Salad** (page 151)
1 medium Peach
Coffee, Tea, or Mineral Water

DINNER
1 serving **Scallop 'n' Cheese Broil** (page 211)
6 Cooked Asparagus Spears
½ cup Cooked Sliced Carrot
1½ cups Mixed Green Salad with 1½ teaspoons Olive Oil mixed with 2 teaspoons Red Wine Vinegar plus Seasonings
Coffee or Tea

SNACKS
2 x 3-inch wedge Watermelon; 1 cup Skim Milk

Optional Calories: 5

DAY 4

BREAKFAST
1 serving **Banana Pancakes** (page 244) topped with 2 teaspoons Reduced-Calorie Raspberry Spread
⅓ cup Cottage Cheese
½ cup Skim Milk
Coffee or Tea

LUNCH
Tofu Salad (3 ounces diced tofu with ½ cup *each* broccoli florets and sliced zucchini, ¼ cup sliced radishes, and ½ teaspoon *each* soy sauce, Chinese sesame oil, and rice vinegar)
2 slices Melba Toast
Coffee, Tea, or Mineral Water

DINNER
1 serving **Sweet 'n' Sour Chicken** (page 76)
1 cup Cooked Cauliflower Florets
½ cup Cooked Spinach Leaves
1½ cups Tossed Salad with 1½ teaspoons Thousand Island Dressing mixed with 2 tablespoons Plain Low-Fat Yogurt plus ¼ teaspoon Dijon-Style Mustard
1-ounce Roll
½ cup Strawberries, sliced, and topped with 2 tablespoons Plain Low-Fat Yogurt
Coffee or Tea

SNACKS
1 serving Reduced-Calorie Vanilla Dairy Drink; 1 small Orange

Optional Calories: 30

DAY 5

BREAKFAST
½ cup Orange and Grapefruit Sections
¾ ounce Cold Cereal
½ cup Skim Milk
Coffee or Tea

LUNCH
Fish Salad (2 ounces fish with 2 teaspoons chopped celery, 4 tomato wedges, ¼ cup sliced cucumber, and 2 servings **Cilantro Mayonnaise** [page 154] on 4 lettuce leaves)
6 *each* Celery and Carrot Sticks
1 cup Watermelon Chunks
Coffee, Tea, or Mineral Water

DINNER
1 serving **Pork Fajita Pitas** (page 31)
6 Cooked Asparagus Spears
½ cup Cooked Diced Red Bell Pepper
1½ cups Mixed Green Salad with 1½ teaspoons Italian Dressing mixed with 2 teaspoons Red Wine Vinegar
1 cup Skim Milk
Coffee or Tea

SNACKS
½ cup Fruit Salad topped with 2 tablespoons Plain Low-Fat Yogurt

Optional Calories: 5

DAY 2

BREAKFAST
¼ small Cantaloupe
⅓ cup Cottage Cheese
½ cup Skim Milk
Coffee or Tea

LUNCH
Egg Salad Sandwich (2 hard-cooked eggs, chopped, with
  1 teaspoon diced onion and 2 teaspoons reduced-calorie
  mayonnaise on 2 slices reduced-calorie multi-grain bread)
6 *each* Zucchini Sticks and Red Bell Pepper Strips
Coffee, Tea, or Mineral Water

DINNER
1 serving **Crunchy Oven-Fried Chicken** (page 121)
1 cup Cooked Broccoli Florets
½ cup Cooked Sliced Celery
Lettuce Wedge with 3 Tomato Slices and 1½ teaspoons
  Russian Dressing mixed with 2 tablespoons Plain Low-Fat
  Yogurt plus ¼ teaspoon Dijon-Style Mustard
1 serving **Puddin' Parfait** (page 157)
Coffee or Tea

SNACKS
¾ cup Beef Bouillon; ¼ cup Canned Crushed Pineapple topped
  with 2 tablespoons Plain Low-Fat Yogurt

Optional Calories: 30

DAY 3

BREAKFAST
½ medium Grapefruit drizzled with ½ teaspoon Honey
½ cup Hot Cereal
½ cup Skim Milk
Coffee or Tea

LUNCH
Tuna Salad in a Pita (2 ounces tuna with 1 teaspoon
  each chopped celery and onion, 2 lettuce leaves and
  1½ teaspoons mayonnaise in 1-ounce pita bread)
6 *each* Cucumber and Carrot Sticks
1 medium Peach
Coffee, Tea, or Mineral Water

DINNER
1 serving **Lamb Steaks with Yogurt-Mustard Sauce** (page 101)
½ cup *each* Cooked Cut Green Beans and Sliced Mushrooms
1½ cups Torn Romaine Lettuce with ½ cup Sliced Yellow
  Squash, 3 Sliced Radishes, and 1½ teaspoons French
  Dressing mixed with 2 teaspoons Lemon Juice plus
  ¼ teaspoon Dijon-Style Mustard
Coffee or Tea

SNACKS
1 serving **Berries with Sweet Yogurt Sauce** (page 132); ½ cup
  Skim Milk

Optional Calories: 30

DAY 6

BREAKFAST
1 cup Honeydew Chunks
⅓ cup Cottage Cheese
1 slice Reduced-Calorie Rye Bread
½ cup Skim Milk
Coffee or Tea

LUNCH
1 serving **Cheese Wedges** (page 49)
1 serving **Hot Vinaigrette Vegetables** (page 107)
½ cup Reduced-Calorie Vanilla Pudding
1 medium Banana, sliced
Coffee, Tea, or Mineral Water

DINNER
1 serving **Pineapple-Veal Kabobs** (page 170)
¾ cup Cooked Bamboo Shoots with 1 teaspoon Diced
  Pimiento
¾ cup Cooked Cut Green Beans
¾ cup *each* Torn Arugula and Sliced Belgian Endive with
  1 teaspoon Olive Oil mixed with Lemon Juice plus
  Seasonings
1-ounce Roll
Coffee or Tea

SNACKS
½ cup Strawberries, sliced, and topped with ¼ cup Plain
  Low-Fat Yogurt

Optional Calories: 5

DAY 7

BREAKFAST
1 medium Peach, sliced, and topped with ¼ cup Plain
  Low-Fat Yogurt
1 slice Raisin Bread, toasted
Coffee or Tea

LUNCH
1 serving **Sloppy Joes** (page 260)
Mixed Green Salad with 1½ teaspoons Caesar Dressing mixed
  with 2 teaspoons Lemon Juice plus ½ teaspoon Dijon-Style
  Mustard
6 *each* Carrot and Celery Sticks
½ cup Low-Calorie Strawberry-Flavored Gelatin
Coffee, Tea, or Mineral Water

DINNER
1 serving **Glazed Swordfish Steaks** (page 165)
1 serving **Creamed Mushrooms** (page 262)
¾ cup Cooked Broccoli Florets
½ cup *each* Torn Chicory, Escarole, and Lettuce with ½ cup
  Diced Tomato and 1½ teaspoons Thousand Island Dressing
  mixed with 2 tablespoons Plain Low-Fat Yogurt plus
  ¼ teaspoon Dijon-Style Mustard
½ medium Grapefruit
Coffee or Tea

SNACKS
1 serving Reduced-Calorie Chocolate Dairy Drink; ¼ small
  Cantaloupe

Optional Calories: 35
Total Optional Calories for Week: 140

Week 2

Three all-time favorites — potatoes, pasta, and rice — are new this week, and you'll find them on our Week 2 Menu Planner.

If you've never tried brown rice, you have your chance on Day 5 with Brown Rice and Vegetable Medley. This colorful side dish combines the rice with mushrooms, zucchini, red bell pepper, and scallions. Rice and Oriental cooking usually go hand in hand, but you can substitute pasta with excellent results. Chicken 'n' Broccoli-Topped Orzo is a delicious stir-fry of chicken, broccoli florets, and a rice-shaped pasta called orzo. Pasta is also the star of our Mexican Pasta Salad.

Pass the potatoes, please! New Potato Salad on Day 6 is a wonderful way to enjoy small, new red potatoes. They're cooked and gently combined with fresh dill, mayonnaise, and yogurt, then served warm or chilled.

DAY 4

BREAKFAST
¼ small Cantaloupe
⅓ cup Cottage Cheese
½ cup Skim Milk
Coffee or Tea

LUNCH
1½ ounces Tuna
1 serving **Mexican Pasta Salad** (page 195)
1 small Apple
Coffee, Tea, or Mineral Water

DINNER
1 serving **Chicken à la King** (page 122)
¾ cup Cooked Mushrooms
Spinach Salad (1½ cups torn spinach with 6 cherry tomato
    halves and 1½ teaspoons Italian dressing mixed with
    2 teaspoons red wine vinegar)
½ cup Reduced-Calorie Vanilla Pudding
Coffee or Tea

SNACKS
1 cup Strawberries

Optional Calories: 25

DAY 1

BREAKFAST
½ medium Banana, sliced
¾ ounce Cold Cereal
¾ cup Skim Milk
Coffee or Tea

LUNCH
Cottage Cheese and Fruit (⅔ cup cottage cheese mixed with
    ½ cup canned pineapple chunks)
6 Zucchini Sticks and ¾ cup Cauliflower Florets
1 Rice Cake
Coffee, Tea, or Mineral Water

DINNER
1 serving **Seafood Stew** (page 26)
1 serving **Yogurt-Baked Eggplant** (page 173)
6 Cooked Asparagus Spears
1½ cups Mixed Green Salad with 1½ teaspoons Caesar
    Dressing mixed with 2 teaspoons Lemon Juice plus
    ½ teaspoon Dijon-Style Mustard
1-ounce Roll
Coffee or Tea

SNACKS
1 serving Reduced-Calorie Vanilla Dairy Drink; 1 small Orange

Optional Calories: 5

DAY 5

BREAKFAST
½ medium Banana, sliced
¾ ounce Cold Cereal
½ cup Skim Milk
Coffee or Tea

LUNCH
2 ounces Sardines
1 serving **Greek Eggplant Salad** (page 193)
1-ounce Whole Wheat Pita Bread
6 *each* Carrot and Celery Sticks
Coffee, Tea, or Mineral Water

DINNER
1 serving **Prosciutto-Wrapped Shrimp** (page 73)
1 serving **Brown Rice and Vegetable Medley** (page 127)
½ cup Cooked Whole Green Beans
1½ cups Tossed Salad with Lemon Juice plus Herbs
½ cup Fruit Salad
½ cup Skim Milk
Coffee or Tea

SNACKS
1 small Orange; 1 cup Skim Milk

Optional Calories: 10

DAY 2

BREAKFAST
½ cup Orange Sections
⅓ cup Cottage Cheese
1 slice Raisin Bread
½ cup Skim Milk
Coffee or Tea

LUNCH
Tofu Salad (3 ounces diced tofu with ½ cup *each* cauliflower
    florets and sliced zucchini, 6 green bell pepper strips, ¼ cup
    sliced radishes, and 1 teaspoon *each* soy sauce, Chinese
    sesame oil, and rice vinegar)
6 *each* Celery Sticks and Cherry Tomatoes
1 small Apple
Coffee, Tea, or Mineral Water

DINNER
1 serving **Chicken 'n' Broccoli-Topped Orzo** (page 167)
¾ cup Cooked Red Bell Pepper Strips
1 serving **Sprout Slaw with Ginger Dressing** (page 61)
½ cup Reduced-Calorie Chocolate Pudding
Coffee or Tea

SNACKS
1 medium Peach; ¾ ounce Cold Cereal; ½ cup Skim Milk

Optional Calories: 25

DAY 3

BREAKFAST
½ medium Grapefruit
1 ounce Muenster Cheese
½ English Muffin, toasted
½ cup Skim Milk
Coffee or Tea

LUNCH
1 serving **Vegetarian Pita Melt** (page 118)
6 *each* Zucchini Sticks and Radishes
½ medium Banana
Coffee, Tea, or Mineral Water

DINNER
1 serving **Apple-Glazed Ham Steak** (page 125)
1 serving **Vegetable Hotchpotch** (page 219)
1½ cups Mixed Green Salad with 1½ teaspoons Russian
    Dressing mixed with 2 tablespoons Plain Low-Fat Yogurt
    plus ¼ teaspoon Dijon-Style Mustard
½ cup Blueberries
½ cup Skim Milk
Coffee or Tea

SNACKS
½ cup Low-Calorie Strawberry-Flavored Gelatin topped with
    2 tablespoons Plain Low-Fat Yogurt; ½ cup Skim Milk

Optional Calories: 35

DAY 6

BREAKFAST
½ cup Raspberries
1 Poached Egg
½ English Muffin, toasted
¼ cup Skim Milk
Coffee or Tea

LUNCH
1 serving **Roasted Vegetable Bisque** (page 22)
1 serving **Cottage-Ham 'n' Apple Quiche** (page 210)
1½ cups Tossed Salad with 1 tablespoon Reduced-Calorie
    Italian Dressing
1 serving Reduced-Calorie Vanilla Dairy Drink
Coffee, Tea, or Mineral Water

DINNER
1 serving **Seasoned Skillet Burgers** (page 168)
1 serving **New Potato Salad** (page 108)
¾ cup *each* Cooked Spinach Leaves and Diced Red Bell
    Pepper
½ medium Grapefruit
Coffee or Tea

SNACKS
¾ cup Chicken Bouillon; ½ cup Low-Calorie Lemon-Flavored
    Gelatin

Optional Calories: 70

DAY 7

BREAKFAST
1 cup Strawberries
⅓ cup Cottage Cheese
½ cup Skim Milk
Coffee or Tea

LUNCH
1 serving **Baked Clams Iberian** (page 282)
1 serving **Nacho Potato Wedges** (page 80)
¾ cup *each* Cooked Broccoli Florets and Sliced Carrots
½ cup Fruit Salad
Coffee, Tea, or Mineral Water

DINNER
2½ ounces Roast Beef
1 serving **Fiesta Pasta Salad** (page 153)
¾ cup *each* Cooked Sliced Zucchini and Yellow Squash
½ cup Skim Milk
Coffee or Tea

SNACKS
Peach Yogurt (½ cup plain low-fat yogurt mixed with ½ cup
    canned peach slices)

Optional Calories: 30
Total Optional Calories for Week: 200

Week 3

And now for a little sweet talk about the Food Plan. No, you don't have to give up desserts, and the Week 3 Menu Planner proves it — ever so sweetly — with an array of dessert recipes.

Top off dinner on Day 1 with Maple-Banana Parfaits. This luscious, layered dessert combines yogurt, pancake syrup, graham cracker crumbs, and bananas. Out of bananas? Any fresh fruit will do. Serve up an old-fashioned goody at dinner on Day 3: Apple Crisp; it's easy to prepare and out of the oven in half an hour. Our dinner on Day 5 features Ricotta-Peach Pie, a perfect ending for a weekend meal. And because it calls for canned peaches rather than fresh, you can serve it any time of the year.

DAY 1

BREAKFAST
Peach Yogurt (½ cup canned peach slices mixed with ¼ cup plain low-fat yogurt)
1 slice Raisin Bread, toasted
Coffee or Tea

LUNCH
Roast Beef Sandwich (3 ounces roast beef with 2 lettuce leaves and 1 teaspoon mustard on 2 slices reduced-calorie rye bread)
6 each Carrot and Celery Sticks
Coffee, Tea, or Mineral Water

DINNER
¾ cup Chicken Bouillon
3 ounces Broiled Flounder Fillet
½ cup Cooked Noodles
1 teaspoon Margarine
¾ cup each Cooked Spinach Leaves and Sliced Fennel
1½ cups Mixed Green Salad with 1 tablespoon Italian Dressing
1 serving **Maple-Banana Parfaits** (page 38)
Coffee or Tea

SNACKS
1 small Orange; ½ cup Skim Milk

Optional Calories: 90

DAY 4

BREAKFAST
½ medium Grapefruit
1 Scrambled Egg
½ small Bagel
½ cup Skim Milk
Coffee or Tea

LUNCH
1 serving **Greek Vegetarian Pitas** (page 71)
6 each Celery Sticks and Radishes
1 small Nectarine
Coffee, Tea, or Mineral Water

DINNER
1 serving **Chicken Loaf with Tomato Sauce** (page 213)
6 Cooked Asparagus Spears
1 cup Cooked Cauliflower Florets
2 teaspoons Reduced-Calorie Margarine
1½ cups Mixed Green Salad with 1½ teaspoons Italian Dressing mixed with 2 teaspoons Red Wine Vinegar
½ cup Reduced-Calorie Chocolate Pudding
Coffee or Tea

SNACKS
20 small Grapes; ½ cup Skim Milk

Optional Calories: 35

DAY 5

BREAKFAST
¼ small Cantaloupe
⅓ cup Cottage Cheese
½ cup Skim Milk
Coffee or Tea

LUNCH
1 serving **Kidney Bean Salad Olé** (page 220)
1 Rice Cake
½ medium Pickle
10 small Grapes
½ cup Skim Milk
Coffee, Tea, or Mineral Water

DINNER
3 ounces Broiled Scallops
1 cup Cooked Spaghetti Squash
1 teaspoon Margarine
¾ cup Cooked Red and Green Bell Pepper Strips
1 serving **Fennel Salad** (page 292)
1 serving **Ricotta-Peach Pie** (page 63)
1 serving Reduced-Calorie Vanilla Dairy Drink
Coffee or Tea

SNACKS
2 cups Plain Popcorn; 1 large Tangerine

Optional Calories: 20

DAY 2

BREAKFAST
1 cup Strawberries, sliced
¼ cup Part-Skim Ricotta Cheese
¼ cup Skim Milk
Coffee or Tea

LUNCH
1 serving **Garbanzo Salad** (page 145)
1 cup Broccoli Florets and 6 Red Bell Pepper Strips
1 small Apple
Coffee, Tea, or Mineral Water

DINNER
2½ ounces Roast Chicken
3 ounces Baked Potato topped with 2 tablespoons Plain Low-Fat Yogurt
1 cup Cooked Brussels Sprouts
¾ cup Cooked Sliced Beets
1½ cups Tossed Salad with 1½ teaspoons Olive Oil mixed with 2 teaspoons Red Wine Vinegar plus Seasonings
1 cup Skim Milk
Coffee or Tea

SNACKS
1 serving **Chocolate Egg Cream** (page 158); 2 cups Plain Popcorn

Optional Calories: 30

DAY 3

BREAKFAST
½ medium Banana, sliced
¾ ounce Cold Cereal
½ cup Skim Milk
Coffee or Tea

LUNCH
Tuna in a Pita (3 ounces tuna mixed with 2 teaspoons *each* chopped celery and onion and 1 teaspoon *each* reduced-calorie mayonnaise, pickle relish, and mustard in 1-ounce pita bread)
1 cup Cauliflower Florets and 6 Carrot Sticks
Coffee, Tea, or Mineral Water

DINNER
1 serving **Eggplant Soup** (page 206)
3 ounces Roast Lamb
¾ cup *each* Cooked Cut Green Beans and Sliced Zucchini
1 Lettuce Wedge and 3 Tomato Slices with 1½ teaspoons Thousand Island Dressing
1 serving **Apple Crisp** (page 224)
½ cup Skim Milk
Coffee or Tea

SNACKS
1 cup Strawberries; 1 serving Reduced-Calorie Chocolate Dairy Drink

Optional Calories: 45

DAY 6

BREAKFAST
1 cup Strawberries, sliced
¾ ounce Cold Cereal
½ cup Skim Milk
Coffee or Tea

LUNCH
1 serving **Cauliflower-Rice Torte** (page 93)
1½ cups Mixed Green Salad with 1½ teaspoons Thousand Island Dressing mixed with 2 tablespoons Plain Low-Fat Yogurt plus ¼ teaspoon Dijon-Style Mustard
1 small Nectarine
Coffee, Tea, or Mineral Water

DINNER
4 ounces Broiled Chicken
½ cup Cooked Noodles
1 teaspoon Reduced-Calorie Margarine
¾ cup *each* Cooked Spinach Leaves and Sliced Kohlrabi
1½ cups Tossed Salad with 1½ teaspoons Blue Cheese Dressing mixed with 2 tablespoons Plain Low-Fat Yogurt plus Garlic Powder
Coffee or Tea

SNACKS
1 large Mandarin Orange; Chocolate Milk (1 cup skim milk mixed with 1 teaspoon chocolate syrup)

Optional Calories: 20

DAY 7

BREAKFAST
1 serving **Festive Fruit and Cheese Fondue** (page 178)
1 slice Raisin Bread, toasted
½ cup Skim Milk
Coffee or Tea

LUNCH
1 serving **Italian Cheese and Egg Bake** (page 209)
1 serving **Italian Potato Casserole** (page 24)
1½ cups Tossed Salad with 1 teaspoon Imitation Bacon Bits and 1½ teaspoons Italian Dressing mixed with 2 teaspoons Red Wine Vinegar
1 small Orange
Coffee, Tea, or Mineral Water

DINNER
2½ ounces Baked Swordfish Steak
¾ cup *each* Cooked Brussels Sprouts and Sliced Beets
¾ cup *each* Torn Boston Lettuce and Sliced Belgian Endive with ½ teaspoon Olive Oil mixed with 2 teaspoons Red Wine Vinegar plus Seasonings
½ cup Reduced-Calorie Butterscotch Pudding
Coffee or Tea

SNACKS
½ cup Low-Calorie Cherry-Flavored Gelatin; 1 large Prune, pitted and diced, mixed with 2 tablespoons Plain Low-Fat Yogurt

Optional Calories: 50
Total Optional Calories for Week: 290

Week 4

What's new this week? Cream cheese, sour cream, sesame seeds, tomato juice, and beef sausage, to name a few, all coming to you courtesy of Week 4.

If the hearty taste of frankfurter or beef sausage is a favorite of yours, you'll enjoy Chili Dogs on Day 3 and Sausage, Chicken, and Rice Soup on Day 7. We've used tomato juice to flavor Roasted Red Pepper Sauce, a delicious accompaniment to a Day 6 dinner of broiled scallops. And sesame seeds add zest to Oriental Chicken and Green Beans on Day 2.

Cream cheese lovers, rejoice! This Week 4 food shows up in Stuffed Cherry Tomatoes, Cheese-Topped Shrimp, and, believe it or not, Mexican Eggs. And Baked Crab Creole, Sliced Steak with Gorgonzola Sauce, and Broiled Chicken Breasts with Red Pepper Sauce all contain sour cream, another food that is new this week.

DAY 4

BREAKFAST
½ medium Grapefruit
Cheddar Melt (1 ounce Cheddar cheese with 3 tomato slices on ½ English muffin, toasted)
½ cup Skim Milk
Coffee or Tea

LUNCH
Cottage Cheese and Fruit (⅔ cup cottage cheese with ½ cup canned crushed pineapple)
6 Saltines
6 *each* Carrot Sticks and Green Bell Pepper Strips
Coffee, Tea, or Mineral Water

DINNER
1 serving **Broiled Chicken Breasts with Red Pepper Sauce** (page 284)
½ cup *each* Cooked Hominy Grits and Sliced Mushrooms
1½ teaspoons Margarine
¾ cup Cooked Chinese Pea Pods
½ medium Tomato, sliced, with 1½ teaspoons Italian Dressing mixed with 2 teaspoons Red Wine Vinegar on 4 Lettuce Leaves
½ cup Blueberries
Coffee or Tea

SNACKS
½ cup Skim Milk; ½ cup Reduced-Calorie Chocolate Pudding

Optional Calories: 35

DAY 1

BREAKFAST
½ medium Banana, sliced
¾ ounce Cold Cereal
1 cup Skim Milk
Coffee or Tea

LUNCH
Bologna in a Pita (3 ounces bologna with 4 lettuce leaves and 1 teaspoon *each* reduced-calorie mayonnaise and mustard in 1-ounce pita bread)
1 serving **Stuffed Cherry Tomatoes** (page 184)
6 Celery Sticks
1 small Orange
Coffee, Tea, or Mineral Water

DINNER
¾ cup Chicken Bouillon
1 serving **Baked Crab Creole** (page 257)
¾ cup *each* Cooked Spinach Leaves and Sliced Beets
1½ cups Mixed Green Salad with 1 tablespoon Thousand Island Dressing
½ cup Reduced-Calorie Butterscotch Pudding
Coffee or Tea

SNACKS
½ cup Applesauce

Optional Calories: 110

DAY 5

BREAKFAST
½ medium Banana
¾ ounce Cold Cereal
½ cup Skim Milk
Coffee or Tea

LUNCH
Sardines in a Pita (3 ounces sardines with 1 tablespoon reduced-calorie mayonnaise and 4 lettuce leaves in 1-ounce whole wheat pita bread)
6 *each* Green and Red Bell Pepper Strips
Coffee, Tea, or Mineral Water

DINNER
1 serving **Sliced Steak with Gorgonzola Sauce** (page 216)
3 ounces Baked Potato topped with ¼ cup Plain Low-Fat Yogurt and Chopped Chives
¾ cup Cooked Broccoli Florets
1 cup Torn Iceberg Lettuce with ¼ cup *each* Shredded Red Cabbage and Grated Carrot and 1½ teaspoons Caesar Dressing mixed with 2 teaspoons Lemon Juice plus ½ teaspoon Dijon-Style Mustard
1 cup Strawberries
Coffee or Tea

SNACKS
1 serving Reduced-Calorie Chocolate Dairy Drink; 1 small Pear

Optional Calories: 40

DAY 2

BREAKFAST
1/3 cup Cottage Cheese with 1 serving **Pear Butter** (page 222)
1 slice Raisin Bread, toasted
1/2 cup Skim Milk
Coffee or Tea

LUNCH
Egg Salad Sandwich (1 hard-cooked egg, chopped, and 3
    ounces tofu with 1 teaspoon *each* mustard and mayonnaise
    and 4 lettuce leaves on 2 slices reduced-calorie wheat
    bread)
6 *each* Carrot Sticks and Pickle Spears
Coffee, Tea, or Mineral Water

DINNER
1 serving **Oriental Chicken and Green Beans** (page 99)
1/2 cup Cooked Rice
1 3/4 cups Sliced Fennel and Belgian Endive with 1/2 teaspoon
    Olive Oil mixed with 2 teaspoons White Wine Vinegar plus
    Herbs
1/2 cup Orange Sections
1 serving Reduced-Calorie Vanilla Dairy Drink
Coffee or Tea

SNACKS
Nectarine Yogurt (1/4 cup plain low-fat yogurt mixed with
    1 small nectarine, diced)

Optional Calories: 50

DAY 3

BREAKFAST
1/2 cup Orange Juice
1/2 cup Hot Cereal
3/4 cup Skim Milk
Coffee or Tea

LUNCH
Tuna Salad (2 1/2 ounces tuna with 4 tomato slices and
    1/2 teaspoon mayonnaise on 4 lettuce leaves)
3/4 cup Broccoli Florets and 6 Radishes
1 small Apple
Coffee, Tea, or Mineral Water

DINNER
1 serving **Chili Dogs** (page 53)
3/4 cup Sauerkraut
1 1/2 cups Mixed Green Salad with 1 1/2 teaspoons Blue Cheese
    Dressing mixed with 2 tablespoons Plain Low-Fat Yogurt
    plus Garlic Powder
Coffee or Tea

SNACKS
10 large Cherries; 1 cup Skim Milk

Optional Calories: 10

DAY 6

BREAKFAST
1 cup Low-Calorie Cranberry Juice
1/4 cup Part-Skim Ricotta Cheese
1 slice Raisin Bread, toasted
Coffee or Tea

LUNCH
1 serving **Mexican Eggs** (page 233)
1 Corn Tortilla with 1 serving **Salsa** (page 131)
1 1/2 cups Tossed Salad with 1 1/2 teaspoons Ranch Dressing
    mixed with 2 tablespoons Plain Low-Fat Yogurt plus
    1/4 teaspoon Dijon-Style Mustard
1 small Orange
Coffee, Tea, or Mineral Water

DINNER
3 ounces Broiled Scallops with 1 serving **Roasted Red Pepper
    Sauce** (page 172)
1/2 cup Cooked Whole-Kernel Corn
3/4 cup *each* Cooked French-Style Green Beans and Sliced
    Mushrooms
1 1/2 cups Mixed Green Salad with 1 1/2 teaspoons Blue Cheese
    Dressing mixed with 2 tablespoons Plain Low-Fat Yogurt
    plus 1/4 teaspoon Dijon-Style Mustard
1/2 cup Reduced-Calorie Vanilla Pudding
Coffee or Tea

SNACKS
1 small Nectarine; 1/2 cup Skim Milk

Optional Calories: 50

DAY 7

BREAKFAST
3 medium Prunes, stewed
3/4 ounce Cold Cereal
3/4 cup Skim Milk
Coffee or Tea

LUNCH
1 serving **Cheese-Topped Shrimp** (page 164)
3/4 cup *each* Cooked Cut Asparagus and Cauliflower Florets
1 3/4 cups Mixed Green Salad with 1 1/2 teaspoons Thousand
    Island Dressing mixed with 2 tablespoons Plain Low-Fat
    Yogurt plus 1/4 teaspoon Dijon-Style Mustard
10 small Grapes
Coffee, Tea, or Mineral Water

DINNER
1 serving **Sausage, Chicken, and Rice Soup** (page 68)
6 Saltines
1 3/4 cups Tossed Salad with 1 serving **Creamy Blue Cheese
    Dressing** (page 243)
1/2 cup Low-Calorie Strawberry-Flavored Gelatin
1 cup Strawberries
1 cup Skim Milk
Coffee or Tea

SNACKS
1 serving **Orange-Cran Cooler** (page 180)

Optional Calories: 65
Total Optional Calories for Week: 360

Week 5

Cooking with wine has been popular for years, but here's a new twist — cooking with whiskey. It's sensational, as you'll discover on Day 7 when you try our Flank Steak with Whiskey Sauce. This marinated steak slices up tender and tasty, and it's festive enough for guests.

A cornucopia of delicious side dishes makes up our Week 5 menu. Bulgur Pilaf combines apricots and raisins with the whole-grain nutrition of cracked wheat (bulgur). Buckwheat groats (kasha), Granny Smith apples, and raisins are the basis of Kasha Stuffing. And Pasta with Roasted Pepper Sauce combines spaghetti or fettuccine with a flavorful sauce made of roasted red bell pepper, anchovies, olives, and tomatoes.

For the fish and seafood lovers out there, we offer creamy Scallop Chowder on Day 1. Day 5 brings a catch of Red Snapper with Anchovy Butter, while Seafood Salad is served up for lunch on Day 7.

DAY 1

BREAKFAST
1 small Orange
¾ ounce Cold Cereal with 1 tablespoon Raisins
½ cup Skim Milk
Coffee or Tea

LUNCH
Open-Face Canadian Bacon Sandwich (2 ounces Canadian-style bacon with 3 tomato slices, 4 lettuce leaves, and 1 teaspoon reduced-calorie mayonnaise on 1 slice reduced-calorie wheat bread)
6 *each* Pickle Spears and Radishes
2 medium Apricots
Coffee, Tea, or Mineral Water

DINNER
1 serving **Scallop Chowder** (page 229)
2 ounces Roast Veal
1 serving **Pasta with Roasted Pepper Sauce** (page 34)
1½ cups Mixed Green Salad with 1 teaspoon Olive Oil mixed with 2 teaspoons Balsamic Vinegar plus Seasonings
1 cup Skim Milk
Coffee or Tea

SNACKS
Pineapple Yogurt (¼ cup *each* plain low-fat yogurt and canned crushed pineapple); ¼ small Cantaloupe
Optional Calories: 85

DAY 4

BREAKFAST
1 cup Strawberries
1 Scrambled Egg
½ cup Skim Milk
Coffee or Tea

LUNCH
⅔ cup Cottage Cheese on 4 Lettuce Leaves with ¼ cup Alfalfa Sprouts and 1 serving **Celebration Salad Dressing** (page 129)
¾ cup Broccoli Florets and 6 Fennel Sticks
Coffee, Tea, or Mineral Water

DINNER
1 cup Tomato Juice
3 ounces Roast Chicken
1 serving **Bulgur Pilaf** (page 290)
¾ cup *each* Cooked Chinese Chard and Sliced Mushrooms
1½ cups Mixed Green Salad with 1½ teaspoons Italian Dressing mixed with 2 teaspoons Red Wine Vinegar
1-ounce Roll
1 teaspoon Reduced-Calorie Margarine
½ cup Skim Milk
Coffee or Tea

SNACKS
2 cups Plain Popcorn; ½ cup Plain Low-Fat Yogurt

Optional Calories: 45

DAY 5

BREAKFAST
½ medium Banana, sliced
¾ ounce Cold Cereal
½ cup Skim Milk
Coffee or Tea

LUNCH
Reuben Sandwich (1 ounce *each* turkey and Swiss cheese and ½ cup sauerkraut with 1½ teaspoons Thousand Island dressing mixed with 2 tablespoons plain low-fat yogurt plus ¼ teaspoon Dijon-style mustard on 2 slices reduced-calorie rye bread)
6 *each* Carrot and Celery Sticks
3 medium Prunes
Coffee, Tea, or Mineral Water

DINNER
1 serving **Cream of Tomato Soup** (page 205)
1 serving **Red Snapper with Anchovy Butter** (page 95)
½ cup Cooked Sliced Turnip
6 Cooked Asparagus Spears
1¾ cups Tossed Salad with 1½ teaspoons French Dressing mixed with 2 teaspoons Lemon Juice plus ¼ teaspoon Dijon-Style Mustard
1-ounce Roll
1 teaspoon Reduced-Calorie Margarine
½ cup Reduced-Calorie Butterscotch Pudding
Coffee or Tea

SNACKS
½ medium Grapefruit

Optional Calories: 65

DAY 2

BREAKFAST
2-inch wedge Honeydew
¼ cup Part-Skim Ricotta Cheese
1 slice Raisin Bread, toasted
½ cup Skim Milk
Coffee or Tea

LUNCH
1 serving **Cobb Salad** (page 148)
6 *each* Carrot and Celery Sticks
2 Dates
Coffee, Tea, or Mineral Water

DINNER
1 serving **Mexican Joes** (page 54)
½ cup *each* Cooked Diced Eggplant and Spaghetti Squash
1 cup Mixed Green Salad with ½ cup *each* Dandelion Leaves
    and Artichoke Hearts and 1½ teaspoons French Dressing
    mixed with 2 teaspoons Lemon Juice plus ¼ teaspoon
    Dijon-Style Mustard
½ medium Grapefruit
Coffee or Tea

SNACKS
½ cup Skim Milk; ½ cup Reduced-Calorie Vanilla Pudding

Optional Calories: 75

DAY 3

BREAKFAST
1 medium Kiwi Fruit, sliced
½ cup Hot Cereal
½ cup Skim Milk
Coffee or Tea

LUNCH
Tuna in a Pita (3 ounces tuna with 1 teaspoon reduced-calorie
    mayonnaise and 4 lettuce leaves in 1-ounce pita bread)
6 *each* Green and Red Bell Pepper Strips
Coffee, Tea, or Mineral Water

DINNER
1 serving **Ham and Cheese Custard** (page 287)
¾ cup *each* Cooked Chinese Pea Pods and Cauliflower Florets
½ medium Tomato, sliced with 1½ teaspoons Olive Oil mixed
    with 2 teaspoons Red Wine Vinegar plus Basil Leaves
1-ounce Roll
1 teaspoon Margarine
1 serving Reduced-Calorie Vanilla Dairy Drink
Coffee or Tea

SNACKS
½ medium Papaya; ¾ cup Chicken Bouillon

Optional Calories: 10

DAY 6

BREAKFAST
¼ small Cantaloupe
1 serving **Ham 'n' Cheese Muffins** (page 69)
½ cup Skim Milk
Coffee or Tea

LUNCH
1 serving **Party Bologna Stacks** (page 23)
Lentil Salad (2 ounces cooked lentils with 2 tablespoons *each*
    chopped onion and celery and ½ teaspoon olive oil mixed
    with 2 teaspoons red wine vinegar plus seasonings)
3 Pickle Spears and 6 Radishes
Coffee, Tea, or Mineral Water

DINNER
3 ounces Roast Cornish Hen
1 serving **Kasha Stuffing** (page 33)
¾ cup *each* Cooked Cauliflower Florets and Sliced Zucchini
¾ cup *each* Sliced Belgian Endive and Torn Watercress with
    Lemon Juice and Herbs
½ cup Raspberries
½ cup Skim Milk
Coffee or Tea

SNACKS
2 Graham Crackers; 1 serving Reduced-Calorie Chocolate
    Dairy Drink

Optional Calories: 70

DAY 7

BREAKFAST
½ medium Papaya
½ cup Hot Cereal
½ cup Skim Milk
Coffee or Tea

LUNCH
1 serving **Seafood Salad** (page 189)
¾ cup *each* Cooked Chinese Pea Pods and Eggplant Strips
2 Graham Crackers
1 large Tangerine
Coffee, Tea, or Mineral Water

DINNER
1 Cooked Small Whole Artichoke with 1½ teaspoons French
    Dressing mixed with 2 teaspoons Lemon Juice plus
    ¼ teaspoon Dijon-Style Mustard
1 serving **Flank Steak with Whiskey Sauce** (page 286)
3 ounces Baked Potato topped with ¼ cup Plain Low-Fat
    Yogurt and Chopped Chives
¾ cup *each* Cooked Sliced Yellow Squash and Red Bell Pepper
    Strips
1½ cups Tossed Salad with ½ teaspoon Olive Oil mixed with
    2 teaspoons Red Wine Vinegar plus Seasonings
Coffee or Tea

SNACKS
1 small Pear; 1 cup Skim Milk

Optional Calories: 115
Total Optional Calories for Week: 465

Week 8

On Week 8 we have some special surprises in store for you. Toast your weight-loss success with a spirited refresher, Silver Jubilee Sparkling Punch. This bubbly beverage is a mixture of champagne, wine, liqueur, and raspberries. And while you're in a party mood, be sure to try Gala Fruit and Nut Cookies, chock full of dried apricots, raisins, dates, and walnuts. Anniversary Apples with Spiced ''Ice Cream'' is another festive dessert that's special enough for a company dinner. It's not made with ice cream at all, but with its lower-calorie relative, ice milk.

Nuts are also new, so do sample our Jelly 'n' Nut-Topped Muffins on Day 2. Their crunchy brown sugar and almond topping is soooo good. No time to bake during the week? Bake them when you have the time, then wrap and store them in the freezer. Thaw at room temperature for a quick breakfast.

DAY 4

BREAKFAST
½ medium Grapefruit
1 Scrambled Egg
½ English Muffin, toasted
½ cup Skim Milk
Coffee or Tea

LUNCH
1 serving **Garbanzo Salad** (page 145)
1-ounce Pita Bread
¾ cup Broccoli Florets and 6 Radishes
Coffee, Tea, or Mineral Water

DINNER
1 serving **Chicken Cacciatore with Green Beans** (page 237)
½ cup Cooked Spaghetti
½ cup Cooked Chinese Pea Pods
¾ cup *each* Sliced Belgian Endive and Torn Arugula with 1½ teaspoons French Dressing mixed with 2 teaspoons Lemon Juice plus ¼ teaspoon Dijon-Style Mustard
1 serving **Anniversary Apples with Spiced ''Ice Cream''** (page 270)
½ cup Skim Milk
Coffee or Tea

SNACKS
½ cup Reduced-Calorie Vanilla Pudding; 1 medium Kiwi Fruit, sliced

Optional Calories: 70

DAY 1

BREAKFAST
1 medium Kiwi Fruit, sliced
¾ ounce Cold Cereal
¾ cup Skim Milk
Coffee or Tea

LUNCH
Roast Beef Sandwich (2 ounces roast beef with 3 tomato slices, 4 lettuce leaves, and 1 teaspoon *each* mustard and mayonnaise on 2 slices reduced-calorie rye bread)
6 *each* Carrot and Celery Sticks
Coffee, Tea, or Mineral Water

DINNER
1 serving **Rumaki-Style Date 'n' Cheese Bits** (page 207)
3 ounces Broiled Flounder Fillet
1 serving **Brown Rice and Vegetable Medley** (page 127)
¾ cup *each* Cooked Spinach Leaves and Sliced Turnip
1½ cups Mixed Green Salad with 1½ teaspoons Thousand Island Dressing mixed with 2 tablespoons Plain Low-Fat Yogurt plus ¼ teaspoon Dijon-Style Mustard
Coffee or Tea

SNACKS
½ medium Banana; 1 serving Reduced-Calorie Vanilla Dairy Drink

Optional Calories: 45

DAY 5

BREAKFAST
½ medium Banana, sliced
¾ ounce Cold Cereal
½ cup Skim Milk
Coffee or Tea

LUNCH
1 serving **Anniversary Party Pâté** (page 28)
6 Saltines
6 *each* Carrot and Celery Sticks
1 small Orange
Coffee, Tea, or Mineral Water

DINNER
1 serving **Pan-Fried Swordfish with Tomatoes and Roasted Pepper** (page 235)
4 ounces Baked Acorn Squash
6 Cooked Asparagus Spears
1½ cups Mixed Green Salad with 1 tablespoon Blue Cheese Dressing
½ cup Low-Calorie Lemon-Flavored Gelatin
½ cup Skim Milk
Coffee or Tea

SNACKS
2 medium Plums; 1 serving Reduced-Calorie Vanilla Dairy Drink

Optional Calories: 75

DAY 2

BREAKFAST
¼ small Cantaloupe
⅓ cup Cottage Cheese
1 serving **Jelly 'n' Nut-Topped Muffins** (page 85)
Coffee or Tea

LUNCH
Tuna in a Pita (1½ ounces tuna with 2 tablespoons *each*
    chopped celery and onion, and 4 lettuce leaves in 1-ounce
    pita bread)
1 serving **Leek Salad** (page 82)
1 small Apple
Coffee, Tea, or Mineral Water

DINNER
3 ounces Roast Cornish Hen
½ cup *each* Cooked Barley and Sliced Mushrooms
¾ cup *each* Cooked Sliced Fennel and Red Bell Pepper Strips
½ cup Hearts of Palm on 4 Lettuce Leaves with 1½ teaspoons
    Italian Dressing mixed with 2 teaspoons Red Wine Vinegar
½ cup Reduced-Calorie Chocolate Pudding
Coffee or Tea

SNACKS
10 large Cherries; 1 cup Skim Milk

Optional Calories: 55

DAY 3

BREAKFAST
½ medium Papaya
½ cup Hot Cereal drizzled with 1 teaspoon Honey
½ cup Skim Milk
Coffee or Tea

LUNCH
1 serving **Marinated Shrimp and Cucumber Salad** (page 146)
1 serving **German Potato Salad** (page 171)
Coffee, Tea, or Mineral Water

DINNER
1 serving **Blue Cheese-Stuffed Burgers** (page 77)
½ cup *each* Stewed Tomatoes and Cooked Sauerkraut
1½ cups Mixed Green Salad with 2 servings **Basil Mayonnaise**
    (page 196)
20 small Grapes
½ cup Skim Milk
Coffee or Tea

SNACKS
Tangerine Yogurt (½ cup plain low-fat yogurt mixed with
    1 large tangerine, peeled and sectioned)

Optional Calories: 75

DAY 6

BREAKFAST
½ cup Orange Sections
¼ cup Part-Skim Ricotta Cheese
1 slice Raisin Bread, toasted
Coffee or Tea

LUNCH
Open-Face Cheese Sandwich (2 ounces Cheddar cheese and
    3 tomato slices on 1 slice reduced-calorie multi-grain
    bread, grilled)
1¾ cups Mixed Green Salad with 1½ teaspoons Olive Oil
    mixed with 2 teaspoons Wine Vinegar plus Seasonings
½ cup Reduced-Calorie Butterscotch Pudding
Coffee, Tea, or Mineral Water

DINNER
Relish Tray (6 *each* celery and carrot sticks and 2 green
    olives)
3 ounces Roast Chicken
¾ cup *each* Cooked Spinach Leaves and Sliced Turnip
1 serving **Rice-Stuffed Tomatoes** (page 174)
1 serving **Gala Fruit and Nut Cookies** (page 296)
Coffee or Tea

SNACKS
1 small Pear; 1 cup Skim Milk

Optional Calories: 60

DAY 7

BREAKFAST
2-inch wedge Honeydew
1 Poached Egg
½ English Muffin, toasted
1 teaspoon Reduced-Calorie Margarine
½ cup Skim Milk
Coffee or Tea

LUNCH
1 serving **Shrimp-Stuffed Shells Appetizer** (page 139)
1 serving **Endive, Pepper, and Blue Cheese Salad** (page 81)
1-ounce Roll
½ cup Fruit Salad
Coffee, Tea, or Mineral Water

DINNER
1 serving **Pork Chops in Tomato Sauce** (page 58)
½ cup Cooked Cracked Wheat
¼ cup *each* Cooked Broccoli Florets and Sliced Mushrooms
1½ cups Mixed Green Salad with 1½ teaspoons Thousand
    Island Dressing mixed with 2 tablespoons Plain Low-Fat
    Yogurt plus ¼ teaspoon Dijon-Style Mustard
1 serving Reduced-Calorie Chocolate Dairy Drink
Coffee or Tea

SNACKS
1 serving **Silver Jubilee Sparkling Punch** (page 298); Pineapple
    'n' Yogurt (½ cup canned crushed pineapple topped with
    2 tablespoons plain low-fat yogurt)

Optional Calories: 120
Total Optional Calories for Week: 500

Appendix

Menus for Men and Youths

The menus in this book were designed for women. Since the daily food requirements differ slightly for men and youths (males 10 to 18, females 10 to 15), the menus should be adjusted as follows:

Week	Add
1 & 2	1 Fruit Exchange 2 Bread Exchanges 2 Protein Exchanges (Youths only) 1 Milk Exchange
3, 4, & 5	1 to 2 Fruit Exchanges 2 Bread Exchanges 2 Protein Exchanges (Youths only) 1 to 2 Milk Exchanges

About Weighing and Measuring

■ Always take time to measure and weigh ingredients carefully; this is vital to both recipe results and weight control. Don't try to judge amounts by eye.

■ To weigh foods, use a scale.

■ To measure liquids, use a standard glass or clear plastic measuring cup. Place it on a level surface and read markings at eye level. Fill the cup just to the appropriate marking. To measure less than ¼ cup, use standard measuring spoons.

■ To measure dry ingredients, use metal or plastic measuring cups that come in sets of four: ¼ cup, ⅓ cup, ½ cup, and 1 cup. Spoon the ingredients into the cup, then level with the straight edge of a knife or metal spatula. To measure less than ¼ cup, use standard measuring spoons and, unless otherwise directed, level as for measuring cup.

■ A dash is about ¹⁄₁₆ of a teaspoon (½ of a ⅛-teaspoon measure or ¼ of a ¼-teaspoon measure).

■ In any recipe for more than one serving it is important to mix ingredients well and to divide evenly so that each portion will be the same size.

■ Weights in recipes are given in pounds and fractions of a pound. See below for ounce equivalents.

1 pound = 16 ounces	½ pound = 8 ounces
¾ pound = 12 ounces	¼ pound = 4 ounces

Pan Substitutions

It's best to use the pan size that's recommended in a recipe; however, if your kitchen isn't equipped with that particular pan, chances are a substitution will work just as well. The pan size is determined by the volume of food it holds. When substituting, use a pan as close to the recommended size as possible. Food cooked in too small a pan may boil over; food cooked in too large a pan may dry out or burn. To determine the dimensions of a baking pan, measure across the top, between the inside edges. To determine the volume, measure the amount of water the pan holds when completely filled.

When you use a pan that is a different size from the one recommended, it may be necessary to adjust the suggested cooking time. Depending on the size of the pan and the depth of the food in it, you may need to add or subtract 5 to 10 minutes. If you substitute glass or glass-ceramic for metal, the oven temperature should be reduced by 25°F.

The following chart provides some common pan substitutions.

Recommended Size	Approximate Volume	Possible Substitutions
8 x 1½-inch round baking pan	1½ quarts	10 x 6 x 2-inch baking dish 9 x 1½-inch round baking pan 8 x 4 x 2-inch loaf pan 9-inch pie plate
8 x 8 x 2-inch baking pan	2 quarts	11 x 7 x 1½-inch baking pan 12 x 7½ x 2-inch baking pan 9 x 5 x 3-inch loaf pan two 8 x 1½-inch round baking pans
13 x 9 x 2-inch baking pan	3 quarts	14 x 11 x 2-inch baking dish two 9 x 1½-inch round baking pans two 8 x 1½-inch round baking pans

Dry and Liquid Measure Equivalents

Teaspoons	Tablespoons	Cups	Fluid Ounces
3 teaspoons	1 tablespoon		½ fluid ounce
6 teaspoons	2 tablespoons	⅛ cup	1 fluid ounce
8 teaspoons	2 tablespoons plus 2 teaspoons	⅙ cup	
12 teaspoons	4 tablespoons	¼ cup	2 fluid ounces
15 teaspoons	5 tablespoons	⅓ cup less 1 teaspoon	
16 teaspoons	5 tablespoons plus 1 teaspoon	⅓ cup	
18 teaspoons	6 tablespoons	⅓ cup plus 2 teaspoons	3 fluid ounces
24 teaspoons	8 tablespoons	½ cup	4 fluid ounces
30 teaspoons	10 tablespoons	½ cup plus 2 tablespoons	5 fluid ounces
32 teaspoons	10 tablespoons plus 2 teaspoons	⅔ cup	
36 teaspoons	12 tablespoons	¾ cup	6 fluid ounces
42 teaspoons	14 tablespoons	1 cup less 2 tablespoons	7 fluid ounces
45 teaspoons	15 tablespoons	1 cup less 1 tablespoon	
48 teaspoons	16 tablespoons	1 cup	8 fluid ounces

Note: Measurements of less than ⅛ teaspoon are considered a dash or a pinch.

Metric Conversions

If you are converting the recipes in this book to metric measurements, use the following chart as a guide.

Volume

1/4 teaspoon	1 milliliter
1/2 teaspoon	2 milliliters
1 teaspoon	5 milliliters
1 tablespoon	15 milliliters
2 tablespoons	30 milliliters
3 tablespoons	45 milliliters
1/4 cup	50 milliliters
1/3 cup	75 milliliters
1/2 cup	125 milliliters
2/3 cup	150 milliliters
3/4 cup	175 milliliters
1 cup	250 milliliters
1 quart	1 liter

Weight

1 ounce	30 grams
1/4 pound	120 grams
1/2 pound	240 grams
3/4 pound	360 grams
1 pound	480 grams

Length

1 inch	25 millimeters
1 inch	2.5 centimeters

Oven Temperatures

250°F.	120°C
275°F.	140°C
300°F.	150°C
325°F.	160°C
350°F.	180°C
375°F.	190°C
400°F.	200°C
425°F.	220°C
450°F.	230°C
475°F.	250°C
500°F.	260°C
525°F.	270°C

Index